THE CAIRNGORM GATEWAY

The Author

ANN GLEN is the author of a number of books on aspects of Scotland, including railway history, and is a regular contributor to *The Scots Magazine*, among other periodicals. A geographer and economic historian by profession, she has a special enthusiasm for the geography of Scotland and Scandinavia – her knowledge of the latter countries fostered by the fact that her husband is Danish.

The Cairngorm Gateway features a popular and remarkable region in Scotland which has been a focus of Dr Glen's research since student days and on which she has spoken to a variety of organisations. She has acquired a close knowledge of the region both through living there and as a result of intensive investigation. Railway preservation is one of her leisure interests, which also include hill-walking, photography and painting. She is active in publicising the scenic, but under-utilised, lines of the Highlands through the Highland Railway Heritage group.

Dr Glen is a member of the Local Government Boundary Commission for Scotland and of the Rail Passengers Committee, Scotland. Her concern for environmental and planning issues, and her contribution to geography, have recently been recognised when she was made a Fellow of the Royal Scottish Geographical Society.

The
Cairngorm
Gateway

A N N   G L E N

SCOTTISH CULTURAL PRESS
www.scottishbooks.com

First published 2002 by

SCOTTISH CULTURAL PRESS

Unit 13d, Newbattle Abbey Business Annexe
Newbattle Road, DALKEITH EH22 3LJ Scotland
Tel: +44 (0)131 660 6366 • Fax: +44 (0)131 660 6414
Email: info@scottishbooks.com

website: www.scottishbooks.com

COVER ILLUSTRATIONS: Loch Morlich (John Peter) *front cover, main image;*
front, top to bottom: On the Strathspey Railway (John Peter); The old 'Bridge of Carr'
(Ann Glen); The CairnGorm Mountain Railway (John Peter)
back, top to bottom: A Sale in the 1950s (A. E. Glen); Path Repairs on Cairn Gorm
(John Peter); Mountain Bikers in Rothiemurchus (Ann Glen)

BRITISH LIBRARY CATALOGUING IN PUBLICATION DATA
A catalogue record for this book is available from the British Library

ISBN: 1 84017 027 1

Printed and bound by Bell & Bain Ltd, Glasgow

CONTENTS

ACKNOWLEDGEMENTS

Many friends have given information, or have helped in providing photographs or in identifying people and places. Thanks, therefore, go to: Jim Barton, Peter Bruce, Alan Cameron, Joy Cameron, Vanessa Collingridge, David Conner, Thomas Coombes, David Cox, Martin Davidson, Paul Devlin, Nancy Eaglesham, John Fisher, Irene Galasso, Jessie Garrow, John Goodwin, Irene Gordon, Mairi Grant, Sheila Grant, Nick Halfhide, David Hamilton, May Harper, David Hayes, Chrissie Highmore, Peigi Higson, Yolande Hodson, Bill Howard, John and Hamish Johnstone, Robert Lambert, Andrew McCracken, William McEwan, Alph McGregor, Martin MacGregor, Muriel Mackay, Tom Mackenzie, Jock Mitchell, Greig Munro, Cathair Ó Dochartaigh, Chloe Randall, Colin Riddell, David Rose, Jennifer Scott, Syd Scroggie, Neil Sinclair, Ken Smith, Ann Wakeling, Neil Wakeling, Helen Watson, James Waddell and Jocelin Winthrop Young. Thanks also go to Neil and Helen Clark for their generous hospitality, and to Margaret Grant for her kindness.

Photographs taken by my father, A.E. Glen, or collected by him have also been used, but I am also greatly indebted to my friend Walter Dempster for permission to reproduce views taken by his grandfather and by his father.

Special thanks are due to Jimmie Gray and Jock Hay for railway information, to Mairi McSween and John Sam Macdonald for sharing recollections on many occasions, and to Duncan Sanderson and other local history enthusiasts for their companionable investigations in the field. James Grant (Seumas Grannd) has contributed sound advice on Gaelic names plus expertise on heritage themes.

Assistance was also received from staff at Aviemore Library, the British Library, Edinburgh University Library, Glasgow University Library, Inverness Public Library, the Mitchell Library, the National Library of

Scotland, the Aviemore Partnership, Badenoch and Strathspey Conservation Group, The Cairngorms Campaign, the Cairngorm Chairlift Company, the Cairngorms Partnership, the Highland Folk Museum, Highland Regional Council and Highland Council Archives, Historic Scotland, the Imperial War Museum, Landmark (Carrbridge), the National Army Museum, the Registers of Scotland, Rothiemurchus Estate, Scottish Natural Heritage, Scottish Record Office, the Scottish Rights of Way and Access Society, the Scottish Youth Hostels' Association, the Signet Library, St Andrews University Library and the Stakis Organisation. The editors of the *Herald*, *Scenes* (Scottish Environmental News), *Strathspey and Badenoch Herald* and *TGO* (The Great Outdoors) are also thanked for the updates on developments within the Cairngorms region which have appeared in their columns.

Over many years papers given at conferences have been a stimulus to further enquiry – from the seminal 'The Countryside in 1970' event in London thirty years ago to 'Rothiemurchus: Nature and People on a Highland Estate' held in 1997 (the papers of which were subsequently brought together in a book, also published by Scottish Cultural Press), plus gatherings of the John Muir Trust, meetings of the Association of Scottish Visitor Attractions and of the Scottish Association of Geography Teachers. Pioneering researches in local history have come from George A. Dixon, former Archivist to Central Region to whom a well-deserved tribute is due; his letters and guidance have been invaluable. The writings and observations of Adam Watson, an acclaimed authority on the Cairngorm mountains, and the work of David M. Munro, Director of the Royal Scottish Geographical Society, on aspects of the Strathspey Estates, are also acknowledged with appreciation. Neil MacGregor has made intriguing contributions to local place-names and traditions, which have been published in the Transactions of the Gaelic Society of Inverness. Material gathered by William C. Wonders, Emeritus Professor of Geography at the University of Alberta, on the Canadian foresters of the Second World War, has been most helpful.

Permission has been kindly given by the respective authors or publishers for leave to quote from the following: O. S. Nock's *The Highland Railway* (Ian Allan Ltd); A. R. B. Haldane's *New Ways through the Glens* (International Thomson Publishing Services Ltd); George Blake's *Mountain and Flood: The History of the 52nd (Lowland) Division, 1939–1946* (Jackson & Sons); Nigel Hamilton's *Monty Master of the Battlefield, 1942–1944* (Hamish Hamilton); and Charles McKean's comments in *Heritage: Conservation, Interpretation and Enterprise* edited by J. M. Fladmark (Donhead Publishing at Robert Gordon University).

Some quotations have also been taken from old local newspapers. All these sources and any others who may not have been traced are acknowledged and thanked.

It has been a signal honour to have my friend, Tom Weir, the doyen of Scottish mountaineers and writers, prepare a preface to *The Cairngorm Gateway* and I record my warm gratitude to him for his participation and for his wise comments. Special thanks are also due to my husband, John Peter, and to our son, Bruce, who have given valuable help with the photography and who have patiently been part of the support team on many forays to the north.

Field, archival and library research has received timely support from the Carnegie Trust of the Universities of Scotland which is thanked for its generous assistance. The Aviemore Partnership, as part of Moray, Badenoch and Strathspey Enterprise, has made a welcome contribution towards the publishing of this book for which acknowledgement is made. The views expressed, however, are the author's own.

The form of the place-names follows the usage on Ordnance Survey maps with the preferred Gaelic version given in brackets.

FOREWORD

by *Tom Weir*

When I was de-mobbed from the Army in 1946, a book of mine about my early climbing adventures with the title Highland Days was accepted for publication. An invitation to write another book soon arrived from the publishers. Covering prehistory, the centuries of the clans, the Jacobite risings, the making of the military roads, the coming of the stage coaches and the railways, it was also to be the story of the Caledonian forest and of the timber floating on the Spey from the mountains to the sea. I agreed to write the book but soon had second thoughts – I did not have the knowledge or the gut feeling for it at that time – and given my experiences there were other subjects I could write about more easily. Better to write about something you know and leave someone else to embark on what would be a labour of love.

A wise choice is Ann Glen who since childhood has grown up in war and peace in Badenoch and Strathspey. With a background in geography and economics at Glasgow University, then subsequently in economic history, she has lectured and written not only on environmental topics but also on railways and transport history. As a professional geographer she supports many outdoor causes – the John Muir Trust, Scottish Rights of Way and Scottish Youth Hostels – and pursues a range of varied activities such as photography, painting and hill walking for good measure. She has spoken on the pressure and controversies surrounding the Cairngorms in recent times and so I opened the draft of *The Cairngorm Gateway* with keen interest and I was not disappointed.

Badenoch and Strathspey became holiday districts with the coming of the railway and, with the inevitable construction of villas and hotels, their villages began growing. Before the First World War the visitors were mainly well-to-do but in the inter-war years, with the onset of depression, the first generation of working-class folk took to the hills rather than walk the streets. A shilling (8p) a night bought a bed in a youth hostel, the use of a kitchen and a common room. When the Second World War intervened, the Cairngorms area became a vast training ground. In the post-war years the holiday-makers soon came back. The winter sports boom of the 1960s sparked off a rash of development in the district including the Aviemore Centre. Of all the villages in the gateway to the Cairngorms, Aviemore has grown most and altered most. The funicular railway has put the spotlight on ski pressures versus environmental issues and a National Park for the Cairngorms is now imminent.

The Cairngorm Gateway traces the story of this strategic corridor and explores the challenges facing both people and places in and around Aviemore and further afield. It is based on an immense volume of research but is easy reading. Enjoy *The Cairngorm Gateway* and add your voice to mine in recommending this book to anyone interested in the area.

Tom Weir

INTRODUCTION

In the year 2000 tourism was one of Scotland's leading activities, the largest employer of its people and one of its greatest sources of earnings. Even before the severe impact of the recent outbreak of foot and mouth disease, Scottish tourism was experiencing a serious downturn, yet 15 per cent of the workforce of the Highlands and Islands was still engaged in the industry. Over the years, tourism and leisure have made the Cairngorm gateway and its settlements, especially Aviemore, well known. It is not the only approach to the Cairngorm Mountains but it is the most obvious one on any map and its popularity continues to grow. It has, however, become a place of conflict and contrast. Yet, from a hilltop, the sweeping vistas of the plateaus with their corries and summits seem unaltered. The lochs with their fringes of Scots pines are still set off by the lighter tones of birch woods. The russet moors are bright with patches of pasture, although farming folk and working farms are now fewer than ever. Meanwhile, the villages and small towns keep expanding relentlessly and residents are far outnumbered by a floating population.

While numerous books and reports have been produced on the Cairngorms themselves, there is little available on their bordering districts in Badenoch and Strathspey. *The Cairngorm Gateway* seeks to redress this balance and especially focuses on the Aviemore area, Rothiemurchus and Glenmore. It draws on a wide variety of source material, such as estate papers and plans, railway archives, newspaper files, official reports, valuation rolls, contemporary accounts and journals, letters and interviews, together with the knowledge which only lengthy acquaintance can bring. An apt description for its content might be 'a study in human ecology', as it traces how people have used the environment and adapted to it through the years.

This gateway to the Cairngorms has long been a mixing ground for people of different origins – from Buchan, the Moray coast, the Mearns, the Lowlands and other parts of the Highlands, folk have come to settle or move on. The twin arteries of the highways and railways hastened these processes. People may be shy about their origins or unaware of their roots but their surnames are revealing. Now, increasing numbers of folk from south of the Border and from abroad are choosing to make a home in the area and thus the cultural blend is continually enlivened.

My interest in the gateway's history and geography began with tales told by the fireside in childhood and was developed by further research during school days in the 1950s. My family's links with the Cairngorm gateway go back about a century earlier when grandfather Glen journeyed there en route to view activity at the Helmsdale goldrush. My father and mother first met in Kingussie and so there is a great affection for the gateway and its people. Phases of residence and holidays have only strengthened these bonds.

Although Kingussie is acknowledged as the capital of Badenoch, and Grantown-on-Spey has a similar claim to the strath, undoubtedly the most controversial settlement is Aviemore. Like it or loathe it, it is a place with which almost every Scot and most visitors to the Highlands have become familiar. Will the sheer numbers of tourists and the inevitable provision for them spoil, or even destroy, what they come to experience and enjoy? The funicular railway on Cairn Gorm has polarised opinion from local to international levels and now a National Park has been signalled early in the new millennium.

There must be a recognition that sensitivity is essential to ensure that the same mistakes are not made with the holiday business as were once committed with heavy industry. Aviemore has come nearer to the brink than any other inland resort in Scotland. As seen today, it is almost entirely a creation of the twentieth century but its recent rapid growth has been bought at a heavy price: 'Instead of ennobling nature and benefiting from it, we are close to reducing our natural heritage to valuelessness.' (Charles McKean in *Heritage: Conservation, Interpretation and Enterprise.*)

It is encouraging that there is a new determination to match the superb landscapes of the Cairngorms with a built environment that does them some credit. Using a light touch, *The Cairngorm Gateway* seeks to combine a historical approach with a geographical perspective.

In the 1930s people were 'going to the hills' in increasing numbers. Here walkers view the Garbh Choire and the Cairntoul massif from the summit of Braeriach (A. E. GLEN)

SUGGESTED EXCURSIONS

It is hoped that the excursions will enable you to get to know the Cairngorm gateway with all its variety and interest. They are of varying length and although none is arduous, they are done at the reader's own risk. It is wise to remember the changeable nature of the weather. The Cairngorm gateway is in many ways the most 'continental' part of Scotland with extremes of temperature and records ranging from a sizzling 27°C in July to a bitter -27°C in January. Listen to the weather forecast before setting out and be sure to have adequate, preferably windproof, clothing and strong, comfortable footwear. The Ordnance Survey maps of the 1:50 000 Landranger series, sheets 35 Kingussie & Monadhliath Mountains and 36 Grantown, Aviemore & Cairngorm Area, are indispensable. If you are going to the hills, know how to use a map and a compass and remember to leave a note of your route and your time of return. Countryside rangers are available to assist you and many additional routes in the district are way marked.

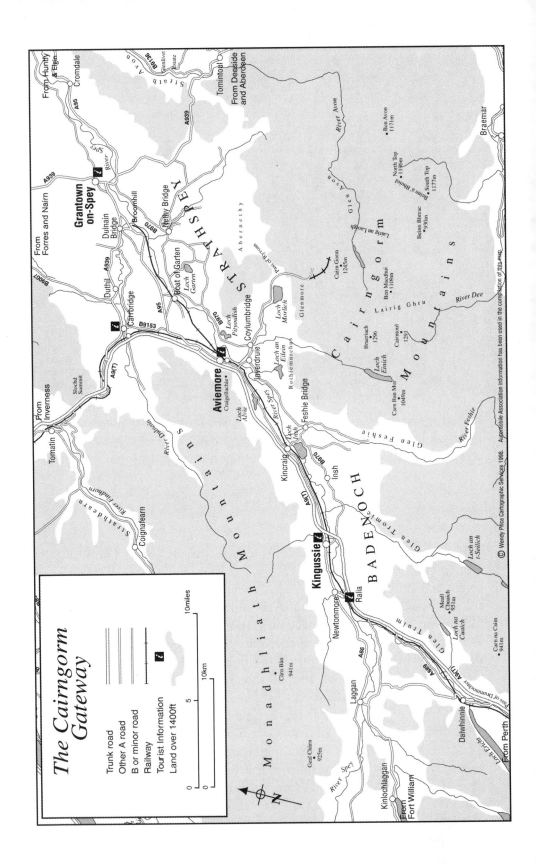

The Cairngorm Gateway

Legend:
- Trunk road
- Other A road
- B or minor road
- Railway
- *i* Tourist Information
- Land over 1400ft

0   5   10miles
0   10km

N

© Wendy Price Cartographic Services 1998. Automobile Association information has been used in the compilation of this map.

Place names and features:

From Huntly, X Elgin, Glenlivet, Cromdale, Strath Avon, Tomintoul, From Deeside and Aberdeen, River Avon, Ben Avon 1171m, Braemar, North Top 1119m, Beinn a' Bhuird, South Top 1177m, A339, A95, River Spey, Grantown-on-Spey *i*, Dulnain Bridge, Broomhill, Nethy Bridge, Abernethy, Glen Avon, Cairn Gorm 1245m, Ben Macdhui 1309m, Beinn Bhreac 930m, Cairngorm Mountains, From Forres and Nairn, A939, Duthil, A938, Carrbridge, Boat of Garten, Loch Garten, STRATHSPEY, Pass of Ryvoan, Lairig an Laoigh, River Dee, B907, B9153 *i*, A95, Loch Pityoulish, Coylumbridge, Loch Morlich, Glenmore, Lairig Ghru, Braeriach 1296m, Cairn Toul 1291m, B970, Slochd Summit, A9(T), Aviemore *i*, Craigellachie, Inverdruie, Loch an Eilein, Rothiemurchus, Feshie Bridge, Loch Einich, Carn Ban Mor 1049m, From Inverness, Tomatin, River Dulnain, Monadhliath Mountains, Loch Alvie, River Spey, Loch Insh, Kincraig, B970, Insh, Glen Feshie, River Feshie, Coignafearn, Strathdearn, River Findhorn, Kinlochlaggan, A9(T), BADENOCH, Glen Tromie, Loch an t-Seilich, Kingussie *i*, Ruthven, Ralia *i*, Newtonmore, Meall Chuaich 951m, Loch na Cuaich, Carn na Cairn 941m, A86, Carn Ban 941m, Glen Truim, A889, A9(T), Laggan, Geal Charn 925m, River Spey, Pass of Drumochter, Dalwhinnie, Loch Ericht, From Fort William, From Perth, Monadhliath Mountains

CHAPTER 1

From Early Times to 1770

Looking at a map of the Highlands of Scotland will show the great mass of the Grampian Mountains that occupy about one quarter of the whole country. The Cairngorms form their eastern citadel and, skirting this high wilderness, is a natural 'gateway', which has long been a focus of routes. From Drumochter, Lochaber and Badenoch these merge to continue northwards to the coast of the Moray Firth. Through this corridor, or strath, runs the Spey, a fast-flowing and temperamental river. Interlinking paths lead into the bordering mountains but until the early nineteenth century or so it was a remote and inaccessible region with relatively few people travelling through it or living in it. Yet there has been settlement there for a very long time.

Folk had been slow to appear in the Highlands compared with China, India or the Middle East. Scotland had been overwhelmed by a colossal ice sheet hundreds of metres thick at its maximum. Even when this shrank as the climate improved, glaciers – rivers of ice – occupied the valleys of the Grampians and left their mark on the landforms in indelible fashion. When the ice slowly melted away about 12,000 BC, a cold tundra emerged. The lofty plateau of the Cairngorms shows what conditions would have been like there: harsh and forbidding. Low-growing Arctic vegetation attracted herds of reindeer, followed in time by nomadic hunters using the continental 'land bridge' from Europe, which was still in place at that time. To date, no trace remains of these folk in the gateway region.

Billions upon billions of tons of rock waste – silt, sand and boulders – had been scraped from the mountain sides by the glaciers. As the ice decayed, huge melt-waters spread the debris over the valley floors, dumping it, even under the ice itself, in mounds and terraces, and creating the undulating terrain that covers so much of Strathspey today. There is possibly a greater proportion of level ground on the plateau tops than in the valleys beneath. The climate then wavered between icy tundra and more genial temperate conditions, which can be traced from lake clays and pollen deposits in peat. Gradually, as temperatures climbed, the tundra gave way to juniper scrub, then to woodland, especially of birch, rowan and aspen, which in turn developed into an extensive forest of Scots pine. The fluctuating dry and then wet climate caused peat deposits to accumulate; in places the pine roots were swamped and the trees collapsed, leaving only heathy bog. Sparse groups of humans were dependent on that forest and its animals – red deer, elk, wild pig, wild ox, brown bear, beaver, wolf and lynx. The fragments of pine wood in Rothiemurchus, Glenmore and Abernethy give only a hint of what this vast wilderness was once like.

Farming came to the strath about 6,000 years ago. Folk cleared parts of the forest by felling and burning the trees and they then sowed grain in the ashes. These first husbandmen settled in family groups and relied on the woods, lochs and rivers for their existence. They left strange megalithic monuments, such as standing stones and circles in mathematical precision, as they had some knowledge of astronomy; yet they had only stone or wood for their implements. If you saunter among bungalows at Muirton on the northern boundary of Aviemore, you may be surprised to find an impressive stone circle or ring cairn, disclosing the worship place of folk of the Bronze Age. More surprising, perhaps, is the fact that nearby standing stones were removed for a farm building over a century ago; despoiling the environment or heritage is nothing new. A stone circle also lies near Granish and there are other prehistoric sites in the district. These provide the oldest evidence for a human presence and date from 4,000 BC when bronze, the first of the metals, was coming into use in Scotland. Sources of the alloy, which contains copper and tin, could only be obtained by trading with Southern England or the Mediterranean lands. Obviously, such very long links required good organisation and a strong ruling class. Bronze was a breakthrough. Having metal tools and weapons gave far greater scope for clearing trees and for hunting animals. Bronze Age people thus had more control over their environment as they not only grew crops but also raised livestock for they had learned to tame cattle, sheep, goats and pigs.

Recent underwater investigations in lochs have taken Scottish archaeology into a new realm. Crannogs, or lake dwellings, built with alder or oak for the piling, alder for the floors, hazel for the walls and reeds for the thatch appeared in the late Bronze Age. They gave the farming people protection from the wolves and bears which roamed the forests. These circular structures had an inner core for the families and an outer one where the animals were kept. A reconstruction of a crannog may be seen near Kenmore on Loch Tay. The folk grew a primitive form of wheat and barley, gathered nuts and berries in the woods and fished from dugout canoes. Abandoned crannogs can be detected in shallows such as in Loch Pityoulish; other lochs in Badenoch and Strathspey may yet reveal more secrets.

In its turn, bronze was replaced by iron about 500 BC. The latter mineral occurs widely in the Highlands but it is usually of poor quality – the so-called 'bog' ores which can be dug out of the rusty-red 'pan' layer in certain soils. Iron goods were long held precious, whether they were crude nails or cooking pots, and remained so until the metal could be mass-produced in the nineteenth century. The hill forts of the gateway date from the Iron Age. These are always located on vantage points near liveable areas and overlook hospitable valleys. They, too, must have provided refuge and security against wild beasts, troublesome neighbours and marauders. Some have single walls, some triple ones formed of the local stone or timber construction inset with rubble. Clambering up to such a site at *Creag a'Chaisteil* on the shoulder of Pityoulish Hill can lead to arguments about their 'vitrification', the process whereby they were burnt in a heat so intense that the rocks fused together. Was this accidental or the result of a fire during an attack, or was it done on purpose to strengthen the wall? The structure of the hill forts remains a mystery to archaeologists.

By the first century AD, the valley of Strathspey was cultivated in patches and settled; the forerunners of little hamlets or clachans were established. Raising crops, herding cattle and utilising the resources of the forest were to be the basis of existence for the future. Locations meeting all these requirements for survival were valued – a sheltered sunny site, good water, a light soil, timber for building and peat for fuel. The rolling terraces left by the melt-waters from the long-vanished glaciers gave free draining, if stony, ground for the early farmers. Clean burns trickled off the surrounding hills and provided an assured water supply. The protective rock of Craigellachie might offer shelter from rampaging westerly winds, but the widening strath was open to bitter storms from the north-east. The lower ranges are of schist and on the west are appropriately named *Am Monadh Liath*, the grey-topped hills.

On the south and east the great rampart of what was known as *Am Monadh Ruadh* – the red mountains, formed of pinkish granite – rears up. Seen in a sunset, the name fits well, but today the range is more commonly known as the Cairngorms from *An Càrn Gorm*, the blue hill. They have no foothills in the gateway area and their appearance is deceptive because they have defences in depth, namely, the greatest proportion of surfaces over 4,000 feet (1,200m) in Britain. The plateaux are of massive extent in all directions and a journey of 28 miles (45km) awaits the walker bound through the Lairig Ghru (*Làirig Dhrù*) from Aviemore to Braemar. There is no mistaking the Lairig – it is the great cleft that splits the Cairngorms into eastern and western massifs. In early times these high wildernesses must have been of limited interest to the dwellers in the glens for the mountain tops were places of tempests and blizzards, only attracting the attention of hunters. The upper valleys, however, were suited to summer pasturing for herds and the passes were a means of movement from one strath to another. Folk became well acquainted with the mountains and their dangers, indeed, an intimate knowledge of the high ground was reflected in the detailed naming of its features.

The expansionist Roman Empire sent expeditionary forces to explore the Highlands. Great forts such as Caputh on the Tay were built on their margins, but contact with Rome's armies was brief. The Romans recorded a Pictish society north of the Forth: traces of its language are evidenced by the sprinkling of 'pit' or 'pet' place-names (meaning a farmstead) found in Northern Scotland, such as Pitlochry, Pittodrie and others. Soon the warrior Celts were in ascendancy and they were organised in tribes. It was a pattern that would evolve into clans and Gaelic became the pre-eminent language. In those early centuries, Celtic missionaries brought the Christian belief to the strath, choosing the dry hillocks at Alvie and Insh for their cells. As in Rothiemurchus or Kincardine, the sites were dedicated to Celtic saints. St Tuchaldus is linked with Rothiemurchus and St Tomhaldaidh with Kincardine. With settlements being scattered, pathways poor and distances often lengthy, chapels of ease were built in order that clergy could more easily minister to the people: Chapelton near Kinveachy is evidence for one of these places of worship. The ancient religion of the strath had been a form of Druidism and its rituals were slow to disappear. Up to the 1860s it was thought appropriate that the parish minister should light the Beltane fire on the first of May as though he were assuming the role of the high priest. Burning brands were carried from the bonfire to every house, further emphasising the ritual's pre-Christian overtones in its symbolism.

The Dark Ages as far as the gateway is concerned are little known in archaeological terms. Upper Strathspey seems to have been thankfully remote from Viking raids. Strongholds, or '*rathad*', were set up on defensive sites, such as the hill by the Doune in Rothiemurchus. The latter name means 'the fort of Murchais' and recalls an ancient warrior of whom no other evidence has survived. By the tenth century, the tree cover, which is estimated to have clothed two-thirds of the Highlands at one time, had been much reduced by both farmers and pastoralists. The families targeted the better sites where brown forest soils (often indicated by the presence of oak trees) gave the promise of a worthwhile crop. The Scots pine forest, however, was greatly valued for its game and for its timber; it was also prized for its hawks, which could be trained for hunting. The Province of Moray was conveniently split into lordships, two of these being Badenoch and Strathspey. In 1226, Alexander II gave Rothiemurchus to the Bishop of Moray in exchange for other lands, and he in turn left it to Elgin Cathedral to provide fir torches and candles. The bishop ensured that the territory was occupied and protected by putting noblemen or 'thanes' in charge of certain stretches. The oldest 'road' in Strathspey is identified as the 'Via Regia' with which Alexander II's name is also associated. Following the grain of the country over Drumochter and holding to the east side of the Spey, it probably had a military purpose in moving troops to forestall Norse attacks on the coast. In Tulloch, a track has long been known as *Rathad an Rìgh*, literally, 'the King's Road'.

Out of the confused times of the Dark Ages, tribal groups or clans began to emerge. They were led by chiefs or rulers who, in many instances, claimed rights of first occupation of the land for their people. There were blood ties at least throughout the chief's extended family. To take the Grants as an example, they developed into an offshoot of the complex network of Clan Alpin, of which Clan Gregor was a leading element. Sir Lawrence Grant was a Sheriff of Inverness in 1263 and this was a tradition maintained by their first Chief, Iain Ruadh, who was a knight in the fourteenth century. The opinion is that they had Norman ancestry with their name being *Le Grand* at the time of the Conquest and that they came into Strathspey in the fourteenth century from Stratherrick. They acquired three 'davochs' (a measure of land) at Dreggie, Glenbeg and Gaick. A century later their link with Freuchie (close to the site of Grantown) had been established: in 1493 it became a barony and a castle was erected there with the hamlet of Ballachastle (*Baile a' Chaisteil* − 'the township of the castle') beside it. Gradually, through additions, their territory comprised much of Strathspey, described as 'ane great Hudge Estait'. (The name has been attributed fancifully but erroneously to the extensive moor of Granish, possibly from Grianais, 'the Place of the Sun', just north of Aviemore. It is not unusual for a window of blue sky to let the sunlight through on Granish when all

A Highland township, c.1730. The folk of Badenoch and Strathspey lived on 'davochs', portions of land supporting a 'baile' or township. Crops were grown on strips of 'run rig'. Beyond lay the rough grazing for herds of cattle and goats (LANDMARK, CARRBRIDGE)

around the mountains are covered in lowering clouds.) The Grant name was readily adopted by the folk over whom these overlords held sway – it was a sign of belonging, of duty and of protection.

Nearby towered Craigellachie, the rock of the alarm, which was chosen by the Grants as their beacon hill in time of trouble. (This should not be confused with the village of Craigellachie 25 miles (40km) to the north where the Fiddich joins the Spey; it is sometimes referred to as Lower Craigellachie to distinguish it from the rock.) The writer, John Ruskin, who visited Aviemore in the 1880s, explained the clan's attitude so well in *Two Paths*:

> The main road winds round the foot of a broken rock, called the Crag or Craig-ellachie . . . it is a headland, a sort of initial letter to the mountains. The Clan Grant have taken it as their rallying cry, 'Standfast, Craigellachie!' You may think long over these words without exhausting the deep wells of feeling and thought contained in them – the love of the native land and the assurance of faithfulness to it.

To this imposing massif Aviemore owes its name – *An Aghaidh Mhòr*, meaning 'the great hill face' in Gaelic.

At the top of Highland society was the clan chief to whom all within the clan or tribal area owed allegiance. It was really a bond based on kinship, no matter how distant. A Lord Lyon King of Arms, the authority adjudicating on matters relating to genealogy and armorial insignia in Scotland, once estimated that half the Scottish nation thought of itself as aristocracy and many still do so. Scots also continue to feel the pull of 'forty-second cousins' in family affairs. Below the chief were the tacksmen holding land either from him or for him. They were men of status and substance in the system and were often closely related to the chief. Then came the clansmen, tenants and cottars, working plots of land for which they paid rent in kind. It could be livestock, wool or eggs; they were also expected to labour on the tacksman's or the chief's land. They had rights to graze animals on the hill ground and to cut peat on the mosses. As a system it was just sustainable and it was held together by mutual obligations. It did not produce abundance and, sadly, it did not remove the risk of famine.

A chief's power and wealth centred upon having both men and cattle. These tribal arrangements gave the chief a 'tail' of followers to protect the clansfolk and their lands in times of conflict or in quarrels with other clans over such matters as cattle thieving. The tacksmen also benefited because they had a position of prestige, an income in kind and labour on demand. The clansfolk had fewer gains – they had little learning, little means, primitive implements and no incentive to make any improvements to their lot. They could win only meagre harvests from land exhausted by constant cropping. It was often a precarious existence. They could also be called away from their own plots to sow or gather for the tacksmen or the chief at the most inconvenient times.

The chiefs had another powerful lever over their clans – heritable jurisdictions or the right to administer rough and ready justice. When the King's laws were only effective where his authority could reach, and that was not far in difficult terrain, the clan chief was the sole legal arbiter. This situation applied in Highland districts. The Chief Grant of Grant held such a Sheriffdom. Wrongdoers were summoned to appear before 'Baron Baillie' courts. In 1663, the lands of Strathspey were given further status as a Barony of Regality, which meant that the chief was practically king in his own territory. In addition to punishing offenders, he could also regulate trade through stipulations about weights and measures. After 1745 these arrangements were abolished, proving a damaging blow to the power of the chiefs and to their social status. At the same time, 'ward tenure', or military service as payment to a feudal superior, was also stopped. Wealth plus new titles and honours, originating often in England or in the expanding empire, came to mean more to clan chiefs than their hereditary rights and responsibilities. Money and position took over from the old clan values in Highland society.

In addition to Freuchie, the Grants in time focused on Glenchernich, largely the modern Duthil. They were not the only Anglo-Norman interests which the tribal society of the Celts began to encounter from the 1100s onwards and that ancient organisation was partly absorbed into the feudal system of these incomers. From the twelfth century the Comyns (now Cumming), who were Norman in origin and a forceful feudal family, were Lords of Badenoch which lay to the south. (The latter name means 'the drowned land' in Gaelic on account of its liability to flood.) They had a fortress at Ruthven, a former motte site, where a clachan grew in its protection. Rothiemurchus became a source of contention between the Comyns and the Shaws, who claimed descent from the Celtic Thanes or Earls of Fife. The Comyns once had a stronghold at Loch an Eilein (the lake of the island) where the ruined castle dating from the thirteenth century stands. They built a hall there with a tower and a vaulted basement beneath it. Now flanked by trees and partly clad in ivy, the islet site may have been a crannog long ago; a causeway giving a shallow link to the shore has recently been detected. Two centuries later, so savage were the Comyns' actions that the clan was proscribed and their lands lost. It is probable that Castle Roy near Nethybridge, which is small in size and of simple design with walls seven feet thick, was also constructed for the Comyns or Cumins. Tom Bigla (Tom Bigleig) is an earthwork just north of Boat of Garten whose name commemorates a Comyn heiress of the early fifteenth century. It may once have been the site of a motte and bailey castle but the mound and ditch have long been eaten away by the Spey and in the 1860s cut through by the railway. To the Comyns' displeasure, the Laird of Grant married the heiress and thus got her land – a useful method of aggrandisement. As to the Comyns themselves, the chiefship is now in the family of Gordon-Cumming.

Through Strathspey there passed one of the most fearsome characters in Scottish history – the Wolf of Badenoch, otherwise known as Alastair Mor mac-an-righ, the Earl of Buchan, who was a son of King Robert II. In 1382, he was gifted the Lordship of Badenoch and the castle of Lochindorb; this warlord also had the fortress at Ruthven. Earlier he had secured the lease of Loch an Eilein castle from the Bishop of Moray but the relationship turned sour. With 'wild, wikkid hielandmen' he wrought havoc on the Moray plain. In 1390, Elgin Cathedral was burned in an act of medieval vandalism. Eventually, the Wolf did penance and made sufficient amends to find a resting-place in Dunkeld Cathedral.

Then came the Shaws who were a sept of the Clan Mackintosh and obtained lands in Rothiemurchus in the latter fourteenth century. Some claim that their old fortress was located on the hill at the Doune of

Rothiemurchus (*dun* being 'a fort' in Gaelic). In time they, too, displeased the Scottish king and nobility by their misconduct and acts of defiance. Their great hero was Farquhar Shaw (*Seath Mòr Sgor-fhiaclach* or 'Big Shaw of the Buck Tooth') who fought in the clan combat at Perth in 1396. There was a recurring dispute between two clans, or branches thereof, Clan 'Kay' and Clan 'Qwhele' (historians cannot identify exactly who these were). King Robert III's son, David, Earl of Carrick, had been on an expedition in the north and he may have organised the brutal contest. The argument appears to have been settled by thirty men from each side in gladiatorial style before the king and his court on the North Inch of Perth. Politically, there were two outcomes – the king's capacity to dominate clans was displayed and there was an interlude of peace between the warring parties for a time. Farquhar Shaw also led his warriors when they ambushed a band of Comyns at *Lag-na-Cuimeanach* (the hollow of the Cummings), near the north march of Rothiemurchus, with Pityoulish.

In 1464, Rothiemurchus was described as 'kirklands' held by the Bishop of Moray as feudal superior and its token annual rent was one 'fir' sapling on request. From the 1500s the yearly demand was for 160 trunks of pine trees to be available for floating out. Financial difficulties rather than warfare may have forced the Shaws to hand over the estate to the Gordons who, in turn, surrendered it to the Grants of Rothiemurchus. Another version suggests that the last Shaw of Rothiemurchus, Allan by name, was outlawed for the murder of his step-father, Sir John Dallas. The Chief of Clan Grant then secured the forfeited land for his second son. The clans were frequently at each other's throats and such acts typify their rivalry for position and power in the Highlands.

Enter Patrick Grant of Muckerach. He was assigned Rothiemurchus in 1570 'gin he could win it' but obtained a Crown charter of resignation for the land within a decade. For long, the Grants there were in a perilous situation with the Shaws intent on recovering their lands. The Mackintosh, as the Shaws' chief, considered that the place should have fallen to him and so the first Patrick's claim on Rothiemurchus was by no means certain. The Grants, however, held resolutely on to their 'duchus' or homeland, which they do to this day. The present John Grant is sixteenth Laird of Rothiemurchus (or the fourteenth according to another counting method); few Highland families have such a lengthy record of inheritance.

The wide valley of Glenmore, in which Loch Morlich sits like a jewel, was for centuries a remote corner. Access was possible via the Slugan an Eas gap (the pass of the waterfall) from Kincardine, in which parish it lay,

Muckrach, a sixteenth-century tower house, is near Dulnain bridge. It was associated with Patrick Grant who obtained Rothiemurchus about 1570. Ruinous for three centuries, it is now restored as a holiday home (left: A. E. GLEN; right: STRUTT & PARKER)

or through the Pass of Ryvoan from Abernethy. For thirty years from 1394 the lands of Glenmore, which were part of the Lordship of Badenoch, reverted to the Crown. So Glenmore was once a royal forest and hunting ground. In 1618, John Taylor, the Water Poet, on a visit to Scotland described one of the great hunts in which the nobility, attired in Highland dress, took part. In the month of August and part of September they came to the 'high-land countries' to hunt 'for their pleasure'. Hundreds of men covering a front of many miles formed a ring (or 'tainchel', from the Gaelic word for plunder or spoil). The deer were driven towards a defile or *eileirg* by the deer hounds, where they were easy prey for hunters with bows and arrows, spears or other weapons. Coming as it does from the same word, the hill *Càrn Eilrig* at the mouth of the Lairig Ghru recalls these times and its former use.

In 1685, Glenmore fell into the hands of the Gordons. As Earls of Huntly, and later Dukes of Gordon, they held immense lands stretching from Ben Avon almost to Ben Nevis. The Earl earned the famed title

'Cock o' the North', and was one of the most powerful noblemen in Scotland. By 1451, Alexander Gordon, the first Earl, had acquired the old castle which stood at Ruthven and by the 1500s the Gordons were heritable sheriffs and effectively governors for the Scottish king in the territory where they held sway. In a few decades, they were out of favour but the castle seems to have been reconstructed for their use in 1590, wisely, perhaps, as they were involved in many foreign intrigues. Nevertheless, the Earl became a Marquis, heading a clan that was pro-Jacobite and formidable.

Abernethy, however, which bordered Glenmore, was the property of the Laird of Grant. Within a few years, Robert Stewart of Fincastle, near Pitlochry, came to Glenmore, continuing an association of that family name with the area, as there had long been Stewarts in the Barony of Kincardine to the north. Robert Stewart was in Argyll's Regiment but had refused to take part in the Glencoe massacre of 1692. So he fled north where the Duke of Gordon gave him protection and, as he could not appoint him an officer, he made him keeper of his forest in Glenmore. This was a position of consequence with a fair income at the time. Dark pines interrupted by glades and mosses carpeted Glenmore, while on the slopes of the Kincardine Hills, where there was a good southerly aspect, several clachans were located.

There was a phase from the seventeenth century onwards when the Cairngorm gateway was left relatively unmolested. Protected by the bleak ranges of *Am Monadh Liath* on the west and by the fast-flowing tributaries of the Spey and *Am Monadh Ruadh* on the east, it was a marginal area to both the Clan Grant lands in the strath and to Macpherson territory in Badenoch. The Chief of Clan Grant must have slept peacefully at night in his castle at Freuchie near the site of Grantown in the knowledge that the stretch was a buffer zone and that a scion of his family was keeping a grip on Rothiemurchus.

Taking one of today's best-known settlements as an example, Aviemore together with Balladern was a davoch or 'doch'. Like most cultivated areas on the Grant of Grant domain, this measure of land was not a precise area because the nature and quality of the soil was so variable. A small community comprising a few families living in a clachan usually had eight 'horsegangs', for which each household contributed a pony or an ox to the plough team. The extent of a davoch was based on the level of subsistence that the ground might be expected to yield for its folk. Rothiemurchus, for instance, had six davochs. Balladern was probably the *baile* (meaning 'a township') or the clachan itself. The place-name seems to combine the former word with *eadarn* meaning the 'in-between' location, which was very appropriate for a site lying on the border of Badenoch and Strathspey proper. Today, old Balladern is remembered in the name Loch Puladdern, which is now split by the A9 trunk road.

The wealth of the clans lay in the ownership of cattle. The aim was to have as many beasts as possible; herds were traditionally numerous but of doubtful quality. The cows were small in size, horned but less shaggy than the Highland cattle of today. They were dark coloured and some descendants of the old breed could once be seen among the cattle of the Laird of Rothiemurchus. Horn and hides were the main items of trade. The beasts were moved to the hill pastures for summer grazing around the shielings or bothies on the moor where the folk camped out. There the women and young folk milked the cows, prepared salt-butter and made cheeses. These were the happier times extolled in poem and song. The cattle were brought back to the shelter of the valleys in autumn where they had to struggle to survive through the winter.

The herds were also used as pawns in skirmishes between warring clans and cattle-lifting became the stuff of legend. The Laird of Grant kept the peace and controlled rustling in his lands by means of 'great violence'. The *Rathad nam Mèirleach*, the path of the robbers, who were almost certainly cattle-rustlers, came through the Pass of Ryvoan to Glenmore where it skirted Loch Morlich and the entrance to the Lairig Ghru, before following Loch an Eilein's south-eastern shore. It saw men from Lochaber and elsewhere come to steal the black cattle and drive away their booty. Moonlit nights required special vigilance; an armed watch had to be set to protect the animals and such herdsmen were known as 'bowmen' in the Cairngorm gateway long after they had ceased to carry weapons. The Grants of Rothiemurchus were glad of the mutual protection arrangements made with the MacGregors, their blood brothers through Clan Alpin.

One of the most remarkable of the Grants of Rothiemurchus was Patrick, the sixth laird, who was born in 1665 and known as 'Macalpine', perhaps because of his special bond with Rob Roy MacGregor. To Macalpine's dismay, Mackintosh men set up a mill just beyond the west march of Rothiemurchus and threatened to divert water from the Rothiemurchus lands to it. (By the 1630s, 'water millis' had been established in 'Abernathie, Kincardin and Glencarnie' in Strathspey. Water rights became a touchy subject after 1658 when, for some years, the laird leased the woods for felling to a burgess in Nairn and small saw mills were built on several streams.) Having ensured support from Rob Roy, Macalpine wrote a contemptuous letter to the Mackintosh, who thereupon resolved to raid Rothiemurchus and set the Doune on fire.

Macalpine hoped to have a message from his ally but time wore on and no messenger appeared. Soon the Mackintosh and his men began to gather and they far outnumbered the Grants of Rothiemurchus. While contemplating this threat, Macalpine was amazed but alarmed when Rob Roy at last arrived on the scene all alone. Where were all the MacGregors? In answer, Rob Roy called for a piper and had him play 'MacGregor's Gathering'. As the tune rang out, MacGregors in twos and threes emerged on the Kinrara lands across the Spey until 150 of the finest men at Rob Roy's command were standing there fully armed. On seeing each group of MacGregors appear, the Mackintosh raiders slunk off in fours and fives. It was astutely done – the Mackintosh band had time to withdraw without losing face and no blood was shed.

Before Rob Roy returned south, he left two of his clansmen, who were renowned for their fleetness of foot, in Rothiemurchus. He reasoned that it was 'a far cry to Balquhidder and no one here knows the way'. To one of them, Macalpine gave the farm at Aultdrue (*Allt Drù*) where MacGregors lived until 1853. The outline of the old house is on a high bank protected by the river and the clearing, which was once tilled, is now crossed by the path to the Lairig Ghru.

By the seventeenth century, Scottish politics were focusing on supporters of the Stewart succession, Jacobites or Royalists, and adherents to the Covenanting or Reformed tradition who looked to the monarchs William and Mary of the House of Orange. On the Royalist side was John Graham of Claverhouse, Viscount Dundee, who was related to the Marquis of Montrose, and he was likewise very active in suppressing the rebellious Covenanters. Several Highland clans – Camerons, MacGregors, MacDonalds and Macleans – rallied to his cause. Even so, the power of the house of Stewart was flagging. At the battle of Killiecrankie in 1689, William's troops, led by General Hugh Mackay of Scourie, were overwhelmed in the defile where the River Garry surges through a gorge. Although the Highlanders were victorious, their leader Dundee perished, the campaign lost co-ordination and when the clans sought to carry the Stewart cause southwards, they were defeated at Dunkeld. Meantime, other Jacobite forces captured and burned the castle at Ruthven, probably to prevent its falling into enemy hands. In May the following year, General Mackay's troops, under Sir Thomas Livingstone, routed the Highland forces of Major-General Thomas Buchan at Cromdale near Grantown. It would not be the last time that folk in the district would see the passage of Jacobite soldiers through the strath. The Grants of Rothiemurchus felt threatened but there was a refuge near at hand. By the sixteenth century, the castle at Loch an Eilein seems to have been ruinous

Ruthven Barracks in 1929; a government stronghold near Kingussie, it was left a blazing ruin by retreating Highlanders loyal to the Jacobite cause in 1746 (A. E. GLEN)

but the first Lairds of Rothiemurchus wisely restored it in case the Shaws should again prove troublesome. The island stronghold was caught up in the conflict of 1690. After the battle of Cromdale, there were skirmishes on Granish Moor. Giorsal Mhòr, mother of the laird, another Patrick Grant, together with her family and retainers ensconced herself in the castle, which was held successfully against General Thomas Buchan and a party of Stewart supporters. The brave Giorsall is said to have busied herself making lead bullets. Meanwhile, the laird and his allies beat off MacDonell of Keppoch and his clansmen to save the day for Rothiemurchus. Once purely defensive, the castle is now the romantic centrepiece in a sylvan setting where the birches of Ord Ban contrast with the canopy of Scots pine around its shores.

In the early eighteenth century, the Highlands were to face great turmoil – the Jacobite Risings of 1715 and, more significantly, that of 1745. These were to be catalysts for profound change. As a punishment after 1715, Jacobite lairds had their lands forfeited, but within Strathspey the gentry remained, if not actively loyal to the Protestant succession, at least non-committal. Independent Highland Companies of men were recruited locally to supply garrisons and Ruthven was repaired to give such a company a sheltering base. Their purpose was to preserve peace and to check the plundering of cattle. The gateway area probably provided some recruits for these duties. Certainly, the Laird of Rothiemurchus had his own 'watch' or homeguard to prevent any theft of his cattle. A Disarming Act was passed in 1716 but it was unsuccessful as clansmen presented quantities of rusty weapons (some even being imported) in order to claim the rewards. The Glenshiel affray of 1719 in which Spanish troops were joined by disaffected Highlanders gave further cause for concern to the Hanoverian side.

Men in privileged positions, such as the Laird of Rothiemurchus or Rob Roy MacGregor, could pen letters but at that time literacy had long been the prerogative of leaders in Scottish society who were taught by tutors. After 1560 with the Reformers at the forefront, a national system of education for all Scots was devised with the declared aim of having an elementary school in every parish, a grammar school in every town and arrangements for progress to university levels. An Act of 1696 laid tax on the heritors, namely the landowners, in order to maintain a school and a qualified schoolmaster in each parish. Essentially, schools relied on the lairds to pay up and provide, and it was an over-ambitious aim. In the Minutes of Duthil and Rothiemurchus Kirk Session of December 1719 (at which the lairds 'Elder and Younger', were present), education was given attention:

> This day the Session did constitute William Martine alias Cameron to be Catechist in the parish of Rothiemurchas; The sd. William is also to teach the children of the parish to read and write, if they be sent to him. And the Session promises him a peck of meal out of each auchten part of land in Rothiemurchas and twenty pound Scots money out of the penalties.

This school was an initiative by the Society in Scotland for the Propagation of Christian Knowledge (SSPCK). From 1709 that organisation worked hard to support education in the Highlands, filling gaps in provision, but at a cost to Gaelic culture and language which at that time it too often equated with 'ignorance and superstition'. Its founders clearly had worries about a resurgence of Jacobite sentiment with its risks of Catholicism. Kincardine's school dated from 1721 and a schoolmaster was engaged to teach the tenants' sons in Glenmore about the same time. Two years on, Aviemore also got a school when both premises and master were 'transported' there from Kincardine. In 1725, with only 24 boys and 3 girls attending, the master was moved to Glen Feshie.

In 1723, Simon Fraser, Lord Lovat, wrote a submission to the government on the state of the Highlands, which caught the attention of King George I. In the same year, an early venturer north of the Grampians was Captain Edward Burt, an officer of Engineers. He compiled a remarkable account of his experiences in the mountain fastnesses and in surprisingly modern idiom mentions 'heath-scapes' and 'rock-scapes' as the dominant scene. Conditions of travel went from bad to worse. He advised taking a guide or 'conductor' to assist the mountain explorer: 'for if he once go aside and most especially if Snow should fall (which may happen on the very high Hills at any Season of the Year . . .) he may wander into a Bog to impassable Bournes or Rocks.' Those unaccustomed to the wilderness and a 'seeming Sameness in all rocky Places' could easily lose their way.

Crossing rivers was especially fraught. In Himalayan fashion tree trunks were laid across ravines to serve as bridges. A notable exception was on the River Dulnain. In 1717 at the Linn of Dalrachney where rock outcropped, foundations could be laid for a high-arched bridge of stone and lime, 'with such ane Reasonable Breadth and height as will receive the water when in the greatest speat . . . '. It is now the oldest surviving bridge in the Highlands and a dramatic symbol for the village of Carrbridge. Funds for the 'Bridge of Carr' came from unused stipends (ministers' salaries) as there was no incumbent in Duthil parish at the time. Acts of the Scots Parliament permitted such sums being put to 'pious uses', such as facilitating access to the parish kirk. On the wider channels, people had to use currachs – simple craft made of hide stretched over a wooden frame – as ferry boats; horses had to swim when towed across such streams. According to Burt, occasional fords were not without their dangers: 'the Bottom being filled with large Stones; the Current rapid, a steep rocky Descent to the Water and a Rising on the further side much worse'. Mosses, of which there were plenty, could bear the weight of the small Highland garrons but not of the captain's English horses which struggled violently and sank deeper into the morass. The ponies simply waited patiently to be pulled out. Meanwhile, the 'heavy Boots with high Heels' worn by the officers put them in as much peril as their horses. The rocky pass at Slochd Mhuic (*Sloc Muic*') was particularly feared as robbers waited there to ambush travellers in the narrow ravine or to steal cattle from clans folk. As Burt was based at Inverness and was familiar with Slochd, it is likely that he reached the fringes of the Cairngorms but he rarely mentions place-names, presumably because he had no knowledge of Gaelic and could not record them.

As a result of Lord Lovat's intervention, Major-General George Wade was asked to investigate and accordingly he set out for Scotland in the summer of 1724. His family background was a military one; Irish born, he joined the army at the age of seventeen and rose rapidly to high rank. He retired as a Field-Marshal. It was on an expedition to Minorca that he became dismayed by the lack of roads and so he had proper ones made to the serve the military. He was never a man to waste time; he did not marry but had four children, three by the same lady to whom he was said to be devoted. Within six months Wade was reporting on his Highland sortie. His report also showed that barracks such as Ruthven were seriously understaffed, but the most worrying matter was that 'The Highlands are still more impracticable from the want of roads and bridges.' Not surprisingly, Wade was given the job and the following year, having been appointed Commander-in-Chief, North Britain, his great road-building enterprise began. The rapid government response shows that the Jacobite cause was considered a real threat. The construction of the military roads was to change the locational value of Badenoch and Strathspey out of all recognition.

Before the general and his troops came to the Highlands, the glens and straths were served by only the roughest and most primitive of tracks, sometimes cobbled in places with the result that they were fit only for foot traffic or for ponies laden with panniers or dragging sleds. From October to May, they were quite inadequate, often just impassable watery ditches. The military plan was to link up the government fortresses. A key route would stretch from Dunkeld across the Pass of Drumochter to be joined at Dalwhinnie by a road coming from Fort Augustus over the Corrieyairack Pass. It would then lead north-eastwards to Ruthven Barracks and onwards via Aviemore and Slochd Mhuic to Inverness. The purpose was entirely strategic, namely to allow troops to be moved quickly between government strongholds and to quell any trouble spots. In the longer term the King's new highway transformed access through the Cairngorm gateway.

By 1725, the first military road was being formed and twelve years of astonishing achievement followed. The logistics and engineering of the routes called for careful planning. Surveying parties equipped with compasses, plane tables and chains went over the ground to be covered in the forthcoming year. Military practice prevailed for the road builders: the provision of tools and food, the setting up of camps, the marking of the line of the route and the positioning of forges for blacksmiths became routine. The preferred camps were 'hutts' of stone rubble and peat blocks thatched with heather. The men, who might have been recruited in Kent or Hampshire, were rostered on a rota system as roadwork earned extra

*This view shows the Wade Stone by the old A9 route in the 1930s.
Now it is preserved near the southbound carriageway* (A. E. GLEN)

pay – effectively double pay for non-commissioned ranks. A ten-hour day
was common.

For Wade's part, he seems to have got some satisfaction, even
enjoyment, out of his summer expeditions to the Highlands. Duncan
Forbes of Culloden, the Lord Advocate, wrote in a letter to the general,
who was then in the wilds of Drumochter, 'Never was a penitent
banished into a more barren desert for his sins'. Doubtless Wade's
'squaddies' labouring in the cold, driving rain or perhaps in sweltering
heat, would have agreed with his lordship. The soldiers hacked out the
roadway, digging ditches and clearing boulders with the simple but
effective tools with which they were issued – shovels, pick-axes, spades
and crowbars plus wheelbarrows. Occasionally, gun powder had to be
used. Civilian craftsmen had also to be employed; masons, pavers and
carpenters were engaged to tackle cross-drains and the numerous bridges
spanning burns and rivers.

Wherever possible, Wade adopted the Roman principle being mindful
that the shortest distance between two points is a straight line – thus, his
routes went over high ground rather than round it. Their width was 16
feet (5.3 metres) which was an extraordinarily generous size in Wade's day.
They kept away from the bigger rivers by contouring along the terraces
on the valley sides. From Garvamore (*Garbhamòr*) north, Wade found it
impossible to span the Spey as rock exposures were lacking. He had to rely

on a ford to reach Ruthven Barracks. After some fruitless attempts at rebuilding, it had been completed by 1724 to house officers and men; there was a bakehouse and brewhouse for their supply and later came a guard house with stables for dragoons and their horses. The troops made use of another ford on the Dulnain at Inchluin, which is now known as the Sluggan, where the surviving bridge has been incorrectly attributed to Wade. In upland areas marker stones were set up at five-mile (8km) intervals to aid travellers in winter – much like the poles now planted to assist snow clearance. One of these great stones survives as the Wade Stone close to lay-by 70 off the southbound carriageway on the A9 trunk road near Dalnaspidal. The general is said to have placed a golden guinea on its top and was surprised when he returned a year later to find it still there. He attributed this to the honesty of the Highlanders and not to their lack of stature!

The military camps for the road makers were pitched at approximately ten-mile (16km) intervals. The line of the road went through the davoch of Aviemore and Balladern. Whether Wade placed a camp there is not known, but about 1728 he certainly seems to have spent some time in the area because he became a regular, but unwanted, visitor at the old Doune where his host was the Laird of Rothiemurchus, Macalpine Grant. Maybe the general was just looking for a square meal for Rothiemurchus had an

The Inchluin or Sluggan Bridge on the River Dulnain, 2 miles (3.2km) from Carrbridge, is where the military road crossed that stream by a ford en route from Aviemore to Inverness (A. E. GLEN)

abundance of tempting game. Determined he must have been, as he had either to cross an awkward ford on the Spey to get to the Doune or look for a boatman with a currach to take him over the river. One night Macalpine took matters in hand. Locking the door when the two were alone, he drew attention to a carafe of water and suggested that they should deceive one another no longer. He then proposed that they toast 'The King over the Water' – in other words the Stuart claimant to the throne. Wade was horrified at being so compromised and never returned.

Whilst the general enjoyed the hospitality of the laird's table, his 'highwaymen', as he termed his soldier road-builders, were also encouraged and rewarded. Feasts of roast ox and camp-brewed ale marked the completion of sections of the route. Such celebrations must have been welcome relief from the tedium of dry biscuit and cheese interspersed with such treats as fresh eggs or fish, which could be got locally. Who knows, such rejoicings may have been held in the gateway district. Although the Redcoats may have arrived smartly uniformed in tricorn hats, bewigged and gaitered with the sound of fyfe and drum to cheer them, road construction in the Highlands must soon have told on their appearance. Each man had just a blanket, a haversack, a tin flask and a stock of 'camp kettles'. Any hill walker will readily appreciate that they were in sore need of the extra allowance of shoes and stockings, plus a new issue of clothing, when they returned south in the autumn.

Lairds were expected to help in providing materials such as timber for the construction of the general's huts. They were also asked to convey meal and malt for the military's use. Local folk were often not at all pleased to see the roadworks or the soldiery. It was a sign of government interference in Highland affairs and of increasing domination. Completed work could be mysteriously spoiled overnight or the programme sabotaged by the disappearance of the tools. Yet Wade and his troops persisted; 300 men were at work on the route in the summer of 1728 and by the following year it was possible for the general and the Lord Advocate to drive in a carriage from Inverness to Ruthven in Badenoch. The military road reinforced Ruthven's position as a major route centre with tracks from Glen Feshie, Glen Tromie, and one along the east side of the Spey, meeting Wade's highway there.

But the chiefs were not always happy about the roads. They feared that 'suggestions of liberty' would weaken their clan's attachment to them and that their lands would be laid open to risks of attack as the roads and bridges would allow easier movement for their enemies. The existence of bridges would make the men effeminate and less able and willing to take risks in crossing rivers! The gritty road surfaces were disliked as it meant having to shoe ponies, and how was this to be done when iron in quantity was lacking? In any case, there were no forges or blacksmiths in many areas and no money to pay for them. The poor country folk had no shoes either and hated the stony highway, while those who had brogues argued that they were too fine for every day use and would soon wear out. The greatest danger foreseen was the impact of strangers coming into the Highlands and destroying the ancient way of life of the clans. So it was to prove.

The locations of some of the huts became recognised stopping off points for the refreshment of travellers on the new roads. Encouragement was also given to the setting up of proper inns on the King's highway. In some places, a government subsidy was offered to foster inn-keeping as a business – in fact, a public service – in districts where travellers were few and income bound to be meagre. Such places earned the name 'King's House' and examples can be seen at Balquhidder and Glencoe. The Cairngorm gateway also got its first inn at Aviemore but it was an initiative of the Laird of Grant. It was a primitive affair, constructed of rubble with garrets above and covered with a roof of heather thatch. Crude as it was this 'howff' at least gave some shelter in what was then a cold, bare place for much of the year. A Post Office of a kind appears to have opened, too, as an 'Avemore' postmark survives from 1727.

In autumn, drovers with their cattle became frequent customers. The beasts needed a rest each night plus food and water at regular intervals – some was snatched on the way as they moved but slowly. Over Slochd Mhuic they came into Strathspey, and Aviemore was on the trail. There was a choice of routes southwards from there. One went via the Lairig Ghru and then by Glenfernate to Kirkmichael; it continued by Ballinluig and the Sma' Glen to Crieff. Alternatives were to go by Glen Truim to Drumochter or to follow Glen Tromie to the Minigaig or Gaick routes. Even Glen Einich was preferred to the menacing Lairig Ghru. Stances were formed for the beasts beside the rough inns. With a menu of oats in various guises – porridge, bannocks or brose – washed down with a dram of whisky, they were very basic places.

Travellers accustomed to better appointments and higher standards made scathing comments about such inns. Captain Burt described one with an earthen floor, most of it wet, the peat fire blackening the walls and rafters, the interior resembling a furnace, with smoke belching out, or a dunghill 'and pretty near the same colour, shape and smell'. It was most uninviting but Scots complained less. They made fewer journeys and those who did travel were usually the nobility or well-to-do who made sure that they enjoyed the hospitality of friends or relations en route. Even so, a Scottish gentleman visiting the Highlands in 1737 was astonished to find the roads completed and gratefully noted the presence of 'civilised places for the entertainment of travellers' where there had been nothing before.

At Aviemore in those early years the tenant innkeeper was James Cumming. One of his sons had great dexterity and this attracted the attention of influential lodgers at the inn. Recommendations led to the young Alexander receiving the backing of the Duke of Argyll and he was involved in the building of an organ for Inveraray Castle. He attained greater fame however as a clock maker in London and, with patronage from King George III, he designed and constructed an imposing clockwork barometer. A more practical invention of this forgotten genius from Aviemore was the world's 'first modern type of water closet . . . heralding a new and more sanitary age', an appliance which he patented in 1775.

Where there were cattle there were also cattle thieves. After the Jacobite insurrection of 1689, as part of its policy for controlling the Highlands, the government had gone along with the raising of three independent companies of men from clans thought to be trustworthy such as the Grants. Their disbanding occurred in 1717 as those in command fiddled the pay returns and the units were not subject to martial law. But Wade recalled the Highland Companies in 1725 and, having secured a new Disarming Act, he set about trying to neutralise the fighting power of the clans. Regular soldiers gave the Highland Companies some basic training for their patrol duties and Wade instituted annual reviews at Ruthven. The general was much displeased on learning that, when the summer was over and he had left Scotland, the men of the Highland Companies set off for home. The calls of the harvest may have been the reason, however, and not insubordination. Nevertheless, the three companies soon became six (one of which was Colonel William Grant of Ballindalloch's Company of Strathspey men) and in time grew to be a regiment, the Black Watch. It was in effect a police force against the reivers but mustering kept men in particular places and not in the remoter districts. So the reivers took care to avoid areas where the companies were on guard. Indeed, they became even bolder and raids were mounted on adjacent lowlands from parts of Badenoch, Braes of Lochaber, Glengarry and Strathdon.

In 1730, local gentry sent a petition to Lieutenant-General Jaspar Clayton, then a commander in Scotland, with 'Proposealles to be laid before the Gentlemen of the Shires of Murray, Banff and Aberdeen for preventing Theft and Depredations by means of the Highland Regiment'.

After deploring 'Oppression by Thieves and Villains', it explains that many areas had suffered more in one year than in twenty from rustling. Accordingly, lists of suspects 'in respect of Habit and Repute' should be drawn up, although the reivers were adept at 'proving themselves alibi'. To stem the raids, Aviemore figures as a strategic point where a sergeant and six to twelve men should be based which highlights the locational significance of the place but the idea was not taken up.

The ring-leaders among the cattle thieves were alleged to be mainly MacGregors, Macdonells of Keppoch and Macdonalds of Glencoe. So infuriating were their actions that even the pro-Jacobite Mackintosh of Borlum was forced to protest to Wade about them. The Laird of Rothiemurchus had agitated correspondence with Macdonell of Glengarry about arrangements to stop cattle-lifting in their respective territories. Although the reivers' numbers were small, the threat they posed was taken seriously. So drovers were made exempt from the Disarming Acts of 1716 and 1748 and with their fierce dogs they were thought a formidable deterrent to most reivers. Not just cattle but horses, sheep and goats were also targeted. A computation was made by Nicol Graham of Gartmore of the loss of this livestock to the Highland economy. The value of the stolen stock, the expense of trying to recover animals, 'watch money' paid out for the guarding of the beasts, the so-called 'black mail' (derived from 'black meal'), which could be described as a protection racket, and understocking as a result of thefts – all this was reckoned to amount to £37,000 a year in the 1700s. It was a very considerable sum at the time.

When the King's highway from Dunkeld to Inverness was complete, other schemes were considered. General Wade had plans (1734–40) for a road through Glen Feshie to link Braemar with Aviemore via Ruthven, but it was never begun. This proposition has reared its head from time to time, most recently in the 1960s when remote countryside and wilderness were less appreciated than they are now. Despite being a great achievement, the military roads were little better than the forestry ones of today. They soon deteriorated with floods and frosts taking their toll. In 1740, Lord Lovat, travelling south along Strathspey in his 'chariot', encountered numerous problems with the passage. He brought his wheel wright with him the length of Aviemore Inn and had no sooner dismissed him than the rear axle broke – such was the state of the road.

A track ran between the Chief of Grant's domain at Freuchie and the southernmost corner of his clan lands at Aviemore. Its line skirted Dalfaber and made north across Granish Moor to near Avielochan and so to Boat of Garten. Now linked via the King's highway to Inverness and to

Dunkeld, this made Aviemore a junction of routes. The site was set on course to be a hub for people coming and going along the corridor of the strath. Aviemore folk knew it as the Captain's Road but there is no record of its having any military associations in Wade's time. By the early nineteenth century, it had been abandoned and soon became the preferred path for whisky smugglers keeping them well away from the new Great Highland Road and the eyes of excisemen.

One unforeseen consequence of the military roads was the good use which the Jacobite army made of them during the Rising of 1745. Prince Charles Edward Stuart and his forces crossed the Corrieyairack Pass on their march south. In August of that year, Lieutenant-General Sir John Cope made a rapid advance with more than 2,000 government troops up the military road over Drumochter to Inverness; after three days of forced marches, his army was reported as fatigued and very frightened. By the time the gateway was reached there were not only desertions but threats of sabotage by Jacobite sympathisers. Cope did not raise extra support – not even men to act as scouts or form raiding parties joined him. In February 1746, the Prince's army passed by Aviemore on its way to Inverness and Culloden. The old inn must have echoed to the skirl of the pipes as the weary clansmen in tartan tatters wound their way north. Only stirrup cups may have been taken there for the prince did not overnight at the inn, possibly a reflection on its unwholesome condition for a royal personage. He chose to billet himself on local gentry, he and his officers opting for the comforts of Inverlaidnan House which stood near the River Dulnain. The lady of the house was a Grant by marriage and was far from pleased to have the prince lodge with her and worse still his army of rough Highlanders in the vicinity. No wonder, she not only had Hanoverian sympathies but also had a split new house. The old dwelling at Inverlaidnan had been burned down in 1739. After some delay it was rebuilt and in 1746 was recently completed. At that time her home was rather unique in the district as it was constructed of stone and lime, no less, instead of random rubble. Thankful she must have been when the prince and his troops soon left for Moy.

The attitude of the Grants to the Jacobite cause was contradictory. Although the clan was raised by the Chief of Grant, the men soon discovered that he was pro-Hanoverian. This led to wholesale desertions and Grant enthusiasts for the Stuarts had to help in less obvious ways. The Rothiemurchus branch followed their chief's lead, if somewhat ineptly, since James, the seventh laird, was court-martialled for surrendering Inverness Castle (then known as Fort George) to the rebels. Aviemore Inn must have witnessed the return of the dejected Jacobites fleeing the disaster of Culloden. They were en route to sack Ruthven Barracks which they left a blazing ruin in April 1746. The worst forest fires of the century were set going, possibly deliberately, in Abernethy that year. The question remains as to whether this was a Jacobite protest.

In the absence of that barracks and with 15,000 troops of the Hanoverian army in Scotland, most regiments were deployed widely and in small numbers to suppress and control any attempt at renewed insurgency in the Highlands. Detachments were positioned at strategic centres and those places with inns, such as Aviemore, Blair Atholl, Dalnacardoch, Dalwhinnie and Garvamore, were sought out by the quartermasters. In September, the commander of Loudon's Regiment, which was based at Fort Augustus, stationed a subaltern and thirty men at Aviemore. This was a Highland regiment raised by the fourth earl in response to the heavy defeat of the British army at Fontenoy in May 1745. The Earls of Loudon, although Ayrshire landowners, were Campbells by descent, and had been zealous Covenanters and staunch supporters of the Protestant succession. Thus, clan hatreds found a fresh outlet in the official persecution and repression of the Jacobites. The troops were still at Aviemore the following year.

A local hero of the uprising was John Roy Stuart, a descendent of the last Stewart of Kincardine who had been inveigled into parting with the ancient barony to his brother-in-law; it then passed to the Earl of Huntly, later the Duke of Gordon. (Like some chiefs, the latter acquired ever more land by paying off the owners' debts.) The first Stewart of Kincardine was a son of the Wolf of Badenoch and a charter of the lands there was obtained from King Robert III in 1400. Kincardine had once boasted a baron's castle near Pityoulish and it had many clachans of which the largest was 'Am Baile Mòr' where some field investigations have been done. John Roy was born at the Upper Knock in 1700 to Barbara Shaw of Guislich.

John Roy – from the Gaelic *ruadh* or 'red-haired' – had a good education and pursued a military career in the Royal Scots Greys which was a regiment of dragoons. He rose to be a lieutenant and quartermaster, a position of consequence with money to spend on billets and supplies. When the Independent Companies of Highlanders, later known as the 'Black Watch', were formed in 1729, he was refused a commission therein and so he resigned from the army. He became a Jacobite agent; with the old family name of Stewart, it can perhaps be appreciated where his sympathies lay after such a rebuff. He was imprisoned in Inverness Jail in 1736 but got out with the connivance of the Sheriff who happened to be Simon Fraser, Lord Lovat. John Roy then fled to the continent where he was entrusted with a mission to Rome, a centre of Jacobite intrigue.

In 1744, John Roy followed the practice of so many Scots adventurers abroad and continued his military career with the Royal Écossais, in the Duke of Perth's Regiment, serving the King of France. He fought against the British forces at the battle of Fontenoy. When the Forty-Five began he made a hasty return to Scotland to join Prince Charles Edward Stuart, whom he had earlier met in France, and with whom he had a close and valued friendship. Using his army contacts, he raised the Edinburgh Regiment and as a colonel took part in all the major engagements of the campaign. His knowledge of the workings of the Hanoverian army would have been invaluable but his advice was often ignored. After Culloden, there was a price on his head. For a time he was a fugitive in Kincardine itself, in Glenmore and elsewhere, having some hairsbreadth escapes. From vantage points in caves high on the hills such as Craiggowrie, he must have watched uneasily while the patrols by the red coats of Loudon's Regiment searched the countryside, but he was able to elude them. He eventually met up with the Prince and his party and together they made good their flight from Moidart in a French privateer. Although John Roy was esteemed as a brave and intelligent Highland officer, it is for his Gaelic poetry that he is best remembered. It is moving and perceptive. The strength of the oral tradition ensured its survival as, sadly, he was unable to write in Gaelic.

Within two decades of the Forty-Five, the old inn at Aviemore was outworn and outdated. An age of improvement and of increasing mobility was beginning. The gentry, the military and government officials were making regular journeys to and from Edinburgh and further afield. The young James Grant of Grant had succeeded as laird and he was related by marriage to Colquhoun of Luss. Hearing that the latter was building a superior inn on Loch Lomondside, James Grant took notice. At Blair, the Duke of Atholl was active in another inn project. An expenditure of £250 on such a building could yield a worthwhile rent of £25 a year, so the laird considered new premises for Aviemore.

By 1765, James Grant of Grant had set masons to work on the new hostelry. A site was chosen immediately in front of the old inn; the idea was that the new premises would hide it and form a spacious courtyard. The old inn was retained for the innkeeper's family as that arrangement would ensure that the new premises were kept 'neat and clean for passengers'. By the side of the Wade road, William Forbes, the grieve from Castle Grant, putting his arithmetic to good use, marked off the simple structure. It was 42 feet (12.8m) in length and 22 feet (6.7m) in breadth; there were two parlours on the ground floor with the main bedrooms, complete with powder closets, above. There was space for a stable on the west side and for a kitchen and 'brew-house' on the east. Aviemore ale in the form of porter, a dark-brown bitter beer, was certainly brewed. Accounts for 1774, run up by the laird's family and servants during a stay at Aviemore Inn for the benefit of his children's health, record the frequent consumption of porter during their residence there. Ale was in general use in Scotland – it was so much safer than most water supplies as it required cleanliness and care in its making.

It was no easy matter to erect such a building at Aviemore; stone and lime construction was rare and the supply of many materials was a headache. While boulders of granite or schist were good enough for random rubble walls, they were very difficult to shape into dressed stones for lintels, doorways, windows or chimneys. Accordingly, quantities of sandstone for these purposes had to be brought from a quarry at Kilravock in Nairnshire by horse drawn carts. The laird's tenants, for such his clansmen had become, were obliged to convey a number of loads for their chief every year. These 'long carriages', which were thoroughly unpopular, could involve carting coals from Findhorn for use at Castle Grant, a distance of some 25 miles (40km). As for the construction site at Aviemore, the tenants' Highland ponies were too weak after the harsh winter to haul weighty loads of sandstone up Strathspey on an even longer journey. The emaciated beasts, half-starved, could scarcely stumble along the roads. To let the masons begin work, the laird was requested 'to give Orders for carrying the Lyme from Rothemurchus', where that rock outcropped on Ord Ban near Loch an Eilein. This meant extra heavy carriages for the tenants which, not surprisingly, they were slow to fulfil. A few valuable bands of crystalline limestone cross the Highlands but the rock had to be quarried and burned, or calcined, into quicklime, prior to its use. A massive lime kiln may still be seen beside the visitor centre at Loch an Eilein.

Great attention was paid to the facilities at the new inn. Politely the grieve refers to 'the little house' (*taigh beag* in Gaelic) – in other words, the two dry closets where the masons were instructed to make a window and 'put a small Funnel or Vent in one of the Corners of the little house beginning below the Seat to prevent there being any bad Air when the Brodds [boards] are lifted off the Boxes' – draughty and chilly it must have been. Wooden pipes were laid to bring water to the wash house and there was a pit for ashes, a peat yard, and paving for spreading dung. It was hard work for the labourers with rocks on the site being first drilled, then blasted to pieces with gun powder. The planting of crops to supply the inn was in hand too; potatoes, turnips, grass for hay and bere, an inferior form of barley to be used in brewing, were sown.

As Castle Grant was being rebuilt at the same time, good tradesmen were scarce. Even food for them was lacking because of poor harvests, and so oatmeal had to be imported from the Lowlands to feed the joiners. Glass came from as far away as Tyneside. Problems arose through shortages of timber. As James Grant had been lax about arranging for sufficient wood to be on hand, flooring and roofing timber had to be got from Rothiemurchus and not from his own forests. Local timber had been much in demand for shipbuilding. Due to the scarcity of timber in the Lowlands, as early as 1631 the pine forests in the Highlands were being targeted by the Commissioners of the Scottish Navy. They struck a bargain with the Laird of Grant when his forest was leased for forty years at 'fiftie merks the hundred' for deals of wood. Furthermore, free transport was guaranteed 'doune the river Spey to the sea without paying toll or tax to any persone'. The flow of logs was controlled by men in currachs who walked back carrying their craft on their backs. The remote location was always to prove an obstacle, although further efforts by outsiders to profit from the woods were made in the 1650s in both Abernethy and in Rothiemurchus. An old man recalled that in his youth in the early 1700s he could travel from near Aviemore in the shade of the forest and hardly ever see the sun until he came to Cawdor Castle near Nairn. Fires by accident or intent had made some inroads, as had local needs, but inaccessibility had allowed the forest and its wildlife to survive in sanctuaries such as Abernethy, Glenmore and Rothiemurchus.

Another early venture into forest exploitation in Strathspey was that of the York Buildings Company, which had an ambitious project to raise water from the Thames for use in London. A few years after the Jacobite Rising of 1715, with a long eye to the supply of minerals and other resources, the company became Scotland's biggest landowner through its purchase of the forfeited estates. As timber was becoming ever scarcer in England, Scottish forests were a big attraction. In 1728, the Laird of Grant sold some 'of the Best and Choysest of the Fir Woods Besouth the River Spey' in Abernethy Forest to the company. Strong rafts were constructed to float logs down the river. An unlikely entrepreneur, who, after visiting the Highlands, urged the company to get involved, was Aaron Hill, the manager of the Drury Lane Theatre in London. He penned the poem, 'The Golden Glades of Abernethy' and is said to have taught local men how to make proper rafts. The scheme did not prosper and within three years the company had collapsed; by 1780 the laird had still not been paid in full for his trees. The company also tried iron-ore extraction near the Lecht, where the mine building may still be seen. Using the Scots pine to make charcoal, the furnace was located at Nethybridge.

Glenmore was also targeted and from 1709 a partnership of a Banff merchant and a Londoner had contracts with the Marquis of Huntly (later the Duke of Gordon) there and with Patrick Grant, alias Macalpine, the Laird of Rothiemurchus, for timber extraction. To assist floating, the laird was urged to consent to 'cleaning and streightning' the Luineag, flowing from Loch Morlich, as in its natural state, it was unsuitable for the purpose. As most of the stream's channel was in Rothiemurchus, this was acceptable, always providing that the laird's meadow and corn lands were preserved and compensation was given for any trees cut down. It was an amicable arrangement with advantages for both parties, but only part of the bed appears to have been cleared as it proved too difficult and expensive. A 'dam-dyke' and sluice were installed on the Luineag and later across the mouth of the loch. Nevertheless, labour relations in Glenmore seem to have been tense with the overseer complaining that he had never had such trouble in his life over wages and stolen planks.

By 1715, land carriage seemed a better option, which meant forming a road across Rothiemurchus: 'Mr Grant was prevailed upon to give them no interruption to the road which was accordingly made by the purchasers, and passes to this hour by the name of the Englishmen's road.' It went from Glenmore to Camismore (now Cambusmore) on the banks of the Spey and its line is closely followed by the modern route from Loch Morlich to Coylumbridge. The largest logs 'fit for masts' were thus hauled out by wagons while the smaller spars were floated down the stream. In 1718, the Duke of Gordon sold the woods of Glenmore to John Smith of Stockton, who was a shipwright, and William Francis of Durham. The duke and the laird enjoyed such friendly co-operation, perhaps helped by their relationship as 'cousins by marriage' (the laird's wife being Jean Gordon), that a saw mill to process Glenmore wood was built at Stronamain on Rothiemurchus ground on the Luineag near Loch Morlich. In return, Macalpine Grant had permission to graze his own cattle – his Highland stots, which, he argued, would not, unlike lowland beasts, disturb the deer – at Lyneburrack (or *Rennaberach*), a shieling on Gordon land in Glen Feshie, where he had the use of both pasture and the bothy. In 1723, they even attempted to alter the course of the Spey between Rothiemurchus and Kinrara which was also Gordon territory. The families were on the best of terms with the laird acting as factor for Kinrara of which he had a tack or lease.

In 1754, the Dowager Duchess of Gordon, on behalf of her son the young duke, began negotiations again with James Grant of Rothiemurchus. She sought the same favours of channel maintenance, the landing and stacking of timber 'as oft as they may have occasion for it' and 'of building saw mills on any convenient stance above the stone-bridge and making leads and way-floods therefor'. The 'stone-bridge' was the one at Coylum. A bridge is shown there on Roy's map circa 1750 and Rothiemurchus traditions relate its construction to the generosity of John Corrour Grant, a son of the Laird Macalpine, who was born while the family were at their summer shieling at Coire Odhar in Glen Einich. He had made his money through military service. Between the Grants and the Gordons all appeared harmonious and the favours were continued, any loss or damage sustained 'by cutting ground, frequent inundations or pilfering of woods by people employed in any part of the work' being taken care of by 'two honest men at arbitration'. Nothing much was done with the forest of Glenmore, however, except for 'several parcels of wood floated down in the usual way' for the new Gordon Castle at Fochabers. There was 'a trifling sawmill' at 'Rennachan' (Rieunachan) in Glenmore, 'manufacturing on the spot' for local use and there matters rested.

Glenmore was, however, a likely proposition for timber exploitation on a greater scale; a map of 1762 shows the extensive woods and the small farms near Loch Morlich, one of which belonged to the forester. The Duke of Gordon's factor stated that it was 'without doubt one of the prettiest places in Britain'. Even before the young duke came of age, action was taken. The painful consequence was the eviction of Patrick Grant, the tacksman of Lynmore and Rienachan (Rieunachan) who feared that the duke's advisers desired to create a deer forest. But no; the purpose was to make way for the duke's servants 'for the more convenient manufacture of the Fir Timber in Glenmore'. This expulsion involved not only the tacksman but ten other tenants in addition. They were warned in 1761 'to flitt and remove yourselves, wives, bairns, Family, servants, subtenants, cottars, goods, Geare, and all other from Whitsunday next'. But Patrick Grant did not go quietly. He fought the dispossession, pursued compensation for improvements that he claimed he had made to his quite substantial house at Rieunachan with wood from Rothiemurchus and asked for access to pasture for his nine or ten horses. Two years later he was still in partial occupation at Glenmore.

In 1766, the Duke of Gordon was reported to have had an 'uncommonly good crossroad' formed from Glenmore to assist the timber trade – possibly the old waggon way had been remade – as he wished 'to enter a bargain' for the woods. In 1767 he was advised to seek a perpetual servitude or right, over the Luineag and its banks but after a legal tussle he was confirmed only in their use. By this time Grant of Rothiemurchus was also active in 'wood manufacture' and so he was jealous of water supplies which were crucial for his saw mills. (One on the Beanaidh had failed 'for want of water' as the channel had shifted.) As the duke had 'of late held forth in a very different language', the dispute turned acrimonious. Relationships went from bad to worse and in 1779 the parties were engaged in further litigation.

About forty years earlier Hull merchants had Rothiemurchus forest assessed as capable of producing timber 'as good as the best Norway wood' but the reality was that they were soon disappointed by its puny size and gave up. Improved accessibility by road and river gave the forests a monetary value to the lairds which was to bring successive bouts of exploitation with variable profits. In 1763 an overseer was appointed for the Laird of Grant's woods where there were already foresters to guard the trees and supervise felling. But wrangles about floating, about the use of the beach at Garmouth for timber awaiting transhipment, and other matters were to embroil the lairds and the Duke of Gordon for many years.

By August 1766, the new inn at Aviemore was virtually complete. It was described as 'a fine house' and had a peel-like appearance for it was a solidly foursquare structure, harled against the elements. There was a large walled garden across the Allt Balladern (now the Aviemore burn) on the east side of the King's highway. Standing on rising ground beyond the valley of the burn where the military road took a slight bend to the north, the inn was the reason for the initial rise to fame of Aviemore as a place of resort. That the Laird of Grant had 'no view but to accommodate travellers' was said to be amply demonstrated from 'his demanding nothing from his tenant but serving his guests well'. The inn thus became a key element in attracting early visitors to the Cairngorm gateway.

Once the new inn opened, Aviemore was again thought to merit a school. So application was made in 1767 to the SSPCK for another charity one. School master Alex. Harvey was appointed but the classes were soon in need of finance from the Laird of Grant as the place was too poor to maintain any teacher, far less one with a wife and five small children to support. It therefore did not last long. A SSPCK school however was active in Rothiemurchus in 1744 and had 36 boys and 19 girls as pupils. Society lists show that Alexander Allan was master at 'Inverey of Rothiemurchus' for eight years until he was 'transported to Kirkmichael & succeeded by David McBean'.

A notable landlord at Aviemore Inn was old John Grant, a veteran of the '45 Rising. He had fought at Culloden among the Clan Mackintosh. Old John recalled that his first sight of the enemy was the long line of white gaiters belonging to an English regiment which was suddenly revealed on a gust of wind blowing the smoke of battle away. He was tenant at the inn for almost forty years helped by a succession of wives, his reign only being interrupted for four years when a Mr MacGregor of doubtful competence took over. The latter wished to keep chaises but this required a licence for which he was reluctant to pay, arguing that the road was impassable for four months of the year and so bringing him little business. The bold fellow therefore asked the Laird of Grant, who was also a Member of Parliament, to present a petition at Westminster to secure him a reduction in the fee.

The track between Castle Grant and Aviemore was upgraded. The minister of Duthil parish, in which Aviemore lay, wrote:

> Grantown to Aviemore, 13 miles (21km) in length, was repaired in 1779 to 24 feet (7.3m) in breadth (being formerly 12 feet) by the country people at the request of the proprietor, James Grant.

The scheme was again typical of a chief obliging his tenants to make road repairs as part of the hated statute labour system; generally all those over 16 years of age had to gather to work on a project with spades, picks and crowbars before the harvest time. But such efforts allowed Aviemore to retain its position as a junction of routes. A few years earlier the Duke of Gordon's people had been required to make the public road through Kincardine where a surveyor was employed 'to inspect the line' as the route went through cornfields and over moss.

Easier accessibility was matched by a new mystique. In 1760 James Macpherson, a Badenoch 'lad o' parts' and schoolmaster, had published 'Fragments of Ancient Poetry Collected in the Highlands', the so-called poems of Ossian. This caused a sensation in literary circles and although there were questions over the authenticity of the work, he became a celebrity with patronage in high places. For that or other reasons, from the 1770s onwards there was a notable increase in the flow of travellers going north. Thomas Pennant, writing in 1772, praised the military roads and likened General Wade to Hannibal as 'he forced his way through rocks thought unconquerable' and 'subdued their obstinacy with gunpowder'. He observed that the new routes did not follow the tracks used by clans folk but even so they had gone far to render the Highlands accessible and hence 'contributed much to their present improvement'. Like most travellers (Johnson and Boswell among them) he chose not to go by Badenoch and Strathspey probably because this would have involved crossing the wastes of Drumochter. Other stretches were also risky. Not long after the new inn opened, its keeper John Grant had received an angry letter from a customer who had very nearly lost one of his postillions and two of his horses in a deep moss 'in the very middle of the King's high road' about five miles (8km) north of Aviemore.

Maps were few in number and thin on detail. The most complete survey was by General William Roy, a Scot born at Carluke, and his team of military surveyors but it was deposited and forgotten in the King's Library at Windsor. Dating from 1747–55, it was on a scale of 1,000 yards to the inch (1:36,000) and was delicately hand coloured. Details of those matters considered of importance to the army and its movement – hills, rivers, woods, farm land, roads and settlements – are carefully shown. Woods were a 'plus' for concealment, a 'minus' for ambush, farm land might give produce for rations and quartermasters sought out settlements as billets for troops. While hills and rivers were potential barriers, the principal roads were of prime strategic significance and shown in red. It was the first large-scale map of Scotland or of any part of the British Isles for that matter. Even so General Roy described it as 'a magnificent military sketch rather than a very accurate map of the country'. It gives a fascinating picture of the Cairngorm gateway with many features marked amid mountains dramatically delineated by hill shading.

It was hardly surprising that knowledge of the Highlands was sparse. It was said that Ministers of the Crown did not know much more of Scotland than they did of Tartary and that was precious little. One of the few travellers to pause a while in Strathspey was the redoubtable Colonel Thomas Thornton of Thornville, a Yorkshireman by birth, who made a sporting tour of the Highlands in 1786. His expedition seems today as elaborate and costly as any venture to the Yukon or Tibet. He was a gentleman with an ample fortune who set off with servants and baggage wagons laden with provisions, bed linen, tents and weapons. Horses and hunting dogs – pointers, setters and deer hounds – made up the cavalcade. The colonel was not unacquainted with Scotland; from the age of 14 he had spent five years at Glasgow University. He had a passion for hunting, especially for falconry, and was an outstanding athlete.

Colonel Thornton was a keen observer, noting how 'the ride between Raits and Aviemore is delightful, the road pleasing and differing from all the Highland ones . . . not in the least hilly'. There were views to 'the noble, winding, rapid Spey' and to the woods of Rothiemurchus and Glenmore 'in melancholy shades' contrasting with 'the pearl covered mountains' around them. This showed a new attitude to wild landscape. Sixty years earlier Captain Burt had found them 'gloomy spaces, different rocks and heath high and low . . . dismal brown', 'dirty purple, most of all disagreeable when the heath is in bloom'. So much for the bonnie purple heather.

The colonel's party approached Aviemore through an avenue of trees from where the inn came into view. He remarked on 'the large wide even plain' bounded by 'grey rocky stupendous mountains' intermixed with woods, yellow corn fields, pastures and 'black unprofitable heath'. Of the inn itself, he was sorry to report, 'found the inn I now put up at differing from those I had passed, it being very indifferently kept, the rooms very dirty; whereas when I was here before, no inn could be in better order'. He was referring to a student excursion made in his younger days but it was ever thus with inns, hotels or any other accommodation. If the rooms were scruffy, the landlord Mr MacGregor proved to be 'civil and attentive' and the provisions 'tolerable . . . mutton particularly good and the claret and cheese incomparable'. Breakfast consisting of 'some tolerable good tea, excellent cream and fresh eggs' also helped to make up for the inn's other shortcomings. Usually innkeepers were highly regarded as key members of a community; the Aviemore innkeeper was known as a supplier of wine to the lairds and in return he purchased hay for his horses and cattle from them.

The Thornton party made use of the ford and the ferry on the Spey to enjoy an outing to 'Loch Neiland' (Loch an Eilein), praising it as 'one of the very first rides in the world'. They climbed into the hills taking champagne and porter with them to be chilled in the snow fields. Everything was done in grand style. The colonel refers to the Cairngorms, an early use of that name for the mountain range. He plundered the game of the district and had a tussle with an immense pike in Loch Pityoulish and with another monster at Loch Alvie – it was over 6 feet (1.8m) in length but the colonel confessed that anglers are proverbially prone to exaggeration. He was received at the Doune of Rothiemurchus where a real taste of the Highlands awaited him. Like Wade, the colonel found the menu of the laird much to his liking. A 'well serviced table' was set with dishes of fine char, roebuck, hare, black game, dotterel, white game, partridge, ducks, snipes, salmon, pike, trout, parr and lampreys – all of which were in abundance upon the estate at that time. Whether this groaning board was a special feast to impress the visitor or whether it was normal practice in the Doune kitchen is not on record. Contemporary evidence shows that it was a time when the hills teemed with moor fowl, ptarmigan and mountain hares plus red deer and roe but numbers could soon diminish, not so much from the 'havock of the sportsman' such as Colonel Thornton but from the inclemency of the weather during the hatching season and from hard winters. The laird presented his guest with a goshawk, a bird prized for falconry, but now extinct in Scotland.

So taken was the colonel with Aviemore's setting, that via the innkeeper he approached the Laird of Grant as he wished to build a house there for his use in the shooting season. Accordingly he suggested that MacGregor give up part of his farm to allow several acres to be enclosed to make a good garden around the house but nothing came of the proposal. Colonel Thornton also negotiated with the Duke of Gordon for 'part of the land of Linovuilg (Lynwilg) called Kannapole lying to the south of the publick Road leading from Aviemore to Pitmain' doubtless with the intention of having a small sporting estate there. A tack or lease for thirty years was drawn up but was never signed.

While Robert Burns was on his tour of the Highlands in September 1787 he also passed through Strathspey and called at Aviemore. He probably overnighted there as he records, 'Breakfast at Aviemore, a wild and romantic spot'. He was amazed to see the snow patches on the hills reckoned to be 18 feet (5.4m) deep in places. Beyond Aviemore, Burns made his way to Grantown where he dined with the Laird of Grant who

The clachan of 'Leneivelg', near Aviemore, in an area which is now known as Lynwilg, as shown in an old sketch of the latter eighteenth century (HIGHLAND COUNCIL ARCHIVES)

had succeeded to the baronetcy in 1773 as Sir James. His experiences however did not inspire any poetry about Strathspey or the Cairngorms which might have added considerably to the allure of the gateway in popular imagination.

When the ministers of the Kirk wrote their parish accounts in the 1790s, they gave an invaluable insight into the many changes which were set to transform the Highland countryside not least in the Cairngorms region. Glenmore, Rothiemurchus and the Strathspey estates of the Laird of Grant were cushioned from the most desperate results of the break up of the clan system by the wealth of their forests and by their location on or close to the new road network. Apart from the chief Cluny Macpherson in Badenoch, who had been loyal to the Jacobite cause, they escaped the vengeance and 'ethnic cleansing' exacted after the Rising of 1745 having been either Hanoverian sympathisers or on the sidelines in that conflict but even so momentous events were in store. [1]

EXCURSION

Craigellachie

This National Nature Reserve is remarkable for its birch woods, unique insects and fungi. The approach to the nature trails is from the car park beside the dry ski slope in the Aviemore Centre where a finger post points to a path running alongside the A9 trunk road and Loch Puladdern (Balladern) for 300m. From some steps, an underpass gives access to paths which form a lower and an upper nature trail – the lower skirts a small reservoir while the upper climbs steeply past a viewing platform. Both lead to the track which goes to the summit of Craigellachie from where superb views over the strath may be had in clear weather – best seen in afternoon light.

For further information contact Aviemore Tourist Information Centre on 01479 810 363.

CHAPTER 2

A Countryside Transformed
1770 – 1850

In 1763 young James Grant of Grant, having taken over the management of his inheritance from his ailing father, was a very large landowner in the vicinity of the Cairngorm gateway. He had been given a good education, attending Westminster School in London followed by Cambridge University – presumed a fitting preparation for a man who would be a politician and a social leader. He quickly showed promise and was a Member of Parliament by the age of twenty-three. Further cosmopolitan polish had come from a Grand Tour of Europe. Long and expensive support for the government plus money spent on these and other indulgences had left the Grants in debt to the tune of £100,000. This was a very large sum. Additional costs were also involved in estate management, in paying taxes and in providing the salaries for a factor, schoolmasters and ministers. There were big arrears of rent too – £7,262 Scots in 1764. (£12 Scots was equal to £1 Sterling). How could income possibly be augmented? Although some properties in Moray were sold off, the Grants had a reluctance to part with land as they 'lament letting the thought of anie but a Grant have a footing within the two Craigellachies' on territory that must be 'preserved for the Clan'.

James Grant had a remarkable former tutor, adviser and friend, William Lorimer, who was also far travelled. He had been to North America, had ventured along the Hudson valley and made a study of the forests there. His family background was in the factoring of estates and so he was knowledgeable about land management. Encouraged by Lorimer and by the example of other influential landowners, James Grant became an improving laird. With increased receipts in view and intent upon advancing the condition of his tenants, every corner of his estates was surveyed and schemes were drawn up for the most appropriate and profitable use of his lands. For him the commercial imperative would be tempered by humanity and a host of projects gathered pace in the 1780s. The aim was the complete re-organisation of the old clachans or 'bailes' with their open field systems in 'runrig' or ridges. New, enclosed farms would in time be leased to progressive farmers instead of impoverished clansmen. Enclosures were in fact very rare, only the great houses, such as Castle Grant or the Doune of Rothiemurchus, showing such features round them on Roy's map.

The young laird was also pre-occupied with the development of New Grantown, known as *Baloor* in Gaelic (from *Am Baile Ùr* -the new township) a model settlement begun in 1765, which was planned as a focal point for industries and as a service centre. By advertising, manufacturers and tradesmen were offered 'lots' on which to settle and the making of textiles and other crafts were encouraged. Stone houses with glass windows where people could see during the winter were central to this plan as dark smoky cabins were 'indisposed for industry and

General Roy's surveyors faced almost as severe difficulties in the Highlands as General Wade's troops did. This sketch by Paul Sandby shows a survey party at work in the Grampians. The making of estate plans involved similar activity (THE BRITISH LIBRARY)

work'. James Grant was to witness the village grow to some 400 inhabitants, some of whom were as 'good tradesmen as any in the Kingdom . . . shoemakers, taylors, weavers of wool, linen and stockings, blacksmiths, wrights, masons and 12 merchants keep regular shops in it'. Manufacturing however was to prove disappointing in the longer term. Nevertheless, by the 1780s New Grantown was reported to be 'in a very thriving condition' – not only did James Grant live beside it taking the closest interest in its progress but the place had no competition. He also had plans for villages based on allotments or crofts of two or three acres but instead of the villagers' income mainly being earned in craft or factory employment, as he had hoped, it ultimately had to be got through forestry, farm labouring or road works. Skye of Curr was an example of such a settlement and another was located at 'the Bridge of Carr' on the Dulnain where Carrbridge has prospered.

James Grant and his officials faced a tough assignment in the countryside. It was hard to break the ancient mould to which the clansfolk were accustomed. They were very poor, their holdings small and 'their habitations wretched'. Peat or rubble huts, with earth floors and turfed or thatched above, housed people and animals under one roof. The soot impregnated turf was stripped off every few years and used as manure. So much fresh turf was cut for roofs and other purposes that the improving lairds were angered as it spoiled pasture for grazing. To see what one of these clachans may have looked like, the Highland Folk Museum, 'Turus Tim' (Travel through Time) at Newtonmore, should be visited. It is modelled on the reconstructed Baile Gean township at Raitts from information obtained at a site excavated there; it shows what conditions were like about 1700. The folk worked hard for a bare existence, 'treading superstitiously in the footsteps of their ancestors, disregarding every new mode of improvement'. The shortness of their leases discouraged initiative; yet 70 per cent of the tenants – the better off – had leases of 19 years or longer before James Grant took over but many had none at all. In 1756, wresting rents from poverty stricken tenants on the estate even caused mobbing and stoning at Craggan (south of Grantown). Recurring starvation haunted the strath. *The Gort Rìgh Uilleam*, the famine of King William, which lasted for seven years from 1695, had left a cruel scar on the folk memory. The starving had tried to survive on boiled nettles. So many families perished that not a 'smoke', a sign of habitation, was left.

Almost a century later, in the early 1770s and again in 1782–3, the threat of starvation returned. Only James Grant's concern and government assistance ensured supplies of imported grain for the people;

no wonder that he became known as 'the Good Sir James'. The cause was the destruction of the oats crop by an early frost in August but the rudimentary road network must have been of some assistance in the distribution of emergency food stuffs. The total population of the key parishes of the gateway – Duthil, Rothiemurchus, Abernethy and Kincardine – was about 3,000 at the time. There were to be repeated shortages in the opening years of the nineteenth century. As for Rothiemurchus, so much land was under forest that it 'could not supply itself with grain'. On the Laird of Grant's estate, oats, rye, bere and potatoes were usually enough but with memories of the 'short years', the prudent and the wealthy tried to store a six month's supply of meal. Potatoes had appeared in the district by 1736 when a few were sent as a gift from the Laird of Rothiemurchus to Macdonell of Glengarry to encourage him to apprehend cattle thieves who had taken three animals from Rothiemurchus. Frost was this plant's enemy and as sub-zero temperatures could occur late or early this was 'a great bar to the cultivation of that most useful crop'. Thankfully, Highlanders did not come to rely on the potato as much as the Irish and thus when the crop failed in the 1840s they did not suffer so badly – at least in Strathspey.

Far from being a golden age, malnutrition was only too apparent. Despite the climate having a name for being healthy, the people had many problems. Fevers and consumption (tuberculosis) were prevalent but the threat of smallpox was already being tackled by vaccination. Swollen joints, allegedly caused by the wearing of 'Highland garb' in cold weather, were common. To ease their miseries, a chance to make some cash was offered by illicit distilling and the folk were 'much addicted to it'. There were dozens of whisky bothies where 'uisky' (uisge), a beverage 'fit only for daemons', was sold 'to the very great prejudice of the purse, constitution and morals of the natives'. The Laird of Grant tried to suppress many of these sordid premises by the simple expedient of knocking them down and evicting the occupants. A brewery was set up in Grantown 'immediately at the building of it on purpose to keep the people from drinking spirituous liquors . . . '. Public gatherings were frequently marred by squabbling, fights and debauchery – human nature appears to alter little.

The most promising area for improvement, and it was by no means good land, was the lower ground. Taking the davoch of Aviemore and Balladern as an example, between 1767 and 1770 it was closely examined. A surveyor, Peter May, with an assistant armed with paper, pens, ink bottle and chain, made rough sketches of the clachans and the land around them. Every landscape feature was named in Gaelic, either from its appearance, its use or from some happening there. So there was 'knockan a' breachan', the speckled knoll, and 'knockan cardich'(cèardaich), the mill knoll; the intervening hollows or 'laggan' also had names such as 'lag each', the horse hollow. The stretches of wet ground near the Spey, often liable to flood, were entered as 'ellans', 'dells' and 'saughs'. The principal stream was shown as the 'Allt Balladern'. The davoch's moss, heath and poor pasture around Dalfaber were marked hopefully 'seems to be improveable'. 'Moor ground' was especially targeted and uneven, stony and rocky areas, of which there were plenty, identified. Although a substantial plantation of 'Scots Firs' was growing on Granish Moor, the folk went to the moss of Aviemore high on Geal-charn Mòr in June to cut peats for fuel. A peat road, shown as the track of 'Carnary' (from *càrn àirigh*, 'the cairn of shielings') led over to the Dulnain valley, to the summer grazings and the shielings.

After 1750 south country farmers with new breeds of sheep had appeared in the Highlands but the Laird of Grant did not approve of sheep farms and so 'no large tracts of land were laid waste' on that account. By 1770 each household in Aviemore kept 40 to 70 sheep and one family had 25 goats. The latter were also common in Glenmore which was noted for

Prior to the completion of estate improvements the cottages of country folk in the Cairngorm area were self built of rubble with a roof of turf or heather thatch. This example was near Kinveachy (SPECIAL COLLECTIONS / GLASGOW UNIVERSITY LIBRARY)

its flocks; they were carefully managed and highly valued as their milk was supposed to have curative properties. The hill Craiggowrie (*Creag Ghobharaidh*, 'the goat's rock') may recall their presence. Generally cattle rearing was preferred. John Grant at Aviemore Inn had six cows and Alex. Grant in Balladern had eight for milk. It was a struggle to maintain the beasts through the winter; although some grass might be cut off the saughs, neither hay nor turnips were grown and the stock fared poorly. The people lived mainly on oatmeal with milk, cheese, a little mutton or goats' meat, and the blood of their cattle.

Improvements were time consuming; they were painstaking and laborious taking several decades to produce results. James Grant of Grant believed in liming the soil; after 1715 lime had been brought into use because Strathspey men had seen the benefits it conferred on acid land in Fife. Limestone outcropped conveniently at Kincraig in addition to Ord Ban at Loch an Eilein. About 1770 James Robertson, one of the first naturalists to visit the Highlands, invited other gentlemen to imitate the Laird of Grant:

The old bridge at Coylum in Rothiemurchus, seen in the 1890s, owed its existence to John 'Corrour' Grant of Rothiemurchus. Lairds had bridges and roads constructed with a view to improving communications on their lands (WALTER DEMPSTER)

Instead of naked hills & dreary mosses, the eye would then survey with pleasure, woody or verdant mountains raising their heads amidst cultivated fields, while the industrious Tenant, tho' his rent were tripled, would live better than he does at present & be under no temptation to quit his native land.

From 1711 the old rents in kind had been given a money equivalent on the Laird of Grant's lands – a sheep such as a wedder was worth 30 shillings (£1.50) and a hen 2s 6d (12.5p). Sometimes these 'custom' rents were resumed to help supply the laird's table which was famed for its ostentation. By the 1750s three-quarters of the rents in the Highlands were being paid in cash which was really hard to find.[2] Whisky bothies might disappear but the 'uisky men' or smugglers whom Captain Burt had met, were as busy as ever because illicit whisky was a staple commodity and its sale helped to pay the new rents. Otherwise folk had little to sell except coarse plaid and bundles of firewood with which they trudged as far as Inverness to earn a few coins. Trading in cattle and pelts was more rewarding.

Estate plans were also drawn up for the Laird of Rothiemurchus; in 1762, William Anderson surveyed the 'Mains of Down' (Doune). A plan for the whole of Rothiemurchus was prepared in 1789 by Archibald Tait. Improvements began in sporadic fashion – a piece of ground drained here, stones cleared there or a boundary or two straightened. There was a limit to what could be attempted when the potential cultivable land was so restricted and the forest mattered so much more. 'Mr Grant of Rothiemurchus' was said in 1795 to have the most trees in the district. The woods were the greatest potential resource in the gateway although farming was catching up.

In the 1760s the woods at Abernethy had been leased to local contractors with limited success. The Laird of Grant advertised 20,000 'full grown fir trees' plus a saw mill and a boring mill at the Dell of Abernethy but the response was slow. Boring mills, which prepared tree trunks as pipes making them suitable for use as water mains, were unusual enterprises into which he had been lured by the Rothiemurchus Grants. Eventually Alexander Cumming, the innkeeper's son from Aviemore in a partnership, tried the business but despite a 15 year lease soon abandoned it. Another attempt to dispose of the forest was made in 1778 and then at ever more frequent intervals during which time thousands of trees were on offer usually close to streams to assist their floating out to Garmouth. The local contractors again met with varying success and Sir James Grant (by then a Baronet) complained that the cost of sending timber to Leith was 'intolerably high'. Floaters got a half penny for each deal or spar they took to Garmouth to which they might also carry bark, hides, skins, cheese and other produce on the rafts. The place grew into a thriving market and port. By 1811 there were seven saw mills in operation on the Laird of Grant's lands alone and the forest probably netted him £8,000 a year.

Both Sir James and his adviser William Lorimer had realised that any sustained yield from the woods would call for a programme of afforestation. It was normal forest management however to leave some seed trees when an area was cleared which led to good germination. In the 1750s the planting of thousands of Scots pine seedlings had begun around Castle Grant for 'ornament & benefit' but most were devoured by sheep and cattle. The lesson was learned. Within a decade planting was progressing in the neighbourhood in a more purposeful fashion when a tall earth dyke was constructed to protect the seedlings and a man deputed to guard them. The object was again both amenity and profit with exotic species such as silver fir and spruce being combined with larches and hardwoods – ash, elm and even laburnum – in the 1800s. Tree growth was encouraged in gardens and along road sides. Pine seed gathered in Abernethy forest was sown at various farms on the estate to produce a supply of seedlings but many were brought from Aberdeenshire and the Lothians. In the early 1800s over 1½ million trees were planted on the moor between Aviemore and Boat of Garten alone. The outcome of so much effort was that by 1814 about one-third of the woodland cover was the result of the estate's forestry policy – principally on the poor quality moorland – and Scots pine was supreme.

Regarding Glenmore, from the latter 1760s onwards, further approaches were made to the Duke of Gordon by traders wishing to purchase timber; in 1771 a merchant, who had examined the forest, wrote regretting that its timber was not manufactured:

> when it would be very advantageous to the proprietor & to the country & such an advantage to the nation . . . many thousand masts, beams – & the finest plank of any lengths for shipbuilding can be had there.

Some activity ensued with deals being supplied for the new Gordon Castle at Fochabers which was still under construction. A bargain was struck with John Stuart, the forester in Glenmore, to cut down 400 trees and cross cut them into logs of different sizes. Soon he had the tenants from Kincardine on the job, working the sluice at Loch Morlich while sixteen horses and six oxen were busy hauling timber in the forest. This arrangement was renewed annually for several years.

By the 1770s owners of forests were more litigious than ever as woods were perceived to have money-making potential; accordingly, there was the vexed question of boundaries to be sorted out and there was renewed tension over this matter between Glenmore and Rothiemurchus. If forest was to be sold, surveys had to be made, and plans drawn, then 'marches' agreed and marker stones carved or set up between estates. Negotiations between the Duke of Gordon and the Grants of Rothiemurchus did not always go smoothly and the duke's staff actually considered having a canal cut to float timber out through the Sluggan pass via the 'Miln burn' over Kincardine to the Spey. This would avoid having to cross Rothiemurchus land or use its water courses, but it ignored the fact that there were three mills on the stream, a ridge of high ground on the Glenmore side, and that Loch Morlich stood 350 feet (120m) higher! Another grandiose but absurd suggestion at this time was the proposal to drain Loch Pityoulish.

There were also arguments over shielings; tenants were strictly assigned to these but when Rothiemurchus folk occupied 'a shealing on the duke's ground in Glenmore', it left the forester there in a quandary. Should he intervene and remove them? The Laird of Rothiemurchus had no such qualms in 1781 when he sent servants to dismantle a Gordon bothy on his land – an act which the Glenmore forester said 'breathes more spirit of defiance at war than any disposition towards peace'.

By 1784 William Osbourne, a Hull merchant, and his partner Ralph Dodsworth, purchased Glenmore Forest from the Duke of Gordon. Presumably it had recovered from the fellings in the early decades of the century. The forest was first offered to the Laird of Rothiemurchus for £10,000 but he declined it. Over a period of twenty years practically the whole of Glenmore was cleared. The duke got his £10,000 and in return he was supposed to have the streams of the Luineag and other burns straightened to facilitate floating. A small dam was again placed at the outflow of Loch Morlich to increase the head of water in the latter. Many men were employed to cut and haul the timber. The best season for the job was spring when the snows melted and the floaters or 'collies' (from *coille*, a wood) were hard at work. They were tough and daring but a decade earlier John Stuart, the forester in Glenmore, had cautioned, 'Most floaters are great knaves' and advised that 'Gordon' should be a sufficient mark on logs 'if cut deep'. These were times of good wages which supported families comfortably but some resented the wholesale destruction of the forest, expressing their feelings in a Gaelic poem:

> Now instead of the song of birds and the murmur of the deer in the
> thicket, our ears are stunned by the crash of falling trees and the
> clamours of the Sassenach.

Rafts were again used to convey the logs to Garmouth, a perilous journey
on the Spey taking 12 hours. A cargo of planks could be piled on top.
Although having a name for being fast flowing, the river only ran at some
three feet per mile (1 in 1800) between Kingussie and Grantown where it
is effectively in a basin but northwards its channel is five times steeper and
strewn with rocks. At Garmouth 47 ships of up to 1,050 tons were built
for the Royal Navy or for the East India Company and it also became a
prosperous harbour for a fleet of vessels engaged in the timber trade.

In Glenmore the landscape was ruined. Despite the arrangement that
solely trees with trunks over 18 inches (46cm) in girth should be felled,
only inferior trees were left; observers agreed that it was 'grandeur in
ruins . . . the axe having laid low the ancient towering pines'. The
partners' manufacture of timber ceased in 1805 and two years later the
contract was bought out. A policy of replanting was not pursued –
regrowth was left to nature – and the commentator Christopher North
(Professor John Wilson) who visited the district about 1815 wrote:

> It is the wreck of an ancient forest which arrests the attention and
> which renders Glenmore a melancholy spectacle.

Under ancient rights of servitude, tenants could also remove trees. These
were required as structural timbers for constructing their 'cruck' houses,
for fencing and other uses. Woods were left mangled and spoiled by their
carelessness. On the Grant of Grant lands, the laird took a merk a year for
what a man chose to cut and manufacture with his own axe but in
Rothiemurchus in the 1700s the laird preferred five shillings (25p) and a
pound of tobacco by way of recompense. Nevertheless, lairds made extra
income from this local trade and the timber was taken to Inverness or
floated out.

Attitudes altered however and by the 1770s James Grant of Grant was
furious with his tenants over 'the pernicious practice of stealing and
destroying' the woods. Notices were pinned to kirk doors condemning
their malice, negligence and thoughtlessness and warnings read out at
services. William Lorimer had recommended that they should have to
purchase all their timber needs. Some spent so much effort in stealing and
selling timber that they had no time for farming; the inhabitants of
Abernethy were infamous for such thieving. Especially objectionable was

their 'cutting Pieces from the Body of large and thriving trees for Candles and other uses'. So conservation had to be promoted and this was partly done by having tenants of 'credit and honesty' as wood watchers or 'poindlers' committed to the care of trees. No one was allowed to go to a wood with an axe. There were similar arrangements in Gordon territory where watches were kept and tenants fined at the Barony Court at Kincardine in 1709 for damage done to the woods in Glenmore and over a century later they were still at it. Even peeling alder bark was met with a summons.

While Scots pine was plentiful, hardwood, such as oak, was so scarce that there was not enough available to make decent ploughs and other implements or even spokes for cart wheels. It was also proposed that birch woods be preserved as birch was valuable for making bobbins, spindles and harness. The rising sap was tapped in the spring by means of a gimlet and a quill to give an agreeable drink but this caused injury to the trees. At Aviemore it was suggested that birch seed should be sown and sheep kept out, possibly by having folk build a dyke, in order to revive the ancient Wood of Aviemore.

With an estimated forest area of 20 square miles (5,180ha), timber was the staple of Rothiemurchus although its extraction was mainly a scattered and small-scale activity. The laird acted as his own forester and overseer which helped to control cheating. The drilling out of whole logs to make water pipes for London took place at two boring mills; one is remembered at Aldracardoch (*Allt na cèardaich*, 'the stream of the works') near Inverdruie. Dr William Grant, the laird's brother, was an inventive gentleman with an interest in timber extraction devising 'an engine for rooting up trees'. In 1770 he had set up the New River Company for water supply in London but the business was mismanaged on the estate and failed within four years. A timber trade with local merchants was less risky than such pretentious schemes. During the Second World War, London's blitz revealed wooden pipes marked with the letters 'P.G.' for Patrick Grant, the eighth Laird of Rothiemurchus; logs had to be clearly identified by a branding iron to prevent fraud by tenants and floaters. Lack of financial wisdom was the not infrequent cause of the disappearance of landed families in Scotland but Rothiemurchus survived intact. The estate was 'entailed', a legal device to prevent it being sold off in lots or seized by creditors, although the woods were partly exempt from this provision. For a time the Gordon and Strathspey estates were similarly protected which made the lairds basically tenants of their own lands.[3]

Felling took place in late autumn; the trees dried out in the winter months when loppers removed the branches and lads leading ponies drew the logs to the river sides. In Rothiemurchus both the rushing streams of the Beanaidh and the Druie were used to power little mills where single saws removed the bark or 'backs' and cut up one log at a time into planks or deals. Each had a small mill pond and wooden cabins for the folk. The carting of the deals to the Spey was tried in Rothiemurchus but floating proved a better and cheaper method. Embankments were raised at the end of Loch Einich where sluices were constructed to control the water. By the 1790s new mills with double saws had been placed near the river banks. A log run was exciting with the turbulent waters sweeping the tree trunks downstream, a scene so well described in Elizabeth Grant's 'Memoirs of a Highland Lady'. Undoubtedly, timber extraction was becoming larger in scale and more devastating within the gateway but the Lairds of Rothiemurchus had a notion of sustainability. As in Glenmore, only trees over a certain girth were to be felled at that time:

> Only the ripest fruit was to be taken and the rest was left to mature
> down the years while natural regeneration continued.
> — SHERIFF J. P. GRANT OF ROTHIEMURCHUS

This method of extraction was a protection against soil erosion but there was also self-interest — if too many trees were cut, the main source of income would dry up. Replanting was also done, with larch being favoured by the gentry. A visitor in 1801 noted that 'Mr Grant cuts down perhaps £1,500 of timber a year — yet riding through his woods not a tree to the eye is missing'. It was probably a conservative opinion as there were sufficient funds to construct a splendid new Doune mansion, 'a most excellent one . . . in great taste' with grounds cleared around it. Cottages with lattice windows in the English style, which may still be seen on the estate, also date from this time.

With the decay of the clan system and the turmoil it caused, the population in the strath was falling, although families of seven or more children were usual. Sir James Grant himself had eleven. In the 1790s a substantial decline had been noted in Duthil and Rothiemurchus parishes. This trend was even more pronounced in Abernethy and Kincardine. Causes were identified as the re-shaping of the land, military recruitment and emigration — the desire to go abroad where men could be their own masters was strong. Tacksmen, who were the element in the community with enterprise and leadership, were especially attracted to the latter and their departure was a severe handicap to progress. Many migrants were to win distinction overseas and in years to come President Ulysses Grant of the United States and Premier John MacDonald of

Canada could both claim local ancestry. Sir James Grant however wished to retain people on his lands; consequently there were no clearances at this time – so Strathspey is less tinged with those bitter memories. Subtenancies which tacksmen arranged were regularised by changing them into direct leases from the laird in order to keep people on the land.

Meanwhile, the gentlemen were sending their children away to be educated, a practice which 'gave them a taste for southern ways and ensured that they would not return'. So began the absentee landlordism and the anglicised leadership which has typified so much of the Highlands. Sir James Grant, who viewed Strathspey as his home, was rather an exception. Yet what were the lairds to do? In the upland parishes teachers were so poorly paid that no one wanted the job. They were expected to teach grammar, arithmetic and Latin. As the Gaelic language and culture were dominant, teaching such subjects was not a success and few ordinary folk could read or write. Sir James used his patronage in kirk affairs to try to better the situation; teachers often hoped for preferment as clergymen and as laird he was the superior, virtually controlling such appointments to several churches. In turn ministers were instructed to 'exercise superintendence' of the schools and scholars on his lands – an early form of inspection.

Sir James Grant's political interests as a MP continued into the 1790s when his attention was increasingly drawn to military matters. There had been a profound change in attitude towards Highlanders after the storming of Quebec in 1758 when they were British troops; after this episode they were no longer perceived as possible rebels but instead feted as heroes. Regarding the army, enlistment at the laird's request to fight European or colonial wars was 'neither popular nor entirely spontaneous'. Yet in 1793 Sir James mustered the Strathspey or Grant Fencibles so successfully that some volunteers had to be declined; fencibles were regiments for the internal defence of the United Kingdom. The following year he raised the 97th or Strathspey Regiment. After serving as marines with the fleet, an extraordinary posting for such Highlanders, they were shortly drafted into different regiments and some found themselves bound for the West Indies. Inveigling men into the army and then breaking the terms of their engagement by sending them overseas was deplored and mutiny was not unknown. The year 1794 also saw the Duke of Gordon, with the help of his enchanting duchess, gather the 100th, later the 92nd, Gordon Highlanders. It was reported that the men made 'hardy, clean, tractable soldiers' and many were excellent marksmen. By the time of the Napoleonic Wars, Highland regiments composed one-quarter of the British army. The patronage of Sir James produced commissions and, combined with valour and perseverance, this could lead to rank and wealth. Badenoch and Strathspey were known for their 'galaxy of military stars'.

The government appeared wise in making the Highland regiments 'provincial', such was the attachment of the recruits to fellow clansmen and birth place. Those who returned were often maimed or invalid pensioners but retired officers were thankful for their 'half pay' which gave them status and allowed them to eek out a living on their hill farms in a harsh land. 'Reduced' private soldiers were encouraged to take up 'lots' on reclaimed land in Strathspey. There were some other gains – habits of cleanliness, of order and of getting up promptly owed much to army discipline which even service in the Strathspey Volunteers could confer. It has been suggested that the Highland regiments became surrogate clans but this is a half truth; the military adopted the trappings of the Highlanders – civilian use of Highland garb was of course forbidden after 1747 to all but officers and soldiers in regiments. Some of the clan traditions were applied to regimental ends – their music, tartans and above all their loyalty. William Pitt the Elder made some cynical observations on the matter. The British army would use 'the courageous qualities which had come so close to restoring the Stuarts'. From the American War of Independence onwards, the 'hardy and intrepid race of men' were to pay the price for the loss of their roles within the clan and the strath gave its share.

Difficult as journeys were, a few travellers kept coming. By 1764 there was a double-arched stone bridge in place of the ford at Inchluin on the Dulnain, but its existence was brief: within four years floods had destroyed it. The Mackintosh chief wrote that 'a float of wood coming down the river, then greatly swelled by late rains, carried off the bridge'. The present single-span at the so-called Sluggan, about 2 miles (3.2km) from Carrbridge, has been in use since 1770. Local efforts maintained the Aviemore to Grantown route for another two decades with a little help from the government in 1796 towards the repair of bridges. Although Sir James Grant of Grant had intervened to improve it, that route was judged 'an imperfect military road'; maintenance of the proper military roads was by then a headache as work parties of soldiers were no longer available owing to the war with France. By a variety of means, the Laird of Grant had over 130 miles (208km) of 'remarkably good' road constructed including an 'excellent bridge' over the River Nethy at what is now Nethybridge. Dulnain Bridge was erected in 1791 when the military were still active in road works.

Far from admiring the mountains from a distance, the curious were beginning to explore them. They sought the amber-coloured Cairngorm stones exposed after thaws or floods, although as gems these were worth little. Local folk quarried for them on the hillsides by Loch Avon where the 'Quartz Diggers' Cave' route now challenges rock climbers. Others ascended Cairn Gorm for the view, stretching in clear weather to Ross, Sutherland and even Caithness. By the 1790s the Shelter Stone with its cave was being visited but the pièce de résistance was Loch an Eilein with its ospreys and five echoes – the latter doubtless contributing to the unsettling of the poor birds and their ultimate departure.

At the opening of the nineteenth century there were no public coaches in service in the Highlands. Only the intrepid travelled for pleasure and very few women travelled on their own initiative. One who did was the undaunted Mrs Sarah Murray (or Aust) who made a lengthy tour of Scotland in 1796. What is more, she kept an account of it and repeated her journey in 1801. The first requirement she advised was a strong and roomy carriage, 'have the springs well corded', and a comprehensive tool kit with stop pole, chains, shackles and much else. Having your servant with you would help in opening gates and assist in the event of accidents; it would also prevent him loitering at inns. Mrs Murray modified the carriage's interior for a Highland expedition with places for wine bottles, tea, sugar and other provisions. As accommodation might be lacking, she suggested overnighting in the vehicle when 'a blanket, thin quilt and two pillows' would do.

After crossing the 'bare, black, tremendous mountains' of Drumochter, she was thankful to draw close to Aviemore through 'the widening strath, rich and well ornamented with wood and sheltered by mountains'. Rothiemurchus and the Cairngorms were greatly admired; although it was August their 'never melting snows' were such a contrast to the 'luxuriant and smiling summer' below. Soon Aviemore Inn was in sight and she was thrilled at the prospect of spending a night there.

> My heart jumped at the idea of passing the night in a spot so grateful
> to my sensations because nature there shines in its natural garb and in
> high beauty.

Little did she know what was in store. If Colonel Thornton, accustomed to rough and ready army ways, was prepared to make excuses for the inn, Mrs Murray was not. Casting a womanly eye over the premises, she looked in vain for cleanliness and comfort:

> No sooner had I put my foot within the walls of that horrible house

than my heart sank and I was glad to escape from its filth and smoke very early next morning.

So early, in fact, that she left without breakfast. The sun was high and she gazed on the 'white patched hollow sides of Cairn Gorm' as she set off. Eight miles on, this resourceful lady stopped at a cottage and obtained boiling water and milk. She produced her teapot and had a meal in her chaise. (From 1790 there was another Grant inn at the new Carrbridge and thought was also given to setting up a second hostelry at Easter Aviemore, now Granish, 'for Soldiers and such passengers complaining of very ill treatment at Aviemore', perhaps an attempted cure by competition.)

On Mrs Murray's return visit in 1801 she spent a fortnight with the Grants of Rothiemurchus; with a ferry boat capable of loading a carriage installed on the Spey near Inverdruie, the traveller could now cross at all states of the river. The Boat of Rothiemurchus was to become as well known as the many other ferry points from the Boat of Insh (now Kincraig) northwards. Mrs Murray made excursions on pony including one to Glenmore where the party breakfasted at Mr Osbourne's house before ascending Cairn Gorm. In spite of being thrown off her mount while exploring Glen Einich, the indomitable lady completed her tour of the district by riding through the Lairig an Laoigh (*Làirig Laoigh*, 'the pass of the calves') to Glen Derry and Braemar.

By the early 1800s the new farms were taking shape on the davoch of Aviemore and Balladern. The inn had the biggest share of the land, with 'Eight Auchtenparts of the Davoch of Bulladern' thought sufficient for it. No innkeeper could exist without a holding in order to provide food for travellers and for his family. Fodder was also essential as were parks or stances for drovers' cattle. So 'mine host' was usually a farmer first and much of the inn's activity was left to the womenfolk. Customers could be astonished to find horses getting as much attention as they did. Former employees of the Laird of Rothiemurchus had taken over the inn and by dint of hard work they had transformed the place. Supplies had to be ordered from a distance, peats prepared in vast quantities and the farm carefully managed. Linen, blankets and clothing had to be made but the premises, kept by an industrious English woman, were again 'commodious and clean'.

Hardly surprisingly among the tenants on the davoch Grants were the most numerous – at Easter Aviemore, Dalfaber, and the Milltown of Aviemore where the tenants' oats and barley were ground. Small holdings were worked by Stewart, Dallas, Davidson and Macpherson families while there were MacDonalds at Knockgranish and Camerons at Sluggan Granish. Whereas observers might be impressed by the new appearance of the landscape, the first enclosures or fields with walls of turf or stone were disliked by the country folk; they had been used to allowing their cattle to range at will watched by herdsmen, except of course in summer when crops were growing on the infield and on patches of the outfield. The beasts were then moved up to the shielings to graze in the hills. The new farms were connected to the main routes by proper tracks and so the planned homesteads tended to follow the road pattern like beads on a string. Meal mills were reconstructed and trades such as those of masons and joiners were encouraged. Regular markets were established at Kingussie and of course Grantown, the special project of Sir James Grant. The intention was that the growing settlement would have six fairs from January to November in addition to a weekly market.

Against this background of change, the 'Great Military Road' was going from bad to worse. A journey from Perth to Inverness was long and hazardous taking several nights on the way. Road building at high speed and by unskilled soldier labour was bound to lead in due course to costly bills for repairs. There were 1,000 miles (1,600km) of such road in Scotland with over 900 bridges 'insufficient . . . injudiciously constructed and ill-executed' according to General Mackay in his report to the Treasury in 1785. Off the King's disintegrating highway, only passage on foot or pony was possible. Through much of the year, the folk in each glen or strath could be considered prisoners 'strongly guarded by impassable mountains on one side, by swamps and furious torrents on the other' – a description which suited much of the Cairngorm gateway very well. Winter journeys were especially gruelling as it was 'hardly agreed by the traveller which is the line of the road, everyone making one for himself'. Almost two decades were to pass before any action was taken. Perhaps the shocking state of the road was the cause of the closure of the Post Office at Aviemore in 1793.

Military road construction had not stopped when General Wade left Scotland; there were successors such as Major William Caulfeild who was also of Irish descent. Appointed Deputy Governor of Inverness Castle in 1747, he continued the great endeavour. New links stretched across Dava Moor via Ferness to Dulsie Bridge and beyond, while east of Grantown another went by the Lecht and Cockbridge to Braemar. From Aviemore, which was described as 'the head of Strathspey', the military road fed into a route along the north side of the Dulnain which was known as the Duthil Road and so a useful network had been growing.

Meanwhile, Sir James Grant was striving to develop better roads through his lands. In the early 1800s, his 'district roads' were hailed as among the best specimens of Highland road making; he tried to persuade the County Meetings of the Commissioners of Supply for Inverness and Elgin to pay half the expense of the bridges. This was a shrewd plan as secure crossing points over major streams attracted settlement and numerous Highland villages today show such origins in their 'bridge' names. In 1803 a road surveyor, James Donaldson, was appointed to oversee an improvement in the route from Carrbridge to Slochd Mhuic. The Carrbridge Road had been begun in 1754 as it was a significant link via Dulsie Bridge to Fort George. As the original Bridge of Carr was too narrow for carriages, it had been widened in the 1760s when James Grant of Grant had a notion to re-route the King's Highway to Inverness across it.

Donaldson negotiated with proprietors to settle on a scheme and a price; Sir James was willing to co-operate. A diversion was made from the Wade road near Kinveachy; it climbed to Carrbridge and then swung up Bogroy brae over the heathy Black Mount in the direction of Slochd Mhuic. These road building efforts of 1804-6 were sufficient to produce a staggered delivery of mails but it was a risky matter in winter because Slochd was such a notorious snow trap. Together with Drumochter, it gave the Post Office an excuse for refusing to provide a direct mail service between Perth and Inverness for several decades.

Something had to be done and done it was. In 1803, Parliament set up and supported with finance the Commission for Highland Roads and Bridges. The state of the Highland economy was a cause for concern; emigration, especially from the Far North, was running at an alarming level. It was believed that better transport would open the whole region to trade, and employment in public works, such as road building and harbour construction, would also be beneficial. The indefatigable and ingenious Thomas Telford was appointed engineer to the Commission. He soon observed that the military roads were 'inconveniently steep . . . nearly unfit for the Purposes of Civil Life . . . (and) laid with other Views than promoting Trade and Commerce'. It was not until 1814 however that they were transferred to the care of the Commissioners. Soon major repairs were being carried out from Badenoch to Moy which involved 50 miles (80km) of road but 'the very unfavourable season' stopped work.

It was a story that was to be oft repeated. Just what was involved? First ditches had to be cleared and sharp ridges cut down; cross drains were inserted instead of paved fords, hollows were filled and retaining walls built against slopes. The surface had to allow for cattle droving and small stones were laid on dry bottomed ground as a base followed by up to 14 inches (35cm) of gravel 'of a proper quality, out of which all stones above the size of a hen's egg shall have been previously taken'. Soon the traveller could experience 'as much convenience as the original imperfections of the several lines admit of' but Telford and the Commissioners had more ambitious plans in store.

Rivers sorely taxed the Commission's engineer. Although the Spey had been bridged at Ralia since 1763, a venture by the Duke of Gordon, the river was otherwise a problem within the gateway as 'no convenient situation could be found for a bridge' as it was impossible 'to foresee the variations to which the channel . . . is liable'. Furthermore bridges were costly and the Commissioners were worried about expenditure; over half their money came from the government, the rest from the Highland counties and individual 'heritors' or landowners. In spite of these problems by 1818 it was possible to travel all the way to Inverness without having to ford a river, board a ferry or negotiate a descent where drag chains had to be used on a vehicle to arrest its speed. A fair road system was developing in and around the gateway too; a westwards link was also being constructed along Loch Laggan-side. This was first urged by the Duke of Gordon in 1804 but it was an laborious matter, not being completed until 1818.

Spare a thought for the work force; in all weathers, the men had to live in canvas tents which were often torn to shreds by the wind and in which the bedding was constantly wet. Inns such as Aviemore must have been merciful havens with the prospect of a warming dram. No wonder labourers were noted 'seldom (to) persevere long in such employment'. In 1825, caravans described as 'moveable wooden houses' were purchased, the first of such to make passage through the gateway. Inexperienced and often unreliable contractors engaged to carry out the projects caused the Commissioners endless anxiety. Yet the latter:

> succeeded in effecting a change in the state of the Highlands perhaps
> unparalleled in the same space of time in the history of any country.
> – JOSEPH MITCHELL IN *MY LIFE IN THE HIGHLANDS*

It was a remarkable achievement by any standard.

These were hard times in the gateway. There had been a high point in land improvement during the Napoleonic wars; with blockades in place and demands for home produced commodities at record levels, farm prices soared and much land was taken into cultivation on the moors and lower slopes.. After 1815 with the cessation of war, demand slumped, prices collapsed and there was unemployment and great hardship in the countryside. Improvements in people's living conditions were patchy as the poet Robert Southey discovered on his tour in Scotland in 1819 when he described the homes on Dava Moor:

> peat stack, peat sty and peat house being altogether; the roofs also covered with turf and peat on which grass and heather grow comfortably . . .

In Badenoch returning army officers took the bigger farms, the folk were evicted and the land put under sheep in the 1820s – Phones, Etteridge, Ruthven and Glen Banchor were cleared. Some landowners viewed emigration as a solution to poverty and welcomed it, but there were no such events in Strathspey at this time. From 1811 the Grant of Grant lands had become part of an immense estate stretching from the margin of the Cairngorms to the Moray Firth. Through a cousin the eldest son of Sir James Grant had inherited this great possession as fifth Earl of Seafield and Findlater with the family name of Ogilvie-Grant. Owing to his incapacity arising from a serious illness, the territory was managed by a guardian, Colonel Francis Grant. The Seafield earldom (which can descend in the female line) retained the lands but was parted from the title of Chief of Clan Grant. The Chief received a peerage in 1817 becoming Baron Strathspey of Strathspey.

At the height of the Napoleonic wars when there was a heavy duty on foreign timber, John Peter Grant, the ninth Laird of Rothiemurchus, was reputed to earn very handsome returns each year from the forest. There was again contention with the Duke of Gordon as the laird and others asked permission to float wood down the Spey after 15 May each year – an activity which sorely interfered with the ducal salmon fishings at Tugnet on the river mouth. In the 1820s exploitation was stepped up with a big saw mill in action near the mouth of the Druie; it was capable of setting ten circular saws in motion and an upright frame of eight plain saws. Ten to fifteen men worked there plus a boy to regulate the flow of water taken from the Druie by a sluice. Deals of Scots pine and barrel staves of birch were produced and were floated out on rafts; to assist their passage, the laird had a troublesome rock at Arndilly removed by blasting.

Much of the wealth from the forest, however, was dissipated on the laird's attempts to be a Member of Parliament, first for Grimsby ('a thoroughly rotten borough') and latterly for Tavistock. He also chose to send his sons to Eton and favoured town houses in Edinburgh. Bankruptcy ensued but his timely appointment as Chief Justice of Calcutta brought financial rescue. The estate was left burdened with hefty debts. The forest of Rothiemurchus was ravaged 'with only a few remnants' standing but, if some seed trees were saved, the natural regeneration was thankfully remarkable on the dry stony ground. Properly managed, the woods were invaluable to both landowners and tenants; the latter earned enough to cover their rents easily and the pattern of forest work in winter fitted in with their tasks on the land in summer.

From 1827, with patience and thrift, William Patrick Grant of Rothiemurchus, the judge's son, set about restoring the family fortunes. His future mother-in-law, the great actress Sarah Siddons, had serious misgivings about his proposed marriage to her daughter Sarah (known as Sally) who was to have a dowry of £10,000 – a veritable fortune in those days. Although the Grants were gentry, they were an impoverished variety and William was bound for Calcutta to try to make good. However, objections were overcome, they were wed in 1830 and the marriage endured. After a questionable career in India – a banking scandal was involved – laird William returned almost penniless in 1848. Meanwhile, he had managed the estate by lengthy and detailed letters to a factor, revealing that he knew virtually every stick and stone there. He was reckoned to put the then considerable sum of £3,000 into the 'duchus' each year. Farmhouses, steadings and miles of stone dykes were built. William had a notion that cattle prevented the re-growth of the pine forest and so must be kept out of it at all costs. His programme took many decades to complete and continued into the 1860s. The limited cultivable land was re-organised in regular fields, usually six per holding to fit the six-course rotation which he introduced and which was so long practised in the district. Near the Doune the streams were straightened, embankments constructed, drainage ditches cut and fertile fields formed. His efforts were the wonder of the countryside. Today the old fields are useless and overgrown with rushes; the powerful Feshie has brought down such volumes of sand and gravel that the bed of the Spey and the water table have both risen, inundating the land. Nevertheless, the 'look' and the layout which distinguish Rothiemurchus owe much to his imprint.

In 1824 tolls had been suggested by the Commissioners for Highland Roads and Bridges as a means of boosting the amount of money available for road works. Toll bars or gates were first installed in Caithness but these were so unpopular that a mob destroyed ones at Wick in September 1827. Would tolls raise enough cash in thinly populated country such as Badenoch? The very month of the troubles at Wick, toll gates appeared on the Great Highland Road, a new description for the highway, and Aviemore was a chosen site. Initially there were six locations between Badenoch and Inverness where travellers had to stop and pay up but these were eventually increased to eight. The collecting of the tolls was let by auction; by the 1850s the Badenoch tolls raised £800 of which the collector got two and a half per cent. The toll keepers themselves were often poor folk who were at first accommodated in huts. As traffic was so sparse they found it difficult to make a living, finding even road repairing more rewarding. By 1834 a permanent toll house had been erected at Aviemore at a cost of £42; it was on the west side of Grampian Road near the bridge over the Aviemore burn. Latterly used as outhouses and a private garage, it stood until 1969 when, ironically in the cause of road improvements, yet another historic element in the gateway's story was swept away.

Telford ('not having visited the Highlands for some years past' as he had so many other schemes on hand and consequently left matters to his capable Inspector of Roads John Mitchell) was invited to consider a completely new alignment for the Great Highland Road between Inverness and Aviemore. His survey gave an estimate of over £30,000 – an unthinkable sum for the Commission to find. It would have continued south from Aviemore either via Glen Feshie and Glen Tilt or via Glen Tromie and Glen Bruar to join the Atholl road at Blair. The intention was

The defile of Slochd Mhuic was a serious hazard on the Great Highland Road. Thomas Telford's embankment was a major improvement. In this view from the 1930s, the main road and railway to Inverness focus on the pass (A. E. GLEN)

to shorten the long detour west at Drumochter and in 1837 Joseph Mitchell, John Mitchell's son and his successor as the Commission's chief inspector, was to present a further report on the possibility but it was not pursued.

Other public works also advanced under Telford's wing. Many churches were in a neglected state, bordering on tumble down. The Commission for Building Churches in the Highlands and Islands of Scotland was set up and completed thorough repairs to the old kirk of Rothiemurchus. In 1828 they also had a single storey manse constructed as a minister was assigned to the ancient parish when it was 'disunited' from Duthil. The old manse still exists set back from the road to Loch an Eilein. Originally a byre and dairy occupied one end, as the minister's family kept a cow, and the rest was the modest dwelling house.

Damage to the roads caused by freak Highland weather was not uncommon but in 1829 there was a major crisis. Both the road system and the improving agriculture suffered a cruel attack from the elements. Floods are a recurring theme in Strathspey, sometimes brought by winter squalls when rapid thawing of snow is followed by prolonged rain and sometimes in summer when intense convectional storms can match them in ferocity. Bulwarks of timber were constructed on some river sides, such as the Druie and the Nethy, to try to counter such problems. 'The Great Floods' of August 1829 have become a standard by which other inundations have been measured. Furious storms centred on the Monadh Liath where in excess of four inches of rain (100mm) is thought to have fallen in 24 hours. The most severe effects occurred in the catchment of the Spey and its tributaries, the Druie, Nethy and Dulnain. The mountain burns became raging torrents and the main rivers burst their banks. A naval captain said that he might have sailed a fifty-gun ship from the Boat of Balliefurth near Grantown to the Boat of Garten for the floor of the strath was converted into a lake. Sir Thomas Dick Lauder left an account of the effects of the floods on the gateway area:

> An entire river poured itself over the rugged and precipitous brow of the hill Craigellachie, converting its furrowed front into a vast and diversified waterfall.

In Rothiemurchus the Druie broke from its channel (a not unusual event as the stream formed a delta and could have many channels near its mouth). Sweeping all before it, the floods surrounded the Dell of Rothiemurchus in a loch. The Aviemore Inn and the few dwellings about it were safe above the turbulent flow on the stony terraces. The big garden of the inn was under water as high as its upper wall. The innkeeper lost two bullocks and several sheep but some did survive in the branches of trees at the foot of the garden. Such a flood was bound to devastate the roads and bridges so painstakingly reconstructed to Telford's plans. It was a weather pattern which has been repeated many times.

The Commissioners were appalled by the destruction. They reported that:

> Within the reach of the Spey . . . trees, crops, stock, dwellings and outbuildings, even the soil itself, were carried down together, and many fields completely and irredeemably overwhelmed with sand, stones and rubbish . . .

Estates in Badenoch and Strathspey were severely hit and 'the advancement in the prosperity of the Country . . . received a lamentable check'. Nevertheless, transport was given a priority and emergency arrangements for the Highland coach were completed so quickly that it was only held up for a day and within a week wheeled traffic was once again moving along the Great Highland Road.

Since 1809 a direct coach had been running the 117 miles (187km) from Perth to Inverness three times a week in summer and twice a week in winter, weather permitting; in addition to its driver and guard, it carried three passengers inside and five on the roof. Nor was it cheap – the fare was four guineas inside and three outside and luggage space was limited. With the publication of Scott's novel *Waverley* in 1814, many travellers were curious to see the wild mountain fastnesses for themselves although, according to some, the book presented a romanticised view of the Highlands 'so utterly at variance with the truth'. By 1820 the Caledonian coach could do the journey in 17 hours. Inverness was a hub of coach activity – seven coaches drove to and from it daily, plus a swarm of post chaises, private carriages and gigs as wheeled vehicles came to the fore in the Highlands. Road surfaces suited to 'light and desultory traffic' were soon showing the adverse effects not only of the rapid stage coaches but also of 'heavy agricultural carriages' and commercial wagons

Royal Mail coaches however were another matter. Over the high stretches of the Great Highland Road, snowfall and storms were alleged to make travel in carriages impossible for months at a time. So the Post Office refused to provide a direct service. The mails from the south came by Aberdeen and could take over a week to reach Inverness. The Duchess of Gordon, who resided at Kinrara, had long been urging improvements in the service because of her interest in Kingussie's development and she

In the 1820s stage coaches opened a new era of travel in the Highlands. The last to run in Britain in 1908 was the Duchess of Gordon from Kingussie to Kinlochlaggan. Its successor was this waggonette which continued on the route until 1915 (HIGHLAND COUNCIL ARCHIVES)

was an influential lady. A serious obstacle stood in the way – the pass at Slochd Mhuic which was an infamous snow trap. From 1831 this hazard was targeted after a serious accident to the Caledonian coach which overturned there. So dangerous was that part of the road that a causeway carrying the road in a reverse curve was formed to negotiate the defile. After as many as 250 men, labouring over several seasons, had cut rock, excavated deep pockets of peat and built embankments, it was completed in 1835. This cleverly shortened the route, 'by removing by far the greatest impediment to an easy and rapid transit along this important line'. That left one other shocking section just north of Aviemore where 'hechs an' howes', some as steep as 1 in 9 over hummocky ground, made the journey very uncomfortable; the hillocks were shovelled away and the hollows filled in. After winter storms primitive wooden snow ploughs pulled by horses were dragged along between snow poles placed to mark the line of the road to try to clear a passage.

Royal Mail coaches began to come across Drumochter in July 1836; in their scarlet livery with well matched horses in the best of harness, these dashing vehicles opened a new era in Highland travel. Speed was a priority and as they did not pay tolls, toll keepers had to have the gates open in good time. The drivers and guards wore a uniform of red coats with yellow collars. While the mail coaches passed the very door of Aviemore Inn, that establishment was not then a Post Office. From 1827 there was a sub-Post Office at Lynwilg to which letter bags to or from Perth, Inverness, Carrbridge and Kingussie were conveyed. A mail gig ran daily to and from Grantown. It was up to local folk to collect their letters from the Post Offices of which another was later opened at Granish.

For all coach traffic, stages were about 10 to 12 miles (16 to 19km) in length. Coaches then pulled up at an inn where horses were changed; it was a job done with such speed that it might take only a few minutes.

> What a scene of commotion a stage house presented on the arrival of the coach! What rattling of chains and harness would there be as the freed horses cantered off to the watering shoal on the nearest stream! What shouting of ostlers! What hurried interviews on every side! What expectation of news!
>
> – THOMAS SINTON IN BY LOCH AND RIVER

Such sights must often have been witnessed at Aviemore Inn. Soon with fresh horses attached and passengers once again in place, the coach would clatter off into the distance. In addition to the Caledonian and the Royal Mail vehicles, Duke of Wellington, Defiance and Princess Royal were the names of other coaches that regularly drove through the strath. The drivers and guards were firm favourites with folk close to the Great Highland Road as they performed many a 'commission' for them. Travellers admired their skill in driving a four-in-hand or a 'unicorn' team of three. A steady pace of ten or more miles per hour (16kph) was not reduced by either unruly horses or the darkness of the night. Sweeping down a hill could give momentum to come up another. Turns were taken within inches of the margin of the road or a bridge corner. Such speed was seen as 'alarming and stupendous'; the shaking of the passengers caused fears for their health and worries too about the coinage of the realm (it was real gold, silver or copper then) being worn away by so much jingling and rubbing in pockets.

The high point of coaching was in the 1840s when the Edinburgh-Inverness run usually took 18 hours and the Glasgow-Inverness one 20 hours. Instead of the coaches, the gentry had their chaises, chariots and sociables and travelled 'post', hiring successive teams of horses at posting inns such as Aviemore. The better off used their own dog carts and ponies for their journeys and faced a long day on the road to Inverness. Travel in summer could be enjoyable but a winter sortie with the threat of blizzards was feared. On dark nights the tales of 'bogies' lurking in avenues of trees at Kinveachy as the coach rumbled past, lit only by flickering lamps, made travellers wary.

News of the better highways soon spread; they were described as a 'luxury in travelling compared with the execrable roads in the Lowlands'. By the 1830s, the improved quality of the inns was also being remarked upon and Aviemore Inn was no exception; it was quite acceptable to people 'with good temper' and 'powers of reflection' – just as well as curiosity about the Highlands was bringing an increasing flow of travellers:

> The poet, the journalist and the ordinary citizen had come to visit, to study and to admire an area hitherto virtually unknown.
>   – A. R. B. HALDANE IN *NEW WAYS THROUGH THE GLENS*

No longer were mountains thought 'fearful' and forests 'horrid'. Travel for enjoyment had begun and tourism was on the horizon for the Cairngorm gateway.

The growing traffic in summer strained the capacity of inns to the utmost. Grouse shooting became very popular in the 1820s and so early autumn was the fashionable season for travel to the Highlands. At times the arrival of shooting parties would coincide with an influx of cattle drovers on their way south to the trysts. Many a night travellers must have been disturbed by their noisy arguments; inn keepers were embarrassed by their rough behaviour and penniless state. Drovers had a fine appetite for food and drink and often little money to pay for it. September was a particularly busy time with trysts at Pitmain near Kingussie to suit droves on their way through Badenoch and for a time another was held at Dalraddy near Kincraig.

Peaceful conditions after 1745 had made it possible to walk cattle to the Lowlands by long and arduous routes. There was a demand for meat from the expanding towns of Central Scotland, from English cities and from the Army and Navy for salted supplies. Until the railways came, early autumn saw herds of cattle moving in leisurely droves from every corner of the Highlands to the principal markets at Crieff and Falkirk or on across the Border. The drovers preferred routes with a soft surface for their beasts which might include ponies for use in the pits of coal field areas. Hence Telford had plenty of small gravel put on the northern roads to save the wear and tear on hooves. Hard surfaces literally wore them out and it was not unheard of for cattle to be shod.

The cattle trade was speculative. Would the cost of a beast bought from an upland farmer be recovered once the long trek was over? Most were sold for fattening on the lusher pastures of the 'south country'. Money was quickly made and quickly lost. Drovers were mainly Lowlanders and hard bargainers too but none questioned their ability to judge cattle. From the gateway, the most daunting route was through the Lairig Ghru in the heart of the Cairngorms. It led to Castletown of Braemar. There was 'a footpath formed with much trouble by the removal of immense blocks of granite . . . fallen from the adjoining precipices' but it was a shorter route to southern markets than by the Great Highland Road. 'Pedestrians' choosing the route would also have their toils repaid if they were 'fond of the grand in nature'. It is amazing to think of groups of women from Rothiemurchus taking baskets of eggs carefully balanced on their heads across the Lairig for sale in Braemar. Folk also went through to help with the Braemar harvests which came earlier there. The Lairig an Laoigh from Abernethy or Glenmore over the shoulder of Bynack via the Fords of Avon to Glen Derry was thought easier, if longer. Each year parties of men from Rothiemurchus went up to repair the Lairig Ghru route while similar work was done on the Lairig an Laoigh by Kincardine folk.

In keeping with Sir James Grant's vision of improvement was his founding membership of the Highland Society of Scotland in 1784. This organisation has since evolved into the Royal Highland & Agricultural Society of Scotland and has had a profound influence on Scottish farming over the years. In 1787, the Strathspey Farmers' Club for 'gentlemen of the district interested in the improved mode of husbandry' was set up. A Badenoch and Strathspey Farming Society, with the Duchess of Gordon as patron, followed in 1803. Cattle beasts had hitherto been allowed to breed without much attention to the selection of the best. Winter fodder was insufficient – the scanty meadow grass of summer augmented perhaps by crushed whins bruised in a stone 'cnotag'. The result was livestock 'destitute of symmetry, size and of flesh'. Later the Highland and Agricultural Society tried offering prizes at shows to encourage improvement but until small farmers saw the advantages of quality animals which would fetch better prices the problem could not be solved. By 1856, however, a champion Highland bull from Strathspey was being exhibited in Paris. Local agricultural societies encouraged good farm produce such as 'cured butter' and 'sweet milk cheese' by giving awards.

Although a cattle and timber economy was in place, the folk of the strath were still very vulnerable to adverse weather. Unfavourable conditions in the short growing season could wreak havoc as happened in 1807, 1808 and 1816; the latter was 'the year without a summer' when the Tambora eruption in Indonesia sent clouds of dust into the atmosphere. Poor families had again to exist for several weeks in the spring 'on the tops of nettles, mugwort, turnip thinnings and milk without any corn food'. The temptation to poach was irresistible – game from the hill and salmon speared with leisters in the rivers.

The distilling of illicit whisky continued. Demand for drams from little pot stills was universal in the Highlands and the Scottish towns. In 1819 a boll of barley converted to whisky represented a cost of around £2 but an anker (about 30 litres) of whisky sent south could earn £10, so that every anker which escaped the excisemen easily repaid the loss of a couple seized. There were other advantages too – the waste grain or draff fed cattle and poultry and there was always the pleasure of tasting the product! In 1822 an Illicit Distillation Act which carried severe penalties was introduced. This was a watershed as it was followed by the Excise Act of 1823 making 'small scale' distilling in pot stills permissible on payment of a modest licence fee of £10. Alexander, the fourth Duke of Gordon, acknowledged as the monarch's 'greatest subject' on account of the size of his rent rolls and the number of people who relied upon him for protection, played a leading part in these revisions. Yet no licensed distillery arose in the gateway area at that time and the poor tenants were hard hit when their lucrative smuggling escapades were finally suppressed. Even so the knowledge of the craft lingered on in Rothiemurchus; old Davie Cameron of Coylumbridge, a former postman, remembered his father's sma' still somewhere near Airgiod-meall (*Airgead-mheall*, the silver hill) in Glenmore. Another smugglers' bothy was for long present deep in Rothiemurchus forest where it lay against a bank. The structure was fair-sized. At one corner a stream entered where the roof rose. All around the room were nooks and crannies for storing gear. Well off the beaten track, the structure may be there yet. Similar hideaways have been found in Glenmore and elsewhere in the gateway area.

Just as the landscape in the strath was being transformed, so were the customs and language of the folk changing. Until the 1830s, only Gaelic had been spoken but as Lowlanders began to settle and trade, Highlanders attempted to speak 'a kind of imperfect English'. Elderly folk could not read – they had no requirement to do so as Gaelic had a rich oral heritage and books were rare. Along with the erosion of Gaelic went the traditional pursuits of the Highland games; the young men were content to practice 'shooting at a target' instead of the old skills of tossing the caber (to form a primitive bridge over a stream) or putting the shot (usually a boulder to be thrown at an enemy). These were martial arts and prizes were in kind – a pistol, a powder horn, a sporran, a sword belt or a skein dhu, or for personal adornment, shoe buckles, a cocked bonnet or a tartan scarf. Penny weddings were also disappearing. These were an old custom whereby wedding guests, probably the whole community, brought gifts of food and drink to give a young couple a rousing send off with a big ceilidh or party. These made sense when so many were poor but being uproarious and lengthy incurred condemnation from a clergy of censorious and narrow outlook

Educational efforts in the Highlands continued to depend on both charity and private schools. In 1807 the school in Rothiemurchus was at Coylumbridge where routes met at a safe river crossing. It was again an initiative by the SSPCK. The schoolmaster had to make do 'with his poor, very poor Government allowance', some assistance from the Laird of Rothiemurchus and the small fees paid by 'a mob of scholars'. Within a few years, Elizabeth Grant of Rothiemurchus described it as 'a very good one' where all the boys were taught and could learn Latin 'if they liked it'. The laird himself examined the pupils and prizes were given. The master received £10 from the laird, a house and garden, plus £5 extra from 'Queen Anne's Bounty'; his wife earned £4 a year from teaching girls to sew. Later the laird had a school and a house for the schoolmaster constructed at Inverdruie. This choice was probably wise as in the early Censuses of Population, Rothiemurchus figures as a township presumably because there was a concentration of people at Inverdruie. After 1818 landed proprietors were obliged to provide such facilities for 'the education of the lower order' and had the right to ask tenants to pay half the teacher's salary. The master had again to look for fees and, if free education had been possible, double the number of youngsters would have been attending. Boys always outnumbered girls – male learning had precedence – and each pupil had to bring a peat each day to supply the fire.

In 1839 the Reverend Charles Grant, the well-meaning parish minister of Rothiemurchus, had engaged a temporary schoolmaster and paid his salary, only to find that the trustees on the estate would not recompense him. The official teacher had emigrated to Australia a year earlier. It was well known 'in the county' that the laird (now Sir John Peter Grant and in India) had arranged to build and maintain the school on his own land, thus avoiding any liability to the parish. But where was the minister to find the 'unquestionable evidence' to satisfy the trustees and ensure his own repayment? By 1842, the laird's school at Inverdruie was 'centrically situated . . . the salary attached to the office, and paid by the proprietor, is L.10 per annum . . . The attendance at school averages from 50 to 70'.

Most children had only a couple of years of schooling, a little longer if their families could afford it. Learning to write was always more expensive than learning to read and hence, according to an enquiry which the minister made in 1837, only half the Rothiemurchus people could both read and write while many could only read. This was probably typical of the gateway parishes at the time. There were SSPCK schools at Kincardine and Kinveachy, indicative of a widespread and popular demand for literacy in English. Gaelic however was not entirely overlooked as records show that in some places pupils were taught to read it. Both young and old came to the Sabbath schools, held in both English and Gaelic, although attendance was often 'irregular' and the fees paid to the masters paltry.

Population was rising in the gateway parishes peaking at 4,000 about 1830 but in the following decade economic depression gripped the country. In the latter 1830s there were crop failures and 'short corn', which only compounded the distress. Highland parishes presented pictures of 'severe unmitigated want and misery'. In 1837 a committee was formed in Glasgow (there was another in Edinburgh) to bring some relief and £30,000 was raised with aid coming from other sources, including the government. Emigration was the proposed solution and in Rothiemurchus this was organised by the Reverend Charles Grant. He believed that:

> Emigration or removal in one way or other of many of the Inhabitants can alone effect a change beneficial to the parish . . . and to those to be removed.

In response to enquiries by the Glasgow Destitution Committee in 1841, he reported that of 616 people in the parish, one-sixth were 'totally destitute of the necessities of life' and many more were poverty stricken. Their suffering was attributed to 'the almost entire destruction of the corn and potatoe crops', probably the result of frosts. Only 135 were 'disposed to emigrate' as 'the idea of Australia, which they dislike, led many of them to reply in the negative'. Australia was of course associated with transportation and convict settlements; it was described in a letter to the *Inverness Courier* from a young man who had travelled there as 'the receptacle for the winnowings of the most abandoned and thoroughly depraved of the human family' – hardly a recommendation to prospective settlers. Some tenants sailed to Canada or to New Zealand and their small plots were merged into the larger farms. Others sought employment in the rising industries of Central Scotland. The Destitution Boards were called upon to give further help in 1847, and many lairds did their part too, but relief and charity were judged 'so unpopular and unproductive generally' that they were only a palliative.

In the gateway districts the cottagers or 'cottars' were especially disadvantaged. They often occupied dwellings as the sub-tenants of tenants, being little better than squatters. In Abernethy in the 1830s they were not permitted to keep a cow or a pony and so had recourse to begging or pilfering. According to the parish minister, this 'much neglected class of people' too often found themselves on the Poor Roll or like others, 'forced to a foreign shore by necessity, for want of employment, habitation or ground to subsist on'. It was a sad state of affairs.

Each parish was expected to look after its poor. After 1845 a small poor-house, a cause of shame to Highland folk, was erected at Coylumbridge, where it still stands. Apart from meagre collections in the churches, the destitute had to depend on donations from such wealthy visitors to Rothiemurchus as the Duchess of Bedford who chose the Doune as her favourite summer residence for many years; she spent much effort on improving it and employed many people. Although paid for by her older husband, the sixth duke, it became a hideaway for the duchess and the painter Edwin Landseer during their long romance. She was a great beauty and the daughter of the Duchess of Gordon who resided at Kinrara and who was a determined matchmaker. The marriage of convenience to Bedford did not stop the duchess having ten children, the youngest two being most likely the progeny of the painter, who was many years her junior. From the 1830s Landseer sketched and stalked among the Cairngorms. His famous painting 'The Monarch of the Glen' is said to have been inspired by Rothiemurchus. He also decorated the walls of a bothy in Glen Feshie with frescoes but these have long since vanished due to misunderstanding and neglect.

All was not well with the Kirk. By the 1790s there were tensions between the 'moderates' and the 'evangelicals' in the established church. The former clergy and their supporters were largely content with the status quo, were liberal in outlook and tolerated such varied pursuits as scientific enquiry at one end of the spectrum, and card-playing and dancing at the other. The evangelicals, on the other hand, required Calvin's doctrines to be followed to the letter and called for repentance. They were conservative, clinging to traditional methods, such as bringing sinners before the Session and denouncing frivolities. From time to time the fervour of religious revivals swept the strath. Itinerant preachers of evangelical persuasion, who came with missionary zeal, drew large gatherings and attempted to set up meeting houses.

By the 1840s there were rumours of stronger dissent, some having a 'deep rooted enmity against the Establishment'. The Free Church – free from patronage, in other words having its ministers chosen and imposed upon the congregation by the local landowner, or superior, and the heritors – was on its way. The break came in 1843 with the Disruption when its inspirational leaders led their supporters out of the 'Auld Kirk' or the existing Church of Scotland; free churches subsequently appeared in the gateway, although not without a struggle. Communities were split and the herd boys confused by whose cows were 'free' and whose were not. Some groups had to worship in the open as at Carrbridge but after scraping funds together for a minister's stipend, a wooden Free Church was built in Rothiemurchus between the Coylumbridge and Blackpark roads; the rise past the Coylumbridge Hotel was long known as the 'old kirk brae'.

In the heyday of the stage coaches, the Honourable Henry Thomas, Lord Cockburn, a circuit judge, was a regular visitor to Strathspey when en route to Inverness. He was a forerunner of the professional classes who were to come to the gateway in growing numbers though duty, not recreation, brought him. He thought the wild country magnificent and he adored the Aviemore district. The approach became exciting 'soon after the waters begin to flow Speyward till at last the full prospect of these glorious Cairngorms with their forests, peaks and valleys' opened out. Many of his journeys to Aviemore were in April with snow on the hills and a passage for the coach having to be cut through the drifts on the Great Highland Road. Small wonder that traffic was light on the route; in 1839, between Dunkeld and Aviemore, he saw only 'two gigs, one mail coach and not a dozen carts'. There were few people about as Kingussie and its neighbour, Newtonmore, both planned settlements, were only small villages. The former was intended as a centre of woollen manufacture but this failed while the latter housed folk cleared from former clachans.

Lord Cockburn put up at the Aviemore Inn. Old hostelries such as Aviemore or Pitmain, south of Kingussie, gave travellers a warm welcome amid frenzied activity as the stage coach came rolling in:

> When the enormous vehicle disgorged a cargo of 'beasts', clean and unclean, greater than what loaded the ark . . . and knowing by experience the advantage of first possession, every monster rushed in and seized whatever he could lay his claws upon – meat, drink, the seat next the fire, the best room, the best bed, and awkwardness or timidity were left to shiver or starve.

As for Aviemore, Lord Cockburn shrewdly observed that it only lacked
two things to make it one of the grandest inland places in Scotland. These
were a wood and a house. It was a very bare site in those days and he
fancied a noble castle and gardens to set it off. Apart from giving the
district a milder climate, he would have changed nothing as in his belief
few places needed less improvement at man's hand; the rivers, rocks,
mountains and lochs he found 'all perfect'. Sadly his opinion has been
largely ignored and one can only tremble at what Lord Cockburn would
write about Aviemore today. It was 'the deep and long solitude' which so
delighted him and he was unaware of any other place 'fairly within the
reach and daily use of civilised man in this island which is so utterly
unobtruded upon by the appearance or the sounds of art or population'.
When the time came to leave the inn, he would climb through the
window of the chaise to sit on the cap-box and gaze on the Cairngorms
again; the mountains, clear to the summits in fine spring weather, were
hovered over by 'tracks of gorgeous clouds' in a vista which gave him
undiminished pleasure.

Other well-to-do visitors were also appearing in the gateway. In the
1840s, the letting of shootings became increasingly common. Prior to
that time, while forests and moors might be preserved, they were rarely
let. As has been described, game was for long a perquisite of the nobility
and gentry – for their sport and for their use at table. In the early 1700s,
records of the Baron Baillie's Court on the Grant of Grant lands note
proceedings against those who took 'roedeer, pairtricks and greenwood',
showing that game and trees were protected. Even so, Highlanders
believed that a deer from the hill, a salmon from the river and a tree from
the forest were every man's right. Deer in particular were strictly
preserved and the penalties for poaching were severe; in 1725, both
'master and man' were fined L.50 Scots for such offences in Glenmore but
the punishments did not stop the practice and poachers could be even
bolder. Forty years later, the Duke of Gordon's forester encountered the
soldier son of a Grant of Grant tenant in Rynettin hunting 'fully armed
with Gun and Durk' along with a companion on ducal land in Glen
Avon. (The possibility of identification was usually less likely on another
laird's territory.) He confiscated these items but the men came to his
house by night, broke a window and snatched the weapons back. Thus,
numerous and skilful poachers kept deer numbers in check.

James Grant of Grant assigned special powers to one of his tacksmen in
1766 as he was anxious to preserve game of all kinds in his forests; the laird
gave him the right to carry a gun. He had to ensure that no one entered
'to hunt or fowl' with guns, dogs, nets or 'any other Engine hurtful or

prejudicial to the game' without the laird's 'order and special leave'. As to 'deer forest' only nine areas in Scotland are mentioned as such in the Statistical Account of 1795. Yet the exclusion of tenants' sheep stock had began as early as the 1780s in parts of Glen Tilt and Glen Garry to make way for deer.

The Strathspey lands allowed permits to be issued to gentlemen to shoot in the 1830s and there was a list of conditions attached, 'no Black Game, Pheasants, Red Deer or Roes' were to be taken. The number of other species to be culled was also limited. Influxes of sportsmen encouraged ever stricter control of shooting rights but even so just an introduction or a courteous letter could secure permission and lairds had little notion of the potential value of their terrain. The Duke of Gordon placed an advertisement in The Times in 1812 for shooting, renting out Glen Feshie for just £12. In Rothiemurchus the Grant family, faced with ruin, was letting the Doune and the shootings as early as 1827. Shortly the Mackintosh of Mackintosh rented out moors at Coignafearn to an Englishman named Windsor. In 1830 for 60,000 acres (24,290ha) the rent was just £25 (actually £30 was charged but £5 was returned under the old system of a luck penny). Lairds were slow to latch on to the commercial possibilities of such sport. In 1833 the forest of Abernethy and the Davoch of Delnabo (with the farm of Coulnakyle at Nethybridge as a residence) were offered for rent in exclusive London clubs and in the press. The ranges comprised high and low ground where the game was reported as 'excellent'. The demand, 'so very prolific of English sportsmen', was quite overwhelming. From such small beginnings, moors were soon eagerly sought by those who had money or were making it through industry or trade; grouse shooting became a craze among the affluent.

A recommendation was made to Lord Seafield by his factor in 1847 that the forests of Abernethy and Duthil should be cleared of stock as were they 'more quiet and private' deer would frequent them in large numbers. (This was to have implications for people with holdings in the forest and the outcome was their eventual removal from it.) An embargo should also be placed on tenants wintering livestock in the forest – for which they were paid by the animals' owners; it was argued that these 'gall' (from the Gaelic for 'stranger') cattle and lambs ate out the grazing in competition with the deer. There were to be skirmishes too between drovers seeking passage and pasture for their livestock, as they moved their herds in autumn, and estate proprietors increasingly conscious of their lands' sporting values. Rents soared so much that a moor with a deer forest let for £80 in 1835 was worth twenty times as much by the 1860s. This was a major new source of income for the estates and was to precipitate another transformation in land use both in the Cairngorm gateway and elsewhere in the Highlands.

The whole business was helped along by innovations in fire power. An Aberdeenshire minister was a pioneer in experiments to devise a copper percussion cap for ammunition. Previously the flash from a muzzle loader scared off the quarry and of course it took time to re-load the weapon. By the mid-1820s hunters had a gun which ensured that the powder could be kept dry – a major advantage which encouraged hunting in the Highlands. In the 1850s the breech-loading shotgun with cartridges greatly increased the capacity of sportsmen to shoot game; 'battus' or mass slaughter ensued. This had material consequences for estate management.

The shooters, as local folk described them, came up the Great Highland Road in their own equipages with their servants. At first they had to make do with the inns or such larger houses as they could find. In the 1840s Castle Grant itself was advertised as 'completely & splendidly furnished and a fit residence for a nobleman's family'. Once known as the Castle of Freuchie, it stood on a raised site overlooking landscaped grounds and woods some two miles north of Grantown. On approach it was, and is, a tall, harled building composed of a range of structures grown in piecemeal fashion but not unpleasingly since the 1500s. A severely plain addition of grey granite to the design of John Adam, elder brother of the celebrated Robert, the classical architect, was tacked on to the north side of the castle in 1753-6, and the old towers became the rear. The appearance of the new quarters did not impress Queen Victoria who likened the building to a factory. Soon accommodation specifically designed for the sportsmen was in hand with a plan for a lodge at Dorback in Abernethy in 1849 and others were to follow.

Instead of the hunters ranging over the moors as they formerly did, butts of turf or boulders were set up in lines on the hill sides and the grouse were driven by beaters across the ground in their direction. Quantities of grouse fluctuated widely and in 1833, Captain Dixon of the Grenadier Guards (lodging at the inn at Carrbridge) got a reduction in his bill for renting the Duthil shootings as the results were so poor. Meanwhile, Lord Arbuthnot and his friends over in Abernethy lost patience and went home early; he also got money back. Nevertheless, the business prospered and by the 1840s eight ranges from Aviemore to Lochindorb were being let. Estates preferred longer leases to annual renting – these not only gave a guarantee of income but helped to conserve stocks without which the game supply would face exhaustion. Provisions about leaving a reasonable breeding stock at the close of each season were written into sporting leases and were obviously in the interest of both tenants and lairds.

Hunting in the Highlands received a royal impetus when in 1847, Queen Victoria came with her family for a holiday to Ardverikie Castle on Loch Laggan's shores. The weather was most disappointing. On 21 August the Queen recorded, 'A very wet morning. The country was very fine but the weather was most dreadful'. Accordingly a drier and sunnier venue was sought further east at Balmoral. The Queen did come back to the gateway travelling through Badenoch on her incognito expeditions through the Grampians and she passed through Aviemore when en route to Grantown in 1860.

By mid-century, the transformation of the old Grant of Grant lands was well advanced. The homeland of Strathspey had become a tongue of remarkably varied country – farmed and settled amid moors, woods and forest. This was the legacy of the good Sir James but there were further endeavours to make it prosper. When the sixth Earl of Seafield set foot on his estate at Aviemore in 1847 he was most displeased by the disordered appearance of the holdings and the irregularity of their margins. Apart from the big farm assigned to Aviemore Inn, the davoch of Aviemore and Balladern had been split into separate lots of 15 to 20 acres (6 to 8ha), each with its own farmstead. Piles of stones cleared from the land with tremendous effort were memorials to the tenants' struggle with the unpromising ground. Much waste land had been taken into cultivation. Pairs of horses drawing iron ploughs progressed across the enclosed fields and farm carts rolled along the Great Highland Road with far heavier loads than could ever have been tackled by ponies laden with panniers. Yet the earl was dissatisfied and gave orders for the lots to be enlarged, the boundaries straightened and common pasture carved up; the tenants did not like more work of this kind and the inevitable disturbance which it caused. Wire fences, an innovation of the 1820s, were soon in place, set around the fields with geometrical precision.

The old turf huts were fast disappearing to be replaced by cottages of stone and lime whose white-washed walls and thatched roofs made a pleasing contrast to their dingy predecessors. New long leases encouraged continuing improvement and on the Earl of Seafield's lands the policies of Sir James were being upheld, 'no industrious tenant needed to fear being removed at the termination of his lease'. It was worthwhile to persist in farming and there was compensation for trenching and other reclamation projects. A Drainage Act of 1840 offered loans at low rates of interest to landowners to tackle the flood plains by altering channels and embanking them.[4] New tile drains, made of earthenware and slotted into ditches, were 'much canvassed' among the gentry; this innovation went far to rendering wet land productive. Leased upland farms put an end to shielings and the common grazings were split among those too. The hilly moors, rising into the Monadh Liath and running to over 3,000 acres (1,214ha), would soon be taken over for forestry plantations and hunting grounds by the estate. These had once been a shared resource and the pattern was repeated in Glenmore, Kincardine and Pityoulish. The appropriation of such areas has blighted rural livelihoods in the Highlands; the forester/farmer of Norway is not to be found there.

More profound changes were on their way. As early as 1818 the Highland Society of Scotland had offered a prize for an essay on 'the introduction of railways for the purposes of general carriage'. By 1845, Lord Cockburn had discovered that:

> From Edinburgh to Inverness, the whole people are mad about railways. The country is an asylum of railway lunatics. The Inverness 'patients', not content with a railway to their 'hospital' from Aberdeen, insist on having one by the Highland Road from Perth.

He was astonished at the proposal since there were no towns or even villages of any consequence, few people and hence few potential passengers along the route. The promoters had other ideas; they were pinning their hopes on the carriage of livestock, 'flocks of sheep and droves of nowt' (cattle). Shares were already on offer for the line which would go by Killiecrankie, over Drumochter to Dalwhinnie and Aviemore but two decades were to elapse before it came into being. Lord Cockburn soon found that defending the environment has its perils as 'anyone who puts in a word for the preservation of scenery or relics, or sacred haunts, is set down as a beast' hostile to modern improvements and the interests of the unemployed. A pioneering conservationist, he was the first to recognise that Edinburgh merited efforts being made to maintain its visual attractiveness and the Cockburn Association, founded in 1875, continues his endeavours His beloved Aviemore would begin to alter out of recognition after the railway opened and the old stage house would become only a memory held in great affection:

> There was no such inn upon the road, fully furnished, neatly kept, excellent cooking, the most attentive of landlords – all combined to raise the fame of Aviemore. Travellers pushed on from the one side, stopped short on the other, to sleep at this comfortable inn.
> — ELIZABETH GRANT IN *MEMOIRS OF A HIGHLAND LADY*

It is a worthy tribute to a welcoming hostelry that put Aviemore on the map, accommodated so many travellers on the Great Highland Road, and lured them to come repeatedly to the Cairngorm gateway.

EXCURSION

On the Wade Road

This excursion makes extensive use of National Cycle Track Route 7, part of the Inverness to Dover system. The Ordnance Survey 1:50 000 sheets 35 and 36 are required for this outing and it is described first for cyclists. Make your way north to Carrbridge along the B9153. At that village before crossing the river turn sharp left into a side road, which leads to Dalnahaitnach. Follow this road, which goes under the Inverness-Perth railway and passes a large saw-mill, for 2½ miles (4km) until the line of General Wade's Military Road crosses the minor road practically at right angles at NH875214. A number of gates have to be negotiated along the way — be careful to close these properly. The Wade Road comes across from Kinveachy via the pass above Lethendryveole at this point. Go through the gate on the right on to the line of the Wade Road and continue to the Sluggan bridge over the Dulnain River at NH870220. The ruinous buildings hint at the depopulation of the countryside here. After crossing the bridge follow a grassy track through a dell where the overgrown Wade Road is on your right. The ground soon levels out skirting mounds showing former habitation on each side. Shortly a vehicle track comes in from the left. Follow this vehicle track ahead — it borders extents of moor on the left side and Scots pine on the right — west towards Insharn, a gamekeeper's house. On the way you will gain an appreciation of the straight line geometry of the Wade Roads and see evidence of the big marker stones which were set up by the track side to guide travellers.

At Insharn, there is an example of a possible Wade bridge which is still in use and this is a pleasant place to linger. The route from Insharn however parts from the Wade Road by taking the vehicle track to the right before the bridge is reached. This is largely the line of the Telford or stage coach route and follows the valley of the Allt an Aonaich amid pine woods past Colin's Leap for over a mile (2km) until Slochd Mhuic is approached. This rugged pass was a challenge to engineers for decades and the remarkable Slochd viaduct on the Inverness-Perth railway will be seen on your left; it is at the highest altitude of any such structure on a mainline in Britain. After crossing bridge 248 over that line, Bishop's Cycle Works are on the right beside the row of former railway cottages – a useful place to call in an emergency. Shortly NCT Route 7 is joined again for the mainly downhill run across moorland and through forest to the starting point at Carrbridge 4 miles away (6km).

For a circular tour for walkers, proceed to the starting point on the Wade Road at NH875214 where there is limited parking and follow the route outlined to Insharn. Then re-trace your steps from Insharn until the vehicle track coming up from Inverlaidnan is met at NH854218. Take this track downhill past the present farm buildings. On your left you will see a ruined structure – this is what remains of Inverlaidnan House which Prince Charles Edward Stuart famously occupied in 1746 during the Jacobite Rising. Continue on the farm track leading back across the Dulnain and so on to the minor road going north-east for ½ mile (1km) to the starting point.

For further information, contact Carrbridge Tourist Information on 01479 810281.

CHAPTER 3

The Railway Era
1850 – 1900

Approaching the mid-nineteenth century railways were all the rage. A line to the Highlands was first mooted in the 1840s but it focused on Aberdeen. The thought of railway tracks to the south being entirely under the control of Aberdonians was quite intolerable to the citizens of Inverness. To be fair, a route from Aberdeen along the Moray coast did make engineering sense – it would be easy to construct and to operate as well as giving a short, fast line between the two centres. It would also have the incomparable advantage of serving the main towns in the North East, for example, Nairn, Forres, Elgin, Keith and Huntly. Furthermore it could expect a healthy trade from farming and fisheries along the coast.

Promoters in Inverness however wished a direct, independent link with Perth. From their point of view this would give big savings in time and distance in contacts with the south. Forres and Nairn would be served by it and the tracks would cross Dava Moor to Aviemore and thence over the Pass of Drumochter via Blair Atholl and Dunkeld to Perth – 114 miles (182km) compared with 200 (320) round by Aberdeen. During the 'Railway Mania' of the 1840s, an investment bubble of great magnitude, there were hosts of company promotions. Soon prospectuses for rival schemes to include Inverness were published but the most ambitious project was that involving the route over the Grampians. O. S. Nock, the railway author, describes how a railway working 'at an altitude of nearly 1,500 feet above sea level (450m) bordered on the fantastic in the minds of many people of the day'. Astonishing as the proposal seemed, Joseph Mitchell, the Highland road engineer at the time who was noted for his close knowledge of the terrain, had surveyed the route and pronounced it feasible. He belonged to Inverness of course and local support for his plan was very strong. The great Joseph Locke, the engineer to both the Grand

Junction (London to Birmingham) and the Caledonian (Carlisle to Greenhill) lines also gave the scheme his approval.

Meanwhile, the Aberdeen interests piled in behind the rival proposal of the Great North of Scotland Railway and fought the Invernessians' Bill every inch of the way. Their chief objections were the height of Drumochter (which the railway has always known as the Gaelic, *Druimuachdar*, the ridge of the upper ground) and the long severe gradients up to the summit. There would be another set of formidable grades north of Grantown over Dava Moor. It was argued that steam locomotives would have difficulty climbing such slopes – it had been conceded that two might be required. Even worse was their lack of braking power; engines might get their trains up but would they take them safely down? Yet Mitchell proposed no gradients steeper than 1 in 70. The Aberdeen lawyers also doubted whether a line across the Grampians through largely empty country could be justified at all.

When Mitchell took his proposal to the sixth Earl of Seafield, the proprietor of the extensive Grant lands in the gateway, he found his lordship hostile. The countess made her views about a railway very plain. They were hateful as 'they brought together such an objectionable variety of people'. She stated bluntly that she would much prefer to travel the Highland road in a post chaise with horses. Furthermore, the factor was worried that trains would frighten the grouse. Lord Seafield could therefore not support the proposition. Meantime road works were continuing on the Seafield lands; a Highway Act of 1835 had abolished compulsory labour for road making and repairs, and so by the 1850s the practice was for the factor to collect money for such purposes at 3d (1.25p) per £ of rent. With the proprietor contributing an equal amount, a contractor was then set to work. Roads were seen as the main transportation system. It was very difficult – if not impossible – for a railway project to proceed without the agreement of a key landowner over whose acres the track would pass between Aviemore, Grantown and Dava. The outcome for the Perth & Inverness Railway was that the Bill was rejected and the Aberdeen link of the Great North of Scotland Railway got the go-ahead.

Shortly the railway boom collapsed; enthusiasm cooled and progress was held up for over a decade. Such had been the scale of financial ruin in some quarters that Parliamentary Committees became very wary of sanctioning railway schemes. Owing to the Aberdonians' severe difficulties in raising money, it was six years before the first sod was even cut for the Great North's own line. The rejection of the Inverness Bill was an acute disappointment for the commercial interests of that town. It was equally frustrating for those Highland landowners looking to the railway to open up the country for sport and trade. Any advance by lines into the Highlands was thus stifled – so different from Ireland where railways were given financial support by the government and positively encouraged.

Nothing daunted, the Inverness groups tried again; they had a Bill before Parliament in 1853, this time for a railway to Nairn. It was to be a line just 15½ miles (25km) long but it was the first crucial step along Mitchell's route to the south. The names of the provisional directors' estates and mansions were to become well known to local folk and other travellers as they were chosen for the company's first locomotives – Aldourie, Altyre and Cluny among them. Hardly surprisingly, the GNSR fought the scheme tooth and nail but this time the Inverness promoters were successful. Meanwhile, in 1853, a new Earl of Seafield, with a wife who had a more positive attitude to railways, had fallen heir to the Grant estates in Strathspey. The contract for the line was soon placed and on 2 September 1854, the first sod was cut by the countess at Inverness amid crowds who cheered themselves hoarse. It was declared a public holiday and such exuberance was displayed that what was planned as a dignified occasion threatened to become a mass ceilidh for the excited townsfolk.

In a little over a year, the short line to Nairn was open for traffic and Elgin was now within Mitchell's sights. The Earl of Seafield began to figure as a company director and the prospect of a line over the Grampians was coming nearer. Mitchell had reassessed the route; indeed, he walked every mile of it. With such a close knowledge of his pet project, he convinced the board of the Inverness & Nairn Railway that the new line could be built relatively economically. The surmounting of Shap and Beattock summits had proved that trains could negotiate the gradients shown on his plans. Already Inverness was well on its way to becoming a railway hub with lines to Dingwall and to Invergordon up and running before the Cairngorm gateway saw any tracks.

With growing confidence, in 1860 the Inverness & Perth Junction Railway Company was formed. It was a real Highland effort with a wide range of support from the community, from lairds putting up thousands of pounds to spinsters contributing but a few. The landowners were crucially interested in the line's potential to boost their timber trade. The Great North's fight against the proposal was as fierce as ever but its record in running a railway was so poor and its public relations so appalling that its arguments lacked conviction. The Act for the new line over the Grampians was obtained on 22 July 1861 and Lady Seafield cut the first turf in October of that year in a field outside Forres. The *Inverness Courier* reported:

> Great enthusiasm was naturally excited by the prospect of direct
> railway communication through a long line of Highland territory . . .
> one hundred and three miles from Forres to Birnam . . . A region rich
> in natural advantages and highly picturesque in character.

The line was launched in grand style before 'an immense concourse of spectators' after a procession of 1,000 marched through the town. There were Highlanders 'in tartan array', companies of Volunteers, school children, incorporated trades, Free Masons, the company directors, engineers and navvies, interspersed by bands and pipers. A 30 feet (9m) high arch decorated with flowers and evergreens stood beside a platform for the official party. There was a gun salute from Cluny Hill and the festivities were brought to a conclusion with a dinner and a magnificent ball. The I & PJR, as it became known, crossed substantial tracts of Seafield land in the Cairngorm gateway and Grantown, Boat of Garten and Aviemore, among other places, were marked out to figure in the development as stations.

A district that mattered to the railway promoters was Rothiemurchus for that was where many people were to be found scattered through the estate in hill farms and cottages. An old directory gives a glimpse of it on the eve of the coming of the railway. Its focus was Inverdruie with its smithy and one room school. (The old building, which was for long known as the library, survives. Latterly it was a dining hall for the pupils and after lying derelict for many years, it has been converted into a dwelling house.) After 1864 an assessment of 3d in the £ of rent was being levied in Rothiemurchus to meet the schoolmaster's salary. Until the Education (Scotland) Act of 1872 the poor were too often condemned to illiteracy with little chance of schooling and the advantages which it could bring. A welcome benefaction in Rothiemurchus was Caw's Trust – a bursary for pupils attending the public school who required financial assistance to continue with their schooling or to proceed to higher education. (John Caw had been the trusted clerk of Sir John Peter Grant and even accompanied the family to India. He returned to Rothiemurchus to occupy Inverdruie House as a well-to-do batchelor, but in 1848 he lost half his hard earned savings in the collapse of the Union Bank of Calcutta in which he had invested on the advice of the laird's sons.)

The Boat of Rothiemurchus was in action – it is a name commemorated in the Boat House of today where there was once a small inn kept by a Mrs Cumming, the ferryman's wife; she was 'famed near and far for the art of making her guests feel at ease and comfortable', a

The old inn at Aviemore dated from the 1760s; it was the historic core of the village and the initial reason for the place's rise to fame. In this view from 1953, the building was being used as a farm house. It was demolished in 1969 (A. E. GLEN)

The rampart of the Cairngorm Mountains, viewed across Granish Moor from Avielochan, is split by the valley of the Lairig Ghru into western and eastern massifs (JOHN PETER)

The Bridge of Carr, built to the orders of the Laird of Grant in 1717, is now used as a symbol for the village of Carrbridge (ANN GLEN)

The Lairig Ghru, the great pass which bisects the Cairngorms, rises to 2,733ft (812m) and has been a route way between Deeside and Strathspey from early times (JOHN PETER)

Old houses, restored in Grantown-on-Spey, recall its beginnings as a planned town, promoted by the clan chief, Sir James Grant of Grant, in the eighteenth century (ANN GLEN)

Loch an Eilein, with its ruined castle dating from the thirteenth century, has long been a magnet for tourists on Rothiemurchus Estate. The castle was once a nesting site for ospreys (JOHN PETER)

Most shops in Aviemore were just huts erected on railway land by the side of the Great North Road. Basic as these were, they served the community for many decades until replaced in the 1960s (A. E. GLEN)

In 1951 the road from Coylumbridge to Glenmore was a narrow dirt track where cars were few and hens could cross the water-bound surface with impunity (A. E. GLEN)

In 1953 a 'roup', or auction sale, of scarce household goods at Coylumbridge attracted a crowd of local folk eager for a bargain (A. E. GLEN)

With safety valves lifting, 'The Postal' double-headed by two Class 5s was southbound at Aviemore Junction in August 1953. Postmaster John Sam Macdonald had just put mail bags on board the railway's Travelling Post Office (A. E. GLEN)

In 1967 the first chairlift station on Cairn Gorm with the White Lady Shieling revealed the destruction of thin soils and fragile vegetation as a result of careless construction methods (JOHN PETER)

The chairlift on Cairn Gorm became a two-stage system as ski-ing boomed in the Scottish Highlands during the relatively snowy winters of the 1960s. Here skiers take to the slopes in 1968 (JOHN PETER)

The Aviemore Centre was 'bastardised modernism'. The Osprey Room and sports facilities were welcomed by the community but the structures and materials were of dubious quality. The harsh climate soon took its toll on them (GLEN COLLECTION)

Hill walkers cross the boulder fields of Cairn Gorm towards the northern corries. The Visitor Management Plan (VMP) for the mountain railway prevents its users walking up to the summit when there is no snow cover – the intention is to safeguard the habitats of the plateau (JOHN PETER)

Hill farming has been struggling to survive and there are fewer farmers and fewer individual holdings now. Here families give a hand with the potato harvest at Tullochgrue in 1999 (ANN GLEN)

Livestock rearing country, as here at Corriechullie on the Braes of Abernethy, was hard hit by the BSE crisis. Continental breeds had infiltrated the traditional Aberdeen-Angus herds by the 1990s (ANN GLEN)

tradition which Rothiemurchus folk have long maintained. The sense of isolation was heightened by the absence of a Post Office and there was no letter carrier, the mails being 'left behind (at Lynwilg) to find their way as chance may direct'. The same applied to Glenmore. As for goods, these were handled by carriers on the Great Highland Road with loads going twice weekly to and from Inverness while another carrier served Forres, Kingussie and Dunkeld. Again any items for the local area were just dumped at Lynwilg. There were sixty entries for Rothiemurchus – ten were farmers or crofters, in marked contrast to today's two tenant farmers, Billy Collie of Achnahatnich and Sandy Mackenzie of Tullochgrue, but trades were well represented with saw millers, masons, joiners and carpenters totalling twelve in all. It was a time when under laird William Grant much rebuilding of houses and steadings was taking place. A road contractor, a merchant (there was only one shop) and a weaver were also kept busy. Rothiemurchus had become a hunting ground and there were no less than five gamekeepers listed. A Game Act of 1831 had legalised their activities.

Among the family names on the estate, Grant was completely dominant but the most surprising representative was Robert Grant, professor of Astronomy at Glasgow University, who occupied Inverdruie House and who was one of the early distinguished professionals to holiday in the gateway. He had been Grantown born and educated at the old grammar school there. Through the provision of bursaries, university education was encouraged as a route to achievement and the affluence which this could bring. After Grant, the most numerous names were Collie, McBean, McDonald and Mackenzie. Soon the remote little world of Rothiemurchus and other stretches of the gateway were to feel the impact of the railway which had such a dramatic effect in opening up the country when, in Joseph Mitchell's words, 'primitive and old fashioned ways were quickly supplanted'.

Mitchell's meticulous fieldwork ensured that the I & PJR was constructed with care and economy but there was another obstacle – land acquisition. Parliamentary Committees ensured that land owners would receive adequate compensation for damage which was alleged they might suffer as a result of railways crossing their estates. Such compensation (and legal fees) escalated. In the countryside, land acquisition by a railway company was based on the value of agricultural land but there were extra percentages to calculate. Railways were reckoned to be noisy and dirty neighbours; disturbance arose from construction works, and when fields, roads, or paths were split by the passage of track, there was 'the inconvenience of intersection'. Finally, 50 per cent more was added on for

Timber continued to be floated on the Druie in the 1900s. The floaters or 'collies' armed with cleeks braved the cold and turbulent waters (WALTER DEMPSTER)

'the fact of compulsion' as the seller had little choice in the matter. All this could represent a tidy sum and be a big financial burden on new lines – in some cases, it could have built them. Thankfully for the I & PJR, the lairds and others generally 'met the company in a liberal spirit over compensation', only one-sixth of total costs going on this and legal matters. Lord Seafield received at least part of his compensation in shares but he also had an elaborate bridge and ornamental gatehouse constructed at the entrance to Castle Grant where the line crossed the Nairn road. Other lairds benefited by selling sleepers of larch or 'Scotch fir' at 2s 6d (12.5p) each and fencing posts at 6d (2.5p) each but they too had to be willing to take shares in payment.

Over the whole route there were few large-scale works such as viaducts and tunnels and in particular the stretch from Kingussie to Grantown was judged 'light in character'. The only sizeable river to bridge was the Dulnain but the Spey was of another order preventing many areas being tapped. Timber traffic from such districts as Rothiemurchus and Glenmore would be very welcome on the line. In

1861 there was a proposal by the laird William Grant of Rothiemurchus to have a bridge built by public subscription as there was none across the Spey between Kingussie and Grantown. A place was chosen above the Druie confluence where the channel was 'narrow and not subject to change'. The incentive was that not only would a railway station be erected in the proximity of the crossing but a road could also be expected to be made to it by the District Road Trustees. The bridge was to have three spans of malleable iron girders resting on masonry piers with flooring and side walls of timber, 'Mr Grant of Rothiemurchus will give all the timber and a subscription of £100'. A cheaper, all timber version was also considered but nothing happened – the funds were not forthcoming. Accordingly in 1862, the I & PJR began negotiations with Grant of Rothiemurchus through his agent for the construction of a bridge over the Spey. The railway proposed to erect it if the laird provided the timber 'as has been done by Lord Seafield at Broomhill' (near Nethybridge) where its successor bridge now stands.

A plan was produced; timber sizes were specified but there was a snag – Grant of Rothiemurchus had to agree to send all his timber by the new line. This he would not do; he had other options – floating it out on the river, an alternative which was cheaper than the railway but less reliable, or hauling it to the Great North's station at Boat of Garten. Losing patience, by July 1864 the railway company resolved to have a bridge built by another party. Nevertheless, the Laird of Rothiemurchus got something out of it for he sold sleepers to the railway and at last there was a bridge over the Spey to Rothiemurchus. This wooden structure lasted until 1884 when it was replaced by a girder bridge which now takes only foot and cycle traffic.

Many other matters had to be arranged. Supplies of water at the stations were crucial; in terms of volume, steam locomotives need more water than they do coal. In Aviemore the water came from the Aviemore burn and involved drawing it off through sluices. The railway's requirements seem to have put paid to the water-powered corn and barley mill at Milton, the former Milntown of Aviemore. The amount paid for the water rights was ridiculously small and good use was made of them. In a location which could be relatively dry and where sandy ground made a reliable water supply awkward, nearly every house built privately in Aviemore in the nineteenth century got its quota 'off the railway' as it was so much easier and cheaper that way. The water had not only to be abundant but also clean and so every week as long as there were steam engines at Aviemore, a pair of men from the loco shed went up to the filters and sluices to check that they were clear.

The contract for the Aviemore section of the I & PJR, which ran from Aviemore to Forres via Boat of Garten and Grantown, was let to William Meakin of Inverness for £33,500. This contractor had also worked on the Inverness to Invergordon route. As money was so tight, the contractors had to be enticed into accepting stock in the new railway as part payment. The Aviemore site probably became a depot for the construction work with a camp of navvies close by. Stacks of sleepers, telegraph poles and fencing posts piled up, together with rail shipped from Liverpool at £7 a ton and fish plates (to hold the lengths together) at £9 a ton delivered to Inverness and Dunkeld. Quarries were opened to supply stone for bridges, platforms and ballast for the track. The scale of activity and upheaval was unprecedented.

In 'By Loch and River', Thomas Sinton recalled the arrival of the first workmen in Badenoch. These navvies with odd accents began a section of the new line and shortly the first steam engine appeared:

> This marvellous novelty of which so much had been heard . . . All the world and his wife set out to meet the wondrous machine . . . except those that were suspicious of the whole thing who took refuge on a knoll.

The centre of attention was only a little contractor's engine, a 'coffee pot' with a vertical boiler, drawn to the site by horses. Once set on rails, the engine was soon puffing about, shoving or tugging wagons along the line for many months. It could also skim along the track 'all by itself at a wonderful pace' – a foretaste of things to come. Innocent bystanders asked if the line would be perfectly straight and, if so, would it be possible to see Perth?

Railway construction also had its drawbacks for it introduced as Thomas Sinton noted:

> a new and disturbing element upon a scene erstwhile so peaceful and retired . . . an indescribable charm was broken . . . the noble fir wood, sadly torn and devastated to make way for a rude embankment of naked sand and gravel.

The old davochs along the strath suffered these disfigurements and more. Bridges had to be constructed over and under the lines to accommodate roads, farm tracks and streams. They were solidly built though only to the dimensions of a single line.

With the navvies' camps came trouble. The first policemen to be active in the gateway area were railway police employed to maintain order and acting under the jurisdiction of the Chief Constable of Inverness-shire. The Aviemore Inn was the focus of much disturbance and when the landlord would not co-operate, the mob broke the windows. It was enough; the innkeeper shut the premises. The most convenient alternative was at Lynwilg where at night the road was described as 'fringed' with the legs of drunken and stupified navvies. Often soaked to the skin from toiling in pouring rain, it is not surprising that they sought warmth and comfort there. Some gateway folk used to claim, with a little embarrassment, descent from the itinerant railway builders.

Within the gateway, the choice of Aviemore for a station did not please everyone. It was acknowledged that the new artery would be a stimulus to trade and a station on the line was worth fighting for. Sir George McPherson-Grant argued in favour of a stopping place at Lynwilg. He was also dismayed by the selection of Boat of Insh (later Kincraig) for another. Similarly a petition from Duthil folk, 'praying that the proposed station at Boat of Garten be placed at Peart's saw mill in Granish wood' was also refused. Steam saw mills, which could be moved around the forest areas, had appeared on the scene in the 1850s.

Joseph Mitchell was sorely taxed by the sheer extent of the site – 104 miles (166km) of it – and there were tensions too between him and the I&PJR chairman, the Honourable Thomas C. Bruce. The pressures told on Mitchell and he suffered a stroke, from which he thankfully recovered, while assistants were left to carry forward the project. Into the peaty morasses of Drumochter ton upon ton of gravel was poured until the track bed could bear the weight of a train. The rails had to be repeatedly re-laid as the ballast sank into the moss.

In less than two years the line was available for inspection, a remarkable outcome in such rough and mountainous terrain as the Grampians. When an attempt was made to send a goods train north from Perth, the trip proved too much for the engine which was ominous for time keeping on the route. It came to a stand between Struan and Dalnacardoch. No water was available at the water column near by and it looked as if the engine's fire would have to be dropped. Not for the first time in railway annals, willing hands got to work with pails and tubs bringing water from the River Garry to fill the tender. Steam was then raised again and the train moved slowly onwards but several hours had been lost over this pantomime.

The Forres-Aviemore section was ready for opening on 3 August 1863 and the line throughout from Inverness to Perth on 9 September. The I & PJR had cost just £8,000 per mile but there had been no skimping –

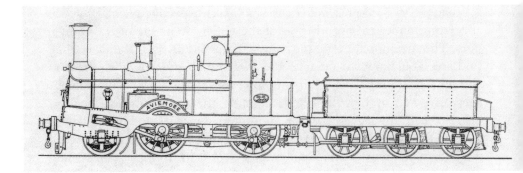

The locomotives which opened the Inverness & Perth Junction Railway in 1863 were similar to this engine, No. 22, named Aviemore (OXFORD PUBLISHING COMPANY)

Joseph Mitchell had seen to that – and observers were impressed by the substantial and permanent character of the civil engineering works amidst such rugged country. The preparations for the opening were fraught with difficulties. The locomotives on order were not available and a crisis loomed. A meeting was held in Perth to discuss the problem as 18 engines were required – eight suitable for passenger work and the balance for goods haulage. The passenger ones at £2,700 each were well behind schedule and so the I & PJR had to get locomotives on loan from the Caledonian and the old Scottish Central companies. When the new engines did appear they were turned out in a gloomy livery of dark green with black borders. No. 22, the first of its class, was named *Aviemore* and there was soon a *Grantown* and a *Kingussie*, a sure indication of places that were going to matter to the railway. The idea of giving locomotives place-names was to emphasise the company's expanding network, although it could confuse the travelling public who could suppose that the name showed the train's destination!

There were plenty of teething troubles. Hardly had the line been declared fit for traffic than a train service, described as 'quite ambitious', was being advertised. On the afternoon of the opening day, an Inverness gentleman chose to travel home from Forres by the very first passenger train from the south. It eventually got to Inverness after midnight to the immense relief of an anxious crowd that had been waiting for hours. There were employee problems too. It was not easy for either local folk or incomers from other parts of the Highlands to adapt to railway life as 'company servants'; railway companies could be quite tyrannical. Errors or omissions were punished by the docking of pay or if serious by dismissal. The staff had a great deal to learn – about new fangled gadgets such as the electric telegraph system; it broke down and consequently passenger trains could not go further north than Struan or come south from Kingussie.

When the new locomotives entered service, they were too lightly built for the long gradients on the new Highland line. Delays were frequent and the railway simply could not meet its timed schedules. A journey from Perth to Inverness, advertised to take six hours, could stretch to a couple of days. Even Joseph Mitchell, the line's enthusiastic engineer, recounted his troubles on leaving Inverness after 10 am (this was probably the train tabled for a 9 o'clock departure) and only reaching Dunphail on the north approach to Dava Moor 'where no other train appeared that day'.

So rapid had been the pace of construction that little thought had been given about cottages for staff. They had to make do through the first winter with huts, presumably left over from the navvy occupation, as temporary accommodation. In March 1864, engineers were instructed to 'immediately advertise for offers for the Station Masters' Houses and Porters' Cottages to be created at intermediate stations between Forres and Dunkeld'. To save time, tracings of houses built at Rothiemay by the GNSR were sought together with 'a note of the expense'. An offer from William Meakin, the contractor for the Aviemore section, to erect the railway's first houses at Forres, Grantown and Aviemore was accepted. The station master's neat little villa there cost £326 while the porters' cottages were just £190 a piece. The latter formed a small row of three dwellings just north of the station on the site of a modern shopping mall. Meanwhile, temporary stations had also been put up along the route at a cost of £80 each but they were little better than wooden sheds. The Earl of Seafield did rather better at Castle Grant with the East Lodge constructed so ingeniously that he could 'step out . . . and get into the train passing' from its upper floor. Soon labourers were reported as attracted to settle near the stopping places on the new line, enticed there by the likelihood of work arising from it.

At the outset, the volume of traffic was very small. The railway was pinning its hopes on freight, especially livestock, but it took time for local folk to switch from droving or carters and carriers to the new line. The winter months saw average takings for the whole route drop to only £1,300 a week. A salvation was the mail contract for the counties of Inverness, Nairn, Moray, Banff, Ross, Sutherland and Orkney. Even with its shocking timetable deficiencies the railway had made very big savings in time. A seven year contract with the Royal Mail had been secured at £5,000 a year. By January 1864, Joseph Mitchell was able to report that the track was 'in a very efficient state' – it was withstanding the onslaught of winter well. There was plenty to worry about for there were 142 bridges over streams and rivers plus 1,700 drains. With his long experience of Highland roads, he wrote:

> We watched during the winter months . . . the effects of heavy floods, severe frosts and sharp snow storms but the works remained entire.

He must have been truly relieved because such had been the hurry to get the line open that slopes of cuttings and embankments had not been properly completed, soiled or planted with grass. So highly praised were Mitchell's engineering skills that in 1867 he spoke on the construction of the Highland Railway (as the I & PJR had become) to the British Association meeting in Dundee. His apprehension about floods was well justified; a year later the long embankment on the GNSR line south of Nethybridge was breached in February, severing the rail link to Boat of Garten for several months. (The GNSR had absorbed the Strathspey Railway of 1865, and within two years the old station at Abernethy was re-named Nethybridge to prevent any confusion with Abernethy in Perthshire.)

When the railway's potential to put money in tills became known, a flurry of enquiries began. William Robertson from Carrbridge requested ground at Aviemore station on which to erect 'a Refreshment Room and Sleeping Accommodation for Tourists'. There were already such rooms at Kingussie which were quickly enlarged and a 'Third Class Ladies' Retiring Room' added; these were all just timber structures. As to the arrangements for 'Gentlemen' at Kingussie, the sheer number of urinals was the talk of Badenoch especially after the station was rebuilt in 1894. Such comforts were essential as carriages had neither lavatories nor dining facilities and lengthy stops were made while whole trains disgorged their passengers. The railway company seems to have been uncertain about how many such refreshment centres to allow. Permission was also sought for similar quarters at Boat of Garten, more understandably perhaps as 'the Boat' became a junction when the Strathspey line of the GNSR opened there on 1 August 1866 and there were transfers of passengers between trains. Its rudimentary inn beside the station eventually became a hotel. The ultimate authority was, of course, Lord Seafield, who had to give the land and approve the plans; the Aviemore project did not get off the ground, although the place had no facilities at all to offer travellers for many years. Owing to the presence of two railway companies, Grantown boasted two stations – Grantown-on-Spey East being GNSR and

Grantown-on-Spey West being initially I & PJR, a rare distinction for a country place. Only the former now survives in a forlorn state.

As for Aviemore, an Ordnance Survey map of 1869 shows the small station with its signal posts and 'fountain' to supply water for the engines. A little way north there was a house at right angles to the tracks – presumably the station master's house – beside the terrace of three dwellings for staff. A long shed marked 'Post Office' stood on what is now Dalfaber Road. Apart from the toll house and the buildings of the old inn, there was nothing on the Great Highland Road west of the railway until the cottages at Wester Aviemore came into view.[5] It was a modest beginning for a village that would become such a key element in the Cairngorm gateway. Kingussie, with its small engine shed for two locomotives used in assisting trains up to Drumochter, was of much greater importance but Carrbridge, which was a route centre of note and a village of some substance, had to wait for almost thirty years until tracks tied it into the network. The railway helped to staunch the outflow of people in Duthil and Rothiemurchus but not in Abernethy or Kincardine where the decline in population continued.

With the coming of the railway and the growing interest in hunting, fishing and field sports, the old Aviemore Inn had found a new purpose – it had been converted into a shooting lodge and dignified with the name 'Aviemore House'. Attitudes had changed greatly since the 1790s when Sir James Grant had been reminding the innkeeper where his first duties lay. A guest had made 'sad complaints' about his reception at the inn and the laird had written:

> I mean Aviemore for an inn for travellers and passengers and that any accommodation he (the innkeeper) gives to gentlemen must be subordinate to and give way to the convenience of travellers.

Now it was a very different story; the preservation of game and deer had become of prime importance to estates because the letting of shooting rights was swelling revenues to the landowners and the existence of the Highland Railway gave a boost to the whole business. Breech loading shot guns could be in almost continuous action – sometimes the barrels became too hot to hold; a record of 100 brace of grouse in a day was set by one tenant in Abernethy. The supply of game was soon shown as inadequate in the face of such barrages. The result was that its preservation quickly evolved into a highly organised strategy. Enthusiasm swung from grouse to deer. These trends had a profound effect on the districts of the Cairngorm gateway. By the 1870s vast extents of the hills and upland valleys, indeed the bulk of many estates, were set aside to provide sport for the wealthy for a few weeks each year. These lessees might be aristocrats or nouveaux riches from Burton-on-Trent or Merseyside and increasingly they included Americans.

Ideally the ranges combined both grouse and deer; the birds were erratic in number and could not be bred in captivity but the deer were more consistent and furthermore made impressive sporting trophies. Abernethy forest was estimated at 'up to 90 stags' a season. It attracted Robert Durning Holt, a wealthy cotton broker from Liverpool, who became one of the first Lord Mayors of that city and who also had connections with Lamport & Holt, the well-known shipping line. In 1869 he agreed to take the forest at £600 a year for two years and for £1,000 thereafter – a very large amount at the time – and to use the Dell of Abernethy as a lodge. Initially he did not fancy deer stalking ('a grouse shooting is all I desire . . . ') but so attached did the family become to Abernethy that they were to occupy the timber Forest Lodge, built in 1887 as a replacement for the earlier Cromalt Lodge, for many decades. Shooting rentals soared – between 1841 and 1883 these rose fourfold in Duthil – becoming the main source of income on many Highland properties and of rates to the counties.

To take Glenmore as an example, up to the 1830s, twelve to fifteen families lived in scattered clachans on the south facing slopes of the Kincardine Hills and in forest clearings. Of the forgotten settlements of Buchonich, Beglan, Rieunachan, Reluig, Badaguish and others, only the latter place-name survives today where forestry houses have been converted to an outdoor centre. Glenmore's population had declined sharply after the years of timber exploitation. In 1836 the Duke of Richmond and Lennox, who was a nephew of the fourth Duke of Gordon, had inherited the estate and took the Gordon name; during his tenure Glenmore's people experienced new and harsh land use policies. Shortly Scrope, in his 'Art of Deer Stalking', was mentioning Glenmore as a hunting ground. It was however also made a sheep run, managed from Auchgourish and Pityoulish in Kincardine; the people were cleared off the land and the old clachans, not only in Glenmore but also around Pityoulish, were swept away. In 1843 John Ross, the schoolmaster at Kincardine (in which parish Glenmore lay), was bemoaning his shrinking fees arising from the clearance of population. Squatters were evicted too, some settling in hovels along the 'Sraid', now the Street of Kincardine. When sheep rearing proved unsuccessful, in 1859 a deer forest in the strict sense was formed in Glenmore. This extended to 15,000 acres (6,073ha) including the west face and corries of Cairn Gorm and in 1899 the yield of stags was reported as between 50 to 60. The first lodge may once have been Mr Osbourne's house but it burned down and a new stone built lodge (now a youth hostel) had been constructed by 1873. It soon attracted the patronage of such rich sportsmen as Sir Edward Cecil Guinness of the Irish brewery family in the 1880s and of the Marquis of Zetland in the 1890s. The shootings alone netted over £1,200 a year. About the same time the duke also had the large farmhouse at Pityoulish, on a bank of the Spey in Kincardine parish, available for rent as it could serve the ranges on the low ground and the fishings on the river.

Rothiemurchus, where sheep farming had been tried unsuccessfully in Glen Einich, was converted to a deer forest in 1843 but there were few clearances on the estate. The hunting grounds in two beats were fenced to keep out farm livestock and to contain deer but in some areas these animals were scarce to the point of being rarities. Consequently in Rothiemurchus calves were got from Mar while some were smuggled into Glen Feshie from Atholl to form nucleus herds.

By 1869 a few families were being moved 'out of the way' in Abernethy when it also became a deer forest, tenants agreeing 'to give up possession upon getting equally suitable and comfortable holdings in the neighbourhood'. Their arable land lapsed into 'sour pasture' and the houses into ruins. This process, carried out over two years, mainly affected folk in high or remote places, such as Rynuie west of the Ryvoan track. Disparaging comments were made about their husbandry but anyone seeing the abandoned homesteads today must wonder how tenants wrested a living on such holdings save by recourse to poaching and the illicit distilling of whisky. What was given in return was often poor land. Tomachrochar, Toberaie and Mains of Tulloch still exist but other sites of resettlement have been long abandoned. (Incidentally crofts, as defined and recognised by the crofting legislation enacted after 1886, were few in number in the Cairngorm gateway – just a handful in Abernethy and Duthil – but they were more numerous in parts of Badenoch.)

Sheep stocks and muirburning were seen as threats to sport – a lessee complained of too many sheep preventing grouse having 'fair play' and so a rotation of muirburning and an allowance of five sheep for every £ of rent was proposed on the Seafield lands. One sheep was reckoned equivalent to two hinds in calf. So the removal of sheep on farms near the pine forest was urged to encourage better quality deer. Enclosures for breeding stock above the forests were to serve the same purpose. With deer numbers soaring not surprisingly farmers on the margins of the ranges began complaining of damage to their crops.

Drumintoul Lodge in Rothiemurchus is typical of the grander 'shooting boxes' erected in the Highlands when deer stalking became popular among the well-to-do in the 1870s (WALTER DEMPSTER)

A deer forest was also set up in Kinveachy but the Earl of Seafield was more interested in his plantations and the reserve was explained as a consequence of the woods being enclosed. Primarily game preservation was aimed at maximising the stock of deer and grouse on estates and the value of the latter became inextricably linked with the size of the sporting bag. The ecological well being of forest or moor was of little significance and it has continued thus on too many estates.

Landowners gained substantially from the letting of sporting rights. By the latter 1870s, Rothiemurchus shootings (over both high and low ground) plus a lodge were worth £2,400 a year, which enabled further improvements to be carried out. Indeed, many of the farmhouses, steadings and other buildings, such as housing for estate workers at Aultnancaber (now a clay pigeon shooting centre), date from the 1860s. On Seafield land it had been the custom for tenants to construct and maintain their own dwellings and byres, such as they were. About 1860 these were taken over at a valuation of two years' rent. Even though the old cottages, which the folk had put up, were often miserable affairs, they felt their loss 'like parting with a right hand'. The proprietor then built replacements, reputedly spending £50,000 on this 'vast improvement' which produced many of the farmhouses and 'offices' which still stand.

Extensive lengths of 'dry stane' dykes were set up as boundaries at a cost of a shilling a yard (about 5p per metre). The funds for such projects were mainly derived from sporting rentals but those were also expansive years for agriculture. Urban markets were growing steadily and farmers engaged in stock rearing had good returns. Consequently there were high levels of investment in farm buildings and machinery until the 1870s when a long downturn in the economy began.

There was much buying and selling of Highland estates too. It is estimated that one-third of the Highlands and islands changed hands (some estates several times over) in the course of the nineteenth century. The ancestral lands of the clans became a negotiable commodity and have continued so. The relationship between chief, people and territory was further weakened and in many instances obliterated. Remarkably, family ownership of the Seafield lands at Aviemore, of the Grant lands in Rothiemurchus and of the Duke of Gordon's in Glenmore and at Kinrara continued unaltered into the twentieth century but other tracts were to see owners come and go. There were visible signs of prosperity in the new shooting lodges, keepers' cottages, stables and kennels which rose on the estates. On Seafield land, Kinveachy Lodge, some five miles north of Aviemore was completed in 1875 and Drumintoul in Rothiemurchus followed in 1877. (The latter had a false start due to problems of water supply; the preferred site was on the slopes of Tullochgrue near Loch an Eilein.) Several others – Dalrachney, Lochindorb, Muckrach, Revack and Tulchan – had also appeared on the Seafield estates by this time. Occasionally lessees had a lodge constructed; Tulchan was one – 'an elegant mansion . . . displaying no small taste in the building and embellishment of a Highland home'. Many smaller shootings, each with a lodge, were viewed as more profitable than a few large ones as large areas encouraged syndicates, 'tenants and their friends', which simply produced a lower rent per capita for estate owners.

The prospect of some regular and often congenial employment for local men, not only on the moors and hills but also in the gardens and grounds of the lodges, was welcome. The positions of gamekeeper, shepherd or other estate worker were much sought after; these not only conferred status and an assured income, but also typically offered a superior house, well found and slate roofed compared to the poor dwellings of so many folk. The downside was that such houses were 'tied' – they went with the job and had to be vacated when employment ended. In the 1900s the great estate of Mar employed about forty outdoor staff and much smaller Rothiemurchus required four gamekeepers while Glenmore had three. The lessees were responsible for the wages which with other expenses probably amounted to more than the rent. Many temporary staff were taken on for the season and there were frenzied preparations – painting and papering, laundering and sewing – even the old bridge at Coylum got a coat of white wash. For women, there was domestic work in the big house. Local shops gained business by supplying the lodges – everything from groceries to tweeds.

The influx of shooting tenants and their house parties plus staff gave rise to a stream of horse-drawn vehicles between the railway stations and the lodges. A note of gaiety and excitement, came to many a strath when there were gillies' balls, treats for staff and the fun of seeing 'society' in their midst. New fashions and manners spread. Royalty's annual migration to Balmoral continues to have the same effects, although on a grander scale and in the media spotlight of today.

To take an example of a typical sporting lessee, Sir Spencer Maryon-Wilson, Bt. of Fitz-Johns, Eastbourne, leased Kinveachy for over fifty years. He hunted over one thousand stags in that time and set a record by disposing of 24 himself in 22 days. For the privilege before the First World War, he paid £1,690 for the deer forest and £100 for the lodge and offices. The fishings only cost him £5 as they were so poor. Sir Spencer therefore stocked Loch Vaa with trout and so tame did they become that they could be fed with crumbs at the water's edge. Poachers found them easy prey but then the baronet put up warning notices inviting informers; local people thought this most objectionable but it never stopped the practice. Ospreys were alleged to pay visits to his preserve even after the birds were 'extinct' in the Highlands.

Overall, whether the sporting estates conferred advantages on local people morally or socially was questioned at the time; opinions were bound to differ on that score. The women, employed as housekeepers, cooks and maids, sometimes found being 'in service' to their liking and progressed to regular work in the south. Men as gamekeepers, gillies, and stalkers, could also earn promotion for there were over 200 sporting estates in the Highlands in the 1900s. For farm folk there was extra cash to be made as ponymen or beaters. By the time the first snows came, the shooting fraternity had usually gone back south. The dust sheets were spread in the deserted rooms of the lodges, the blinds were drawn, the shutters were bolted, the water tanks were emptied to guard against winter's frosts and the mansions of the wealthy hunters went into hibernation. Criticism was levelled however at the subservient attitudes engendered among the once independent and proud Highlanders.

If careers in estate work were advanced by the presence of the shooting tenants, marriages were also made and not just at the upper levels. New blood came to the strath, sometimes legitimately and sometimes not. A distinguished Highlander of regal countenance and noble bearing (and an able piper by all reports) appeared regularly on the platforms at Aviemore station in the inter-war years. When the trains arrived, a tune or two earned some coins for this presumed offspring of the Prince of Wales, later King Edward VII.

Bothies for the hunters to take lunch, often attached to stables for ponies, were built amid the hills; in Rothiemurchus there were once two such shelters in Glen Einich and another at Aultdrue. On extensive estates subsidiary lodges (now mostly in ruins) were placed far into the mountains. Stalkers' tracks which were carefully constructed and regularly maintained reached into the glens and climbed the slopes past many a corrie. Gamekeepers or their assistants turned folk off the hills during 'The Season' which for grouse shooting commenced on 12 August, the Glorious Twelfth, and could continue to December while stag hunting might begin on 1 July and proceed with increasing intensity from 1 September. The new order of priorities meant that timber extraction stopped when the shooting tenants were in residence; an Act of Parliament actually prohibited the floating of logs in summer because angling interests protested that the activity spoiled their sport. Out with the prohibited weeks on the Seafield estates, dams were only to be opened once a week. A network of these dams, forming ponds to augment the flow in tributary streams to the Spey, had been installed especially in Abernethy forest.

After the railway came middle class and professional families increasingly made their appearance in the gateway districts, delighting in Loch an Eilein and the high tops. A variety of naturalists and not a few egg collectors wandered through the forests. Gathering, and then arranging, natural history objects in albums or cabinets was thought educational and not at all pillaging the environment. In 1871 the policy on the Seafield estate was that 'tourists and pedestrians' should be checked from disturbing the best deer grounds 'nicely and in a courteous manner'. Attempts were made to close time-honoured paths, such as the route through the Lairig Ghru, a passage stoutly defended by a Scottish Rights of Way and Recreation Society which had originated in Edinburgh in 1846. The rumpus came to a head in Rothiemurchus in 1882 when a family of English visitors, Martineau by name, was active in having these historic routes recognised. Dr James Martineau, the Principal of the Unitarian College in Manchester and an outstanding preacher, had begun coming with his family of three daughters to the Polchar in Rothiemurchus each summer. He was a determined hill walker and climbed Braeriach at the age of 80. The family was naturally resentful when visitors to Loch an Eilein – including ladies in their long skirts – had to climb over gates with their picnic baskets in order to gain access. So the Martineaus were not above conniving at such sabotage as lifting gates off hinges and unscrewing the locks (he had begun his career as an engineer in Norwich); at the same time, they resided very close to the Doune and carried on a civil but futile correspondence with the laird:

> But he is full of his fancied rights, he despises popular resistance and will never be brought to reason but by the decision of a court.

It seemed hopeless, especially with his gillies 'challenging and terrifying the ignorant' and throwing down finger posts erected by the Scottish Rights of Way Society.

Grant of Rothiemurchus and his shooting tenants objected most strongly to any tracks giving access to the deer forest being open to all – but passage into and through the estate had been getting ever easier. The Duke of Bedford had seen to the upgrading of the route round Loch an Eilein to a carriage drive standard when he and the duchess were tenants at the Doune. The Earl of Stamford and Warrington, while the shooting lessee, had a road made into Glen Einich along the line of the ancient track there and Sir Curtis Sampson had arranged a new bridle path from Coylumbridge to join it. All these were for their own greater convenience but these improvements helped walkers and especially cyclists who were beginning to appear on primitive machines in the mid-1880s.

The lairds' response to popular pressure was to form an alliance: the Highland Property Association was set up 'to spread the truth about the nature and management of Highland landed property, correcting some very gross errors' and pointing out that 'the interest of proprietors and tenants are in the long run identical'. Yet a wind of change was blowing and in June 1887 the Cairngorm Club was begun by a handful of enthusiasts at the Shelter Stone by Loch Avon and was later formalised in Aberdeen. It was matched by the Scottish Mountaineering Club in Glasgow and their members sought access to the ancient tracks and to the hills as of right.

After protracted arguments in 1888 old routes, such as the Thieves' Road (*Rathad nam Mèirleach*) from Loch Morlich to Loch an Eilein, were admitted as rights of way. In retaliation estates placed 'deer watchers' in such bothies as Aultdrue (it was known as the Torr) and Corrour on the Lairig Ghru route to see that walkers kept strictly to the paths. But times were changing. When converting the hills behind Aviemore into a deer forest in the 1860s, Lady Seafield had thought nothing of cutting through the old Wade road with a high deer fence and no one had protested. Now it was different – visitors supporting the Scottish Rights of Way Society were not only penning letters to the press but were also distributing leaflets among local farmers to let them know how the law stood.

In 1894 Sir James Bryce, the Liberal MP for Aberdeen South, promoted an Access to Mountains (Scotland) Bill. A distinguished scholar and widely travelled man, he believed that citizens had 'a right to enjoy the scenery of their own country and (to) seek healthy recreation on their own mountains and moors'. Many new landowners and lessees did not see the matter in the same light at all. Most were accustomed to the English position where unless a right of way was followed, an individual was trespassing.[6] Their intention had been to purchase privacy, even exclusivity, on often vast estates where tourists and mountaineers were viewed as troublesome interlopers. Such a tenant was W. L. Winans, a millionaire American, whose son Walter was a noted marksman. Winans leased a huge area of the North West Highlands, comprising six estates, which stretched from the east coast to Kintail where he had the margins patrolled by an army of keepers. When Sir Hugh Munro was attempting to measure the heights of the Scottish mountains for his famous Tables, two of Winans's employees actually pursued him to the summit of a peak there, presumably to check his veracity.

There was another outburst of protest in Rothiemurchus in 1903 when notices implying that roads were 'private' – the ominous word 'trespass' was used – were put up by the shooting tenant; these were seen as a violation of the ancient right of way to Glen Einich. At Newtonmore that same year 'a great demonstration' took place when the populace marched up Glen Banchor behind a piper to open up all the old rights of way to the hill. The closing of moss roads in the shooting season was preventing folk getting to their peat banks. But the sporting interests continued to fight back as in Glenmore where the shooting lessee tried to inconvenience and discourage tourists going to Cairn Gorm – their ponies and traps had to remain in the open all day and the gamekeeper's wife was prohibited from giving visitors tea.

With regard to forestry, in 1866 the government had removed the duty on imported timber and so supplies from the Baltic countries and from North America recommenced. Gradually the price of home grown timber fell but new plantations, mainly of Scots pine, continued to be established. Two impediments to good forestry were muirburning and what was described as 'promiscuous grazing'. On the Strathspey lands since the 1760s no muirburn had been permitted between 1 March and

29 September when dry weather might allow it to get out of control and cause forest fires. Stopping tenants letting their cattle, sheep, goats and horses browse in the forest was more difficult. Traditionally livestock was supposed to be 'hefted' at night in folds or pens and contraventions were punishable by fines and 'poinding' or confiscation; the process of enclosure should have resolved the matter but it did not.

The Earls of Seafield had an active planting policy; Francis William, the sixth earl, is said to have had 31 million trees planted. Much of this activity was in Duthil parish with seedlings supplied from a nursery at the Doune in Rothiemurchus. His son, John Charles, continued these schemes notably on the Monadh Liath where a vast forest extending from Carn Dearg Mòr to Beinn Ghuilbin and beyond was set out in the 1860s. School children are said to have helped with the planting but an adult worker was supposed to be able to plant 12,000 seedlings in a day.

Somehow a balance was contrived between heavy felling and massive afforestation which maintained the area of forest. The railway's demand for timber was welcome but other contracts were also made. In 1867, the Laird of Rothiemurchus sold over 21,000 trees near Achnahatnich to a Crieff merchant for almost £700 and the whole lot was cleared with even the stunted or small specimens going for pit props. Notwithstanding Abernethy's new status as a deer forest, 'lots of fine old natural grown Scots pine trees' were advertised for sale by private treaty a few years later. A distinction was being made between the upper 'natural' forest, the haunt of deer and the sportsmen, and the lower 'worked' forest on the Seafield estate. Such was the repute of its forests that they were visited by a French government commission in 1881 when the 'management and arrangement' were reported as 'being perfect' with species from the Himalayas and the Rocky Mountains in cultivation.

Once the railway was in action, roads became of secondary importance. They served simply as feeders to the new line or for local access. In 1862 the Commission for Highland Roads and Bridges had come to an end having contributed to a transformation in the Highlands which left it with:

> Profitable agriculture, a thriving population and active industry . . .
> The value of land had been incalculably increased and the condition
> of every class of people improved.

Latterly more and more of its work had been concerned with road repairs rather than new construction.

By 1889 all public roads, which were generally the main ones, were assigned to the County Councils; cottages were put up for roadmen and their families beside the stretch of road for which they were responsible. The trimmed verges and neatly cut drains showed the pride which the men took in their work. At intervals piles of broken stones of various sizes were stored in 'road metal magazines'. The transfer of stretches of private road however was held up for long enough because there were such tough standards regarding bottoming and surfacing to be met; one such route went from Coylumbridge towards Glenmore and was a source of contention for many years.

Turning to the Highland Railway, it lavished the utmost care on shooting parties for summertime was the line's high season and the working of special saloons used by such families and their servants was typical of the cream of the company's business. This was in complete contrast to the spartan arrangements for third class passengers and the decanting of sleepy travellers out of trains at unsocial hours on to draughty platforms.

Many of the special carriages rolled through the gateway on their way north or south. Perth had to wire Inverness full details of the size and composition of such groups to ensure a smooth passage for them. Perth General station was packed and trains ran in several portions; the

Wealth raised from sporting rentals allowed improvements on estates to continue and the Doune, seat of the Grants of Rothiemurchus, was suitably enlarged. This view from 1948 shows the building after wartime occupation by the military (A. E. GLEN)

platforms were thronged with aristocratic and well-to-do families plus their servants, grooms and mountains of baggage. To take an example of a typical train to which the gateway would have echoed in the summer of 1888 – it was the 7.50 am from Perth and at the height of the season consisted of 36 vehicles belonging to nine different railway companies. In addition to ten assorted passenger carriages, typically little six wheelers, there was the Highland Railway's Post Office van, a sleeping car, five luggage vans, thirteen horse boxes, two vehicles to convey carriages and three family saloons. With engines attached 'fore and aft', the procession toiled 'pluckily over the Grampians'. No wonder it took four hours to reach Inverness. If the train struggled up, it raced down the hills and the railway enthusiasts, Foxwell and Farmer, doubted 'if there was any higher speed than that which occurs daily on the descent between Dava and Forres'. It was hair raising stuff.

Mention has been made of the formation of the Highland Railway in 1865; this arose from the first major re-organisation of the Scottish railway companies. Amalgamations were in the air and out of the old Inverness & Nairn, the I & PJR and others, emerged the new company. The Highland Railway was to exist for almost sixty years and it left a lasting impression on the Cairngorm gateway and its people. To a lesser extent the GNSR did the same. The railways really made the villages grow; the remoter places lost out while the villages soon gained in numbers. Before the lines opened, Aviemore was just an inn and a few cottages, Boat of Garten was only a ferry point and Abernethy (later Nethybridge) a handful of dwellings and a public house beside a Telford bridge.

There was great pride taken in working 'on the railway' and there was plenty of work to be done. Steam locomotives and the trains they pulled were very labour intensive. The Highland Railway's practice was to assign an engine to a certain driver and expect 'spit and polish' turnouts. Old enginemen remembered that Highland locos were invariably cleaner than the carriages! In 1883 an engine was removed from its driver's control because it was 'in such a disgraceful state through want of proper attention'. Copper and brass fittings were burnished, black lead was applied to the back plates of boilers, and in the cabs there was a fetish for cleanliness. A penny or two extra a week as a reward encouraged young cleaners, boys who often worked at night and only got a few shillings as a wage. Poor lads, they had ample time to do a good job as they had 12 hour shifts. It was a start from which 12 year olds could progress to lighting up engines and then to firing them by their upper teens. Wiping down the boiler, cab and tender with oily rags was one thing, but tackling the dirt encrusted, greasy wheels and side rods was quite another. The fire box had to be emptied out by a lad climbing through the fire door and enduring the scorching heat from a hot grate or once the engine had stood fireless in a Highland winter, the unbearable cold. There was suffocating dust to brush off the brick arch and tube plate and heaps of choking ash to shovel out of the smoke box. Then the waste had to be carted off in wheel barrows. Even so it was a start and gave promise of a long career as a railwayman.

A youngster might also join as a lad porter or as a lamp boy – the latter being the first step to becoming a signalman. Every signal was lit by an oil lamp and it was crucially important for safety at night or in poor visibility that it was working properly. Thankfully, a laddie did not have to climb the tall signal posts too often as the Highland Railway had a wire hoist or windlass system for taking the lamps up and down the posts and the oil reservoirs were meant to last eight days. Otherwise, lamps had to be cleaned, wicks trimmed and oil re-filled – and not just on the signals – all through the station premises and in the signal cabins, too, in the early years.

The Highland Railway faced many challenges, some of which arose from its position as Britain's highest and most northerly main line and one of these was snow. There was an immense blizzard in February 1865 which blanketed the Grampians and stopped traffic for five days. Men had to be called out from districts near the line to dig it out. Joseph Mitchell was well versed in the ferocity of conditions over Drumochter where heavy snowfalls were invariably accompanied by high winds which caused the snow to be 'drifted with great rapidity into hollows and cuttings'. Having seen it all before on the Great Highland Road, he proposed to erect screening fences of light timber, decayed sleepers and mounds of earth along the track sides where there was a risk of drifting. This was successful and fragments of these once extensive systems may still be seen bordering the old Highland line.

In addition 'proper appliances', or three types of snowplough, had to be constructed. Light ploughs were fitted to all engines in autumn; these could shift up to two feet of snow. A more formidable plough to move drifts up to five feet (1.5m) in depth was put on pilot engines and these were then attached to goods or passenger trains. The largest type of snowplough was a massive contraption reaching to the engines' chimneys which could tackle drifts of 10 feet (3m) or more and required four or five locomotives of the early Highland classes to propel it. In combination these devices could keep the line open in all but the most severe weather and together helped to bring reliable communications to the gateway throughout the year for the first time. The 1880s were notorious for a

When Aviemore became the junction of two major lines in 1898, there was a big increase in employment. Here staff of the Highland Railway gather on the platform. The station master, (probably John Campbell) wearing a frock coat, is seated on the right near the village policeman; it is likely that the locomotive foreman and the carriage and wagon inspector are seated on the left. Around them are clerks, lamp boys, porters, guards, shunters, signalmen, C & W examiners and shed staff (GLEN COLLECTION)

series of fearful winters which beset the North and which tested the resolve of Highland Railway staff to the utmost. Engines were snowed in for days on end in the wastes of Dava Moor, a place enginemen came to dislike more than the heights of Drumochter. At the outset Highland engines had just open footplates over which a tarpaulin was stretched but proper cabs were quickly introduced to give the engine crews some effective protection.

Aviemore was the key station for the gateway area. In charge from the beginning was John Stott Lawrence. This redoubtable station master became a legend in the district. His railway service began with the Perth & Dunkeld line whose employment he had entered at Dunkeld itself. A likely lad, he soon earned promotion and was appointed station master at Guay, a wayside halt in Strathtay that is now long forgotten. At Aviemore he was to hold a similar position for 32 years. At first Lawrence had only a porter to assist him. E. T. McLaren, a devoted visitor to Rothiemurchus in the 1880s, has left a description of the first little station – it was just a small wooden shed, probably resembling the Strathspey Railway's smart reconstruction at Broomhill. With the name 'Aviemore' on a white board framed by honeysuckle, the place was 'an undiscovered delight'. Two bonuses were the uninterrupted view of the Cairngorm range and 'the entire stillness' when the train had gone.

John Lawrence became much more than Aviemore's station master – he was in effect the 'headman'. He built up a general merchant's business in the only store, a low wooden building on the east side of the railway (now Dalfaber Road) where Aviemore's first Post and Telegraph Office was also located. His family eventually took over, as Highland Railway staff were forbidden to engage in trade which might distract them from their duties. Trains were infrequent and there were so few people about that there was no difficulty in walking across the line by means of a level crossing to reach it. Even in the 1960s Aviemorians argued that there was a right of way across the tracks at that point. John Lawrence was to log 50 years' service as sub-post master in the growing community. From Aviemore, a postwoman, Kirsty Grant, covering as much as 12 miles (19km) a day summer and winter, carried the letters round the district.

Lawrence was 'not quite the universal provider' as his store did not sell meat. So three times a week John Mackintosh, alias Jock Groat, and his wife, appeared each carrying baskets. Meat was sold in four pennyworths, equivalent to the old Scottish coin known as a groat – hence the nickname. Only some cuts of mutton and eggs were available. Jock's business grew and in time he acquired a pony cart. Once across the bridge over the Spey, the road to Inverdruie was lined by giant fir trees giving a cathedral like, gloomy aspect to the route. It was here that Jock had an encounter with a capercaillie – the cocks are as big as turkeys and can be madly aggressive. Wielding his whip in defence, Jock cowered in the cart as the big bird – 'the biggest boogar' of its kind he had ever seen – repeatedly attacked him. In time trade prospered sufficiently for Jock to have the handsome villa 'Laurelbank' built about 1900 in Aviemore.

Most importantly John Lawrence began producing a list of houses and other accommodation for the growing number of visitors attracted to the district. Such was the demand that the Doune mansion of the Laird of Rothiemurchus was briefly run as a hotel. By the 1880s Craigellachie Cottage on a two acre site (0.7ha) was newly completed for a Grantown banker and solicitor. The villa part of a new Post Office and store was being constructed for Lawrence. Known as Aviemore Cottage, it was advantageously located by the side of the main road. (This typical

Victorian structure was recently demolished and its site is now occupied by the flats of Grampian Court.) It was the beginning of a building boom in the gateway which lasted until the First World War.

Aviemore, like other gateway settlements, found a new purpose as a railway village. The Highland Railway became its people's main employer and its very life. Every detail of the line's operation impinged on its folk – by means of the Working Time Table, the Appendix to it and the Book of Rules and Regulations. With almost Biblical authority, the company required:

> Every Officer and Servant of the Highland Railway Company to make himself thoroughly acquainted with the instructions and intimations . . . applicable to his particular Duties.

From 'Accidents' and 'Breakdown Trains' to 'Wagons' and 'Wood, Loading of', these set out how the line was to be run. A vast accumulation of knowledge was gathered in the hard school of experience.

Aviemore Cottage was one of the first 'Railway Age' buildings in the village. It was built for John S. Lawrence, station master and post master, as a letting house, shop and Post Office (AVIEMORE LIBRARY)

The Highland Railway was rightly jealous of its territory; the founding company had struggled hard for its line to the south. It was intent on seeing that no other railway served Inverness and tapped any business there. In the 1880s and 1890s there were projects to do just that. Entrepreneurs were impressed by the reports of heavy summer traffic, especially in August when such long trains ran north of Perth. A high proportion of the passengers had first-class tickets with extra revenue coming from the hiring of private saloons and excess luggage. In May 1878 sleeping cars had been introduced on the Highland line and by 1885 Pullman vehicles were running there. For a few weeks, the activity was 'splendidly profitable'. It was perhaps inevitable that rival routes such as the Glasgow & North Western Railway of 1882 should be promoted. This would have reached Inverness via the Great Glen and have been 40 miles (64km) shorter than the combined Caledonian and Highland route by Perth.

The Highland interests fought back; there was great pride in a company which had its roots in the North and which had been constructed 'by the credit and gentry of the Highlands and not by London speculators'. The Bill for the G & NWR was rejected but the Highland again felt threatened when the West Highland Railway Act was passed in 1889. To counter this menace, a direct line from Aviemore to Inverness via Carrbridge was proposed by the Highland. As early as September 1883, its engineers were told to carry out a survey of the route and soon parliamentary powers were sought. It was a move to forestall any advance from Fort William and it has been questioned whether the Highland had any real intention of ever constructing the line.

A danger also came from the east in the form of an old adversary, the Great North of Scotland Railway, a concern with which relations had been strained on many matters. An example was the line into Boat of Garten where separate single tracks had been laid in 1866 and a signal box removed as the parties could not co-operate over joint running. The GNSR's bold project was to go from Ballater via Tomintoul to Nethybridge and thence by the valley of the Dulnain to Slochd Mhuic and beyond. The GNSR had the temerity to try to do a deal with the Highland over a shared effort from Boat of Garten to Carrbridge but the latter would have none of it. It is questionable if the GNSR could have found the resources for this pipe dream but it did have parliamentary sanction for the line. The proposition put the Highland directors on the spot and the GNSR thus rebuffed lodged another Bill for its own route from Nethybridge to Inverness. This was part of an amazing scenario – a railway that would go from Dundee to Ballater and so to the Highland capital. One way or another, the GNSR was determined to obtain running powers into the town.

The Highland Railway's response was the Direct Line scheme which had serious disadvantages for the company. It served no major centres of population as there were no Grantowns, far less a Forres or a Nairn, on the route over Slochd Mhuic. Inevitably, a shorter run would cut fares and reduce revenue by as much as 2s 6d (12.5p) off a third class ticket between Perth and Inverness. The lucrative Aviemore-Forres track was also bound to be by-passed and reduced in importance. Worse still, the Direct Line would be very expensive to build involving major engineering works with three big viaducts – at Slochd and over the deep valleys of the Findhorn and Nairn rivers. Each of these structures would be on a curve and a gradient. At one stage a long and very costly tunnel was also thought likely at Slochd but Murdoch Paterson, the Highland's civil engineer, examined the proposed alignment of the route there again and again. Early one Sunday morning in a flash of inspiration he saw that turning right and using a viaduct to cross the ravine would solve the problem. It was of course out of the question for him to go to his office on the Sabbath in Inverness and so he was on tenterhooks all day until Monday came and he could look at the plans again.

The GNSR kept up the pressure and surveyed its own route. To the horror of the Highland directors it had a Bill for 'The Strathspey, Strathdon and Deeside Junction Railway' drawn up. This quite disregarded the fact that landowners along 30 miles (48km) of the 36-mile (57km) track were in total opposition to it! Parliament preferred the Highland's scheme and an Act of July 1884 approved the new line from Aviemore. Construction was long delayed – trade depression being the excuse. The Highland actually proposed an amalgamation with the GNSR but rows over exchanges of traffic and other issues forced the Highland to go it alone. Late in 1889, the contract for the first section of the Direct Line from Aviemore to Carrbridge was let. With reluctance the Highland Railway had been trapped in a costly game of railway politics.

Earlier the Earl of Seafield's agents had prepared a feuing or site plan for Aviemore. It was deduced that with any railway junction of significance, a sizeable settlement was bound to grow around the new station. With an eye to business and to exercise some control over building, land attached to the farm of the former inn was set aside for the eventual construction of houses and other facilities. A feuing plan shows a dozen quarter acre (1,000m²) feus on the west side of the railway (Grampian Road) where a handful of villas, including a new station master's house, had been pencilled in opposite the station but the largest site of 12 acres (5ha) was reserved for a hotel and an adjacent extent of grazing for a golf course. Several smaller feus to the east of the railway (now Dalfaber Road) were also marked off for houses. In feudal fashion, a landowner would exact a feu duty in perpetuity from people putting up houses on such sites as the ground would still be his property. Feu duties took their origin from the old obligations folk once had to serve their feudal lord in giving labour on his land, in military service on his behalf or in other ways. Such a duty was a fair sum at the outset but inflation made the charge derisory by the time the imposition of new feu duties was abolished in 1974; others have continued to pay up on account of this remnant of feudalism.

With the Highland Railway having been dragged unwillingly into embarking on the Direct Route, it was hardly surprising that the construction of the Aviemore–Carrbridge portion was extremely slow. There were no serious difficulties for the civil engineers, although the track was on a rising grade almost all the way to Carrbridge and big embankments had to be formed at Kinveachy. This time round the navvies' labour could be supplemented by the steam-powered cranes and shovels used by the contractors, John Ross & Son. On 8 July 1892, the so-called Carrbridge branch was at last open for traffic. Since 1862 the location of a station there had been under discussion. The Earl of Seafield insisted that it should serve the district 'at the most convenient site consistent with other arrangements' – hence its 'off centre' position in relation to the present village. Carrbridge got a little engine shed to house the solitary locomotive assigned to the route.

It was not until 29 October 1898 that the official opening of the expensive Direct Line – it had cost almost £1 million – took place and a luncheon was held at Carrbridge. Its crowning glory, the Nairn viaduct, with its twenty-eight masonry arches in pinkish sandstone, designed by Murdoch Paterson and Sir John Fowler, of Forth Bridge fame, is one of the finest monuments in Scotland to the Railway Age. Meanwhile, Aviemore had been transformed into the junction of two major routes with a handsome new station and offices, an island platform, two signal cabins, an engine shed to house eight locomotives and a carriage and wagon department and much more. There were massive water tanks to supply the engines' needs and a reservoir was subsequently made at the foot of Craigellachie. An agreement was drawn up between the Highland Railway Company and the Countess Dowager of Seafield whereby any tenants or feuars of houses on her land, who were not entitled to a supply of water free, could attach a pipe to 'the main iron conduit' with her consent on payment to the railway of 'a sum not exceeding one shilling (5p) per pound per annum', according to the value of the property as entered in the Valuation Roll of the County of Inverness. This was a major benefit for the development of the village but the beneficiaries had to be careful – there was to be no wasting of water through carelessness or defective pipework. Moreover, if they failed to pay their dues, the railway company had the right to sever the supply. The stylish station, which survives practically intact, was designed by William Roberts, a senior engineer in the Highland Railway, and is almost entirely of timber construction. Together with the grid of sidings, the structures were so extensive that they had to be put on tipped ground. The old level crossing to the south of the station was replaced by a 'tunnel' bridge on an awkward S-bend under the tracks.

To many travellers over the years, Aviemore Junction would mean changing trains and often spending time on bleak platforms or huddled in

In 1892 the new Aviemore station was under construction. The old station can be seen in the background (left). A notice advises passengers to change for Carrbridge. At this date the footbridge was north of the station to allow access to the signal box (GLEN COLLECTION)

waiting rooms. For the well-to-do, through carriages were advertised from London to Inverness via the London & North Western, the Caledonian and the Highland Railways – there was no disagreeable changing of trains for such patrons. Although the Highland's passenger numbers rose by some 40,000 in the following year, profits were not in proportion as there were now two main lines to keep up and to operate. These disappointing results were a severe burden on the company and it was forced to become more business orientated as we shall see.

A bonus for the Cairngorm gateway was the new status for Aviemore Junction which helped to popularise the district and travel writers were not slow to mention it:

> The station is large and commodious as all trains stop there, and so it is a very convenient centre for excursions. The morning newspapers from Glasgow, Edinburgh, Dundee and Aberdeen can be obtained before 8.30am! Every year additional accommodation is being provided for the summer and autumn visitors.
>
> – A. I. McConnochie in *A Guide to Aviemore and Vicinity*

The railway community at Aviemore grew very rapidly in the rush of expansion. First one, then another new terrace of railway houses, amounting to fourteen dwellings, were set up fronting the line. With a scullery and water closet integral with each the house, as workers' housing they were really up-to-date for their time; curiously their gardens faced the tracks as if to give a pleasant view from carriage windows. There were two additional villas – the first for the shed master; officially he was the shed foreman but 'shed master' gave him a titular equality which put him on a par with the station master. His surname as a mark of respect was always preceded by 'Mr', though in the confines of the shed bothy, every railwayman knew to whom the words 'the gaffer' or just 'the mannie' referred. The other villa was for the permanent way inspector; he too was a key man as the junction was a focus of track repair and maintenance. It was also an examination point for rolling stock.

The railway village had a very special identity. A Highland railwayman looked upon himself as part of a great system. Almost everyone at Aviemore Junction was an incomer, otherwise how would the station and shed have been staffed? From existing stations and loco depots throughout the H.R. network they came with their families to take up residence in Aviemore. The staff registers reveal their origins – Inverness, Burghead, Dunphail, Brora or Strome Ferry and many more. Some would stay until retirement and others would move on. The drivers proudly referred to 'my engine', the signalman to 'my cabin', the shunter to 'my yard' and the station master to 'my station' – almost oblivious to the fact that these were railway company property. The Highland Railway's official handbooks (as did most companies) described vehicles from other British lines as 'foreign'. It never occurred to Highland railwaymen to strike – they and their wives saw to it that ends were met. Enginemen especially were the best paid skilled 'technicians' in the years before the First World War. They had enormous status at a time when almost all youngsters fancied being an engine driver when they grew up.

To coincide with the Direct Route's opening, a shrewd and experienced man was appointed General Manager of the Highland Railway. Thomas A. Wilson came from England's North Eastern Railway and it was not long before he discovered some of the Highland's deficiencies. He was quite shocked by the lack of regard for punctuality and issued a notice to staff:

> . . . I wish to impress upon staff that punctuality is a rare thing on the Highland line. I do not know whether staff have realised this. Usually our trains start late, lose time on the road, and arrive late at the end of the journey . . . we must make a serious attempt to run the trains at the advertised time.

He commented on the 'leisureliness' which passengers had come to expect on the Highland Railway. A story is told of a visitor enquiring at a station about the likely time of arrival of a train from the south to which the reply was, 'The train before's behind and the train before's behind as well'! To some it was part of the Highland's charm – allowing people to wander about on platforms at intervening stops and converse with their friends. From now on, sharp but polite requests would urge them to take their seats promptly. Clearly 'fragments of time' were not valued highly enough by staff; there were 29 stations between Perth and Inverness in those days and if even a minute was lost at each, the whole system was held up and travellers had to face half an hour of extra journey time. Staff were therefore warned to be ready for incoming trains and be prepared to start them away without the loss of a second. Reports about any delays at stations were to be submitted by the station masters to Head Office in Inverness for investigation. The Highland Railway also faced the formidable task of speeding up services on a single track system; this was a tall order but a doubling of the line was soon in progress from Blair Atholl to Dalwhinnie. In 1897 three extra passing places had been introduced on the track south at Inchlea, Moulinearn and

Inchmagranachan, all being costly as signal cabins and staff were needed at each location.

Under the new regime Greenwich Mean Time was transmitted at 10 am every day along the signal circuits from Inverness. Each station had to respond by means of its station call – Aviemore's was 'T'. Then all clocks had to be adjusted to GMT. Guards and drivers had to check times on their watches before commencing duty – a watch was a real status symbol on the Highland Railway. Local folk, who in many cases had none, soon learned to time their activities by the movement of certain trains on the line. 'She's late the night', referred to trains – these were always female as were locomotives. One of the best known was 'The Johnstone', the local stopping train to and from Inverness commencing at Newtonmore in the morning. Billy Johnstone was its driver for many years and he had a name for running to time – a good thing too when folk were weary and wanting to get home after a day in the town or at the market. Long after Billy had progressed to more impressive trains, such as 'The London' with the sleeping cars for the south, the name stuck.

Over in Rothiemurchus since 1873 there had been a new school (now a visitor centre), with a house for the master, to which the children of the railway families walked making a three-mile round trip. This was the result of the Education (Scotland) Act of 1872 which required compulsory elementary education for children between the ages of five and thirteen; it established school boards and attendance officers. However, fees still had to be paid and even a half-penny a week per child was a burden on poor families. As Rothiemurchus was a pioneer in the provision of a school meal, at least its pupils could look forward to a bowl of broth at lunch-time. Beside the triangular school green, the smithy's clangour always attracted young spectators. Through the generosity of the Martineau family, the old school had been converted to a library and stocked with books. Dr Martineau's 'penny readings' in the library were, according to his audience, 'sae good thae shud hae been two pence'. In addition to their own sketching, painting and writing, his daughters taught wood carving in which Rothiemurchus folk displayed remarkable skill. The family, which contributed so greatly to the cultural life of the community, is commemorated in the Martineau Memorial at the junction of the Loch an Eilein road with the B970. The monument's Celtic tracery was carved by their pupils.

In 1886 St Columba's kirk had been completed for the Free Church congregation at Inverdruie. Sir John Peter Grant of Rothiemurchus, the eleventh laird, had long sympathised with the Free Kirkers. He showed real magnanimity towards them in giving the site and in placing the foundation stone. The Grants were 'auld kirk' but they subsequently became Episcopalian after the laird's second marriage to Lady Mary Augusta Pierrepont, a daughter of the Earl Manvers. The family has continued to follow that persuasion as have many members of the Scottish gentry and aristocracy. By 1900 however most 'Frees' had composed their differences sufficiently with the United Presbyterians to form the United Free Church and so St Columba's became 'U. F'. Nor had the spiritual needs of the railway folk in Aviemore been overlooked for there was a mission building for the Church of Scotland (later St Andrew's) in the village.

The gateway's most imposing edifice was also under construction – the splendid Station Hotel in Aviemore which would be grander than any other in the strath. Thanks to the railway, visitors were coming in increasing numbers and spreading wealth more widely throughout the Cairngorm gateway than ever before.

EXCURSION

Strathspey Railway

Join the train at either Aviemore, Boat of Garten or Broomhill and savour this scenic stretch of the first mainline through the Highlands which went from Inverness via Forres to Perth. As the steam locomotive hauls its train over moor and through forest excellent views open to the Cairngorm Mountains on the 9-mile (14.4km) long trip. A buffet car provides refreshments en route.

For further information contact Strathspey Railway's station at Aviemore on 01479 810725.

CHAPTER 4

Advance and Conflict

1900 – 1919

With the opening of the new century, the Cairngorm gateway was more accessible than ever and Aviemore looked set on course to become a tourist centre of significance. Every year the demand for summer quarters was brisker. The crowning glory of the railway village was the big Station Hotel which opened in 1901. It stood on a commanding site and had terraced lawns sweeping down to the main road.

From the 1880s ground had been set aside for the construction of a hotel and the fact that its name included 'station' might suggest that the Highland Railway had some part in it; the answer is not directly. Encouragement it might give but finance it could not. The Highland Railway did in time have hotels of its own – at Inverness, Kyle of Lochalsh, Dornoch, and by 1911 at Strathpeffer. The Aviemore Station Hotel Company was set up in 1899 with a share capital of £25,000, which was a large sum of money at that time. The directors were Donald Grant, a Grantown solicitor, agent for the Laird of Rothiemurchus, and owner of Craigellachie Cottage, and Augustus Charles Baillie, a Notary Public in Edinburgh. This was a public office for the well educated of good character who on payment of a fee could sign deeds and contracts authenticating these with a certificate and a seal. He was also, however, a younger brother of James Evan Bruce Baillie of Dochfour, who was a director of the Highland Railway, and clearly the company would have been well disposed towards his involvement. Both Baillies were active in the territorial army – James was a colonel and Augustus commanded the Lovat Scouts in the Boer War.

The Baillies were wealthy and well connected. Originally the family came from Lanarkshire but with money made in the West Indian trade, they aspired to be Highland gentry and had links with Dunain near

Inverness. They acquired the estate of Dochfour on the banks of the Caledonian Canal. In 1894 James Baillie married Nellie Lisa, soon to be Baroness Burton of Burton-on-Trent and of Rangemore, who, as heiress in her own right to a brewery fortune, was rich by any standard. (To the old aristocracy, however, they were just 'beerage' who had altered their name from Bass to Burton. The family had a liking for sport in the Highlands and Mr Bass, later the first Baronet, leased Tulchan in 1849.) In time the Baroness also became a director of the hotel company, a position which she held for many years. Other directors were soon appointed, notably Livingstone MacDonald of the Fife Arms Hotel in Braemar, who was the new company's first chairman and, with his 'hands on' experience of the hotel business, a valuable choice. As to the shareholders, a motley collection from the station master and a local gamekeeper to an advocate, a shipbuilder and the Baillies' clergyman brother, plus many others, put money into the project.

The new hotel was hailed as 'a fine house in Scotch baronial style' and was well matched with its setting against the rocky backdrop of Craigellachie. Having a palatial appearance it quite outclassed most shooting lodges and many a castle. Its architect was Robert J. Macbeth of Inverness. Its public rooms with sumptuous carpets, rattan chairs and potted palms were handsome. The hotel was designed for summer use only being open as a rule from May to October. Widely publicised as 'comfortable and spacious', it was said with some exaggeration to be over 1,000 feet (300m) above sea level and although the air was 'less bracing than that at Braemar', it was 'far more impregnated with health giving properties of the pine woods' – a good selling point when chest complaints were so prevalent. The view to the Cairngorm Mountains from its windows were outstanding and it quickly attracted the titled and the wealthy – the Earl and Countess of Southesk, the Earl of Durham, industrialists and shipping magnates who brought their 'accompanying servants'. Clearly its clientele were either used to residing in castles or at least could afford rooms in a near replica while on holiday. Although on a smaller scale, the development was a prototype for Gleneagles.

By 1903, the Station Hotel was recording a profit in excess of £2,500 and accommodation had to be increased. The old inn, its farm and garden were first leased (and later purchased) by the hotel company and supplied its needs for dairy and other fresh produce. For water supply it shared the Highland Railway's cast iron main, a cause of some concern in years to come. Soon it boasted 'an electric power station' and a steam laundry, features which were the talk of the district; people came from miles around just to see the building, which was said to have 100 rooms, lit at night. The owners took great pride in the hotel maintaining it 'in the highest style' amid its gardens, croquet ground and 9-hole golf course. They shortly looked for a young professional to manage the course, but in the interests of economy settled instead for a green keeper at 25 shillings (£1.25) a week. Within a decade the hotel was logging over 14,000 bed nights ('sleepers') in its five-month season.

A small Temperance Hotel owned by the McLauchlan family and frequented mainly by commercial travellers stood on Dalfaber Road but by 1903 it had a larger rival for another temperance establishment was under construction for a Mr Davidson of Kingussie. This was the Cairngorm Private Hotel close to the driveway of the lavish Station Hotel. The Cairngorm was also well planned with commodious public rooms and fourteen bedrooms 'all beautifully furnished'. Scarcely had it opened than it was set for expansion the following year. By all accounts, the hotels were well run and an English observer wrote:

> Scotland . . . is, as regards hotels, like the curate's egg, only 'good in parts' – some are very bad. Two of the good ones, as finely managed as any in Europe, are at Pitlochry and Aviemore. A factor in their excellence is their employment of fully trained Scotch waitresses. At Aviemore . . . the bonnie waitresses, dressed in bright tartans, are a delight to the eye. Why can't we have them in London?

A local newspaper, the *Kingussie Record & Badenoch Advertiser*, had been launched in 1902 and it took notice of 'the visitor season', which was attracting more and more 'health seekers' northwards. It listed houses that had been rented, giving the names of the tenants and their house parties. They brought their own maids or hired local help to run their 'homes from home'; they packed their own linen, cutlery and even ornaments to improve their temporary abodes and incidentally transformed local aspirations. Quite a variety of accommodation was available in the gateway from large villas to 'lodgings with a parlour' or simpler 'rooms with attendance' in the railway terraces. On offer in Rothiemurchus were houses ranging from the laird's Doune mansion, the U.F. Manse or the School House to farms such as the Dell; everyone was on the make when it came to renting out property. Even though rail travel to the gateway was not cheap, it is clear that people of different income levels were being catered for. With their homes let for the summer months, the local occupiers withdrew to a cottage or bothy, usually at the foot of the garden, much as their ancestors had taken themselves to their shielings in summer in earlier times. Apart from the hotels, about thirty assorted premises were available for renting in Aviemore and Rothiemurchus; according to Provost MacBean of Kingussie 'every building was commandeered with the possible exception of the hen house'.

Even so, both Kingussie and Grantown were much more substantial places, finding increasing favour as holiday resorts with their several hotels and many villas. They had administrative and service functions too, such as banks and courthouses; both had a number of fairs but Grantown had a regular livestock market. From 1885 it boasted a weekly newspaper, the *Grantown Supplement*, which in 1907 was joined by the *Strathspey Herald & Grantown Advertiser*. It was perhaps more 'urban' than Kingussie, having a hospital and a gas works. Kingussie had a sanatorium, however, where the chronically ill, especially those suffering from TB, were treated. Neither dominated the tourist market and no spas or hydropathics were developed in the gateway; the former were dependent on the occurrence of mineral springs while the latter were grand hotels offering water cures and indoor bathing for 'genteel hypochrondiacs'. Some springs of the chalybeate variety, and foul tasting, were sampled by local people.

The visitors came predominantly from the Scottish cities, the Glasgow and Dundee folk favouring July (the Glasgow Fair holiday being the second fortnight) and the Edinburgh contingent August. Many were from much further afield – from London and other English towns or the Empire – for example, from Bombay, Chittagong or distant Zanzibar. Their quest for summer quarters began in February when property was advertised in 'the southern papers'. The local press carried advertisements for houses to let at 6d (2.5p) a time and to distinguish them, they had to have names – the numbered 'lots' carved out of the old davoch at Aviemore becoming 'Burnside', 'The Shieling' or 'Lairig View'. Plenty of new houses were being erected too. Tradesmen were invited to make offers to construct a villa 'on a site commanding a most desirable view of the Cairngorms' which would certainly be reflected in its value. A three-public, five-bedroom property on a prime site and near the station could fetch £1,000; such a villa was not thought excessively large at a time when families were big. To keep prices in proportion, a bottle of Scotch whisky cost only 3s (15p) in the 1900s. The idiosyncratic names chosen by the Victorians – 'Aldersyde', 'Clune Villa' and 'Vulcan Cottage' – were superseded by the Edwardian villas taking the names of hills – 'Braeriach', 'Craiggowrie', 'Ord Ban' and, of course, 'Cairngorm', perhaps reflecting the growing interest in hill walking. On returning from the Empire to cooler climes, some chose to remember where they had made their fortunes by giving their new homes in the strath such names as 'Borneo', 'Kimberley' and 'Harare'.

Of the eminent visitors to the gateway one of the best known was Sir George Henschel, a celebrated musician and founder and first conductor of no less than three symphony orchestras – the Boston Symphony Orchestra, the Scottish Orchestra (now the RSNO) and the London Symphony Orchestra. He had his dream house built at Allt na Criche (stream of the boundary or march) near Lynwilg. The upgrading of lodges and mansions was in full swing – £4,000 was spent on Kinrara and both Glenmore Lodge and the keeper's house there were improved at a cost of £2,000. At Drumintoul, 'the sanitary arrangements' had been 'seen to' according to an advertisement offering the lodge plus the shootings and fishings in Rothiemurchus for lease at £1,750 a year. Many farmhouses were also enlarged and bathrooms installed as one of the key demands of visitors was reliable and up-to-date plumbing – something in which Highland properties were noticeably lacking.

The Highland Railway which had been the catalyst for all this activity was again busy on the housing front; in May 1905 it constructed another terrace at Aviemore to supplement its stock. Staff had to pay rent to the company for their houses but had several perks – coal, water and unofficially pails of scalding water from the shunting engine when it came alongside; this was the answer for greasy, soot stained overalls on wash days. They benefited from another service – the youngest lad at the shed was given the job of the wakener. In the days before reliable alarm clocks, he would go round the railway households within a mile of the depot in all weathers by day or night to summon the men to their work but woe betide him if he 'chapped' on the wrong door!

The railway was in full swing; it had become a key element in the gateway and for most folk life revolved round it. On a summer's evening many of the community turned out to take a promenade on the platforms and await the arrival of the evening train from the south amid discussions about who was travelling and why. There were endless movements of vehicles through the station and shunting in and out of the sidings. These were not always without incident. In 1904, 'considerable damage' was done to the Forres portion of an afternoon train. A regular manoeuvre was either the dividing up or putting together of trains at Aviemore Junction, a task which called for canny driving. On that occasion, carriages shunted 'at an alarming speed produced a shock of great violence' damaging rolling stock and causing 'severe shaking but thankfully no injuries to passengers'.

In June of that year, the Highland Railway announced that it would run express trains – a big challenge on a system where trains could only pass at stations, hence their large number, in loops or on the solitary stretch of double track. The Highland became the only single line in the world which attempted such feats. Within a decade, the best Inverness-Perth train was covering the 118 miles(189km) in just short of three hours at an average speed above 40 mph (64 kph). Committed engine crews were showing their locomotives' paces as they 'toiled over the mountain heights'. One enthusiast timed a Castle class engine (admittedly going downhill) between Dalnaspidal and Struan at 72 mph (115 kph). New and powerful engines were imaginatively named. The 'Lochs' were joined by 'Castles' and 'Bens', names which appealed to the travelling public and enhanced the distinctive character of the line. To those ignorant of Gaelic, some were tongue twisters such as *Ben a'Chaoruinn* and *Ben Mheadhoin*. The Glasgow builders, Dubs & Company, were much favoured by the Highland Railway but locomotives were also constructed in its own works at Inverness. The first 'Small Ben' or 'Bennie', as the railwaymen knew them, was proudly named *Ben Nevis*. This was an error of judgement as Britain's highest mountain neither bordered the Highland line nor could be seen from it and there were protests. Accordingly the name was changed to *Ben-y-Gloe*, after the great massif near Blair Atholl. So proud was the shed master at Aviemore of this engine which was under his care – and was also HR No. 1 – that he named his house after it. With a view to improving locomotive performance, tests from Blair Atholl to Dalwhinnie involving the Highland engine *Skibo Castle* and a North British Intermediate were held in 1910. With identical trains, the NBR contender bettered the Highland's schedule. A return match was

Aviemore Junction from the south with the buildings on the island platform nearing completion; the acetylene gas plant and the lamp bothy are on the left (GLEN COLLECTION)

organised in the south and the results were the talk of Aviemore and other sheds for weeks.

There was good running ground on the almost level track between Kingussie and Aviemore where engines often touched 50 mph (80 kph). A high degree of expertise in working the single line had been achieved and 'telephonic communication' between trains and stations was a bonus. On the approach of a train, telephones ringing in the stations heralded many a reunion on the platforms on the Highland line. For the railwaymen there was plenty to learn about the new junction as every station had its peculiarities and Aviemore had some 3 miles (5km) of sidings. 'Down' was towards Inverness and 'Up' was towards Perth. The junction had to be approached slowly – trains entering the 'Up Loop' at Aviemore and passing through the crossovers were not to exceed 10 mph (16 kph) to avoid the risk of derailments. On wet or snowy days, 'Up Stopping Trains' had to be brought to a stand under the station veranda to prevent passengers getting a soaking.

The shed master in charge of the running side had a big team working shifts round the clock; there were coalmen and cleaners, labourers, boiler washers and fire raisers, fitters and, in pride of place, the enginemen – the drivers and firemen. His area of responsibility ran from Slochd summit to the county march at Drumochter. The carriage and wagon department at Aviemore Junction saw that all vehicles were checked by examiners – the tap of their hammers could detect hidden flaws by the rhythmic 'clunk' from the wheels; axle boxes too were inspected and topped up with grease. A long carriage shed to hold two trains of eight coaches each was erected between the main lines in 1910. There was a permanent way staff responsible for maintaining the track from Millburn Junction at Inverness to Aviemore. There was also a senior telegraph linesman with a remit from Aviemore to Daviot on the Direct Line and from Dava south to Dalwhinnie. Each team had its own hierarchy although the 'C & W' inspectors were also answerable to the shed foreman. The nerve centre was of course Inverness but Aviemore Junction was the major base between headquarters and Perth; it is not surprising that railway companies were the most complex business organisations that had ever been seen.

By the 1990s freight had almost deserted the Highland line but Aviemore Junction and the whole network once depended on it. The Highland Railway handled every imaginable type of goods from eggs in boxes, empty petrol cans, timber (peeled, unpeeled and long), pianos in cases, bread in hampers to loads of hay or straw (the latter of course never to be marshalled behind the engine). Livestock was normally sheep or cattle although flocks of sheep were still being driven south by road in the 1900s. So the sounds of bleating and mooing were added to the banging of buffers and the squeal of brakes which reverberated across the gateway from the busy junction. Autumn was a high point for such traffic especially when the sheep sales at Lairg in Sutherland were in progress. Railway men generally disliked horses as these could be tricky. Those known to be excitable or restive – and most were in the presence of steam locomotives – were only accepted at owner's risk and they were carried in special horse boxes which had compartments for their grooms. Both horses and carriages could be taken off railway vehicles or loaded at Aviemore as it had a large loading bank – so convenient for the gentry coming to the shootings.

To help make the railway pay, drivers were always encouraged to take an extra wagon or two over the specified number on their trains – the maximum on the Inverness-Perth route was 35 plus a brake van but on the easy ground between Aviemore and Newtonmore 50 could be hauled and it was a matter of honour to do so. The loco stars were the 'Big Goods', the first locomotives with a 4-6-0 wheel arrangement to appear on any British line. Built in Glasgow in 1895 to the design of David Jones, the Highland Railway's Locomotive Superintendent, they were strong engines for freight work:

> It was some sight to see a Jones Goods, belching smoke and steam as it wrestled with a long train of wagons over Dava – they were such stately engines with their big cabs and ponderous connecting rods – the epitome of Victorian engineering.
>
> – A. E. GLEN

The first of the class HR No 103 has been preserved and may be seen in Glasgow's Museum of Transport. The loads for passenger trains were calculated on tonnage and each locomotive class had its own appropriate loading.

The station master's duties at Aviemore Junction were now considerable and he had a staff of 18 or so including booking and goods clerks, signalmen and lamp boys, guards, shunters and porters in various grades from trainees to foremen. A woman came to clean the office for a couple of shillings once a week. In addition to keeping in touch with Head Office in Inverness by telegraph, the 'Station Agent' (for such was his other title) had to deal with the public in all its moods. He had to ensure that carriages were clean inside and out, notices had to be checked and kept up-to-date, reports written and returns made. He had to school

Highland enginemen were devoted to their locomotives. Here one of the famous 'Big Goods' HR No. 109, designed by David Jones and built in 1894, stands outside the shed at Aviemore (GLEN COLLECTION)

'lad porters' to be active and 'polite and respectful' to passengers. Stores of coal for the offices and waiting room fires and oil for lamps were in his care. Aviemore had an acetylene gas plant but it had to be used so sparingly that the station lights were put out between trains! Windows of waiting rooms had to be opened daily 'for the admission of fresh air' and insalubrious tasks such as inspecting the 'wholesomeness' of water closets also fell to the station master.

The calling of the station name 'distinctly and effectively' at Aviemore Junction was essential as many passengers had to change trains there. At night or in the early morning, such shouting proved an irritating disturbance to householders near the station and they protested. So staff had to go over all the carriages, compartment by compartment, to ensure that passengers were 'properly seated' in the correct trains. As for the intoxicated, a common enough variety on market days or after Highland Games, they had to be put in a separate compartment and the door locked to prevent annoyance to other travellers. It was often easier said than done.

A lookout had to be kept too for the company's directors with gold or silver medallion passes entitling them to first-class seats and the best of attention.

The weather was a regular anxiety; from 20 November to 31 March, the station master became something of a meteorologist reporting morning and evening to the traffic manager in Inverness on the state of the weather and the rails throughout the gateway area. In frost, fires had to be lit in 'choffers'(from the French 'chauffer') to warm the big water tanks and the water columns at the platform ends; then a watch had to be kept on them lest they go out. The permanent way foreman advised whether trains required an extra engine or if snow blocks were likely. From autumn through to spring every locomotive was fitted with a small plough. Being conveniently placed between the heights of Drumochter and Dava Moor or Slochd, Aviemore Junction mounted many a snow clearing mission and one of the biggest snowploughs and a breakdown van were kept at the ready through the winter. You might think that the most experienced drivers would be called out to tackle the snow hazards because it required courage to charge into drifts concealing the track and possibly risk derailment. As the giant snowplough took several engines to push it, there were often simply not enough enginemen 'spare' to man the expedition and volunteers from all grades on the running side were therefore sought. A cleaner in his teens, who had only a few firing turns to his credit, might find himself paired with a young engineman just passed for driving. In the intervals between the running of trains, locomotives with smaller ploughs would make passage day and night to keep the spine of mainline through the strath open for the strategic trains – the Mail, livestock specials and fish traffic. Passengers were not seen as a priority and just had to wait until the emergency was over.

Long railway journeys were usually beyond the means of the bank clerk or the typical foreman and their families, and so it was the better off who were the takers of holidays and thus the railway's principal customers. They could make comparisons between competing lines and sometimes criticism was levelled at the Highland's arrangements. For instance, passengers had to bring their own repast with them or hope for 'a bite and soup' in Kingussie's Refreshment Rooms. In 1910, by placing an advanced order, they could have:

> For a bob . . . a basket all to themselves, containing a pot of tea, bread, butter and jam, or a full meal – breakfast for 2s 6d (12p), dinner for 3s (15p). The Highland Railway have nothing to learn about catering for those who travel on their railway.

Some were not so sure and missed the sumptuous restaurant cars of the West Coast main line, resenting having to 'make the best of a luncheon basket, literally to grub in a not too clean and crowded compartment' but for children it was a novelty and great fun. Chasing up the baskets and cups from such meals however was much less fun for staff up and down the line.

The railway had taken centre stage in the gateway and even in leisure time it was to the fore. The U.F. Church Hall (which still exists) was the venue of the Railway Mission which had the added attraction of lantern slides. Many turned up to see 'Life on the Railway at Home and Abroad – Railway Men at Work: their Hardships, Temptations and Dangers; Strong Incidents of a Disastrous Collision in Scotland, and Railway Scenes in South Africa, India and Japan'. It was a rare blend of the mundane and the exotic.

Aviemore's first policeman was appointed in 1898 and apart from attending sheep dippings and enquiring into gun licences he really had a quiet life. Occasionally he had to deal with problems of drunkenness and assault. The only licensed outlet in the village was at the Station Hotel which had a public bar round the back. This was a thirst quenching refuge like an oasis in a desert for off duty drivers and firemen parched by a roasting in the cab of a steam loco. It was a sore temptation for those who overshot their mark. A brawl could lead to a fine of 10s (50p) or 7 days in jail for the culprit. When hard earned wages disappeared overnight, it was no wonder that 'temperance' was a major issue and efforts were made to start Good Templars and a Cairngorm Lodge was established. The men from the estates and farms also met up at the hotel bar and, with Territorial Army camps at Inverdruie or Loch an Eilein becoming a regular feature of the summer months, a large tap room was opened.

The churches were key elements in the life of the community; each had their staunch members which drew the railway families and the people of the countryside together. The different brands of Presbyterianism might have been thought divisive but railway work tended to encourage tolerance. Folk were part of a team and had to get along together. On the positive side the kirks were the focus of much social activity organising talks, concerts, picnics – the ascent of Cairn Gorm being very popular – and fund raising. Sunday, or the Sabbath, was a sad trial for the younger generation. W. M. Haddow in *My Seventy Years* described how newspapers and books of a secular nature were removed; good clothes, which were generally black, were taken from wardrobes and brushed, boots were polished and the whole family was marched to church. On returning home there was a meal (largely prepared on the

Saturday), the reading of 'improving' books such as *Pilgrim's Progress* and there might be a second service to attend. Children were not allowed out to play. By nine o'clock everyone was indoors; prayers were said and the whole family followed the chosen Bible reading. This was a typical regime for the Free Presbyterians and young folk were thankful when the dreary day was over. Fast days of propriety and prayerfulness were held before communions to which hundreds of folk came. Such were the crowds in some localities that the kirks could not hold the throng and preachings might take place in the open air or in a convenient barn. Close to the stone circle, the Free Presbyterians (known as 'Wee Frees') had a mission hall of galvanised iron erected in 1905 whose cheerful red and white paintwork was in complete contrast to the austerity within. It became known as their 'tin temple' in Aviemore. Visitors too had to tread warily and most went to church – to the old kirk near the Doune in Rothiemurchus or to St Andrew's in Aviemore if Church of Scotland, or to St Columba's if United Free. All this put the English in a quandary but the Scots Episcopalians with the laird's support acquired an iron shed in Rothiemurchus to which both they and Anglicans could go.

In the summer of 1903 a big bazaar was held in Aviemore to pay off the cost of St Andrew's Church. The event was under canvas in a field adjoining Aviemore station and, being timed for August, relied principally on the generosity of visitors. Significantly William Whitelaw, chairman of the Highland Railway, and the Countess of Seafield were guests of honour. The solid, granite kirk, now the parish church for Aviemore and Rothiemurchus, cost £1,000 and was designed to seat 350 inhabitants and summer visitors. Meantime the congregation of St Columba's, the U.F. church in Rothiemurchus, called a Gaelic speaking minister as the language was still used among the older generation and his ability to 'minister to his people in their mother tongue' was greatly welcomed. He had a new house too; a corner site had been offered by the Laird of Rothiemurchus for a villa which subsequently became the Church of Scotland manse.

When motor cars came on the scene, some visitors had an alternative to travelling on the railway. These primitive and unreliable vehicles had first appeared in Scotland in 1896 and soon they were rumbling and jolting along the quiet Highland roads. By 1903, 'Horrified' was protesting in Kingussie:

> Is there such a thing as law and order in the capital of Badenoch? How are motor cars allowed to fly about our streets at lightning speed and no one interferes?

Motor cars began to appear in the 1900s. Here the Glen family pose for a photograph at Loch Alvie while on an excursion from Newtonmore to Aviemore in 1915 (A. E. GLEN)

Exception was taken to 'the furious and reckless driving of motor cars at speeds (without the slightest exaggeration) of 30 miles per hour (48 kph)'. Worse still, the drivers were 'insolent and overbearing'. Wealthy men were reportedly spending their money on 'the new means of locomotion' and agents for the Scottish built Albion and Argyll cars and continental varieties, such as Chenard and Panhard, were to be found in Badenoch. The first motorists were exploring the Cairngorm gateway and the larger hotels, such as Nethybridge, bought vehicles for hire. 'Pratt's Motor Spirit' was on sale and Aviemore's Station Hotel put up 'motor car sheds'.

In the early years of the century, the cycling craze was at its height too and a bike could be bought for £9 or hired for a few shillings a week. When nights lengthened in August, cyclists could be met on every corner 'without lamps or bells'. Even ladies in long skirts took to bicycles, the wheels being protected from entanglement by webs of strong thread. The Highland Railway did not follow the rival Great North's initiative by having special vans for cycles but it did transport motor cars in carriage vans or on trucks. For car owners this service was a wise move. Over Drumochter, the surface had become a mass of boulders and stones interspersed with sand slips and bare rock. In 1903 a venturesome motor cyclist was thrown off his machine four times while negotiating the summit stretches and he feared serious injury if he attempted the route in the dark. As for early motor cars, even when roofed over and enclosed, they had no heating and so for Grampian conditions, driving gloves, fur collars and muffs were essential on cold days while protective dust coats, veils and goggles were advisable in summer. In the absence of windscreen wipers, a half potato rubbed over the glass helped the rain drops to disperse. It was so much safer and faster to go by train than to endure such discomforts. As a result of timber cartage the roads in the gateway districts could be very rough; traction engines hauled logs from Inshriach to the GNSR railhead at Boat of Garten 7 miles (11km) away in preference to the nearer, but dearer, Highland Railway at Aviemore and these machines tore the surface into ruts.

Horses did not take kindly to noisy motor cars and some nasty accidents happened when the nervous animals bolted. Horse drawn vehicles were the norm in the gateway until the early 1930s and they came in all shapes and sizes – landaus, brakes, waggonettes, charabancs, chapel carts, phaetons, spring vans, pony traps and even sleighs. Most could be bought second-hand at sales and second-hand horses were also on offer. As cities were electrifying their tramways in the early 1900s, ex-tram horses at £5 each were eagerly sought because they were strong and well disciplined. There was a problem however – their curious behaviour whenever they heard a bell, be it school or kirk, when they would stop suddenly. In December 1908, the last stage coach in the British Isles made its run from Kingussie to Tulloch and back; its withdrawal was a sign of the times. In a smart livery of yellow and black, it carried the name Duchess of Gordon and set off from the Duke of Gordon Hotel, leading inevitably to ribaldry that 'The Duchess' left the Duke's Arms every morning at 9 o'clock! A waggonette continued to convey mail to Kinlochlaggan until 1915 when a motor vehicle replaced it.

When the Highland Railway began promoting holiday-making in its territory in 1909, it used an Albion motor car – D55 – for publicity purposes. It had advertisements painted all over it for 'The Royal Route via Dunkeld'; 'The Highlands for Fishing'; 'Dornoch Links – Vardon says "Probably the Best in Scotland" – Stop the Car and Enquire'. The vehicle had an itinerary in the North of England and literature about special ticket offers and circular tours was given out. Like the Caledonian and the North British systems, the Highland did try using the cinematograph in its promotions but the film does not survive. The company was determined to win a fair share of the growing tourist traffic but it took a ribbing over its *Strathpeffer Spa Express* which ran only on Tuesdays. Although advertised as offering 'great comfort and speed', patrons discovered that they had to change trains and waste two hours on the way mostly at Aviemore. Other marketing tricks were also tried; 'a noted literary man' was won over and wrote:

> I shall never go anywhere else. I will spend what leisure I have on the Highland Railway. The Continent can take a back seat and the Canary Islands be relegated to the third row in the gallery.

It was very encouraging. London journalists were brought north to see 'popular and picturesque spots' and breakfasted at Aviemore. With every year the districts of the gateway were becoming better known.

On the sporting side, *Golf Illustrated* was penning appreciative comments about the Station Hotel's small golf course ('the links are excellent') but it was for guests only. The popularity of golf was growing and every town or village was proposing to have a course. In Boat of Garten, the railwaymen set about carving fairways and greens out of rough pasture and broomy hillocks near the station. It was widely recognised that a golf course was a pre-requisite for attracting visitors to 'health resorts'. So in April 1906, a golf club was formed in Rothiemurchus and railwaymen were again very active in creating it. The laird gave the ground at Inverdruie and a club house was put up for the following season. A local subscription cost 5s (25p) – a bargain for a course praised as 'a very good inland one and beautifully situated'. It continued until the 1950s when the ground reverted to the estate.

Most visitors came to walk and picnic in the forests and hills. Some investigated the area's natural history, making collections, sketching and taking photographs. The idea of a Scottish National Park was first floated in 1904 and this was a response to a perceived need. Access to the Lairig Ghru and other paths was greatly eased in 1912 when the Cairngorm Club put up the 'Iron Bridge' over the Allt Beanaidh alongside a former ford on that stream. Designed to admit only pedestrians (or cautious cyclists), it continues in use and carries a plaque giving the times and distances between Aviemore and Braemar.

Highland traditions were fading, however, with the decline in the speaking of Gaelic and the playing of what proved to be the last shinty match in the gateway when Rothiemurchus played Aviemore; the game has continued strongly in Badenoch with teams from both Kingussie and Newtonmore being at the forefront. Cricket was an introduction encouraged by the Laird of Rothiemurchus who provided a field and participated in the games; the English influence on upbringing and education was plainly at work among the gentry but not surprisingly 'village cricket' did not take root. Football certainly did. In 1910, railwaymen made up a team and Aviemore visited Boat of Garten and won; there were to be many heroic encounters in years to come.

Although the majority of visitors were summer migrants, a hardy band of enthusiasts was coming in winter to ski. Winter travel was a feat of endurance as conditions on the railway were primitive with just one foot warmer among five passengers. It was barely enough to take the chill off an icy compartment, let alone the passengers' cold feet. In a Ski Club of Great Britain report of 1906, an account of 'A Fortnight in the Cairngorms' appeared. Based at Kingussie, the skiers attracted much attention especially as they taught youngsters to ski using barrel staves. They left a pair of old skis at their hotel as templates to encourage local manufacture and some people saw their advantages for getting about in thick snow. Skiing was forecast to become popular in the Highlands.

> There is one village in Badenoch which, because of its proximity to the Cairngorm ski slopes, should be in the winter months a premier port of call for all who aspire to glide the crystal waste.

The answer was Aviemore. As the livelihood of so many was now linked to the tourist trade, it might have been thought that earnings in the lean winter months would be welcome. But it was not so. Enterprising neighbours such as Carrbridge and Newtonmore were reported as overcoming their locational disadvantages and taking bookings for Hogmanay far in excess of those at Aviemore. Although the latter was nearest the big snow fields, its folk were preoccupied with the railway or their farms and in any case the Station Hotel was shut for the winter.

As the population of the gateway rose, the need for medical services grew. The first doctor was Hugh Crichton-Miller who belonged to a prosperous family. He was born in Genoa and educated at Fettes College. Setting up initially in general practice in the early 1900s he came to Aviemore in the summer and went to Italy in the winter. This was the custom of other fashionable doctors – following an affluent clientele between the Highlands and warmer climes according to the time of year. Needless to say, this migration caused considerable irritation to local G.P.s in the north. It was difficult for a doctor to make a living there; the majority of local people simply could not afford medical attention unless in an emergency and certainly not on a regular basis. This seasonal incursion allowed favoured doctors to look after wealthy patients, such as shooting tenants or other visitors who might suffer from overexertion or overindulgence, while providing an opportunity for country folk to consult them too. The fees were accordingly adjusted and it was a form of subsidy to the less well off. Hugh Crichton-Miller subsequently specialised in psychiatry running a private nursing home near Harrow for which most of the staff were recruited in the Aviemore area. He was also the founder of the renowned Tavistock Clinic in London.

The first resident doctor to serve the gateway's people was the much respected A. C. Balfour, a cousin of the writer Robert Louis Stevenson; he shared his surname with the hero of one of Stevenson's best-known adventure stories, *Kidnapped*. He came to Aviemore in 1905 and together with his wife, Margaret Ellen, made an outstanding contribution to the well being of the community over many years. When he first began his practice in the extensive district he went about on horseback. Then he acquired a bicycle for use on local calls, hiring Willie Hay's car for longer distances; he never learned to drive. Like Dr Orchard in Kingussie, he also tried skis when there was enough snow. Dr Balfour soon became aware of the dangers of railway work and quickly instituted an ambulance class for the staff with tests to be passed and certificates to be earned 'under painstaking examination'. Soon calls on his time began to come from

By 1910 bicycling had become popular and although main roads could be rough they were empty of traffic. In this view Aviemore's villas are on the left and St Andrew's Church on the right (VALENTINE COLLECTION / ST ANDREWS UNIVERSITY LIBRARY)

incidents in the Cairngorms – hill walkers losing their way in the mist and eventually arriving back at midnight completely exhausted. By the time retirement came, he had delivered a fair share of the active population of the district and knew everyone well. When a youngster came with a message from 'Mr McDonald' without hesitation the doctor asked, 'Is it John Sam, Priesty, or Red Jock?' – such was his close acquaintance with the whole community.

The impact of the summer visitors on the local economy and the flourishing station could not disguise the continuing dependence that many still had on farming or forestry. Such folk lived close to nature and tried to produce a goodly portion of their own food. Thankfully, once the railway had been opened, grain prices fell as assured supplies of meal from more fertile districts were obtainable. In autumn a steam traction engine went the round of the farms to supply power for the threshing mill which took the grain off the stalks; a few farms even had their own barn mills. These events were rare occasions for neighbours to gather to help one another in a communal act with plenty of food and drink on hand. Sometimes the harvest in the gateway was much delayed by poor weather – in 1903 it was still being secured in November and in 1905 it was so late that the Harvest Thanksgiving was not held until December.

Hardship and poverty were common and there was no shortage of applicants for assisted passages to North America from the Clyde. In the Canadian prairies, there were tempting opportunities for young men from a countryside of poor soils, small hill farms and big families:

> Young Farm Hands: 160 acres of Farm Land Free.
> A Situation with a Farmer in Western Canada: Guaranteed.
> Advance of £5 Passage Money.
> Apply Canadian Government Agent.

The United States, Australia and New Zealand all figured in such advertisements; many youngsters took up such offers and left the district rarely if ever to return, even on visits. For too long the Highlands and islands suffered an unstoppable haemorrhage of its enterprising young people. The lairds and the shooting tenants (who often saw themselves as quasi-lairds) were not indifferent; they gave support to good causes and practical help in other ways. Charles E. Moreing and his family, who leased Drumintoul Lodge for many years, met the expenses of providing a district nurse. To mark Queen Victoria's Diamond Jubilee in 1897, a Nursing Institute was established to place such nurses in country areas. Other welcome assistance was the distribution of venison to local people;

this was done regularly in Glenmore and Kinveachy while Aviemore station staff received such gifts from Rothiemurchus.

On the social side there was plenty of activity as the railway communities had injected a new vitality. In the years before the First World War, every club or group had its annual 'ball' and dancing classes helped the gateway's folk find their feet. Typically Highlanders had a passion for music and dancing. Long after 'ba-als' had become dances, older people spoke of the fun they once had when the Lovat Scouts' Ball was a highlight. With no hall in the gateway, the usual venue was the library at Inverdruie where the music was home-made with fiddles and accordions. The walk out and back to Aviemore through the woods was a good time for 'high jinks' and a bit of courting. Any excuse for a night out was eagerly grasped and presentations gave such opportunities. The standard gift for a man was 'a gold albert with appendages' – in other words, a watch chain with seals – and the evening would be made merry with songs, stories, supper and a few drams.

The Lovat Scouts became a social institution too. As a result of the Boer War, army reserves were formed and in 1900 Lord Lovat established the Lovat Scouts. Gillies, gamekeepers and shepherds signed up as reservists in this unique rural regiment and quickly proved their exceptional abilities in fieldcraft and reconnaissance. The bounty on offer helped to augment their usually low earnings. Competitions in marksmanship and annual camps varied the routine of the countryside too and brought men together in comradeship. In two World Wars, the Lovat Scouts were to win fame both for their valour and for their unorthodox methods.

New amusements were on their way. In 1903 a 'cinematograph exhibition' had taken place in the public hall in Newtonmore but it attracted so little interest that it was very poorly attended. By 1910 however, the Northern Cinematograph Company gave a show in the School House in Rothiemurchus to a fair sized audience. Soirées, which were another favourite entertainment, were soon enlivened by the playing of gramophones. Although Christmas as a celebration in the church calendar was frowned upon by the bleaker sorts of Presbyterianism, this did not stop both grown ups and school children attending a big party at the Doune of Rothiemurchus where the hostess was Lady Mary Grant. Episcopalians enjoyed such frivolities as Christmas trees and one was the centre piece at the Doune where it was 'dismantled so that each scholar received a gift'. The Episcopalians alone held a service on Christmas Day – otherwise the shops, such as they were, remained open and the postal services continued. New Year was the holiday with parties on

Hogmanay, followed by first footing, and gifts for the children. On New Year's Day, there was a rifle club shoot, then a dinner and dance in the evening. This festivity brought all the gateway folk together with much jollity.

Occasionally there were other excitements. Impressive celebrations took place in Rothiemurchus in 1901 for the delayed coronation of King Edward VII. The whole populace assembled at Drumintoul Lodge. It was August and the shooting season. A huge bonfire was lit, a hundredweight of fireworks was set off and twenty-one rounds fired from a model cannon. Cake and wine were served to the whole company and the evening was rounded off with a torchlight procession followed by dancing on the bowling green – all by courtesy of the tenants of the lodge, the Moreing family. En route to Inverness, circuses began to call at Aviemore. Village children would hear the whistles and puffing of the traction engines, then the plumes of steam would spurt through the birch trees of Craigellachie and the youngsters would run out to welcome the showmen. In 1910, they had a double treat when Biddall's Circus ('on a small scale') and Bostock's Rail Road Circus stopped off for a few days.

As ever the people of the Cairngorm gateway were hostages to the weather. February 1903 brought torrents of rain following a heavy snow fall and vast floods resulted. Huge ice floes cascaded down the Spey on the highest water levels since the railway had opened in 1863. Observers likened the episode to the 'Great Floods' of 1829. The Druie, as was its wont, burst its banks, low lying meadows became lakes and river sides were ripped away; twelve square miles (3100ha) of floods lay between Boat of Garten and Grantown. There have been many repetitions of such events but none so disastrous as that of June 1914 when violent storms assailed much of Scotland. The fury of the elements on the bare hills east of Slochd Mhuic was such that the Baddengorm burn near Carrbridge became a raging torrent. Over three square miles (780ha) of drainage basin were affected by an 'aerial disturbance of quite a phenomenal and unprecedented character' with devastating results.

The 11.50 am train from Perth had left Aviemore with the locomotive *Ben a'Bhuird* at its head. When the train reached the bridge over the Baddengorm burn the structure was in a perilous state but this was not obvious to Driver Ross and his fireman on the footplate. The arch of the bridge was jammed with tree trunks and debris ponding back the water to a depth of 20 feet (6m) on the upstream side. This had undermined the foundations of the bridge. The engine got across but the subsiding track derailed the tender and the train was halted; the weight of the carriages then led to the total collapse of the arch and the vehicles were thrown down the bank. The middle coach was swamped in the flood; five passengers were lost and nine injured. A visitor from the United States was saved by clinging to the branches of a tree; he likened his experience to being swept over Niagara Falls.

The Highland Railway's Civil Engineer George Newlands, hastening back from an inspection in the north, went down on a light engine to Slochd that evening. Taking a lamp, he walked to Baddengorm and was horrified to see that the bridge and embankment had been torn away. A forester who had lived beside the burn for 45 years said he had never seen such heavy rain; it had washed an acre (0.4ha) of sand and stones all over his fields. A road bridge nearby was also destroyed. People were appalled by the Baddengorm disaster, especially as the Highland line had a remarkable record for safety over the half century of its existence. The destructive effects of the deluge became very real to them through the pictures in the national newspapers and through the photographs taken at the scene by Walter Dempster, the son of the Rothiemurchus schoolmaster.

In June 1914 after a freak storm, the Baddengorm burn tore away the railway line and bridge north of Carrbridge with disastrous consequences (WALTER DEMPSTER)

The inquiry revealed the dangers presented by the gathering of numerous burns on bare hills long cleared of their forest cover, and the nature of Highland streams on slopes where any excess of water made their stony beds travel. A watery avalanche of boulders had swept off the hills carrying rocks estimated to weigh as much as eight tons downstream. The foundations of the bridge had rested on hard gravelly boulder clay, not on rock, but these were thought substantial and well protected from being undercut by the burn The nearest rain gauge was reportedly at Aviemore where records going back forty years showed a mean annual total of 30 inches(760 mm) but the maximum could be 60 per cent greater and the minimum 40 per cent less. The summer storms of the Cairngorms region had proved to be quite as fierce as 'cyclonic disturbances in tropical latitudes' – a timely warning to the complacent.

The destruction at Baddengorm was a cruel blow right at the beginning of the tourist season and it was essential that a new bridge be put in place as soon as possible. The contractors were McAlpine's from Glasgow who had considerable railway experience. With men working day and night, in just three weeks new masonry abutments were supporting a steel span from Motherwell and the Direct Line could be re-opened. This was not however to be the last that was heard of the Baddengorm burn; there was another episode in 1923 when mercifully no trains were involved.

In the early summer of 1914 the Highlands had never been so well filled with demands for accommodation far exceeding the supply. It was confidently expected that the tide of visitors would continue to rise year by year, in spite of prices often being thought unreasonable and groceries scarce. The deer forests were at their zenith – these amounted to 3.5 million acres (1.4 million ha) of the Highlands and questions were beginning to be asked about the absence of people in them and about alternative uses for the land. Southern tourists, unfamiliar with these matters, were charmed by the Cairngorm gateway, as was reported in the *Scots Pictorial*:

> Deposited on the station platform, they stretched their legs, inhaled the delicious air, admired the imposing station, the large hotel so finely planted on high ground against the rocky hill, and either stayed or returned.

It seemed as if a golden age for tourism was about to begin. The outbreak of the First World War on 4 August 1914 dashed these hopes; the conflict was not over by Christmas and it was to mark the end of an era. The

The Aviemore Station Hotel was opened in 1901. It was one of the finest in the Highlands with an outstanding setting and extensive grounds (GLEN COLLECTION)

declaration of war with the German Empire had 'an immediate and very injurious effect' on the holiday business as August was the peak month. There was panic and families left for home or cancelled their bookings. Lessees – many of whom had military obligations – were absent from the grouse moors and deer forests. This caused local traders to suffer financially. All special and excursion trains in Scotland were withdrawn. Those for government use had priority as the nation went to war – the instruction was 'all other traffic must stand aside'. The Cameron Highlanders and the Lovat Scouts, the gateway's territorial regiments, were mobilised forthwith. 'Tea Tables' for soldiers and sailors were set up at Kingussie station as canteens for troops in transit. The Highland Railway and its staff were to be put under immense strain by five years of national effort.

Stations resounded with activity and Aviemore being a junction was especially frantic. Numerous military and naval trains had to be run. It was impossible to keep traffic flowing as usual and soon reductions in the published timetable were announced – just four 'up' trains from Inverness and four 'down' trains from Perth each day. Sunday work had to be accepted in the crisis and religious views set aside, like it or not. Due to the threat of possible invasion, railwaymen were warned that all means of transport were to be removed or destroyed if instructions should be issued to that effect; it was a dreadful thought as Highland drivers doted on their engines. Every employee was to become a potential saboteur whether in a depot or out on the line.

With so many of its men enlisting, the Highland Railway began to have problems even maintaining its reduced public service. William Whitelaw, the chairman of the company, was truly alarmed for trains could not be run 'without signalmen, pointsmen, drivers, firemen and engine cleaners'. Indeed the most urgent need on the Highland was for the latter – the efficiency and safety of a steam locomotive owed a great deal to their exertions. Help was sought:

> Strong boys who are willing to work can become good cleaners in a very short time . . . Any boys who have finished their education and are physically strong can serve their country now and at once by offering their services in this way.

The lads were paid 14 shillings (70p) a week and could sign on at the larger depots including Aviemore Junction but there was a problem. Boy Scouts were not permitted to accept any money – they were expected to give every penny to their organisation – and there was already a troop in the village.

The war dragged on and when New Year came in 1915 gifts were sent to the troops at the front – pipes, tobacco and cigarettes for the officers and men from the gateway. Smoking was universal, being seen as a harmless diversion to steady the nerves. Festivities at home were muted; an entertainment for children at the Doune included lantern slides of the war while grown ups were enlightened by a lecture on 'The Spread of the Gospel in Manchuria' in the U.F. Church Hall.

Due to shortages of imported cotton wool for dressings, sphagnum moss, which had sterile properties, was gathered as a substitute on the wet moors. There were sales of hand-painted postcards for the Belgian Refugee Fund – many Belgians had fled to Britain – and flag days for the Red Cross, the French and other deserving causes raised money. Nurses sold these on trains at Aviemore while the Cameron Highlanders' band drummed up patriotic support in the station square. The indefatigable Martineaus and their wood carving class also had sales of their work to assist the war effort.

The strath buzzed with rumours especially when a German was picked up in Carrbridge. Had he been seeking intelligence about freight or troop movements on the railway? The sinking of the Clyde built *Lusitania* and the heavy losses at the battle of the Somme in 1915 provoked revulsion while the return of disabled soldiers made the horrors of war only too plain. Efforts at home were redoubled and, as part of a national scheme, money was raised for a bed in a Scottish military hospital at Bellahouston in Glasgow. Women and girls were hard at work making comforts for the men in France and in the Dardanelles; the combined production of Aviemore and Rothiemurchus was an assortment of vests, scarves, body belts, mittens, shirts and 120 pairs of socks! In the absence of a village hall in Aviemore, concerts and other fund raising activities went on in the garage of the Cairngorm Hotel, heated in winter 'by old stoves and hot pans'. Willing hands made up parcels of soup tablets, chocolate, plum pudding, cigarettes and writing materials there to send to men in the forces. With holiday-making showing contraction, the Aviemore Station Hotel Company bought the Cairngorm Hotel for a knock down price of £2,500, with its furnishings a bargain at £900. The two establishments were then run on the principle of niche marketing – the new acquisition always had lower prices and more basic accommodation.

By the spring of 1915 the Highland Railway was in crisis. O. S. Nock believed that 'it was called upon for a step-up in productivity unparalleled in British railway history'. This was primarily to meet the requirements of the Royal Navy's bases at Scapa Flow and Invergordon. There were severe problems in supplying the latter – there were 4,000 workers in the repair yard itself and 7,000 men in camps around it. While construction was in progress, every siding north of Perth was choked with wagons bound for Invergordon. Worse still, Inverness was selected as the Ammunition Storage Centre for the Grand Fleet. In fact the whole of the north of Scotland was declared a special military area and restrictions were so severe that passengers arriving at Inverness without a permit could not leave the station.

What made matters so much worse was that, of the 272 miles (435km) of main line between Perth and Thurso, only 41 (65) were double track. At least the Forres line gave an option at Aviemore Junction and its railwaymen became accustomed to long hauls to Helmsdale, to lengthy shifts sometimes stretching to 18 hours or more and to overnighting away from home. As the war broke out in August, the Highland Railway's rolling stock and engines, due for overhaul when traffic was light in the winter, had little chance of being serviced. It had only limited numbers of both and all too soon of its 152 locos, one third were withdrawn awaiting repair and another third were in pressing need of attention. A loan of twenty assorted engines from other companies was hastily arranged and the War Office was urged to discharge HR fitters from the forces.

The shortage of wagons was also acute. Forestry camps appeared along the line and timber haulage soared. Coal for the Admiralty was taken north by sea but all other requirements were moved on the Highland Railway – loco coal, industrial and domestic supplies plus coal for fishing boats. The railway had to borrow over 1,000 vehicles. The huge freight trains earned the name 'Jellicoes' after the admiral. Unbelievably, no thought had been given as to how crews would be transported to man the Grand Fleet; it was thus entirely dependent on the Highland Railway for the movement of its men and stores. To handle the mountains of mail for the Navy, three new Travelling Post Office vans had to be put into service. All of these trains went through Aviemore Junction but there were often not enough suitable locomotives to handle them. An order for new engines had been bungled. Six splendid locos – modern in design and of solid construction – had been built in 1915 at Newcastle-upon-Tyne but they never saw revenue earning activity on the Highland Railway. They were alleged to be too heavy and bulky for the line. Ironically, this River class was well suited to hard slogging and in the 1920s, these 'Hielan'men', as they became known on the Caledonian Railway, where they gave stalwart service, came north again to show their paces.

As the war intensified by 1916, 97 per cent of the active men in the gateway districts had either enlisted or were on the reserve lists. Local tribunals had been set up to deal with problems of recruitment and to ensure that men indispensable to industry were left at work. Out of fourteen men of military age employed at the Station Hotel in Aviemore, only the engineer/handyman, who was in charge of the electricity generating and hot water plants, was left and even he was hauled before the tribunal for the Badenoch district.

The folk of the gateway soon had a close encounter with hostile forces. From March 1916, all lights had to be 'invisible from outside' as the risk of air raids by Zeppelin airships had increased. It was timely advice for on the night of 2 May, a Zeppelin appeared over the Grampians. L. 16 came inland at Lunan Bay near Arbroath before crossing Deeside. The sinister shape was seen just south of Aviemore about 11.30 pm pursuing a north westerly course. The great airship could not be ignored because it made a sound 'like the clatter of 100 motor cars' while travelling at about 60 mph (96 kph) and it was assumed that its cargo of bombs was destined for the big naval base at Invergordon. It had missed the other targets of Rosyth and the Forth Bridge as its commander had mistaken the Firth of Tay for the Forth estuary. Turning south then east, it had plainly lost its way but its return passage was again verified at Aviemore. It shed some of its bombs in Aberdeenshire narrowly missing Craig Castle. The craft was finally wrecked in Norway. After the war, a flare from the airship was picked up in the Cairngorms on the Mar Lodge estate; it was given to the

Prince of Wales (later King Edward VIII) for identification by the Admiralty before being returned to its finder, Alexander McDonald, the keeper at Luibeg.

At every turn, the people of the strath were increasingly aware of being at war. 'Daylight Saving Time', introduced in May 1916, was greatly resented although it was put forward as helpful to Highland farmers. Wages rose but so did the cost of living, and liquor sales were subject to restriction and prohibition in some areas. The use of motor cars for pleasure was targeted and exception was taken to 'wasteful domestic establishments' and to 'extravagance in dress for women' – excesses that had only been glimpsed in pre-war days among some hotel guests and shooting tenants. There were food shortages too and meat was rationed; by 1917 a 'Venison Distribution Committee' was active in sending supplies to the south. Visitors were few and far between although the district was publicised as distant from the coast and therefore safe from any risk of possible invasion.

Meanwhile, troops of the Canadian Forestry Corps had arrived at Glenmore. It was rumoured that they would be augmented by 150 German prisoners of war 'under armed guard' but thankfully as far as local folk were concerned, the latter never materialised there. (Prisoners from a camp at Nethybridge were however deployed in felling in Abernethy.) The Canadians established camps at the Sluggan, in Abernethy forest and at Loch Morlich. The first company on the scene was the 110th in June 1916 to be followed in July 1917 by the 121st. The base for the latter, which stood opposite Glenmore Lodge, was impressive with accommodation for officers, 170 men and 50 'Finns' or civilian labourers, plus stabling for 60 horses. The Canadians disliked the weather – the winters were not cold enough to turn the ground solid for any length of time and thus they mostly had to work knee deep in mud or peat. Even so the men began 'scything down the trees like corn stalks' producing sawn timber for pit props, for ammunition boxes and for use on the French railways. It was yet another intense onslaught on the forest. Thankfully the Duke of Richmond and Gordon reserved stands of pines close to the shores of Loch Morlich but in other localities a clean sweep was made – regrettably in the Sluggan and in the eastern portion of Rothiemurchus. Not even seed trees were left.

The Canadian troops came complete with their own machines and set up a three-foot (0.9m) gauge railway to haul timber from Glenmore via Rothiemurchus to the loading bank at Aviemore station. Rothiemurchus woods were no strangers to tramways – rail networks with horse haulage had been used for logging in the 1900s when floating was given up. The

Canadians' railway had little steam locomotives from Bagnalls in Leeds – in railway parlance, narrow gauge saddle tanks – which pulled trains of bogie wagons. From the loading bank at the station the track of the timber railway followed Dalfaber Road and swung across the steel girder bridge over the Spey. At all times trains had to give way to road traffic and to prevent wheeled vehicles becoming caught in the track it was covered with wood to the top of the rails. The line veered to the bank of the Druie where the Rothiemurchus saw mill once stood. A timber trestle bridge carried it across the river and it ran through the Dell woods to Coylumbridge where there was a level crossing. The track continued up by the Luineag to Aultnancaber, then across the moor in a straight run to the Sluggan road where a saw mill was located. Further branches were constructed to serve other sectors of Glenmore, notably on the south side of Loch Morlich. An extraordinary offshoot went along the stream bed in the Sluggan and inclines worked by stationary engines supplemented the system. An empty train left Aviemore about 6 am with some lumberjacks on board and made stops at Inverdruie to pick up others. A halt at Coylumbridge let the engine take water.

The Canadians had a moment to savour in July 1917 when the Prime Minister, Lloyd George, accompanied by Winston Churchill, then Minister of Munitions, was in Aviemore. The pair had been to Inverness (probably also to Invergordon) from where they travelled by motor car to overnight at the Station Hotel. An inspection of the Canadian Forestry Corps was quickly arranged as most conveniently a contingent of 250 men from the Glenmore camps was bound for Grantown to take part in a gala. Captain Hugh A. Calder, their commanding officer – who deserved full marks for initiative – sent a message to the Premier and so the Canadians were summoned to line up on the hotel lawn. Lloyd George greeted them from the steps congratulating them on the 'work of very great national importance' which they were doing. Having inspected the troops, he shook hands with the captain and presented him with a cigar – perhaps it was one of Winston's.

Some of the lumberjacks were merchant seamen who had been trapped in Britain by the war; they were remembered as a rough lot especially when they took a dram too many. They often had little English as some were of Finnish or Russian origin and of course no interpreters could be found in the district when they came to court. In being absent from their camp, they were contravening the Aliens' Restriction Order and faced a fine of £3 or 20 days imprisonment. On a brighter note, local girls found dancing partners among the Canadians and weddings were the outcome, sending in time a share of war brides to the Dominion. One wartime marriage certainly caused a sensation – 'Bride in Uniform' read the headline:

> Miss Mary Anderson, a Sergeant-Major in the WAAC, wed CGMS J N Nyschem from South Africa in Rothiemurchus.

A social revolution was in progress and women were assuming new roles. Early in 1917 the Scottish Women's Land Army was formed. Girls were promised lodgings, 18 shillings (90p) per week in wages and a free outfit – breeches, high boots, two overalls and a hat. It was very daring attire as hitherto only variety stars such as Vesta Tilley had been seen in trousers and then exclusively on the stage. The clothing did not appear to be a deterrent as a year later there were 113,000 women working in the Land Army in Britain. The early recruits had been badly in need of reassurance:

> You are doing a man's work and so you are dressed rather like a man . . . but you are expected to behave like a British girl [who] expects chivalry and respect from everyone.

Only a few of these lasses appeared in Strathspey but women were becoming much more venturesome. A lady 'engaged in war work' wrote in the *Daily Chronicle* that come February with some days of leave, she would be roughing it:

> I'm off rucksack packed, skis varnished, the metal work well oiled, boots repaired, ski bindings dosed with oil and grease, to go by the Highland Railway for its stations are the highest and snowiest in Britain. One can get a decent ski tour in the Cairngorms reached from Aviemore. It's a great days work to cross the Lairig Ghru to Braemar!

With the Continent closed to tourists and winter sports enthusiasts, a fresh look at possibilities at home was being taken.

A greater importance began to be attached to Christmas perhaps because the festival was given national prominence and the idea that gifts should be exchanged on 25 December gradually caught on. The choice had a decidedly patriotic flavour with such winter games as 'The Allies' Flag Day Puzzle', 'Fighting in Flanders' or 'Defending the Coast' for the home based. For men at the front there was 'The Chemico Body Shield' which was 'proof against shrapnel and bullet'. Housewives were dismayed that they were to 'refrain from despatching plum puddings to the theatre of war' as these could only be supplied to troops in France through the Director-General of Voluntary Services.

Meanwhile, there were new arrivals in the gateway who were to have a big impact on its people. Sam MacDonald had taken over as post master in 1916 and the Post Office was moved to Clune Villa conveniently opposite the station. Sam became a leader in the community – chairing meetings, acting as a master of ceremonies at festivities and playing in the football team. The other was William Gault, the new shed master, who became known as 'Parson Bill' on account of a marriage he had once conducted to bring respectability to a household in the Railway Terrace. Originally from Wick, he had been shed foreman at Blair Atholl for 18 years where he had shown his mettle. His was a typical progression in railway service and he was thrown into the frenzy of problems at Aviemore Junction. From February 1917, a direct Euston – Thurso train for the Admiralty had been running. It covered the 717 miles (1,147km) in 21½ hours and very nearly half that time was spent negotiating the Highland Railway system. This giant train of 14 vehicles only had sleeping cars for officers; no wonder that to Navy men it was known as 'The Misery'!

During the war years, over 1,000 troop and naval specials went north and every one of these trains plus many other extra ones went through Aviemore Junction. Mr Gault had to conjure up replacements for lame engines and there were occasions when there was not a single locomotive left at the shed. Apart from coal, timber dominated freight traffic and by the last year of the war, the Highland Railway had carried over 403,000 tons of it – the equivalent of eight train loads every working day compared with its peacetime norm of one train load per day. The gateway re-echoed to the clamour of shunting, the whistling of engines and the roar of steam round the clock.

Major John Peter Grant, the son of the Laird of Rothiemurchus, who was serving with the Lovat Scouts in Gallipoli, was in the news when he was awarded the Military Cross. Many of his men were tenants or estate workers and had known him from boyhood. He was highly regarded for his competence in the field and they nicknamed him 'Bones' on account of his skinniness. Viewing the panorama of Rothiemurchus from the heights of Tullochgrue, one of his old sergeants declared, 'No wonder Bones was so bloody good with a telescope!' He was a lawyer by training and subsequently a Sheriff-substitute of Inverness-shire and adjacent counties but as a laird he is remembered for his expertise in bagpipe music, his knowledge of Gaelic and his love of all things Highland – enthusiasms which might be thought to sit awkwardly with a Winchester education.

The coming-of-age of John Peter Grant of Rothiemurchus in June 1896 was marked by a gathering of family, estate folk and school children at the Doune of Rothiemurchus. Here, the young man, who was to become laird and sheriff, sits between his father, Sir John Peter Grant, and his step-mother, Lady Mary Grant (WALTER DEMPSTER)

A fellow officer who shared a tent with him once said, 'You'd be damned fine company, Bones, if you'd only get rid of your ruddy bagpipes!' Invariably clad in an ancient kilt, 'The Sheriff', as he was more formally known in later years, often appeared at Highland Games as a judge of pipe music.

The end of 'the greatest war in history' at 11 am on 11 November 1918 brought a muted response from the folk in the Cairngorm gateway. Most significantly, there was a joint thanksgiving service for the Armistice organised by all the churches. Only psalms were sung with a precentor raising the tune in the old way. It was a sad and very solemn occasion. Otherwise flags were hung out, scholars had a holiday, bonfires were lit and a dance was held.

For troops returning from France or Gallipoli, an official 'welcome home' was planned. The returning veterans were very different from the lads who had set out – disillusioned and disabled, shell shocked and shattered by the trauma of the conflict and the loss of so many friends. The First World War took a terrible toll of the people in the strath, as elsewhere in the country. The impressive war memorial installed in St

Andrew's Church in Aviemore was made by the wood carvers of Rothiemurchus. Edith Martineau herself carved the dove of peace which once surmounted it. The panels bore 28 names – the measure of the sacrifice made by the most active men in the cause of a nation's freedom. Their absence was to weigh heavily on the gateway's progress in years to come.

The timber exploitation stopped. There was not much left of the Scots pine forests of the gateway. The Canadians went back home with their Highland brides. The small locomotives were sold off; stacks of logs awaiting removal by rail still lie rotting on the moors where they were abandoned by the lumberjacks. Their little railway was torn up leaving a deplorable road surface so rough that pupils could not reach the school in Rothiemurchus with dry feet 'unless there was either frost or drought'. Social considerations which had been shelved by the war came to the forefront and the visitors were coming back. The house lets for 1919 were practically up to pre-war standards and the shooting lodges had their tenants again. And, as for a Channel Tunnel, a subject of considerable interest to railwaymen, it was forecast that within a decade there would be four in use.

EXCURSION

Loch an Eilein

Loch an Eilein with its ruined castle has been a visitor attraction for several centuries. It is reached by the B970 from Aviemore; branch southwards at Inverdruie for 1½ miles (2km) to a junction at NH891097 where a minor road leads to the loch side. There is parking available (a charge is payable) and a visitor centre which is run by the Rothiemurchus estate. The path of 3 miles (5km) round the loch passes through pine and birch woods and interlinks with other routes for walkers and cyclists.

For further information contact the Rothiemurchus Visitor Centre at Inverdruie on 01479 812345.

CHAPTER 5

From Peace into Combat

1919 – 1939

The folk of the gateway tried to pick up the threads of their pre-war activities and in the summer of 1919 there were sports and a picnic for children when they went to their accustomed venue for outings, Loch an Eilein, in a cavalcade of farm carts. That beauty spot had long been a favourite with tourists – excursions by waggonette being advertised from Kingussie and Nethybridge in the pre-war years. An attraction had been the ospreys but these had last nested on the castle in 1899; sadly they were driven out not only be disturbance but also by repeated nest robbing.

Such an event out of doors – given decent weather – was possible but gatherings out with the kirks were very much restricted by the lack of a hall. Unlike Boat of Garten or Carrbridge, Aviemore had none. So early the following year, war veterans met to try to secure an army hut. Through the generosity of a donor suffering from grievous war losses a hut was purchased. The men prepared the foundations for what became 'The Comrades' Memorial Hall', a wooden structure with a veranda, which stood on the southern approaches to Aviemore. It was a homespun effort led by Bert Davidson, a local postman and sergeant in the Lovat Scouts. Basic as it was, this hall transformed community life and older Aviemorians have happy recollections of it. The hall became the centre for the British Legion when that organisation was formed in 1929. What was left of the building, which had latterly been set on fire, was dismantled in 1996.

The county council also began to consider problems deferred by the war. Foremost of these was an urgent road repair programme plus improvements to its schools – 'the primitive sanitary conveniences' – dry toilets – which were in use in Rothiemurchus and many other rural schools were to be replaced and not before time. Road traffic was beginning to grow. In August 1911 a survey of motor vehicles at Slochd Mhuic had counted just 376 over seven days but by 1922 a similar census gave over 1,000 – a trebling of the number – and Kinveachy with a road junction reported over 1,500. What was worrying, goods tonnage on 'mechanical vehicles' was 94 per cent of the total because cartage by horses over any distance was in severe decline. Surplus army lorries were available second hand at low prices and, crude as they were, these vehicles had a far bigger range than any horse. So the inadequate state of the roads was a source of strong protest and dominated public debate for years.

From 1889 onwards the county councils had taken over the care of the main roads but many routes did not fall into this category. A Central Road Fund was set up by the government in 1910 using money raised from motor taxation and sums were made available to local authorities for road improvement but this did not bring much benefit to the Highlands. Piecemeal repairs simply filled up the big pot holes with crushed rock. The Great Highland Road through the strath was little altered since Telford's time, indeed, it may have been worse – just a narrow, water bound ribbon of grit and stones. For motorists it was an achievement to cover 100 miles (160km) in a day and they were left with sore arms and shaking hands. Surfaces were cut into deep ruts by the solid tyres on their cars. When pneumatic ones came into use, nails from horses' shoes which littered most roads caused frequent punctures and it was not at all unusual to have a couple of flat tyres on any long journey. There was a breakthrough in 1923 when stretches between Aviemore and Kinveachy were tarred. A ploy that caused great indignation was the fettling up of roads before 'The Twelfth' – that is before the grouse shooting season commenced and the 'toffs' arrived at the lodges. The county council then sent 'a steam road roller, a tar boiler and a whole camp of stone breakers' to tackle the worst stretches.

Such was the pressure for improvement that a new 'Great North Road' was proposed and was shortly sanctioned, as the *Badenoch Record* reported:

> Soon the 20-foot (6m) highway with all its advantages will be a wonderful reality . . . fancy, shooting over the Grampians in a balloonette-shod Rolls-Royce!

The Aviemore-Newtonmore section was let to Shepherds of Rochdale and there were more protests as the contractors brought their own workmen with them and gave no jobs to local men. Stone from an unsuccessful distillery in Kingussie supplied much of the road bottoming. It was estimated that 'to bottom, metal, roll and tar a Highland road' cost

£1,000 per mile (1.6km); the surface was then supposed to last ten years but maintenance was always hefty eating up grants of £19 a mile. By 1927 construction was in full swing in the gateway where big excavations and new gradings were essential south of Aviemore. After 'macadamisation' a speed of 25 miles per hour (40 kph) in comfort was promised all motorists; the pale concrete bridges of modern design caught the eye along the route and the new highway was reckoned a notable achievement.

For those who did not have a car or aspire to one, motor vehicles were seen as 'an intolerable nuisance disturbing the peace of the Highlands'. Petrol stations and garages were also springing up. Aviemore soon had two – Hay's and Mackay's – which together with those at Grantown and Kingussie emphasised the gateway's significance as a touring region. Exception was taken to these premises in some quarters:

> The terrible curse of petrol filling stations is decried by landowners as the colours of the pumps clash painfully with their surroundings while the verges are damaged by careless motorists.

Hay's garage was just a wooden shed with a couple of petrol pumps outside it. Dave Mackay's was a former army hut but he had been trained as a motor mechanic at Beardmore's on Clydeside. Willie and Jock Hay were brothers who came from a railway family but they were as unlike as chalk and cheese. Willie was always gentlemanly in suit, collar and tie with a cloth cap; Jock, bespectacled and in oily dungarees, was usually wrestling with the innards of some recalcitrant car. From the shed venerable bicycles could be rented for a few shillings a week. Willie would drive a hired car to unlikely places including Loch Einich and he soon had the first lorry in the district.

Into the 1920s, the number of cars was rising by 3 to 5 per cent every year as motoring found a new market. Whereas cars had once been built individually and in small numbers, consequently being very expensive, they began to be mass produced and vehicles of small size rolled out of factories in their hundreds. They became affordable. Take the Austin Seven for example; it became a popular choice in the gateway:

> £149 complete – Runs at 1d per mile – Unequalled value – Seats two adults and two children – Four cylinder engine – Water cooled – Automatic lubrication – Three speed gear box – Spare wheel and tyre – Brakes on all Four Wheels – Electric Lighting and Starting.

The old disadvantage of just one door, through which the whole family had to clamber before the driver could take his seat, had been replaced by doors on both sides. For Highlanders, the 'all weather body' was a big attraction. Even better, the little car did amazingly well on icy roads and one Rothiemurchus owner boasted that it would climb up a telegraph pole if put to the test! The availability of such cars added up to greater mobility for townsfolk and ever easier access to the countryside with the inevitable consequence of putting new pressures upon it.

In step with the new enthusiasm for motoring from 1927 the Aviemore Station Hotel Company began placing advertisements in the Dunlop and Michelin Road Guides and also in the AA and RAC Handbooks. The following year decisions were taken to market its premier attraction as 'The Aviemore Hotel' and to include a map of Scotland highlighting the position of Aviemore in its publicity. Its garage and chauffeur accommodation had to be regularly augmented. So many brightly painted vehicles were seen on the Great North Road that tartan cars to suit any clan were thought likely. Morris tourers were much admired but exotics from the Continent were also spotted – the long forgotten Donnat Zedels and Chenard Walckers among them. At the other end of the scale, there were bargains to be had at £10 which a handyman could fettle up – a blacksmith would soon repair a broken spring. A policeman on a bike was no match for the motorists and so the county council bought a motor cycle and sidecar which was based at

An assortment of cars gathers at Loch an Eilein in 1930 when new makes were being mass produced and motoring was becoming affordable for many holidaymakers (A. E. GLEN)

Kingussie; it caused quite a stir when it puttered through the gateway. Caravans added to what was described as 'the ceaseless traffic' on the main road in high summer. People marvelled at:

These houses on wheels, their dainty windows bedecked with curtains, a cross between a bathing machine and a Waring & Gillow van.

Some folk feared for their house lets if the trend continued. Everyone now had a bicycle and there was a wide range available – New Hudson, Hopper, Hercules, Fleet, Rudge Whitworth, Royal Enfield and Raleigh – on sale from £4 10s (£4.50). School children longed to be big enough to have a bike to take them to school instead of having to hitch a lift on the milk 'cairtie' going back to the dairy at Upper Tullochgrue in the mornings. Otherwise many faced a walk of several miles each day and short cuts across the railway line were very tempting.

There were changes on the railway too. In January 1923 came the amalgamations of the private railway companies. They had been operated basically as one unit during the First World War and even before that conflict 'nationalisation' had been discussed in some quarters. The Highland Railway became part of the London, Midland & Scottish Railway Company (or LMSR) and its olive green engines were painted maroon if passenger ones, otherwise they should have been black. The Highland reasoned that all its engines pulled passenger trains at some time or another and turned the lot out in maroon! The submergence of the old Highland in a new entity with a southern and obviously a London emphasis, brought real regrets. Seniority became all important on the railway – even a day could make a difference and competence or reliability took second place. Men could be in their forties before they were appointed as drivers. New locomotives arrived from the former Midland Railway and very effective they were too but they earned the nickname 'Crabs' on account of their ungainly appearance.

Scarcely had the LMSR begun to impose its identity on former Highland practices and territory in the summer of 1923, than the newspapers of 9 July were carrying the front page headline 'Carrbridge Cloudburst'. Mercifully, it was a Sunday when the storm struck and passenger trains were not being run. This episode was much more destructive than the pre-war one – eye witnesses spoke of floods of turbulent water coming off the hills like a wall, carrying trees away as though they were straws. The Bogbain, Baddengorm and Foregin burns, of which the first was the chief culprit in the affair, were normally just minor streams but their combined waters rose over 40 feet (14m). Despite the re-modelling of the rivulets' channels after 1914, they returned to their old beds, as rivers are wont, with catastrophic effect. Two railway bridges of the trough girder type and a steel girder bridge over the main road were swept away and engulfed in the debris, together with a long stretch of embankment and a timber siding, plus other structures. This left the new bridge at Baddengorm standing firm, but battered, in isolation. In several places, long lengths of rail were left hanging in mid air. Overall, the washouts involved two miles of track (3.2km) which in civil engineering opinion was the most serious destruction to have happened on any British line and it was another blow in a peak holiday month.

Again McAlpine's won the contract and shortly a camp of 250 men, working in shifts through the day and with acetylene lamps at night, were restoring the system. They toiled to rebuild embankments, construct temporary timber bridges and lay light railway lines to bring in supplies. As the feverish activity to reopen the route continued, owners of motor lorries ('not exceeding two tons') were notified that they might travel 'with great caution' to Slochd via the bridge at Dalnahaitnich higher on the Dulnain. Downstream of the flood in the lower Dulnain valley, it took years for the croft and farmland strewn with the waste of sand, boulders and tree roots to recover.

Meanwhile, the GNSR outpost at Boat of Garten had also been absorbed into a new entity – the London & North Eastern Railway – which allowed 'the Boat' to retain its status as a junction between two major companies. There was fresh competition too when a motor coach service started between Glasgow and Inverness in 1928. The 'beautifully upholstered and luxurious vehicles', which cost £1,800 each, took almost nine hours on the way and carried just 26 passengers. They had heating to allow all year use and sported a MacGregor tartan stripe in deference to their Inverness owner. The railway fought back by offering cheap excursions from the gateway districts – 11s (55p) for a winter day trip to Edinburgh or only 33s (£1.65) for a trip to London for a football international at Wembley but it took over twelve hours to get there.

Railwaymen had a perverse attitude to cars and motor vehicles of any sort; very few had one any way. They held them in some contempt – steam locomotives could go faster – and they argued that if they could drive an engine they could easily handle a motor car. One or two did have motor cycles and the younger men would gather in the station square to take turns of trying them out.

Cashing in on the motoring boom were new tea rooms and bakers' shops conveniently placed near the garages and petrol pumps where touring parties called and where motorists would take a break. Grant's in Boat of Garten, McCook's in Aviemore and Wade's in Kingussie were all set up in the inter-war years and prospered. The gateway suffered less from the restrictive attitudes of landowners or the bureaucracy of local authorities which could throttle local initiatives in some areas. There were complaints from parts of the Highlands that enterprising individuals could:

> Not build a hotel, not put up a motor garage and start a motor service, not enlarge their cottage and take in visitors, not serve teas or food to tourists . . .

Such commentators longed for popular tourism of the Swiss kind if the Highlands were ever to develop and support a larger population of independent folk in 'a pleasure ground for many' and not just for a few. In this lay the seeds of conflicts in years to come. Numbers in the gateway parishes had been rising between 1911 and 1921 but they then began to fall; emigration was again an option for folk determined to try to better themselves without such constraints.[7]

Although motor cars were bringing more people to the Highlands, Strathspey was to many a well kept secret – relatively few people knew about it or the Cairngorms. An enthusiast who had discovered the gateway wrote:

> It has beauty, grandeur, extent, fascination, that kind of charm . . . and Aviemore is set to be the head and font of the whole thing.

Despite the number of letting houses on offer, amenities for holidaymakers were lacking. Warnings were given that if Aviemore was to retain its place as 'one of the finest health resorts on Speyside', the community would have to provide recreational facilities for its summer visitors. In 1923, plans for new tennis courts were drawn up. (There were already ones at the big hotel but exclusively for its patrons.) Courts in the village would have been preferred but the asking price for a site on the Seafield estate was £800 – a steep price compared with £400 in Rothiemurchus close to the little golf course. The choice was obvious. It was again down to local effort by means of whist drives, prize draws, bazaars and dances, to raise the money. Visitors also gave freely and within a year the courts were open. Soon there were tournaments and trophies to be won as the game grew in popularity.

At the top of the visitor scale, at least in terms of wealth, were the

The opening of the tennis courts at Rothiemurchus in 1923 sees a group of the main organisers and fund raisers in their 'Sunday best'. Among the group are the minister, the doctor, the post master and the railway's telegraph engineer (J. S. MACDONALD)

American lessees in the lodges. By the mid-1920s, shootings were being taken up at a record level. To encourage wealthy U.S. citizens to come to Scotland, the Cunard Steamship Company rented several estates, such as Glentromie, Gaick and Castle Grant. Attention was given to improving deer stocks by feeding hay and mineral supplements in the hope of providing larger stags and finer heads for the hunters. The historic pattern of deer being scarce had long been broken and herds had become numerous through being strictly preserved. Rentals ranged from £750 (usually for low ground) to £5,000 for a proper deer forest. But deer forests were under scrutiny and a committee appointed by the Secretary of State for Scotland, which was taking evidence in 1920, had found:

> among all concerned a marked reluctance to return to a system under which large tracts of country were almost entirely devoted to the amusement of a few rich people.

Alternative profitable land uses had been the subject of debate for long enough but options appeared limited. There were Highland parishes such as Alvie and Laggan where shooting estates were still yielding over half the rates' income to the county – funds that were indispensable to local government. In a community context, youngsters employed to drive grouse on the moors could earn between 6s to 8s per day (30 to 40p) which was a useful addition to family income but fines awaited employers who hired under-14 year olds.

The hotels were full at the height of the season and their charges reflected this demand being several guineas dearer per week than in the quieter months. Patrons were becoming more choosy about hotel facilities and demand for water at Aviemore Hotel was rising inexorably with wash basins in every bedroom and extra bathrooms putting pressure on the supply off the railway's main. So a little lochan at the foot of Craigellachie was converted into a supplementary reservoir by the hotel company for its exclusive use. Dry weeks in summer worried the railway too as bigger and more powerful locomotives consumed more water.

Most hotel owners kept up with the changing fashions and the Aviemore Hotel converted its smoking and billiard premises into a ballroom. The Highland theme however was by no means forgotten – plaques of clan crests were commissioned for display, waiters wore tartan jackets of 'Red Grant' and enquiries were made for a piper, preferably one who could teach Highland dancing to the guests.

Intellectual families specially favoured the gateway and rented its houses every year. In August, professors were said to be 'as common as gooseberries' and there was an abundance of ministers in the area ('hopefully their theology is better than their golf'). Whole families of visitors filled the churches and formed discerning congregations. Both Boat of Garten and Newtonmore outdid Aviemore in the number of reverends. When the principal of a divinity college preached in Kingussie, the roads leading to the church were choked with cars and cycles. At the other end of the visitor spectrum was the growing number of campers – guides, scouts, wayfarers and climbers who put up their tents 'notwithstanding the heavy rain' at recognised camping grounds at Dalfaber, Coylumbridge or Loch an Eilein as 'tramping' had come into vogue. Contingents of the Territorial Army were also back at their summer camps.

With the onset of the Great Depression in 1929 there was a reverse. The Americans disappeared. The majority of the larger villas remained unlet for several years. Business shrank on the railway. Hotels deferred investment. This demonstrated if any proof were needed that tourism was fickle. There was continuing demand however for more modest accommodation, which helped the gateway folk to make ends meet. The women on the farms and the railway wives were a hard working lot. Think of Mrs Sutherland; her husband and four sons were all on the railway, mostly as guards. With three shifts in action, Mrs Sutherland and her like ran a round-the-clock service of main meals and sandwiches. In addition she took in summer visitors, displacing some of her family to a tent. It was doubted if Mrs Sutherland ever slept. Mrs Mackintosh at Cragganmore was of the same mould. Her husband and eldest son were engine drivers. In a little cottage which lacked a bath she looked after her visitors so well that they returned year after year. Cragganmore was always spotless, the food delectable and the good wife like a new pin. On the Lairig Ghru route Mrs Garrow cared for generations of mountaineers and walkers in her simple home. In Aviemore warm-hearted Mrs Graham from Glasgow ran the guesthouse, Cairnallan. Her husband was the gateway's plumber, methodically tackling the eccentricities of Highland installations. Everyone was 'dearie' to Mrs Graham and she expected folk to be as cheerful and energetic as she was, memorably in a busy shop reminding a girl assistant that she would be 'as bonnie as her mother if she didnae have such a soor look on her face'!

In spite of the hardship, the Royal Northern Infirmary in Inverness was well supported – concerts raised funds for it, flowers and fruit from the Harvest Thanksgiving were sent to it and in 'Egg Week' in 1933 the gateway district gave no fewer than 261 dozen eggs to the infirmary. The loco men presented a clock 'to the female medical ward' and womenfolk sewed night clothes and bed linen for the patients. Short as cash was, dutiful collectors went round for Heather Day, Poppy Day, for the Lifeboats, the Lepers and the District Nursing Association among other charities. Jumble sales drew the hard pressed – old clothing being in great demand for wear in the byre or in the fields. Big fund raising ploys such as the kirk sale of work were kept for the summer months when visitors could contribute to their success as they amply did.

In 1930 came the union of the Church of Scotland and the United Free Church; the old kirk in Rothiemurchus, which had been a place of worship from time immemorial, closed with 'an edict of demission of office'. St Andrew's in Aviemore was joined by St Columba's at Inverdruie, the former U.F. church, as the two Church of Scotland kirks in the gateway. That same year, the Scots Episcopal Church of St John the Baptist was opened in Rothiemurchus. In addition to the laird's family, it served incomers predominantly from the south and consequently was, and still is, known as 'the English church'. Meanwhile, Alvie kirk attracted crowds to hear Sir George Henschel play the organ and to listen to the choir he trained; he also found time to give concerts to assist good causes. He had two daughters, Helen and Georgie, both of whom had distinguished careers in broadcasting but it was his second wife, an American lady, with the forthright and determined character of many of the breed, who is remembered as an enthusiastic county councillor. She was a passionate supporter of the League of Nations and, of course, Aviemore had to have a branch of the association. After a promising start, about 1928 apathy set in and there were thin attendances for lectures on solemn subjects, especially when there was a competing attraction such as the comic Harold Lloyd in the film 'The Kid Brother' in Kingussie.

For the Grants of Rothiemurchus funds appeared slender. On the estate, every possible house was let to summer visitors to supplement their income. In the circumstances, the appointment of the laird as a Sheriff-Substitute of Caithness, Orkney and Shetland at Lerwick, something of a legal outpost and far from his home, was very welcome. A transfer to Inverness, Elgin and Nairn in 1927 was the beginning of over thirty years of service on the bench. In the Grant family, the girls wore the boys' cast-off clothes, including their boots, allegedly; even the Doune, which was the ancestral home of the family, was leased out. It was occupied for some months by Dr Kurt Hahn, the founder of Gordonstoun School, after he fled from Nazi Germany in 1933 with some of his pupils. The daily routine included an early morning run and the now notorious cold bath.

A teaching programme was improvised and even the Rector of Grantown Grammar School helped out with mathematics. A local lady took the boys on forest rambles to learn about the flora and fauna on which she was very well informed. On encountering estate folk, however, when she explained what she was doing, she was greeted with hoots of laughter – it transpired that she was a habitual poacher. When Dr Hahn got to hear of this, her services were promptly terminated. Meanwhile, he was looking for suitable permanent accommodation in the North of Scotland but the Doune was not to be the choice. The mansion was then run as a hotel between 1935 and 1942; a key part in this venture was played by John Johnstone, an Edinburgh solicitor and secretary of the Aviemore Station Hotel Company, who also rented a holiday home in Rothiemurchus. Notwithstanding his knowledge and contacts in the business, the hotel met with only limited success.

Walter Dempster, the school master in Rothiemurchus for 32 years, had a pivotal role in the community. With many lacking much formal education, he was in demand for writing business letters. To oblige a tenant farmer he agreed to write to the laird to ask for a reduction in rent but closer enquiry revealed that none had been paid for years! There was a similar pattern on the Seafield Estates – rents being paid in instalments or perhaps not at all when the Depression was at its worst.

Poverty in the community led to poor nutrition. In 1936, milk was issued to pupils and shortly a soup kitchen was set up in Rothiemurchus with the library serving as the canteen. A collection raised only £3 to finance it but farmers helped with gifts of 'neeps' and 'tatties' for the broth. Some family incomes were augmented by the small allowances paid for keeping children in need who were 'boarded out' by Glasgow Corporation on farms and crofts in the Highlands and islands.

By October when all but the tenacious visitors had gone, the gateway's people could revert to normal. The younger children were back at school in Rothiemurchus while the older scholars went up by train to Kingussie on Monday mornings to live in 'digs' there during the week. How they counted the days until they could catch the 6.18 evening train home on Fridays. Glenmore was reckoned so inaccessible that the keeper there campaigned successfully to have a teacher assigned to educate his children in a room in the lodge. For grown ups, the exertions of summer time were replaced by some relaxation although the routine work on the railway, farm or croft was unrelenting. The Great North Road was almost deserted and it was easy to get a seat on a train. The gateway might seem very quiet but its folk knew how to enjoy themselves and there was plenty on offer – a badminton club, a choral society, the Women's Guild, the British Legion, a gun club and a miniature rifle club which met in the hall – illuminated by thoroughly dangerous petrol lamps considering that the building was wooden. The few Masons had to journey to Lodge Spey in Kingussie. In 1924, weekly film shows began in Aviemore with 'The Snow Bride' launched by the Badenoch Cinema Company which travelled round halls in the district. A sure success in the railway village was 'The Iron Horse', a thrilling drama of early railroad days in America in nine reels which was shown to packed houses in 1928. Those in the know became accustomed to bringing their own cushions to ease the discomfort caused by the hard wooden seats during such long performances.

The railwaymen had taken over the holding of a Christmas treat for the local children and given it a decidedly Highland flavour. Throughout the year they raised money by dances and whist drives to finance the big party. There were carols, games and recitations but the highlight was the arrival of Santa Claus led in by a piper; there was a gift for every child from a Christmas tree and on leaving 'baggies' of fruit for all. It was the result of prolonged effort by the whole community. New Year continued to be the principal festival being ushered in with a chorus of whistles from the engines lying at the shed. Only in the 1930s did Christmas become a holiday in the gateway with the shops firmly shut. Scottish traditions were not neglected though. Hallowe'en brought out the guisers in their home made costumes, eager to entertain with their well rehearsed 'turns'. Burns

*Although car ownership was increasing from the 1920s onwards, it was still possible to
stroll along the Great North Road in Aviemore and the other gateway villages*
(VALENTINE COLLECTION / ST ANDREWS UNIVERSITY LIBRARY)

Night was marked with a supper in the hall which was packed to capacity
with young and old. 'The Sheriff', Colonel Grant of Rothiemurchus,
took the chair, led off a Grand March and dancing followed into the early
hours. Maybe a few remembered hearing that Robert Burns had once
lodged in the old inn.

The curlers hoped for sharp frosts but their club had a sporadic
existence; in its glistening snow white garb there was no lovelier or livelier
part of Scotland for the roaring game. The Rothiemurchus folk went to
Loch an Eilein when it was bearing and in the winter of 1925 curlers were
in action on a pond formed on the Station Hotel golf course – a donor
having given funds to make rinks there. A succession of severe winters in
the early 1930s saw Loch Puladdern covered with excellent ice until
March. Tommy Hogg, a Selkirk man, who had opened a tweed
warehouse in Aviemore where he pioneered 'mill prices' and mail order,
became chairman of the curling club. He had the soft brogue of the
Borders and was invariably dressed in plus fours and matching cap in his
favourite cloth. Sheriff Grant, ever one to support Highland traditions,
became president. The changeability of the winter weather was seen as an
obstacle to any permanent winter sports programme – the alternately
rising and falling temperatures being very difficult to forecast at the time.

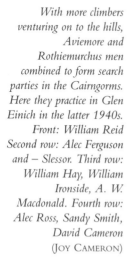

With more climbers venturing on to the hills, Aviemore and Rothiemurchus men combined to form search parties in the Cairngorms. Here they practice in Glen Einich in the latter 1940s. Front: William Reid Second row: Alec Ferguson and – Slessor. Third row: William Hay, William Ironside, A. W. Macdonald. Fourth row: Alec Ross, Sandy Smith, David Cameron
(JOY CAMERON)

Nevertheless, there were pipe dreams that one day there might be 'a motor road from Aviemore to a shelter hut or hotel on one of the many suitable sites at the foot of Braeriach' and thus give access to ski slopes.

Winter lured the unwary to the mountains. Gateway men – shepherds, gamekeepers and stalkers – did not venture on to the heights when conditions were adverse or likely to worsen. There was a general lack of understanding of the weather of the high tops and the closure of the Ben Nevis Observatory in 1904 had been deplored as a mark of a parsimonious government. At New Year 1928, two Glasgow University students, Hugh Barrie and Thomas Baird were lost in the hills. It is said that Sheriff Grant advised them not to go as the mercury in the barometer was falling and he was concerned about their inadequate attire. A search party was called out; it was led by the Rothiemurchus keeper John Mackenzie supported by Constable MacLean and Dr Balfour from Aviemore but blizzard conditions made the rescue attempt impossible. Near Whitewell a monument stands to Barrie with a verse from one of his poems inscribed on it. In January 1933 there was another calamity in the Cairngorms involving young men from Grantown, Alistair Mackenzie and Duncan Ferrier. These tragic events highlighted the ferocious nature of mountain weather and the fortitude of those who formed the search parties. A tradition had become established of the rescue teams being volunteers. If a railwayman was called out to take part in such a mission on the hills, there was always someone willing to cover for him at the shed or the station and so no wages were lost – such was the mutual concern shown by the gateway's people. Willie Hay contributed his lorry as transport for the team of which he was a member. Meanwhile, at the Post Office, Sam MacDonald would keep the telegraph office open round the clock enabling press men to send off their reports at any time.

On a happier note, the railwaymen looked forward to their annual reunion which took place in January and, when tongues were loosened with a dram or two, many a tale was swopped. The old Highland company men remembered the time when a cutting collapsed near Kingussie engulfing the line in sand, or Red Jock's misadventure on a Castle class engine when a wheel came off the tender when he was speeding down Glen Truim, or they argued about how the Barneys, the Highland Railway's smaller goods locomotives, got their name.

The old time balls had given place to dances and by the 1920s these had to have 'jazz band assistance' to attract the crowds although there was piping for the reels. There was a strong rearguard action about the new fangled tunes – bystanders protested when jazz was played at the Strathspey Farmers' Club Show at Grantown where it annoyed the spectators and had 'a most upsetting effect on the livestock'. Traditionalists could take comfort from the practice at Balmoral where King George V and Queen Mary would have no modern dances whatever – only Scottish ones or decorous gavottes and waltzes being permitted. The gateway folk being accustomed to homespun entertainment formed their own concert parties such as 'The Optimistic Amateurs' led by Alex McLaughlan. 'Wee Eckie' helped his grandmother run the Temperance Hotel in Dalfaber Road and he was always immaculately turned out in a white jacket when he met guests off the trains. An accomplished actor and organist, he was latterly an insurance agent. Versatility was the name of the jobs' game in the gateway.

Most folk could turn their hands to several things. For example Peter Macpherson was a railway guard who specialised in measuring men up for suits which were made in the south. Not that he did this very often because his patrons had few outfits by present day standards – just ones for work (which for railwaymen meant uniform or dungarees), a set for special occasions and old clothes for home or garden. Most men had but the one good suit which, if they kept their figures, they had probably worn when they got married. To serve the ladies, Mrs McSween, whose husband was a carriage and wagon inspector, was the village dressmaker and competently tackled dresses for whole wedding retinues. A summer outfit and a winter one did most women and children were happy to get 'hand me downs'. Styles were often years out of date but who cared? Cloche hats and 'earphone' hairdos appeared long after these fashions were just memories to laugh over in photo albums elsewhere.

This adaptability and sense of enterprise was not just a prerogative of railway folk. For example, the Collies of Lower Tullochgrue, a family associated with Rothiemurchus for generations, not only farmed that holding but Willie Collie and his son Jim also worked the old water-powered saw mill at Inverdruie. Its big wheel was still capable of powering three saws; all the ingenious gearing and cogs were made from hardwoods as very little iron, a scarce item, had been used in its construction. The Collies also carted coal round the district from the railway's siding at Aviemore. In summer their farmhouse was let out and by means of such combined exertions, they were able to send two sons to university. Old Willie eventually became a county councillor of Inverness-shire.

There were occasional high points in the social round. The circuses were back and the country folk were always intrigued by the performing animals. In 1925 came 'Sir Robert Fossett's Greatest Show – Circus, Hippodrome, Rodeo and Wild West' complete with fifty horses, ponies and other 'educated animals'. The Royal Continental Circus brought Russian dancers and jugglers balancing a motor cycle on a pole with a lass astride it. Valenza, 'the Strongest Girl on Earth' fired off a huge cannon on her back. Short of going to Inverness which was a regular venue, circus lovers had to wait a decade until 'The Savage South African Jungle Circus' ('direct from America at enormous expense') arrived with its lions, elephant and horses. Its speciality was a troupe from the Gold Coast 'eating fire and dancing on broken glass to a native band'. Athletes were invited to confront 'The Great Zass', a human punch bag who was said to be the toughest sensation of the generation. After such a show, there were gateway characters who tried to emulate the circus acts – like Bob and Dunc, elderly twins of great stature from Rothiemurchus, who were seen trying to teach their old pony to race round a field with one of them balanced precariously on its back.

Into the farming and railway community came distinguished residents. The naturalist, Seton Gordon was one of these. Of Highland gentry by descent, he was a graduate of Oxford University; he and his wife

This aerial view taken in 1932 shows Aviemore from the north. St Andrew's Church is left centre and the station upper left. In the foreground are the Free Presbyterian Church (left) and Muirton farm (right) (AEROFILMS LTD)

purchased Auchantoul, a large villa north of Aviemore which by a strange coincidence is now owned by Scottish Natural Heritage. In 1925 his acclaimed book, 'The Cairngorm Hills of Scotland' was published and it was so well received that it even earned a poem in *Punch* magazine:

'Twixt Aviemore and Braes o' Mar,
There lies a land — and what a land!

Seton Gordon's writing captivated the imagination of his readers and brought the gateway districts to the attention of a much wider public. The great naturalist was a puzzle to local folk; he invariably wore the kilt and had a field glass with him when he explored moor and mountain. The rumour ran that he was a John MacNab character in the manner of the Buchan novel — a gentleman poacher. Nothing could have been further from the truth. He wrote regularly for the *Scotsman*, gave lectures and in 1927 broadcast on the Cairngorms. Unwittingly all this put a media spotlight on the area but it was seen as welcome publicity which was bound to attract active visitors interested in natural history. For her part.

Mrs Gordon sought to enhance the quality of life for women; she started a branch of the Scottish Women's Rural Institute, a movement founded on Canadian lines, and a Girl Guide company, both of which met in Aviemore. All too soon it seemed, Seton Gordon was publishing 'The Charm of Skye' and by 1931 the couple had forsaken the gateway for that island.

Seton Gordon had written about the Gaelic place-names of the Cairngorms and a renewed fascination with the language became evident. Regrettably it was fast disappearing from the strath. In 1932 a Gaelic concert with bagpipe music encouraged over a hundred to sign up to join An Comunn Gaidhealach with Sheriff Grant of Rothiemurchus in the forefront of the revival,. To their great credit, the Sheriff and his wife were staunchly Highland. Mrs Gertrude Margaret Grant, who was of Irish birth, learned Gaelic and was so well versed in Highland dancing that she taught it and he gave instruction in piping; they even engaged a Gaelic speaking girl from the Uists as a nanny for their children. Ceilidhs began to be held in the old library in Rothiemurchus, or at the laird's home Corrour, at which he delighted in playing the pipes. Acknowledged as a foremost authority on piping, the Sheriff became president of the Piobaireachd Society. In 1934 he piped himself on to the air in a concert broadcast from Grantown; the half hour programme was a response to a plea to the BBC for some Scottish music and ironic applause greeted the announcement that 'London had the say in its choice'. He was said never to be happier than when 'fear an taighe', or master of ceremonies, at a ceilidh with folk gathered round a log fire on an open hearth as they joined in the choruses and sat in rapt attention to listen to the stories. Soon there was a flourishing Gaelic class and a local girl, Mary MacDonald, was winning medals at the Mod for her sweet singing.

Football was a passion among the railwaymen and sporadically the gateway could muster a team under the banner of Aviemore to play on the Romach, a marshy piece of ground behind Muirton farm. In 1934, Seafield Park near Seafield Place was chosen as the new football stance. There was a succession of fixtures and trophies to be contested in local derbies; one with Grantown was so acrimonious that a replay was ordered and not for the first time the competence of the referee was called in question. Games were generally sporting even if hard but one against Boat of Garten became an affray when the Boat players, ignoring the visiting team, 'shouted, bawled, quarrelled and fought one another' to the point that police intervention was sought. Teams travelled by train to their matches with a hearty following of supporters making good use of their concession tickets on the railway.

There were other developments too in the gateway. From 1928, Kingussie and Newtonmore had electric street lighting but for many years Aviemore could not guarantee the sum required for such installations. There was consternation however when it was discovered that the Dell of Rothiemurchus was to get a supply. How was this possible? Willie Grant, the tenant farmer there, had a habit of getting his own way and why not? After all, the Grampian Electricity Company's pylons were to cross his fields and his wife ran the big farmhouse as a hotel. Aviemore farm, which continued in the ownership of the Aviemore Station Hotel Company, was unique in having a power line from the hotel's own generating plant to its dairy. A few houses in the village near the route of the hotel cable also got electricity – notably the Post Office and the doctor's villa. The Station Hotel Company, which now owned and managed three establishments for guests – the Aviemore Hotel, the Cairngorm Hotel and the old inn as Aviemore House, seemed almost in a monopoly position. Telephones were scarce, there being but one public phone in Aviemore's Post Office ('You may telephone from here') and only a handful of private ones throughout the district. So few were there that most of the numbers were

Aviemore F.C. were winners of the Dewar Cup in 1926, when shirts had laces and goalies wore 'bunnets'. The majority of team members were railwaymen but the whole community gave support. Dr A. C. Balfour is back row 4th left and Sgt. Bert Davidson is in Lovat Scouts uniform on the far right (A. LEDINGHAM / J. C. HAY COLLECTION)

either single digits or two at most. The Station Hotel, naturally, was Aviemore 1. There were no call boxes and urgent communications were by telegram brought by a lad cycling out from the Post Office.

The first council houses were completed in Aviemore in 1935 when six semi-detached bungalows were built along Seafield Place with three adjacent terrace houses. So scarce was housing that railway families actually took up residence in the waiting rooms on Aviemore station's island platform. In the inter-war years there were few new homes – either public or private. Of the latter, just a handful of properties and some hotel company housing on Dalfaber Road appeared. Railwaymen had to leave their company houses on retirement and only careful saving over many years could produce enough for a modest 'hoosie'; much accommodation could only be described as primitive. Some folk put up their own 'but and ben' as did the Rothiemurchus estate joiner, Charles Wickenden who came from England. Known as 'English Charlie's', the cottage still stands near the Loch an Eilein road and is now a pottery.

Other folk were squatters who were not entered on the valuation rolls and paid no rates. Typically their cottages were made of old railway sleepers and had galvanised iron roofs. Jim Tulloch, the trapper mannie at Avielochan, had one where he 'exercised a permanent proprietary right, limited only by absence of title'. In the inter-war years a hundred old sleepers bought for £10 was usually enough for such a dwelling; railwaymen could get them for half price and ideally the cottages were near the tracks where such sleepers could be dropped off from a ballast train. After a stone or concrete base had been laid, two men hammering in 9 inch (23cm) nails could put up the shell in a couple of days. The chimneys were built of brick or stone and some sleeper cottages were harled which neatly concealed their origins but the smell of creosote from the timber was less easy to hide.

A village council was formed in 1933 with post master Sam MacDonald as chairman. Its first project was to be a bowling green (finally realised in 1998); local clubs took stalls at a bazaar and produced £100 towards it. A new village hall was planned and the Martineau Bequest left for that purpose totalled over £1,700. On a more mundane level, a scavenging scheme was set up – not that there was much refuse by today's standards – recycling was the name of the game. People were frugal but very rarely mean. Edible scraps fed the hens, jars were returned to the shops for a refund of a penny or saved for jam making; paper 'pokes' were used for 'pieces', newspapers lined drawers, protected clean floors, wrapped eggs in transit and kindled fires. Only ashes, broken dishes and tins were thrown on to middens and every farm or cottage had one.

Aviemore was increasingly becoming a service centre. With a big wages bill to meet on the railway, banking had been done in the station Waiting Room with staff coming for a couple of hours once a week from Kingussie – by train of course. About 1928 the Bank of Scotland put up a small office, just a corrugated shed, near the station. This was used until 1935 when a sub-branch was opened in a modest building where the present bank now stands. It only did business in the morning being run by two clerks who came down on the Mail train from Kingussie and left about mid-day. Aviemore people got so used to morning banking that the office staff had little to do in afternoons when the bank first opened on a full-time basis in 1955.

As the railway owned extra ground, stances beside the Great North Road had also been let to shopkeepers. A group of galvanised iron and timber huts appeared and the gibe that the village was just a shanty town of 'tin shacks and chocolate machines' was heard from those who passed through it. In the 1930s first in line from the station was Sandy and Willie Campbell's; they made and sold footwear – the boots were tackety and the laces of leather. They were a kindly pair who through a mouthful of tacks would sorely deride the government of the day. Alongside was 'P. Grant, Chemist', which had formerly housed the bank; it opened in 1936 under pharmacist, Sam N. Mearns. Sammy, who came from Boat of Garten, was well read, an accomplished raconteur and a talented artist in watercolours. Many must be proud to own one of his paintings of local scenes. With his keen wit, few of the foibles of gateway folk or visitors went unobserved. Then came Betsy's. The premises were meant to be a draper's but stock was so minimal that 'One Shirt' became her 'by-name'. McCook's next door was a complete contrast; it was at first a tea room but was latterly transformed into a baker's cum grocer's. The brothers Frank and Pat McCook, ably assisted by Frank's wife Mina, had the business and surely no better name for such a firm could have been devised. It was filled with the aroma of newly baked 'softies', cakes and biscuits. There was also Richardson's which had replaced the Lawrence store where Grampian Court is now sited.

Up the road, genial Sam MacDonald combined a grocer's shop with the Post Office which was in a separate room. His shop had butter on marble slabs, sugar in big blue bags, loose biscuits weighed out by the pound and an impressive coffee grinding machine. Further along the Great North Road there was a rival whose owner was yet another MacDonald – Donald – none of whom appeared to be related. He was known as Speedie. This was said to be due to the lengthy time he took to emerge from the back shop. He had had an adventurous past in the gold

S. G. Macdonald's shop with its post office was a hub of Aviemore. Here the staff are (from left to right) postman Bert Davidson, Bella Hay, Lilian McIntosh, Sadie Gordon, Catherine Dempster, S G Macdonald, unknown, Duffy, unknown, Bobby Gault and postman Donald Fraser (J. S. MacDonald)

rush in the Yukon, had worked in California and South Africa and so he was the most travelled man in the village by far. On his return he opened a 'shoppie' in Tulloch and named his cottage 'Klondyke'. When Sam MacDonald began sending a van round and trespassed on Speedie's home patch, the latter replied in no uncertain terms by setting up a shop in Aviemore. There was a choice of butcher's – Charlie Stewart's beside the Aviemore burn (which some still call the butcher's burn) or Kennedy's in the station square. Once a week the fishwife, Elsie Callie went round the houses with a creel on her back.

Tough as the Depression years were, there were a few new shoots of growth in the gateway. In May 1933, the Scottish Youth Hostels' Association set up simple premises – just a contractor's timber hut – in a magnificent wooded setting to the south of Aviemore. It formed a link in a Cairngorm 'chain' of hostels for climbers and walkers; it proved so popular that it was enlarged the following year. Open from May to the end of September, its throughput of hostellers soon topped 3,000 and it was conveniently close to Mrs Lawrence's Pot Luck Tea Rooms which became a favourite rendezvous. By 1937 it was reported that hikers in droves were visiting the north and 'pedal cycling' had 'enormously increased' with at least four per cent being foreigners.

The hostels encouraged new types of visitor – folk of all ages with little means but a great liking for the outdoors who came for back packing, mountaineering and hill walking. With so many out of work in shipyards, engineering shops and offices, some put their enforced leisure to good use enjoying wild country, the open air and exercise as they had never done before. Aviemore became the recognised 'base camp' for the western Cairngorms. There was plenty to tempt them to the gateway:

> There is no district where there are so many paths, old roads, hill tracks and rights of way in the Highlands.

But the fact that so much land was 'a pleasure ground for a few' was under attack again and there were complaints that lack of access to the countryside was stifling popular tourism. By the mid-1920s, it was estimated that one-third of Scotland had been sold to new proprietors since the First World War and a state agency, the Forestry Commission, was one of these. In 1923 it bought Glenmore, including Loch Morlich and Cairn Gorm, from the executors of the Duke of Richmond and Gordon. Its first task was to set about replanting the forests decimated in the war years. Forestry was seen as a long-term solution to employment and other problems in the Highland economy. It was not however to be on Norwegian lines with individual crofters and hill farmers acting as foresters and managing their own woodlands as a sustainable resource providing alternative income. More is the pity. In 1929 the duke's trustees also disposed of Pityoulish with Kincardine, and Kinrara to new owners. Lieutenant-Colonel Carlyle MacGregor Dunbar, a cavalry officer, became associated with Kincardine and Sir Herbert Kinnaird Ogilvy of Inverquharity Bt, and an advocate, with Pityoulish. The Dunbar family had been lessees of the latter property for several decades. Kinrara went to Sir Theodore Ernest Warren Brinckman of the Life Guards, London.

There had been increasing bitterness over access to Glenmore. The shooting tenants for many years had been the Dennistouns who had originated in the East End of Glasgow where they had a mansion named Golfhill and as landowners they gave their name to a district of the city. James Dennistoun, the founding father had made his fortune in banking. One August morning in Glenmore, Captain Dennistoun, armed with his field glass, had counted no fewer than 143 walkers making the ascent of Cairn Gorm before a solitary individual came to ask his permission to go through the deer forest. His reply was succinct, 'One extra will make no difference – my stalking has been ruined for the day'. By the 1920s the estate complained bitterly about damage done to the roads by motoring parties. Accordingly, gates were padlocked and vehicular traffic (other than estate vehicles) was prohibited. An incensed motorist broke off the locks. Shortly, the tenant lost patience and gave up Glenmore. (In 1924 the Countess of Carnarvon, the wife of Lieut.-Colonel Ian Onslow Dennistoun of the Grenadier Guards, bought Alvie estate for him.)

Meantime, Abernethy Parish Council protested that the Sluggan Pass linking Kincardine and Glenmore was a right of way connecting two areas of the parish. The Forestry Commission has kept it closed to vehicles. Similar problems arose in Glen Tromie and in Glen Feshie where 'a strong, intelligent man' was paid to stand by a gate to turn back 'tired and jaded city dwellers' who drove up in their cars. Locked gates and notices were indications of the arguments over motor cars and perceived rights of way; 'Private – No Vehicular Access', or worse 'Dangerous for Motor Cars', were signs that appeared in order to warn off the strays.

The levels of Highland depopulation continued to cause alarm although numbers rose a little in the gateway parishes in the 1920s. The government was urged to buy out the rentals of the deer forests in the Highlands and islands which were reckoned to employ 880 on a permanent basis and a further 400 temporarily in the course of a year. The press reported that resistance to sporting interests was clearly growing and in some instances it was scarcely surprising:

> They had shut up inns, blocked rights of way, forbidden employees to give shelter to travellers and left nothing undone that could be legally done to exclude and frighten the public.

Consequently, Scots who could afford it were said to be going in increasing numbers to the Alps where they found a countryside open to them. For the rest, many were as yet unaware of the possibilities on their own doorsteps and of the hindrances that might be placed in their way because of the unreformed nature of land ownership. Even A. E. Robertson, the first Munroist, noted:

> A strange tightening on the part of landowners and shooting tenants against what they thought were unwarranted intrusions by the public . . . they were restricting rights of way across their land.

Nevertheless, the Cairngorm gateway suffered fewer restrictions of access for most of the year than did other Highland districts. The inquiry into deer forests had raised the question of their continued use for sporting or for recreative purposes. 'Recreative purposes' however posed a problem when there was frequent disturbance during the stalking months; usually no objection had been taken at other times of year when those climbers and walkers who troubled to ask were given every facility. Under Scots law, owners had no practical means of excluding strangers 'owing to the time and expense of taking out an interdict against every separate person', and in any case were they causing actual harm? A lessee of the Rothiemurchus deer forest even suggested having permits to admit mountaineers and skiers much in the manner in which the estate issued tickets to fishermen.

As long ago as 1924 a National Park was urged for the Cairngorms. The first National Park was established in the United States in 1872; now these are to be found in 100 countries around the world. (Only in 1998 was Loch Lomond and the Trossachs earmarked as the first National Park in Scotland and the Cairngorms are to follow.) 'Hamish Ban' in the *Weekly Scotsman* deplored the exclusive landowners who closed off hills, glens, forests and streams in order to reserve them for a few weeks for privileged English or Americans. He looked for a solution:

> What we want now is a man like Lord Leverhulme to purchase the whole of the Cairngorms and present it to the nation for health, open air and instruction. Such a gift would bestow on Scotland a possession and heritage of outstanding and incalculable value for all time.

Slowly the idea of a National Park began to move up the political agenda. There were moves too for a National Trust for Scotland in which Sir Iain Colquhoun of Luss took a lead. He imagined an area of 100,000 acres (40,000 ha) located in 'the wildest and most typically Scottish section of the Grampian Mountains'. The aim should be to preserve a portion of the Highlands in its primitive state as an exemplar of its flora and fauna. Such action was seen as urgent as road construction and hydro schemes were making obvious incursions into wilderness.

Soon the National Park idea focused on the Cairngorms. Sir John Stirling-Maxwell, the owner of Ossian estate on the Moor of Rannoch, of Pollok estate in Glasgow and a Scottish representative on the Forestry Commission, was equally eager 'to secure a tract of land where nature will remain forever undisturbed and which every citizen will have the right to visit' – aims which he admitted might be difficult to reconcile. The object should not be to attract crowds or to make access too easy. Proposals for motor roads, funicular railways, camp sites, winter sports, hotels at high levels and such like, which he believed would threaten to make the mountain park into 'a tea garden', should be refused. Such ventures could only exist outside the park; otherwise how would 'solitude and primitive mystery' be preserved? At all costs 'the tragedy of Snowdon' should be prevented in the Cairngorms. His vision for the handling of a National Park was low-keyed, with any accommodation or development kept simple and small in scale – a design approach which some gateway tourist projects would have done well to follow. Nevertheless, Sheriff Grant of Rothiemurchus was worried, especially as his estate now marched with state-owned Forestry Commission land in Glenmore. Sir John sought to reassure him – there would be 'no merry-go-rounds or bathing pools' in Rothiemurchus forest and a National Park would only acquire areas by agreement.

In 1929 a Labour government led by Ramsay Macdonald came to power and some at least of the aristocracy feared the appropriation of their property and 'Red Revolution'. By 1930 the Addison Committee had been appointed to consider the matter and the lairds took action. Grant of Rothiemurchus, with his legal background, summoned Cairngorms landowners to meetings in Grantown. They were concerned that land would have to be purchased if a National Park 'more or less on the American model' was established. Other interested parties jumped in on the act – notably Aberdeen Town Council and those county councils which thoroughly approved of the idea. Soon there were angry scenes. It was rumoured that the Duke of Richmond and Gordon, still a major Cairngorm landowner, was prepared to part with upper Glen Avon to form a portion of a National Park. The duke was furious – he had not even been consulted. In a telegram to Grant of Rothiemurchus ('Emphatically deny that I approve of National Park scheme . . .') followed by irate letters ('no excuse be given for pushing through a hair brained (sic) scheme riding rough shod over all sporting rights'), he made his displeasure very clear. He was determined to expose 'the mischievous liar' who had the temerity to put the story about. At the races at Goodwood and in London's Carlton Club, a refuge for Tory grandees, the rumours flew. The King's Private Secretary and the Keeper of the Privy Purse became embroiled in the affair. If Lochnagar was ever part of a National Park it would 'make Balmoral impossible for the King'. After all, he too was a landowner in the wider Cairngorms. The proprietors put up a united front – they were totally opposed to the concept, even if Rothiemurchus was widely recognised as a place 'where nature reserves were most required'.

Seton Gordon was drawn into the discussions for there was 'no better authority on National Parks'. He identified two key issues; firstly, unlike Canada or the United States, Scotland had no virgin land and was a small country. Secondly, if a National Park was to be established any proposals would have to be subject to the owner's consent which he believed was paramount. Avoiding controversy, the pattern of land owning was not considered; his was very much a 'status quo' approach which did not envisage extensive public or state ownership of land at all.

Soon questions were asked in Parliament about National Parks for Scotland and it became known that the Forestry Commission was prepared to co-operate over the project. In 1930 a National Trust committee pledged support for a recreational park and nature reserve in the Cairngorms on any land that was not required for planting. The visitor pressures were increasing every season – between August and October that year over 1,000 people had passed Derry Lodge and over 200 cars had been counted at its entrance. A strong positive interest in a National Park came from the Prime Minister, Ramsay Macdonald. Taking lodgings in Rothiemurchus, he had walked and climbed in the Cairngorms finding there 'a source of spiritual and physical well being' in what he described as 'a national domain'. The manoeuvrings were all in vain. In 1933 came the announcement that a Cairngorms National Park was 'not practicable meantime' – the Depression and resulting economic crisis had put paid to it. The National Park would have incurred running

In the 1930s people took to the outdoors and to the Cairngorms in growing numbers. Here hill walkers use cycles to facilitate access to Glen Einich. They are passing the first bothy which was built for stalkers and shooting parties (A. E. GLEN)

costs estimated at just £5,000 a year By 1935 however substantial falls had occurred in sporting rentals and land in the Highlands was 'almost unsaleable' but the opportunity was still not grasped. The course of the gateway's growth and development might have been very different had the National Park become a reality at that stage.

The fame of the Cairngorm gateway for its natural history brought contingents of scientists to it from time to time. The British Mycological Society had a fungi foray in September 1927 when fifty members investigated a great variety of species, many of them rare. In 1934 came members of the British Association for the Advancement of Science who were conveyed by special train from Aberdeen. The station master at Aviemore said he had never seen so many intellectuals on any platform at one time and he was relieved when his staff, having safely rounded them up, escorted them to their carriages again. Occasionally, packed trains of excursionists drew in – the record was set by one with over 1,000 passengers.

Yet the gateway was seen to be losing out in attracting tourists. A brochure to advertise the district as 'a health and holiday resort' was planned and the support of the LMS and LNER railway companies was sought. Although there was a Scottish Travel Association, Scotland was not publicised as a whole or on its own account which was a serious deficiency when a glance at any national newspaper or periodical showed what other countries were doing. Lectures were given in Glasgow to encourage holiday-making in the Highlands and there was no lack of ideas about what to add to the amenities which villages had on offer. One suggestion for Aviemore was 'a suitable swimming pool and a model yacht pond with a sand bing alongside for infants' play'.

Even if appropriate, projects were starved of investment and had as always to rely on voluntary effort. The village did have a putting green where there was a vacant patch of ground beside the Post Office. (It was originally used for open-air badminton until the post-master's wife had the bright idea of introducing putting and hiring our equipment.) There were complaints that the season was all too short; occasionally the Station Hotel opened at Easter as a favour to the Scottish Ski Club and laid on a programme of 'après ski' activities for its members. Sheriff Grant was very concerned about the use of false pretences to tempt people to come in wintertime because he had done enough hind stalking in February to know that one had to be very fit and well clad to enjoy winter weather on the hills. For their part, summer visitors continued to tolerate the lack of facilities – the houses with outside larders and loos and no baths – because the folk were so welcoming and the scenery was so superb:

> I think it must be the Cairngorms that do it. They are everything by
> turns . . . it's an elusive quality, nearly liquid in strong sunlight,
> mysterious and awful under black clouds, withdrawn and half hidden
> by swirling mists . . .

In 1934 publicity came from an unexpected quarter and put the
Highlands in the headlines. A Loch Ness monster 'photograph' was taken
by a surgeon who had been on holiday in the Inverness area and it was
soon being sold as a postcard by a local chemist. The picture excited great
attention and interest in Inverness-shire received a big boost. Fifty years
later it was rumoured that the picture was just a hoax – a clockwork toy
may have been placed in a bath to simulate Nessie – but by then the
monster's repercussions on tourism had been immense.

Although the visitors were largely unaware of the presence of the lairds
and their families in the gateway – only Highland Games or important
events bringing them into public view – local folk were well acquainted
with them and their eccentricities. The coming of age of Iain Grant, the
son of the Laird of Rothiemurchus, in 1936 was such an affair. There
were rejoicings on the estate where the young man was presented with
numerous sporting accoutrements from a dirk and belt to stalking boots
by the tenants and workers. A bonfire on Ord Ban and a dance in the
library at Inverdruie made it a night to remember. High hopes were
expressed for Iain as his father, the Sheriff, was held in such esteem 'by the
tenantry and by the county' but Iain Grant never achieved such
popularity.

The gateway folk were soon bemused by the Abdication. They might
have heard of divorce but few could have named anyone whom they
knew as having been ensnared in such an episode. Edward VIII, when
Prince of Wales, had walked through the Lairig Ghru under the guidance
of Seton Gordon and had been met by the Laird of Rothiemurchus. The
Prince played the bagpipes and seemed to have a liking for things
Highland. His going meant that he never set foot in Scotland again. The
following year the Coronation of King George VI and Queen Elizabeth
was marked by parades of ex-servicemen, Girl Guides and school children
in fancy dress. There were sports, souvenirs for everyone, 'a very vivid
fireworks display' and another bonfire on Ord Ban.

Against a background of international tension, aeroplanes were being
seen more frequently over the strath. In 1933 the ten seater air liner
named Inverness had called at Kingussie aerodrome at Pitmain – it was
just a field – and offered flights to local people. They marvelled at the
luxurious monoplane with its warm and comfortable cabin in which it

was possible to carry on a conversation while enjoying unrestricted views of the valleys and mountains. It was piloted by Captain Edmund Edward Fresson, an aviator who had been flying in China. He came north from Cheshire to give joy rides and solo air displays in places as far apart as Dumfries and Kirkwall. Earlier he had visited Grantown with a three seater biplane. These sorties allowed him to survey the possibilities for air routes and Inverness was selected as a base. He became managing director of Highland Airways which first opened a service from Inverness to Wick and Kirkwall. The Inverness transport company of Macrae & Dick, who were innovators in new forms of travel, was associated with the venture. A remarkable pioneer, Captain Fresson was the founder of Scotland's air ambulances and launched the first official air mail service in Britain at normal postage rates. In 1935 from a height of 6,000 feet (1,830m) he made an aerial survey of the Cairngorms.

Newsreels and press photos of the bombing horrors of the Spanish civil war and the Italian atrocities in Abyssinia struck new terror and proved that civilians at a distance could now be in the front line in wars. Concerned folk urged that aerial warfare should be proscribed. The disquieting news from Germany aroused the sympathy of Free Church and other ministers for their persecuted brethren there. So in April 1938 Sheriff Grant of Rothiemurchus held a meeting on air raid precautions. Aviemore was reported to be dragging its feet over ARP, notwithstanding the postponement of a big dance and ceilidh to allow training to take place. Enquiries came from a boarding school in Canterbury about moving for safety to the Aviemore Hotel but with the Munich agreement, the infamous 'piece of paper', the crisis with Nazi Germany passed and it was business as usual. Early the following year an Air Raid Defence League was formed and ARP wardens were recruited. Fire and ambulance services were reviewed – not before time as apart from hydrants and hoses in the station the nearest appliances were at Grantown and Kingussie. The provision of gas masks was discussed and anxious questions asked about ARP arrangements for livestock; would there be masks for them too? And should slit trenches be dug in the gardens and air raid shelters put up there?

Although the gateway was not considered a strategic area, defence work had belatedly become a priority. Aerodromes were under construction at Kinloss and at Covesea near Lossiemouth; tradesmen went from the strath to help build them. These sites were to play a key role in the coming conflict. A travelling recruiting bureau for the Cameron Highlanders was busy – with a strength of 1,230 men, it hoped to fill 30 places but got well over that number from Aviemore and Kincraig alone.

It was stated that there would be no 'National Service', or conscription, unless the country went to war. In spite of the 'piece of paper' brought back from Munich, tensions were mounting relentlessly in Europe.

The outbreak of the Second World War on 3 September 1939 numbed the communities of the Cairngorm gateway. The grim news was announced from the pulpits and in places wireless sets were brought into churches. Although it was the Sabbath and some folk were Free Presbyterians they too listened to Prime Minister Chamberlain's speech. Shortly without warning, the sinking of the Clyde's Donaldson liner *Athenia* on the Canada run, the first maritime casualty, spelt out the coming conflict's shocking reality. When the Monday newspapers were collected at the stations they were full of war preparations, warnings and advice.

Within 48 hours of war being declared, the local Lovat Scouts were mustering at Aviemore station. As many men as possible had to bring a pony. The contingent was under the command of Lieutenant Iain Grant of Rothiemurchus, the laird's son. It was a glorious autumn day but it might as well have been heavily overcast, so disconsolate were the onlookers. There was great difficulty in squeezing the garrons into cattle trucks bound for Beauly where the troops were to gather. Subsequently in trying to stop a stampede of these ponies Iain Grant was seriously injured.

Up at Avielochan, folk worried about cottages and galvanised iron roofs painted red. Would a RED roof – no matter how small – not be the first thing that the Jerries would spot from the air should they ever fly over the strath? Messages for grey or green paint were sent by McCormack's bus to the ironmongers in Grantown. This was not as easy as you might think because emergency running was in force – although a wit said that was no different from usual.

'Evacuees', the word soon became well known in the gateway: from July 1939 the government had a scheme in place to move children from vulnerable towns and cities to the countryside. There was plenty to be arranged – transport, meals, accommodation, clothing, schooling and much more for the youngsters. Attempts by the Luftwaffe to bomb the Forth Bridge and Rosyth Naval Dockyard on 10 September gave the whole matter greater urgency; the exodus began in earnest on 30 September. Reception committees had been formed in rural areas but Aviemore's co-ordinating officer fell ill at the last minute – maybe the prospect was too much for him – and substitutes had to be found. Meanwhile, billeting officers had been scouring the countryside for weeks before the expected influx made its descent. It seemed that any property could be considered 'fair game' – the McSweens had a new little bungalow, 'The Glen', under construction in Aviemore and were shocked when it was assessed in its empty state as capable of holding ten! To forestall any takeover, the family organised a hasty removal from Railway Terrace before the plaster had dried on the walls.

After days of expectancy word eventually came down the line that children would be journeying from Edinburgh with both mothers and teachers. This news filled local households with trepidation – mothers had a name for being even more difficult and fussy than their offspring. At the summons, Aviemore and Rothiemurchus folk got busy in the Comrades' Memorial Hall, which was to act as the reception centre, preparing food. The few who had cars loaned them, fitted of course with ARP headlamp shields to reduce the power of their lights, to take the youngsters to outlying places. The afternoon wore on and no trains with evacuees appeared. It became evening, darkness fell and still the train had not arrived. After 11.30 pm word filtered through from Kingussie that 250 children plus helpers had been taken off the train there. The weary

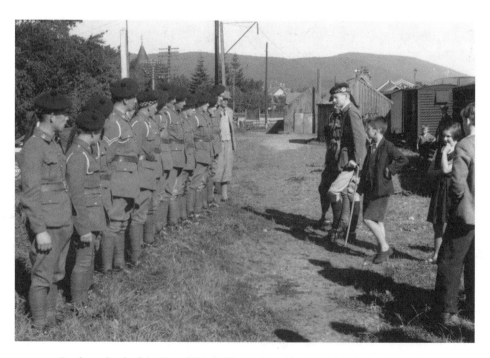

On the outbreak of the Second World War in September 1939, the Lovat Scouts, the local Territorials, were mustered in the goods yard at Aviemore station under the command of Lieutenant Ian Grant of Rothiemurchus (A. E. GLEN)

This shop in Boat of Garten was maintaining essential rural services at a time when these were in decline; petrol stations were shutting and Post Offices were threatened with closure (ANN GLEN)

The Strathspey Railway, which was a volunteer initiative, re-opened part of the original Highland mainline between Aviemore and Boat of Garten in 1978. Here LMS Class 5 No 5025 awaits the signal at Boat of Garten (JOHN PETER)

Friendly to the visitor and to the environment, Boat of Garten Golf Club dates from 1893 and is one of the four challenging courses which feature in the annual Speyside Classic (ANN GLEN)

A water sports centre, set up at Loch Insh by the Freshwaters in the 1960s, continues to attract enthusiasts for canoeing and sailing (JOHN PETER)

The track through the Pass of Ryvoan is one of the many historic routes to be explored on foot or cycle in the Cairngorm Gateway (JOHN PETER)

The alpine nursery at Inshriach was established by Jack Drake in the post-war years on part of his family's estate; it has since become well known to gardening enthusiasts throughout Britain (ANN GLEN)

In Glenmore National Forest Park, non-native species of conifer have been removed, as here on the Kincardine Hills, with the purpose of encouraging the growth of a natural woodland, predominately of Scots pine (ANN GLEN)

Once a place of seclusion, Loch Morlich's storm beach appeals to water sports enthusiasts and visitors. Extra areas of beach have been created to increase capacity but have raised conservation issues (JOHN PETER)

*The lower station for the CairnGorm Mountain Railway, as the funicular system
is now designated, makes use of granite and its design attempts to harmonise
with the mountain environment* (JOHN PETER)

*The CairnGorm Mountain Railway has a two-metre gauge track and is electrically
powered. The two cars can be adapted to carry more passengers in the ski-ing
months than in the summer* (JOHN PETER)

The environment and land use of the Cairngorm Gateway is enhanced by its interpretation. Here Countryside Ranger Ali Trinder from Rothiemurchus Estate talks to a party of students at Loch an Eilein (ANN GLEN)

The Royal Society for the Protection of Birds has become a major landowner in the Cairngorm Gateway and an influential conservation interest. This visitor centre and hide is on its reserve at Loch Garten (ANN GLEN)

The Strathspey Railway's opening to Broomhill in 2002 gave it 10 miles of running line and renewed hopes of reaching Grantown-on-Spey. Here No 9, an Austerity saddle tank engine, leaves Broomhill station (ANN GLEN)

The spread of housing over farm land and into woods (as here at Nethybridge), is causing tensions in the Cairngorm Gateway. Most dwellings will be second homes and a challenge for the National Park authority (ANN GLEN)

Loch Avon, set in a glaciated valley, is one of the highlights of the Cairngorms. This view from Stac an Faraidh shows the Shelterstone Crag, Loch Etchachan and the slopes of Ben Macdui (far right) (ANN GLEN)

A large investment in path construction and repair is projected for the Cairngorm Mountains; such work was in progress on Cairn Gorm in 1997 (JOHN PETER)

Aviemorians were left with gallons of boiling water for dozens of teapots and mountains of bread and butter. There was nothing to be done but share out the latter and take it home. There was a surfeit of sandwiches on local menus for days. Eventually evacuees did appear and the kind village 'wifies' were in tears, overcome at the sight of so many 'poor wee craturs' with their labels and gas masks.

Some youngsters of course came by choice – at least by parental choice. One of these was John Goodwin, formerly chairman of Highland Distilleries. Although Glasgow born, he had three maiden aunts who lived at Lynwilg just south of Aviemore. They were the Misses Gracie (although folk overlooking the niceties of grammar knew them as the 'Miss Gracies'). They were daughters of a former chairman of the Fairfield Shipbuilding and Engineering Company on the Clyde and were obviously well to do; they had a car and servants including their old nannie, a delightful lady, Josephine Muckles. John and his sister were despatched to Lynwilg and put in their care. John was old enough to attend Rothiemurchus school to which he tricycled – yes, the old A9 was so quiet that this was possible. He was forced to wear a leather 'Biggles' type of helmet to keep his ears warm which he thoroughly detested. Once out of sight of the windows of Lynwilg House, he took it off but had the savvy to put it on again on the way back from school before Miss Muckles caught sight of him. Sandwiches were supplied for his lunch but invariably the filling was cheese which he loathed but was too shy to say. So he would stop by the old Spey bridge, pick out the cheese and throw it into the river. Hardly surprisingly his time with the Gracies was brief as both they and nannie found little boys rather trying. At the other end of the gateway's social scale, the Watson children were billeted with their auntie, Mrs Dean beside the Shieling. Bob Dean was an engine driver and had a sleeper house without a bath or any other frills. The Watsons enjoyed much more freedom than John; they guzzled syrupy pieces and got grubby and tired helping Adam McDougal, who was the Shieling farmer, with the hens, the cows and the harvests.

Many evacuees came with inadequate clothing; some had little enough any way and there were wee lassies who had only cotton frocks and gym shoes. Admittedly the amount of luggage allowed to them was exceedingly small. Hurried calls went out for shoes, warm clothing and prams. Within a month of war being declared, some 175,000 persons in Scotland were 'transferred' in 'Operation Pied Piper' as the evacuee movement was code named. An unforeseen problem was the higher cost of keeping children in the countryside – their appetites increased enormously in the fresh air and a 'jeelie piece' was not enough to stave off hunger. Parents were expected to pay only 9s a week (45p) for the support of each child. Tight as cash often was for gateway families, most dipped into their own pockets to see that the youngsters were properly fed. The evacuee mums from the city, far from picture houses and dance halls, suffered boredom and there was a sense of relief when they soon returned home.

When Winston Churchill came back to prominence as First Lord of the Admiralty, he was seen in Aviemore again – this time with whisky glass in hand viewing the scene quizzically from a first-class compartment when en route to visit the fleet in the north. Soon the battle of the Atlantic was at its height with swarms of U-boats threatening the shipping lanes and imported supplies. The greatest upheavals which the folk of the Cairngorm gateway had ever experienced were about to commence as they became absorbed in an all out war effort and the district became part of a vast training ground for combat.

EXCURSION

Glen Einich

This great ice-scooped valley lies in part of the Cairngorms National Nature Reserve. It can be reached by walkers and cyclists from either Tullochgrue (NH915087) or from the car park at Loch an Eilein. The distance from the latter to the mouth of Loch Einich is 7 miles (11km) and should not be underestimated. It involves fording the Beanaidh near the site where the first bothy once stood. Allowing for the return journey by the same route, this it is a lengthy excursion into wild and often stormy terrain. The western massif of the Cairngorms frequently attracts tempestuous weather.

For further information and arrangements to be observed when stalking is in progress, contact the Rothiemurchus Visitor Centre at Inverdruie on 01479 812345.

CHAPTER 6

On a War Footing

1939 – 1945

In contrast to the Depression years when agriculture was doing poorly and much land went out of cultivation, the farmers in the strath were bracing themselves for unprecedented activity – an extra 1.5 million acres (787,000 ha) were to go under the plough in Britain. Local Agricultural Executive Committees, first constituted in 1917 during the First World War, were soon up and running again to target the production of home grown food by co-ordinating the output of Scotland's 70,000 holdings. This was intended to make the nation as self sufficient as possible but it also swiftly reversed the run down in farm economies that had blighted the lives of country folk in the 1930s. For the hill farmer, it was not easy to make a living out of a flock of a hundred sheep or so grazing on the moor in summer and the fields in winter. Two or three cattle beasts were kept for milk. When opportunity offered butter and soft cheese were made. The indifferent soil gave only slim crops – chancy weather and the short growing season as always saw to that. Farmers relied upon oats, hay, tatties (potatoes) and neeps (turnips), with a handful of garden crops and fruit bushes as a bonus. The oats, or corn as it was generally known, was still being carted to local mills such as Mullingarroch in Kincardine to be ground into meal. Some hens scratching in the farm yard were seasonal layers. Gradually farm subsidies, paid from general taxation, transformed the situation giving assured incomes to farmers and low prices to consumers.

All food supplies had to be shared out fairly. The first stage saw enumerators, who in normal circumstances would have been carrying out a census in 1941, giving out identity cards. On that basis ration cards were issued in September 1939 and these soon covered tea, sugar, flour, meat, bacon and butter – all items which Britain imported in quantity in peacetime. People had to register for groceries with chosen shops and had also to sign up for the supply of coal and coke which simply reinforced the gateway folk's reliance on sticks and peat. The 'Dig for Victory' campaign encouraged everyone with a garden to grow their own vegetables. Even eggs were precious as feed for poultry was limited and most of the latter had finished up in the pot. From farm to farm, the countryside was scoured for fertile eggs to put under broody hens but too often the reply was, 'Ah've naethin' but a wheen auld roosters an' nae eggies at a".

Many regular visitors had taken their departure but refugees made their appearance, notably Sammy Nathan and his family. They were in fear of persecution should there be an invasion. Fast talking Sammy developed a drapery business humping bulging suitcases round the district on an old motor cycle with a side car. Inevitably he was dubbed Sammy the Jew, not from any discriminatory standpoint at all, but simply to differentiate him from other Sams in the gateway. The Nathans joined enthusiastically in the local war effort with Sammy active in the first aid team and his wife organising fund raising entertainments with the

The railway was again called upon to make heroic efforts in the
Second World War. Here 'the engines that won the war', LMS Class 5s,
double heading long trains, await the 'right away' at Aviemore south (A. E. GLEN)

children. Elderly visitors from pre-war years also sought sanctuary in the gateway. Some were distinguished and many were characters – like 'auld Crowe', a patriarchal figure, who was said to have been a collaborator with Marconi and had named his son after the discoverer of radio. He lived on the royalties of the innovation. Or Colin the Kiltie – Captain Colin Campbell of Snizort – who wore a tattered kilt and Glengarry bonnet and sped almost daily down the Great North Road in a pair of disreputable gym shoes. Gateway folk were generally accepting; they had to be as so many who were native to the place had their own peculiarities, probably enhanced by varying degrees of isolation from modern conventions. Meanwhile, official advertisements challenged the regular pre-war visitors – 'Is Your Journey Really Necessary?' – and the few folk who could take a break were urged to 'Holiday on the Land' and give assistance with the harvesting of crops.

Aviemore's ARP wardens operated from a wood shed in an odoriferous location between the byre and the stable at the back of the old inn. There they mustered, trained and sometimes held their noses until the 'all clear' would sound. A siren was mounted on the building but it was usually impatient whistles that summoned the squad. Air raid shelters were almost unknown in the gateway as it was a non-strategic area but there were air raid warnings when the siren would wail – mostly at night – and nervous folk going home from a picture show or whist drive would leap off their bikes and make for the nearest ditch. No one was willing to take on the responsibility for fire fighting around Aviemore; the buildings such as the hotels were reckoned to be too big, the railway junction was seen as potentially a high risk area and so much valuable property was widely scattered. When Clydebank was blitzed, the terrible glare of the fires over 150 miles (240km) away was seen from the hills above Grantown.

The ARP training sessions were on Wednesday afternoons – the official shopkeepers' half day. The wardens measured folk for gas masks, took part in first aid competitions and practised casualty evacuation. This involved using an imposing vehicle, an ARP ambulance assigned to the group and garaged at the Aviemore Hotel. There were heated arguments about who should drive this prestigious machine – those who considered that they were better drivers practically coming to blows over the honour. Perhaps to even matters up there was but one size of overalls for all the wardens – big fellows, like Pat McCook, the baker, were bursting out of them while wee Sammy Nathan was lost in his.

The ARP had to ensure total darkness in all dwellings after sun down. Joiners quickly fabricated frames covered with sombre blind cloth to jam into window spaces but these made rooms suffocatingly hot in summer. A chink of light would produce a visit from a warden and a reprimand. Yet a solitary light shone from the heights of Tulloch all through the war. (This was taken as a sign of Tulloch folk's attitude to authority; had they not harboured MacGregor outlaws in the cattle thieving days of old?) The very few cars about the gateway – most had been laid up – had dimmed side lights and head lamps fitted with 'slit masks'. When folk saw how clearly moonlight lit up the valley they were apprehensive. Street lighting was not used – not that Aviemore had any out with the station which as a rule was lit by its own acetylene gas plant. Steam locomotives were supposed to have their cabs so well covered with a heavy sheet that no glow from a fire door showed. This was too much to hope as foot plates became torrid and enginemen simply had to get some cool fresh air.

The railway folk realised just how much the junction mattered. Over many weeks, huge consignments of coal for steam loco use were built into a giant wall along one side of the engine shed right up to roof level. Both men and women turned out to construct this coal bank. So vast was this emergency supply that it projected beyond the ends of the shed where it was painted white to try to prevent staff colliding with it in the blackout. The purpose was to make the depot self supporting for months in the event of lines to the south being severed, thus cutting off trains coming from the coal fields of the Central Lowlands.

By May 1940 both Aviemore and Boat of Garten had Home Guard companies consisting of 20 to 30 men. With the German breakthrough on the Western Front, the defence of the British Isles became paramount. Those who were not liable for military service on account of age or infirmity had become L.D.V.s – Local Defence Volunteers with an upper age of 65. They were a motley collection in civvy clothes who wore an arm band and carried revolvers or shot guns – which ever was available. 'L.D.V.' was said to mean 'Look, Dook and Vanish'! Those that volunteered in the gateway were no strangers to weaponry; gamekeepers and stalkers made first-class recruits for the Home Guard. Many were army veterans, such as Major John Raffles Flint Drake of Inshriach, who was the officer in command of the local company, and incidentally a relation of Raffles of the famous hotel in Singapore. There was a rush of recruits for the guarding and watch keeping duties which were to be performed. Funds had to be raised for uniforms; a dance produced over £150 and giving precedence to Highland loyalties, the first purchases were Balmoral bonnets. The Drakes were typical of the well-to-do families who had made money in industry or commerce and could thus realise aspirations to be Highland landowners. In the inter-war years they leased Revack Lodge and its shootings from the Seafield Estates and clearly became enthralled by the Cairngorms. Owners of Inshriach since 1937, they too had become refugees as their London home in Knightsbridge had been blitzed.

The womenfolk were again playing their part. Throughout the war years, the Red Cross branch made up hundreds of sewn items, thousands of woollen comforts and hospital supplies, plus consignments of sphagnum moss for field dressings. The old kirk in Rothiemurchus was used as a store for blankets, sheets, towels and much else. Stacks of books and magazines were gathered. Work parties toiled to make up parcels for the Jocks – these again contained strange mixtures of cake, cigarettes, chocolate, soap, handkerchiefs and socks. Lassies liked to put a message in the parcels in the hope that it might produce a letter and lead to romance. Before long ladies were taking the place of 'gents' at the fund raising whist drives and demonstrations of wartime cookery taught housewives how to make 'economical egg dishes', 'sugarless date jam' and hearty main courses using potatoes.

The year 1940 was a grim one in Aviemore. On 16 March there had been the tragic loss of an engine crew and the locomotive *Loch Ericht* just north of the village. The engine had been piloting a freight train up the bank to Slochd, as was the usual practice with a heavy load. Ahead the rear part of an Inverness bound goods train laden with coal broke away on the climb and wagons began running back through Carrbridge towards Aviemore with station staff helpless to stop them. The vehicles hurtled down the hill for miles and crashed with great force into the oncoming train. The driver and fireman perished. The guard in the brake van of the runaway wagons had managed to jump clear before these gathered momentum. The brick arch of the wrecked locomotive was set up as a memorial by the lineside which was strewn with coal debris for years. The railway community was devastated by the accident.

Early in June came news from France of the fall of St Valery-en-Caux. This was another calamitous blow to gateway folk. The 51st Highland Division, as part of the British Expeditionary Force, were involved in fighting a rearguard action and had been compelled to retreat to the French coast. Thousands of exhausted troops were surrounded and captured when General Fortune surrendered there. Men of the Camerons, Argylls and others had to face five years in prisoner of war camps in Germany. Among them were Aviemore men from the Macdonald and Lobban families. The lads became the focus of village efforts to send letters (via Lisbon and Marseilles) and Red Cross parcels. A P.O.W. fund was set up. From the prisoners came repeated requests for bag pipes not just to maintain their musical skills but also to keep up their morale and sound a note of defiance. It was in the prison camps that the pipe tune and figures for 'The Reel of the 51st Division' were devised. In the post war years, Aviemore's Willie Macdonald would win distinction as a brilliant piper taking many awards at the Northern Meeting in Inverness.

Across Europe the winter of 1940 was one of the most severe on record. It brought daunting snow blocks on the Highland line with trains snowed in on Drumochter. Aviemore depot played a key role in trying to keep the route clear. A big snow plough kept in the shed there was attached to a 'Barney' whose exposed cab was enclosed by a wooden shelter with a wagon sheet wrapped over it. Then a Class 5, better known in the gateway as a 'hiker', would be coupled on. These powerful locomotives first came to the Highland line in 1935 and soon proved their worth handling passenger and freight trains with ease; they became commonplace – there were eventually more than 800 of them in Britain – and they are remembered with gratitude as the engines that helped to win the war.

No young fireman really belonged to the ranks of the footplatemen until he had been out with the big plough. It was a daunting experience. With snow in the wind, the signalman at Aviemore's south cabin would warn the enginemen, 'The ploughs are out on the hill' – meaning Struan bank up to Drumochter. Charging a drift was terrifying for a new hand. With the regulators wide open and the locomotives belching smoke and steam, the plough would be blasted into the snow. When the drifts were bad, the shed master would be sure to send for the driver 'John L', a bold member of the Mackenzie clan, who was always prepared to batter his way up to Drumochter and beyond. It was a matter of pride for Aviemore men not to let the snow beat them and to go out with the big plough was like an initiation rite. Driver Jimmie Gray of Aviemore recalls such a trip:

> With a tarpaulin tied down over a wooden contraption on the cab, there were only slits left to see out and the heat was ferocious. We would thump into a drift, thrown off our feet by the force of the engine behind us and feeling as if it would burst into our cab. A white blinding hell filled the footplate – you could not see across it for snow – then we would be running free again. We were left soaking and filthy – nothing made you as dirty as snow clearing.

An infamous place for snow blocks was the Bachan, just south of Dalwhinnie, and returning north the engine crew would be astonished to see the thickness of the drifts they had cut through there. A big drift could bring the engines to a halt – the enginemen hoping that the wheels were still on the rails and that they could back off and have another run at it. Once the line was officially clear, Aviemore men would patrol it day and night on a locomotive with a smaller plough to ensure that it was kept open.

As part of their contribution to the national endeavour, gateway folk had flocked to see a 'cinematograph entertainment' in the Cairngorm Hotel; the purpose was to raise money for a canteen for service personnel in transit through Aviemore Junction. The films had been shot by Jean Gracie and John Sam Macdonald, the postmaster's son and a ciné enthusiast, who both organised the event. The canteen began in a caravan in the station square but soon became a Church of Scotland 'hut' on the station platform from which trolleys were replenished with snacks. Aviemore became renowned among the troops. A penny bought a cup of tea and two pence got a filled roll. To service men and women it was 'the second best canteen in Britain' – there happened to be one that was free! Urgent and continuous pleas were made to gateway housewives for 'sandwich spread material' to fill the popular softies baked in their dozens by McCook's. A lettuce, an egg or two, a handful of tomatoes – all was welcome. Even visitors were roped in to help in a succession of shifts and

Various sizes of snow plough were devised by William Stroudley for use on the Highland Railway. Here the largest type is on view outside Lochgorm Works in Inverness with four of the locomotives of the 1860s which were required to propel it into the drifts (STRATHSPEY RAILWAY COLLECTION)

The 'Misses Gracie' – Isobel, Alison and Jean – in August 1948. With community assistance, the latter two ran the famed Church of Scotland canteen for troops in transit at Aviemore Junction during the Second World War (A. E. GLEN)

any denominational hesitancies quickly disappeared. Jean Gracie, assisted by her sister Alison, was in charge. The Aviemore canteen's record was to serve 3,000 service personnel tea and food in one day; all arms of the British forces and almost all allies were represented in the throng. Any extras went to civilian passengers in special need. The *Daily Record* ran 'Jock's Box' which raised money to provide cigarettes and chocolate for troops. These too were given out in their hundreds at Aviemore. 'Thank Jock', was the grateful response as canteen staff tried to race through the packed trains distributing this bounty.

There were plenty of 'coupon free' foods available locally – venison and other game, rabbits and hares, plus fish from rivers and lochs. Folk drew the line at pike but not at poaching for something better. Jim Tulloch at Avielochan made a living by trapping rabbits and cycled weekly to the station on a bike festooned with his catch. The load was sent to game dealers, Carr and Wright, in Manchester. Summer brought fruit in the gardens – prickly gooseberries, black and red currants and raspberries. The linesides grew wild rasps and there were some choice specimens in moist corners. Rose hips were gathered to make rose hip syrup as part of a national campaign. Cranberries from the moors were slow to pick yet many pounds of them were collected in good seasons; blaeberries from the forests grew in ones and twos, and perhaps because too many were eaten off the bush, it was difficult to get enough to fill a fruit tart. Most of the gateway women were assiduous in preserving fruit and making jam or jelly – there was extra sugar for the latter – and hives were kept for honey. By autumn there was pride in having store cupboards that were well filled. Generally food rationing did not hit country folk as hard as it did city dwellers but even so menus had to be eked out with tins of dried milk and dried eggs in the lean months.

Folk struggled to keep the strands of community activities in place. There were children's parties and occasional outings but almost everything was geared to raising money for some war purpose or good cause. In 1941, over a few months, there was a 'War Weapons Week', collections for the Spitfire Fund and 'Aid for China' plus 'Aid for Russia'. Even the sheep dog trials were an excuse for fund raising. A War Savings group was set up and scarcely a week went by without appeals for cash. The Cameron Highlanders' band and dancers came to a packed Comrades' Memorial Hall as the climax to a big fund raising effort. Blood donors were also sought – transfusions were a medical breakthrough which were hailed as a life-saving marvel. There were drives for salvage of all kinds. As Britain was practically cut off from imports, recycling was crucial. There were calls for scrap metal and whereas railings in Inverness disappeared with real regret, Kingussie was only too glad to be rid of German guns from the previous conflict which had been presented to the burgh as trophies. Caches of paper, rags, tin foil and rubber were to follow as cupboards, sheds and lofts were cleared.

The wireless meant a lot to gateway folk. The sets were battery powered and almost every dwelling sprouted an improvised aerial. Folk listened to the broadcasts critically, voicing cantankerous protests when reference was made to 'England' or to the 'King of England' instead of Britain, or when some political viewpoint was put across which they disliked. 'Shut up, man!' might be followed by 'Who asked you, ye silly b . . . ?' and the apparatus abruptly switched off. Just as in the First World War, spy hysteria swept over the district. Any stranger, alighting on Aviemore platforms during a change of engines at the junction, who was seen to consult a map, or worse to use a camera, would be escorted to the station master's office and asked to produce an identity card and other credentials before being told off.

The military were making their presence felt in the gateway in a big way. Many sizeable properties, especially lodges such as Pitmain, Revack and others, were taken over – 'commandeered' was the word – by the War Department with the Treasury paying the bill. The Doune of Rothiemurchus was a regimental headquarters for the 1st Mountain

Regiment, Royal Artillery. In 1942 four mountain battery groups, equipped with 3.7 inch guns, were under canvas in front of the house; with each battery having about 250 men, 50 horses and 130 pack mules plus one lorry, it was quite an assemblage of troops and animals. When 'reveille' rang out at 6am, the men set about feeding, watering and mucking out the long lines of mules and horses, a daily logistical challenge.

It was a very wet summer and the camp suffered flooding when the Spey topped its banks. The crops were still green in September that year. Being in tents when the autumn snowfalls came was thoroughly miserable for both personnel and for beasts in the open. In due course the RA teams demonstrated their skills, honed in the high Cairngorms, for the benefit of brigades of the 52nd Lowland Division. The Royal Army Service Corps and the Pioneer Corps were also in evidence in the area. The job of the Pioneers was to unload hay and fodder from the trains at Aviemore and help fill up the three-ton Bedford lorries which the RASC boys then drove out to the camps in the surrounding area. Where the old ferry had plied at the Boat of Rothiemurchus a chain still hung across the river. For those soldiers, prepared to go hand over hand, this offered a short cut to the nearest pub – the bar of the Lynwilg Hotel – although there was always the risk of falling off on the return journey and having to swim back to base.

Much less obtrusive were the Norwegian commandos at Glenmore where they occupied the former shooting lodge. They also took over Forest Lodge near Nethybridge but their nerve centre was Drumintoul in Rothiemurchus. To give no secrets away, such premises were listed as rented out to the Ministry of Public Works and Buildings. The exiled King Haakon and Crown Prince Olav stayed at Drumintoul after a memorable inspection of the contingent outside Aviemore station.

Among the soldiery the Norwegians were special – usually blond of hair, athletic in build and bronzed by sun and wind, they caught the eye. They also had to be intelligent and resolute for they were being trained in sabotage techniques. In 1942 'ST 26 at Aviemore' took over the training of recruits on a mixture of fieldcraft, military and weapons instruction, unarmed combat and the use of explosives. Just for practice, cars were blown up on the beach at Loch Morlich and glass fragments were for long mixed with the sand there. They also had a go at the famous boulder of Clach Bharraig on the shoulder of Cairn Gorm. Inevitably there were casualties – some of their hazardous practice missions were carried out in pitch darkness. Coylum House was their hospital and it was staffed by Norwegian nurses who would sleep with a pistol under their pillows just

Crown Prince Olav of Norway with men of the Highland Light Infantry in the Cairngorms in 1942 (The Imperial War Museum)

in case a Nazi saboteur should turn up in Rothiemurchus.

With incredible bravery and determination, the Norwegians parachuted into enemy occupied territory in the dark or were put ashore from a boat. The attacks on the hydro-electric scheme at Høyanger on Sogne Fjord, and possibly on the heavy water plant at Vermork, near Rjukan, in February 1943, were planned at Drumintoul Lodge. These were to prove the most successful commando raids of the twentieth century – daring assaults which severely hindered, and ultimately prevented, the Nazi capacity to make atomic bombs.

Everything the Norwegians did, they did well. They swam superbly, they threw stones further than anyone had ever seen before and appeared inexhaustible. In winter time, clad in white battle dress, they flitted through the forest on skis, which it is said were made in Dumfries out of Scots pine from Glenmore. These were the men of the Kompagnie Linge, named after its distinguished founder, Captain Martin Linge. They were officially Norwegian Independent Company No 1, established in 1940, and worked closely with the British Special Operations Executive. Their adventures and bravery led to films such as 'The Heroes of Telemark' and to such books as 'Report from No 20' or 'The Shetland Bus'. A great rock placed at Glenmore by the people of Badenoch in 1973 commemorates their fortitude and sacrifice. It carries these words in Norwegian and English:

You took us into your homes and into your hearts and gave us hope.

On Norway's Independence Day each May a memorial ceremony is held and the Norwegian flag is always flown there.

The Second World War caused another timber crisis in Britain. By the 1930s, home production met only 4 per cent of the country's requirements for timber and wood products, such as paper pulp. Worse still, reliance had shifted from Canada and Scandinavia to the USSR and the eastern Baltic States with over half the supplies coming from the latter areas. German supremacy in the Baltic quickly put a stop to this trade. The British army's needs were colossal – a million chairs, half a million beds, and limitless quantities of ammunition boxes and packing cases. As Forestry Commission plantations sown since 1919 were immature, privately owned forests were perforce targeted again.

An initial request for Canadian assistance was made in October 1939 but it was the following May before the Canadian government took the decision to re-establish the Canadian Forestry Corps. This was again organised as a military unit but, unlike the First World War, the men received combat training too. With mobilisation centres throughout Canada, company ranks were soon filled by experienced lumbermen from timber producing provinces such as Ontario and British Columbia.

Crossing safely by convoy from Halifax to the Clyde, by July 1940 there were 20 CFC companies in Scotland, where all were to operate initially. Their head quarters were first at Blair Atholl but were latterly near Beauly. Each company, which was assigned to a camp, numbered 200 men with a major in charge assisted by three to five officers and NCOs. It is estimated that some companies were 20 to 30 per cent French speaking and a proportion of these were not fluent in English at all. Among the personnel were loggers, sawyers, mill workers, blacksmiths, carpenters, storemen, mechanics, cooks and medical staff, making the companies practically self sufficient, apart from their rations. They arrived with the most up-to-date equipment Canada could provide – rotary sawmills, caterpillar tractors, sulkies (pneumatic-tyred steel arches for log haulage), angle dozers for road making (which incidentally revolutionised snow clearance on Highland roads), drum winches for 'high lead' logging on slopes and transport lorries. This array of modern machinery transformed timber output in the Highlands; the aim was to produce sawn timber from the best material and pit props from the remainder.

The CFC had five camps in Strathspey, which was part of their District 4 extending northwards from Loch Rannoch. These were at Torwood in Glen Feshie, at Insh on the B970 near Kincraig, at Boat of Garten on the same road, at Carrbridge south of the railway station, and in the Forest of Abernethy close to Causar at Nethybridge. Most huts were covered with 'backs', the trimmings when logs were processed. The bark was left on the external thin pieces of timber giving the camps a curiously rustic look but this greatly helped insulation and weather proofing and, if their quarters lacked such a protective cover, the Canadians soon applied it. The companies involved in Strathspey were at various times Numbers 6, 11, 12, 14, 20 and 22 and as many of the Canadians had Scottish connections, they received an especially warm welcome. In fact, it could be said that they were welcomed with open arms and at one stage, No 11 Company at Carrbridge camp was recording a marriage a month. The substantial CFC entertainment hall near Boat of Garten proved very popular with the community for whom the Canadians organised lorry transport to film shows and concerts. It was also lavishly equipped – at least in local eyes – for billiards, table tennis, darts and such games.

The CFC made no lengthy railway this time although they did have narrow-gauge Decauville systems in some timber yards. They were credited with repairing the greater part of the rough road from near Coylumbridge to Glenmore which received a good coating of tar for the first time, transforming it for the better. There were reservations however about their felling technique. The Canadians cut with the axe or saw at waist height, no less. This practice provoked consternation, being both uneconomic and ugly, as it left unsightly 'stump fields'. The Scottish method was to cut timber as near the ground as possible and understandably lairds and foresters were horrified by the destruction which they witnessed. So pressure had to be applied to make the lumberjacks change their ways. Despite working nine-hour days and undergoing military training on Saturdays, the CFC men found time to help bring in harvests and quell forest and moor fires. Some spent their limited leisure hours making toys for children or carved gifts for sale in aid of the Red Cross. As some compensation for their hard work, they at least got regular leave and a tot of rum in severe weather.

Even earlier in February 1940 the first Newfoundlanders had appeared around Carrbridge. The public were informed that 'a great forestry operation has begun in the Highlands under the Forestry Commission department dealing with timber supply'. There were 66 lumberjacks in that party; they selected suitable trees, felled them and built a camp of six log cabins providing sleeping quarters and a mess room in just twelve days.

Timber traffic soared during the Second World War. Newfoundland lumberjacks operated a light rail system with the assistance of muscle power at Carrbridge (Glen Collection / Mrs M. Browne)

When war was declared, offers of help had come from Newfoundland, the great island which at the time was a British colony off the mouth of the St Lawrence in Canada. The islanders' 'available and eager manpower' was quickly utilised 'for the purpose of cutting pit props in connection with coal production in the United Kingdom'. Over 2,000 loggers were recruited as a civilian group, the Newfoundland Overseas Forestry Unit, and sailed in a variety of vessels from St Johns and Halifax. Unlike the Canadians, they had to provide all their own clothing, footwear and tools such as axes and bucksaws. Their pay was just $2 a day – the minimum rate paid by the big Canadian logging companies – one dollar of which was sent off to their families 'back home'. They had to work a 44 hour week with only one week of paid holidays in the year; yet some were to serve in Britain for over six years.

The Newfies, as they became known, had mainly been employees of lumber companies exploiting the extensive forests on the island although some were fishermen. Most were of English origin with a sprinkling of French or Indian extraction. Generally Roman Catholic, they were said to have 'a high devotion to the church' but many were illiterate. The lumberjacks brought with them 'a breath of their backwoods and open spaces . . . with their jerkins, laced high boots and peaked caps . . . '. They were judged to be 'wild, wild fellows'. They had to forego their accustomed logging menus of beans, salt meat and fish, pasta and hard bread. No wonder that game (of dubious legality) became a regular feature in the cook houses where rationing made the preparation of substantial meals a real challenge. The gateway was so important in terms of timber extraction that Carrbridge became the foresters' headquarters controlling all operations concerning the camps (of which there were twenty-five spread out between Laggan and Ballindalloch), sawmills, access roads, plus the allocation of some 500 men and their equipment. There was an additional district office at Kingussie. Four sizeable camps appeared in the stretch from Aviemore to Boat of Garten alone.

Having got the Newfoundlanders into the forests, it was another matter to keep them there. They wanted to join the British forces. So alarmed was the government by the likely mass defection that Clement Atlee, then Deputy Prime Minister, was sent round the camps to persuade the lads to stay on as loggers. Only half did so – some returned home – which meant that further recruitment was essential. Thankfully all the crossings of the Atlantic involving the Newfies were safely accomplished.

The forests themselves were not entirely to the Canadians' or the Newfoundlanders' liking. Despite the fact that they were based in the drier Eastern Highlands, they loathed wet raw weather with drenching rain which washed away the access roads and turned ground into mud. While some timber was on 'fair logging terrain', they soon had to tackle stands planted on 'very steep rough ground' which climbed to the tree line where trunks were small, stunted and damaged by the elements. The Newfies worked closely with the Canadian Forestry Corps, some of whose camps they took over. Caterpillar tractors were virtually unknown in Britain and so the Newfie teams had to improvise with local equipment as best they could. Horses were used to pull slipes (sledges) or pole wagons; chutes, down which the logs could slide, were constructed on steep land. The Newfies struck a bargain – in an advantageous 'swop', they supplied the Canadians' sawmills with logs and in return got machines which they lacked. In time the Newfies received their own fleet of trucks to carry timber to the railway sidings. Train loads, mainly of pit props in up to a hundred sizes, were sent off to the timber yards at Bo'ness and Grangemouth, ports on the Firth of Forth which pre-war had depended on continental supplies from the Baltic. Telegraph poles, railway sleepers and barricades for beaches were also prepared. Little was wasted for pulp mills in far away Kent took any reject material for paper making.

Homesick as many were at first, the Newfoundlanders worked hard and played hard. They scoured the countryside for old bicycles – any boneshaker which could turn a wheel was snapped up. The Canadians did the same. Village pubs were like a magnet and the lads are remembered as 'just daft about dancing'. Wherever a dance was billed they could be seen peddling resolutely along the roads usually with a lassie perched on the cross bar. The Newfies especially were eager for company – at the outset they lacked recreational facilities of their own but soon Camp 11 near Granish became a prime attraction with its commodious hall for films and ENSA (Entertainment National Service Association) variety shows. It was open house there and youngsters relished the fruit drinks and chewing gum that were liberally dispensed. For local girls the lumberjacks represented new dancing partners and some soon succumbed to their trans-Atlantic charms by becoming their girl friends and ultimately their brides.

On the sporting side, while the Newfoundlanders mustered football teams and tug o' war squads, the CFC men, who became known as 'Canucks', preferred baseball and boxing, or arm wrestling as a trial of strength. Neither group had much enthusiasm for climbing or hiking in the Cairngorms, which is scarcely surprising after their strenuous labours on steep ground. The Canadians especially cycled considerable distances on their week long leaves, making for the bright lights of Inverness or visiting Scottish families to whom they were related.

As early as February 1941, the Women's Land Army was looking for recruits. Even though women had made a valuable contribution to farm production in the First World War, there was fresh resistance to them:

> Substituting women for men is absurd . . . They can look after chickens but cannot ditch. They can look after cows but they cannot look after the bull. They can drive a tractor with a lady-sweep but they cannot pitch hay . . . in short, they cannot do any heavy work on a farm – and there is not a great deal of light work.

But the girls were made of sterner stuff. They showed that they could harvest potatoes, shaw turnips, thresh grain, manage horses and muck out with a barrow and plank. Winter work outside was miserable with freezing hands and iron hard ground. There were no weather bulletins on the radio or forecasts in the newspapers – information which would have been only too useful to an enemy. Everyone was thrown back on old weather lore and to tapping barometers if they had one. Double British Summertime was introduced with the clocks being advanced two hours to make the best possible use of available daylight. It put farming routine completely out of gear – hens still laid eggs when they felt like it and cows gave milk at the usual times – and therefore many folk paid little attention to it, preferring the sun's time. In the spring, the Department of Agriculture's 'tractor mannie' came round to give a hand with the ploughing. By 1943 there were 9,000 Land Girls at work in Scotland but there were comparatively few of them in the Cairngorm gateway. One was Eva Holmes at Avielochan who took to farm life and eventually married a local farmer. From being an Edinburgh secretary, after just a month of basic training, she had to learn on the job and her wage of 18s 6d (95p) a week was a pittance, considering the labour involved, compared with a hairdresser's 25s (£1.25) and accommodation costs had to be met.

The gateway saw much more of the 'lumber jills' who were paid even less. The charges for their board and lodgings were also taken off their pay. From April 1942, young women volunteers were recruited by the 'Home-Grown Timber Production Department of the Ministry of Supply' and given a brief forestry training in the Banchory or Brechin districts. They became members of the Women's Forestry Corps and had

The Second World War revived farming as Britain strove to be as self sufficient as possible. Here William McInnes of Dalfaber farm uses horse power to harvest oats near Aviemore (A. E. GLEN)

a uniform much like the Land Army but wore dark green berets instead of felt hats. 'Mair lassies in breeks' was said with a shake of the head. The girls were accommodated in camps of timber huts – one was at Guislich near Pityoulish, another at Inverdruie beside a saw mill in Rothiemurchus. First the introduction of steam power, and then oil engines, had long freed such mills from river side locations. A hut and mess hall, now neatly concealed as cottages, still stand. The girls had to be resilient, felling trees and leading horses hauling logs over the 'corduroy' roads, laid with small tree trunks to give a firm surface, which were formed in many forests. Sometimes they worked alongside the Newfies but often seemed to be left with the nastier jobs. Heavily laden timber lorries ground their way to the loading bank at Aviemore station or through the notorious tunnel bridge under the railway, and along the Great North Road to Fenwick's saw mill just north of the village.

Welfare officers were appointed to look after the girls. Miss Stevenson, a formidable lady who had once run a nursery school in Glasgow's West End, was one of them. Every day one of the lassies, 'a wee thin cratur'

The Newfoundlanders worked hard and played hard. Here they relax with a sing song back at camp (GLEN COLLECTION / MRS M. BROWNE)

(someone less suited to felling timber could hardly be imagined) cycled into Aviemore for rolls to make the pieces (sandwiches) for a camp. She became part of the village scene; then she inexplicably disappeared. After some months she returned thinner than ever. 'Did ye no' ken? Ah wis aff havin' a wean . . . Ah'm awfie sorry for Miss Stevenson . . . she disnae ken much aboot it. Whit did she say? Hoo did it happen, Nellie? Ah sez, hoo dis it usually happen, Miss Stevenson?'

As 'treats' the lumber jills were allowed to have visitors to tea at their camps and the handsome Norwegians were very popular guests. The girls were also permitted a weekly outing to the pictures in the Comrades' Memorial Hall but it was an uncomfortable ride in a truck there and back. These film shows however were forbidden to Free Presbyterian lassies from Skye and so, having chummed up with a local family, they were invited to supper instead. If they missed the lorry back to camp, they faced a long walk in the dark until the Royal Engineers strung a suspension bridge across the Spey, near where the *Lochan Bàn* ferry had once plied. Conveniently linking Dalfaber with Pityoulish, it was a helpful short cut although it swayed alarmingly and sentries had to be negotiated at either end of it.

The railway was hard pressed for men. Many employees followed a local tradition by being reservists or Territorials and some went off on the Friday before war was declared. For those left it meant fast promotion in all grades and men's jobs being done by women. They were employed as porters, guards, ticket collectors and cleaners, handled the duties in signal boxes and took over much of the office work; the girls in the motive power depots had to stand the ribbing they got as 'fitters' mates'. Even the permanent way gangers (or 'clachers' from the Gaelic for stone) were joined by women who helped to weed and clean up the lineside but did no heavy track work. In whatever department they served the women did an excellent job and soon won the esteem of their cynical male colleagues.

It was pandemonium on the railway. Shifts never finished on time and six day weeks had to be faced. Railway employees did not know when they would get home. All the way along the Highland line there were hold ups with sidings packed with vans and wagons. The single line system was again the sole means of moving freight and other traffic. Road transport was almost non-existent and in any case was restricted to just 60 miles (96km) as petrol was so severely rationed. The defence bases in the north – for the RAF at Evanton and Kinloss and for the Navy at Invergordon, Thurso and Scapa Flow – caused a vast upsurge in goods trains. Numerous army training camps and the formation of emergency food stores at Mulben and Culloden Moor only lengthened the procession. Trains carrying mines consigned to a depot at Kyle of Lochalsh were stored in big sidings at Duirinish. Rail traffic trundled on in spite of the difficulties caused by the lighting restrictions, air raid precautions and snow storms. The specials for naval personnel had top priority over all other trains except those for the King and the Prime Minister.

So huge troop trains or 'specials' again wound their way over the Grampians and through the strath and there were long passenger trains too; sixteen coaches were quite usual although the record was set at Aviemore Junction by a train of twenty-one. The old term 'Jellicoes' became common currency among railwaymen for any military specials. There were unceasing calls on the depot for extra engines to assist trains up to Slochd summit or 'The Slochd' as it is known to railwaymen. By afternoon it was usual for a column of six or more locomotives to be lined up there waiting for an opportunity to run back coupled together to Inverness while the Aviemore 'pilots' went south to assist more heavy trains up the hill. At the junction every vehicle continued to be checked by the wheel tappers (who were popularly known as 'greasers' because they packed the axle boxes with tallow); just fourteen minutes was allowed for this job plus taking water or any shunting that had to be done. It was a tall order and it was a considerable achievement if trains got away on time. On the single line, delays simply became cumulative. An episode which could upset the network was the dropping of the tablet – a brass disc in a leather pouch which was carried on the locomotive from one section of track to another to be deposited with the signalman and ensure the train's safe passage. Meanwhile, no other train could enter the section. For years engines had been fitted with a device known as a tablet catcher but it did not always work. To loose the tablet in the dark was the worst scenario involving stopping the train and sending the fireman to scour the lineside with the help of a lantern or torch.

To say that the station and yards at Aviemore Junction were noisy is an understatement. The clangour of wagons as buffers came together, the thump of brake pumps, the blast of steam as safety valves lifted, the screech of wheels over points and of course the engines' whistling by night led to protests from villagers but trains had to be run round the clock. A code of whistles and crows – one being short and the other long – was the language of the locomotive and Aviemore had its own exclusive vocabulary. Trains arriving at Aviemore from Forres for example had to give three whistles and the same again on leaving. Trains to and from Carrbridge had to give two, while those from the south gave just one.

Noise was bad enough but there was also smoke. On windless days a pall, which was visible for miles, hung over the railway yards. It was frowned upon for an engine to make smoke in the station itself and if plumes of smoke appeared there were bound to be complaints. Beside the south signal cabin was a siding known as Bessie's; all the sidings had unofficial names but Bessie was a terror to enginemen and if the least smoke was made, threatening to stain her washing or spread soot on her garden, she was out vowing vengeance. Not surprisingly she was known as 'Bessie Bla-ack Smoke'. There was also Haggerty's siding – there were twelve in the family of whom five were on the railway at one time. New sidings were laid at Aviemore and additional loading facilities installed at Boat of Garten, Kincraig and Newtonmore mainly for the timber traffic. Carrbridge had its station yard remodelled and the Canadians had a light rail system there. From the outbreak of war until 1945 over 2 million tons of timber were sent out from stations on the Highland line. A record was set in June 1945 when 11,747 wagons were despatched – with over 600 in one day.

Old Highland Railway engines – Castles, Bennies, Barneys, Clans and Clan Goods – continued in service; the same went for coaches and other

The Highland Railway sought to run an express service over a single-line system. Such engines as the 'Small Bens' were often 'pilots', assisting by double heading on heavy trains. Here HR No. 6, Ben Armin of 1899 is seen outside Aviemore shed (GLEN COLLECTION)

vehicles and so 'make-do-and-mend' was not just confined to the domestic scene. In addition to the Class 5s, the stalwart 'hikers' which performed miracles on the long, steep routes and won fresh praise from their crews, some big 8Fs appeared on the scene. These freight locomotives were used on timber trains to Grangemouth but their south country drivers, being in dread of the route over Struan bank and Drumochter, earned the name of the 'Grampian crawlers'. Their locos proved such slow movers on the hills that they only made the delays worse and their stay in the north was relatively short. On the other hand, the 8Fs being powerful brutes did have their uses; when a locomotive and its train of wagons was stopped at a signal at Balavil near Kingussie in one of the bitter winters of the early 1940s, it could not restart as it had frozen to the rails – it was an 8F that came to the rescue and administered a mighty heave to free the lot.

Railwaymen became accustomed once again not only to long hours but also to overnights away from home. The pattern of their three shifts could cause complete confusion among Highland landladies, 'First you were late, off early, then you were early, off late, and now you are first at

Aviemore enginemen with LMS Class 5 No 4798, on of the versatile locomotives known to them known as 'hikers' which were firm favourites on the Highland Line. Left to right are: G. Ross and G. Rennie, (firemen), W. Stewart, A. Ferguson and W. Fraser (drivers) (J. C. HAY)

last!' Pre-war Perth men 'booking off' at Aviemore had to make do with an old carriage taken off its bogies and parked beyond the engine shed as a bothy; makeshift it might be, but it was kept spotless. By the 1940s it was supplemented by former sleeping cars as ever more engine crews from Glasgow and elsewhere had to be accommodated at the junction. Aviemore men working through to Helmsdale also found an old carriage, converted into an improvised hostel, for their use. Their log books regularly showed the staff 'booking on' at 10 pm and returning at 4.50 pm the following day from such a trip. Enginemen were frequently asked by the shed foreman at Aviemore to 'do a doubler' – that is a double shift – or after a tiring day, be called upon on a wintry night to go out with the snow plough. In 1943, Aviemore got a large custom built railway hostel located between the two main lines north of the station; latterly a holiday home for railway families and known as Spey Lodge, it is now occupied by the Strathspey Railway.

Meanwhile, the Lovat Scouts had spent time on Deeside, some being stationed on the royal estate of Balmoral itself. They had to wear sand shoes to avoid disturbing the castle's residents, endure conditions of bitter cold in tents and near starvation on limited rations; these they quickly supplemented by poaching in the rivers and forests. A grenade thrown into a pool could produce plenty of fish suppers. Being capable hill men, they thought little of walking through the Cairngorms during brief leaves to return to their homes in Rothiemurchus for square meals. In the course of the war, the regiment was to occupy the Faroe Islands, undergo high altitude training in Jasper National Park in the Canadian Rockies, and to take part in the Italian campaign.

Even greater surprises than Canadians, Newfoundlanders or Norwegians were in store for the gateway people. They first heard of colonial troops coming to the district in 1942 when the minister of Rothiemurchus and Aviemore made an announcement to that effect from the pulpit. He then called on the troops' welfare officer to speak. This gentleman, whom many had taken for a missionary, was Dr Shandra from Ceylon (now Sri Lanka). He had to forge links with the community to ensure a welcome for Indian soldiers. The people were asked to do their best to help boys far from home in a strange land. As few gateway folk had seen anyone darker than Sammy Nathan in the flesh, they were told about their dark colour. They were warned too about the troops' religious observances for most were Sikhs and Muslims coming from what in pre-Partition days was the Punjab. Language would be a major problem. The congregation was reminded – if any was required – that their own lads would also be thankful for friendship and a welcome in foreign lands.

Gateway families were proverbially kind and generous to strangers in the true tradition of Highland hospitality. The welfare officer need not have been so anxious for the Indians' manners were to prove exemplary; in no time at all the soldiers were addressing the ladies as 'mammy', making even the old spinsters feel quite flattered.

Of all places, the Indians detrained at Dalwhinnie in territory more akin to the Arctic tundra than the baking heat of the Indus plains. They were officially Numbers 1 and 2 Pack Transport, drawn from the Royal Indian Army Service Corps as part of Force K6, in support of the 52nd Lowland Division. Men, mules and tents were soon dispersed in almost every thicket of broom or clump of birches around the strath and also in sizeable camps at Kincraig and Boat of Garten. One was located in a clearing on the Lairig Ghru path near Coylumbridge. It was up and running within three hours one afternoon with sentries posted and curries cooking. Heaps of boulders still mark the places where the tents stood. An Indian field hospital was opened on Kinrara estate.

Small, wiry and fierce eyed, how exotic the Indian men seemed. Syd Scroggie, the Cairngorms walker and writer, who trained along with them, describes the 'turbanned Sikhs and charcoal complexioned Mahrattas' who jingled on horse back through the pine forest of Rothiemurchus 'with spur and pennon'd lance'. Their cavalcades would follow the stony path by Achnagoichan to the Iron Bridge where they crossed at the ford, splashing through the icy waters of the Allt Druidh en route to the mountains. There were both British and Indian officers – the former holding King's Commissions and the latter Viceroy's Commissions. The British officers from the Royal Army Service Corps were a dashing lot. Some had been champions at equestrian events pre-war, or at least crack riders. They were allowed to have their own horses so long as they provided the animal's feed. There were gymkhanas on Sunday afternoons at their camps at Pityoulish or Loch Alvie where show jumping and tent-pegging replaced the polo of the Raj.

The Indian troops were always cold and always hungry. The period of self denial of Ramadan, which could fall in winter with its snell winds, snow showers and squalls, was a sore trial to them. The gateway housewives took pity on the shivering lads in the tents. Spoonfuls of tea and sugar were received like gold to be taken back to camp for a cup of char. When they were welcomed into the houses, 'Pull curtain, mammy, sunset!' would puzzle a Highland hostess until she got the message that the visitor did not wish to be spotted by his mates eating a freshly baked scone and drinking hot tea by a blazing fire in the middle of the day.

The harsh conditions told on the Indians' health; bronchitis, pneumonia and even tuberculosis, were prevalent and sadly, there were casualties. The Aviemore Hotel, commandeered by the military authorities, became in part a hospital and folk as far away as the junction's platforms were distressed to hear the patients racked with coughing. A mosque was set up in the foyer of the hotel. Guests honoured with an invitation would arrive to find soldiers at their devotions. If gateway folk learned about religions new to them, the Indian troops just as quickly picked up local expressions. An apology about intruding on a reading from the Koran brought the answer, 'It's OK, mammy, jist learnin' a wee bittie'.

Gateway folk were intrigued by the Indians – and who wouldn't be by the sight of a turbanned subahdur with a splendid moustache and the epitome of spit and polish, with a hen under each arm? For their part the troops were amazed by the natives of the gateway, especially those with blonde or red hair. The Indians were delighted to have company and tried to repay kindnesses. When two secretaries were invited to dine at their headquarters in the big hotel they found that a couple of mouthfuls of a

Indian troops in support of the mountain batteries of the 52nd Lowland Division on manoeuvres at Meall Chuaich near Drumochter in October 1942 (THE IMPERIAL WAR MUSEUM)

fiery curry was more than enough but they could not risk embarrassing their hosts by not eating up. Then one had a face saving idea. She pled for glasses of cold water which sent their hosts – who were ever eager to please – scurrying off to the kitchen during which time the girls decanted the spiciest part of the contents of their plates into their handbags!

To lighten the burdens of hard work and worry, there were weekly programmes brought by the Army Mobile Cinema Unit to the Comrades' Memorial Hall. Betty Grable, Veronica Lake and Olivia De Havilland might appeal to the Jocks and Tommies but they had no charms for the Indians. They did not patronise such shows. Then an Indian film 'Kanga' was booked. The men from the Punjab attended in droves and the level of audience participation was incredible. Every bit of action provoked either shouts, sighs, stamping of feet or threats of revenge. The racket was deafening. The floor shook and the timbers creaked. Nothing like it had ever been witnessed in the hall and although its keeper, Duncan McLeod, a First World War veteran, feared for its stability -'It near fell doon' – the show was a triumph with the troops.

The serious purpose of the Indians' presence was to provide transport and this meant the horses and mules tethered beneath the birches. In particular there was a stretch of land on the west side of the railway in Aviemore which was mule territory. There the Indians and the RASC held sway amid the long lines of animals; it was dubbed 'Shanghai'. The Great North Road through the village became plastered with dung and straw. Mules were fickle creatures causing trouble at the loading bank at the station by biting and kicking, or refusing to budge. Their popularity rating with the soldiery was very low. If an engine should let off a gush of steam like a geyser, the mules would bolt, galloping off along the road with hay bales flapping and their drivers running helplessly after them. Nevertheless, the creatures endured the blizzards and cutting winds of winter in the hills when the skill of their drivers in negotiating sheets of ice, steep bouldery slopes. peat hags and swollen streams enabled the gunners for whom they toiled to put in their practice. Zig-zag tracks hacked out on hill sides to allow access for the mountain batteries and the occasional mule shoe found by walkers are reminders of their sojourn in the Cairngorms. The Indian troops had an impact on the gateway far out of proportion to their numbers or to their length of stay. Yet remembered are the mystical oriental dances they performed before a packed house in a Canadian Forestry hall.

The 52nd Lowland Division had three infantry brigades – consisting of nine infantry battalions – in rotation in the district of which the Highland Light Infantry and the Cameronians appeared in 1942, to be followed by King's Own Scottish Borderers, Royal Scots, Royal Scots Fusiliers and Glasgow Highlanders. All of these troops spent time under canvas either around Loch Alvie or at Loch Pityoulish as they underwent training. Their Divisional Headquarters however were not in the gateway district but at Dunphail House on the north side of Dava Moor. Some units of the Division were also based in Ballater. On a bright morning at Avielochan, a long column of men, tin hatted and in full battle gear, came up the Great North Road led by a piper playing 'The Barren Rocks of Aden', a stirring tune that still brings a lump to the throat. For the lowland lads, the gateway had some resemblance to the barren rocks – it was so very different from the teeming tenements, busy streets and cheery pubs which they knew at home. During such free time as they had, they simply did not know what to do with themselves. Some drank and brawled; some poached. The Sheriff discovered a pair in Rothiemurchus with a pheasant. He demanded to know how they had come by the bird. They pointed to a service rifle and gave the innocent reply, 'Us yins is no' wantin' it, is youse yins?' They were irrepressible and just as well for their training in the mountains was arduous. The dances, the picture shows and the pub at the big hotel in Aviemore were very welcome distractions.

Out with their bridge building projects, the Royal Engineers spent time constructing bothies on the Cairngorms plateau, dumping loads of boulders into streams to make fords, or blowing up a variety of structures (some of which they had only recently put together) just for practice. While attempting to strengthen the timber bridge on the Spey at Boat of Garten, they set it on fire with a blow lamp, whereupon a pontoon ferry had to be re-introduced on the river, recalling Jimmie Boatie of years gone by. In their few idle moments, for amusement they were reduced to watching the endless shunting manoeuvres at Aviemore station, or they might go to the NAAFI, set up in a marquee at Coylumbridge. (Strictly this was the Navy, Army and Air Force Institute, providing catering and recreation facilities for servicemen in place of former regimental provision.) Aviemore was such a small place and was so saturated with military personnel that the engineers looked forward to 'hitting the town' – in this instance, Grantown – for hot baths and a cinema show.

Up to 1942, the task of the 52nd Lowland Division was to repel an enemy attack on British shores but the focus then shifted to a possible aerial invasion. Exercises consequently became more of the commando type. As the war progressed in the Allies' favour, however, the emphasis moved to training for an offensive. Serious manoeuvres saw troops and animals filing past, all wearing gas masks. There were long convoys of lorries, armoured personnel carriers and tanks plus all the paraphernalia of mechanised campaigns on the move. Their track marks were left on the tarmac for months.

The lowland infantrymen were to be transformed into mountaineers and where better than in the Cairngorms?

> The foot sloggers from south of the Highland Line were to learn the art of fighting at high altitudes.
>
> – GEORGE BLAKE IN *MOUNTAIN AND FLOOD*

They moved in small groups in this remote terrain and proudly wore the shoulder badge 'Mountain'. The plan was to switch the troops from relying on vehicles to mule transport and then to backpacks as the ground got progressively higher and rougher. This did not prevent a brigadier from getting his jeep to the summit of Cairn Gorm but some argue that it actually reached Ben Macdui.

The long preparations for D–Day began, although well concealed from the public and possibly spying eyes. Columns of camouflaged vehicles rumbled along the A9 'in the awful panoply of war' while military policemen buzzed about on motor bikes. Dress rehearsals – immense in scale and code named 'Goliath' – plus false information were designed to give the Germans the notion that an attack would come through Norway. This explains why a sprinkling of Norwegian officers and men was posted to the Scottish regiments. There were troops everywhere, augmented by signals, artillery, engineers, transport and ancillary staff; camp sites or other accommodation had to be found for all of them. Gateway folk soon knew the jargon about Bren gun carriers, walkie talkie sets and weasels which could cope with deep snow and work at high levels. The latter were miraculous machines compared with wayward pack animals. The mountain troops learned to use skis and snow shoes, to form igloos and snow holes and to bivvy out of doors in all weathers. The Cairngorms were as near as possible to conditions in the high tundra of Arctic Norway and were thus crucial to their experience. Ironically, in the autumn of 1944 the Division was sent to land and fight across the flooded island of Walcheren in the Scheldt estuary on the Dutch coast, 'up tae the oxters in watter' – an area as flat as a pancake and mostly below sea level.

For the Home Guard there were proficiency tests and the excitement of joint exercises with the army. On one occasion the Aviemore contingent was sent to guard a secret ammunition dump at Loch Garten. This area was so sensitive that only its few residents in the scattered crofts, the postie and the vanman from Boat of Garten were allowed into it. Sentries turned the imprudent back. The adversaries for the Home Guard were the Norwegians from Glenmore and Forest Lodge near Nethybridge. There are no prizes for guessing who won. Suffice it to say that the Norwegians had a novel way of preventing their prisoners escaping – they removed their trousers! This was a terrible indignity for such as Tommy Hogg of the Tweed Warehouse to be left standing in his long johns in Abernethy Forest. He never forgave 'thae furriners'.

The Newfies also joined the Home Guard. Such large numbers volunteered to assist in the defence of the British Isles that a 3rd Inverness (Newfoundland) Battalion was created in just a fortnight when 700 men enlisted. This unit was quite unique as it comprised the only 'overseas' personnel in the entire Home Guard. The foresters took their role seriously even constructing an assault course and a rifle range at Carrbridge, both of which were good enough to be used by the Army. They also participated in commando exercises in the Highlands; the fit young fellows were prepared as a mobile striking force to fight on counter attack lines at focal points in the North East. They therefore gave up 'money, sleep and relaxation' to take part in much rigorous training, bringing strength and youthful enthusiasm to the contingent. They were also something of a liability at times when they took their service rifles out to shoot wild fowl on the lochs – and this in the close season too. One day, the shots re-echoed round the hills as the bullets ricocheted off

Home Guard battalions were active in the Cairngorm Gateway. Here the 3rd Inverness (Newfoundland) Battalion – the only overseas personnel in the entire Home Guard – is being inspected (GLEN COLLECTION / MRS M. BROWNE)

the water at Avielochan. Bob Campbell, the keeper on the Kinveachy estate, who was assisting with hay making in a stack yard nearby, raced to the scene to confront the miscreants with the threat of a well nailed boot until Aviemore's solitary policeman arrived by bike. Bob also had the task of keeping the Canadians at Carrbridge in check but poaching came naturally to such woodsmen and it was a hopeless task.

Constable Duncan Mackenzie also had his work cut out maintaining some semblance of law and order among such a diversity of people and interests. As he was a real countryman who enjoyed fishing and shooting, he had won respect in the community. His leadership of the local search party took on a new and serious purpose – the tracing of aircraft missing in the hills. There were many such call outs. Along the Great North Road came special transporters, known as 'Queen Marys' after the liner on account of their size, which conveyed what was left of aeroplanes, to Kinloss.

If any local men were ignorant about poaching prior to joining the Home Guard, they soon learned the required skills. This put their colonel in a most invidious situation for that honoured rank was held by Sheriff Grant of Rothiemurchus. Being on the bench, he took a very dim view of such goings-on. So in July 1943 he made a recommendation to the officers in charge of the Home Guard battalions that the rifles should be 'put under lock and key' in one location when they were not being used for duty. Such a notion produced a mixture of mirth and outrage. What would happen in an emergency if all the unit's rifles were locked up in one place, or even a number of locations, scattered about the strath? The issue reached the local press where one of his own clansmen took the Sheriff to task. He suggested that the men should not only be issued with rifles but plenty of ammunition as well; he argued that this was in fact being done in towns and cities where it was less likely that a volunteer would be called upon to do single combat than on a lone croft or farm. He concluded, 'If a Home Guard can get a bit of extra meat ration through practice with his rifle, the laird should shut his eyes and thank his lucky stars that the unit has some decent shots!' There was no rejoinder from the Sheriff. His admonitions were all the more frustrating when it was common knowledge that servicemen in training were allowed to shoot at deer. Herd numbers were so successfully held in check in the war years, for example in Glen Feshie, that the Scots pine forest began to regenerate by sprouting an abundance of flourishing seedlings.

Another source of contention was the wearing of Home Guard uniform. When clothing was rationed – trousers took eleven coupons – it was a great temptation to use battle dress issue around the farms. Of course, it should only have been worn 'when on duty' or in circumstances 'where it was absolutely warranted' but no one paid much attention to that order. Apart from the railwaymen, who had their own supplies of overalls, the khaki blouse became the norm for men folk in the gateway long after the war was over.

One alarm which had the Home Guard on the alert was the escape of three German prisoners of war who went on the run in the Grampians. They were from the Afrika Korps, and reputedly clad in that uniform complete with peaked sun caps; they were said to speak little English. Contrary to opinion that 'they could possibly be mistaken for hikers', they must have stuck out like sore thumbs. The hills and moors were combed methodically for them and the escape was the subject of gossip in the strath for days.

From the summer of 1943 local folk had become accustomed to seeing prisoners of war about the place; they were quite conspicuous having yellow patches on their brown battle dress. There was a camp for Italians by Kingussie station and another for Germans at Lynstock near Nethybridge. The 'Agricultural Executive Committee for Inverness-shire' had announced that P.O.W.s from Germany and Italy would be available for any type of work on the land; it was stated reassuringly that there was no cause for concern as farmers sending in applications would receive 'good conduct men' some of whom could even be billeted on the farms. They also assisted the timber squads in the forests. The Germans however were treated with some scepticism until they showed just how hard they could work or what special skills, such as clock or watch repairing, they possessed. The day workers were paid 1s per hour (5p) for an eight hour day and 1s 3d (7p) for every extra hour thereafter. They were to be given only one basic meal but most households treated them more generously. After the war and with East Germany under Communist control, some preferred to settle in the Highlands, married and became part of the community.

With Italy's collapse in September 1943, the last lap of the conflict was at hand. The community accelerated its efforts. A branch of the Women's Voluntary Service had been set up in the gateway and ladies were horrified when a sergeant, speaking about anti-gas measures, gave out phials of poisonous gases for them to sniff. They were doubtless glad of the first aid talk that followed. The raising of money was unrelenting. In the very first week of the Aviemore and Rothiemurchus Savings Group's existence over £700 was collected; £500 was soon produced for the Prisoners of War Fund to be followed by the 'Wings for Victory' campaign when £7,500 was gathered – the target was just one third of that sum. The whole of Badenoch, by the standard of those days, put up an incredible £50,000. People's pockets appeared to be limitless – the war had brought big pay packets to many and little on which to spend it. Salvage continued to roll in – ten loads of paper a year to be used for aircraft construction. Paper and wood ply made parts for the Mosquito light bomber and were also regularly utilised for producing propeller blades for other aeroplanes.

By 1944 it was clear that the tempo of the conflict was altering. British P.O.W.s were being repatriated and people were allowing themselves to say, 'When will the war be over?' In May an odd duty was assigned to Aviemore engineman. It was to go 'light engine to Dalwhinnie for train heating purposes' – that village is one of the highest and chilliest in the Highlands. May can also be a risky month for weather with winter loath to let go its grip on the hills. On the face of it, the railwaymen's task seemed a tedious one – attending to a locomotive attached to the tail of a train to supply the coaches with steam hour after hour. Little did they know that D-Day was only four weeks away. On 5 May General Montgomery left for Scotland in order to pay visits to the Home Fleet and then four days later to have a short holiday in the Highlands. Monty's diary records:

> I garaged my special train (Rapier) at DALWHINNIE and walked the mountains and fished. I had begun to feel the need of a rest and it did me good.

This was no ordinary holiday. While the general strolled in the hills or tried to coax salmon from the Spey, his every movement was being scrutinised by an actor. This was Clifton Jones, who was a serving officer and whose task it was to impersonate Monty in North Africa. It was part of a grand deception to plant the idea of possible Allied landings in the south of France in German military minds. A film was later made about the actor's exploits as Monty's double.

Monty is remembered at Dalwhinnie where the women and children gathered to see him and be rewarded with a friendly wave. He called at the little school at Kinloch Laggan where he enjoyed talking to the 'bairns' in the classroom. As for the railwaymen, their efforts brought some comfort to the occupants of the mysterious train parked in the bleak heights of the Grampians.

D-Day arrived and with it the hope of peace at last. Some companies of the Canadian Forestry Corps were shortly on active service on the Continent. By August 1944 the local Home Guard was stood down. As the gateway men who had served in the battalion had worn the cap badge of the Queen's Own Cameron Highlanders, they were made honorary members of the regimental association. It was a nice gesture. There were other glimpses of normality when 'by permission of the Ministry of War Transport' a bus could begin running more frequently between Kingussie, Aviemore and Grantown but most cars, given up since the start of the conflict, still gathered dust in their garages and sheds. At the end of November, the CFC's No 22 Company, relocated to Boat of Garten, was the last in the district and one of the last to leave Scotland. With the submarine threat in the Atlantic extinguished, the Canadian troops' Scottish wives began to set sail for the Dominion as soon as onboard accommodation was available for them. For the Newfie brides, Newfoundland was a shock as they stepped back some fifty years in terms of domestic facilities. According to a letter sent home to Scotland, it was a place of 'bogs, dogs and fogs'. It was to prove a real test of endurance for them in the face of its dank mists, severe frosts and isolation.

When victory in Europe came at last in May 1945, the folk of the Cairngorm gateway were relieved and very thankful but exhausted by the prolonged war effort. Their clothes were threadbare and their houses had weathered, flaking paint. There was a bonfire on the traditional venue – the top of Ord Ban – and another on Tullochgrue; the Victory Dance in the Comrades' Hall was packed out. There was a service of thanksgiving for deliverance from cruel tyranny in the kirk to which the whole district came. The chorus of whistles which rang out from the steam locomotives at the big shed on VJ Day ushered in further festivities. Even so, the rejoicings were soon tempered by worries over an uncertain peace and the changed attitudes which would shape the post-war years.

In 1948, Glenmore Lodge became a centre for outdoor education and sports after its use as a training base for Norwegian Special Forces during the Second World War (A. E. GLEN)

EXCURSION

Loch Garten Nature Reserve

The Royal Society for the Protection of Birds owns this reserve in the forest of Abernethy where the best known osprey nesting site in Scotland can be viewed. Take the A9153 to Kinveachy, branching right on to the A95 at the junction. Look out for the sign showing 'RSPB Ospreys'. After ¾ mile (1.2km) branch right again at Deshar school on to the road leading to Boat of Garten. Continue through the village crossing the River Spey. At the first T-junction on the B970 go left towards Nethybridge. After about half a mile (1km) take the right turn clearly marked 'RSPB Ospreys'. One and a half miles later (2km), the shores of Loch Garten are reached. There is ample parking at the entrance to the site and a short walk leads to the viewing hide.

For further information contact the RSPB 01479 821409.

This excursion is also possible following the National Cycle Track which borders the road from Kinveachy to Boat of Garten.

CHAPTER 7

Post-War Pressures and the Ski Boom
1945 – 1965

The Cairngorm gateway was suddenly much quieter. Its hill tracks had become well worn under the tramping of soldiers' boots and their 'middens' of rusting tins defiled many a summit. Heaps of stones marked their high level 'howffs' while abandoned army huts plus munitions stores hid in odd corners of the forests. The Aviemore Hotel and big houses like the Doune of Rothiemurchus, which had been commandeered, were left badly run down. The whole district felt the hiatus as business boosted by the military and the forestry camps shrank. Yet the military presence did not disappear altogether as there was a workshop for a unit of the Royal Electrical and Mechanical Engineers or REME in Grantown for several years. They became so much part of the community that they had a football team in the local welfare league.

Priorities which had been postponed by the long conflict began to surface. One of the central issues was housing. Scarcely had the Newfies vacated their camps than folk were to be seen trundling barrows laden with their possessions along the Great North Road in order to claim a hut for their use. Back to this community struggling with the painful realities of peacetime had come Desmond Nethersole Thompson. Of Irish extraction, he had been educated in England. Forsaking school mastering for ornithology, he arrived in the Highlands in 1934, first settling in a remote part of Abernethy forest and latterly at Whitewell in Rothiemurchus. He was large, exuberant and something of a mystery; he believed that gateway folk saw him as 'a hot headed young bird fancier from the bogs of Ireland who was always in too much of a hurry'.

A remarkable lady, Carrie Mackenzie, became Desmond's wife and they had a son, Brock, and a daughter, Myrtle. Carrie was a capable mountain guide having taken visitors over many years to the Cairngorms.

Desmond Nethersole Thompson, the distinguished ornithologist, who as a controversial councillor achieved so much for the Aviemore district (TOM WEIR)

She had a considerable knowledge of Highland birds and must be credited with greatly advancing Desmond's awareness of them. Carrie joined him in spending long hours on the high plateau and the moors charting every move such birds as the dotterel and the greenshank made. She and her children endured the privations of the years when Desmond, an impecunious naturalist, had yet to win recognition. They tolerated a small galvanised cottage on the slopes of Tullochgrue for which a rent of £8 a year had to be paid. It was on croft land where there was protection from eviction. Carrie kept it habitable, despite having to fetch water from a spring. To earn some money they occasionally had to resort to selling the eggs of rare species – Desmond knew those which would nest again. Together with his lifestyle and his politics, this did not endear him to the landowners or to more orthodox ornithologists.

A volunteer in the Second World War, how Desmond ever came to be a captain in the Royal Army Service Corps intrigued those with military links. He was a citizen of the Irish Republic, hailing from a Kerry family and proud of it. He must have been one of the most unconventional soldiers ever to don a uniform. As an expert ornithologist his knowledge however was found invaluable for he was a member of the exclusive War Office Pigeon Corps; his duties led to him being arrested on D-Day as a possible enemy agent – for spying on the cliffs at Dover when he was only looking for the nest of a peregrine falcon, a bird of prey which could cause casualties among carrier pigeons.

Desmond was a confirmed socialist but he was perceived as exotic among the Labour Party faithful who expected shop floor antecedents. His selection as a parliamentary candidate caused ructions in the party in Inverness-shire because his candidature was not endorsed by the National Executive. Desmond was outraged especially as he had supported 'the principles of socialism since boyhood'. It provoked a split producing a Highland Independent Labour Party which was pro-Nethersole Thompson. It got little support but there was an advantage for Desmond – he became well known, even notorious, in the north. To avoid splitting the Labour vote, he withdrew his candidature. His exploits had begun by challenging Lady Katherine Grant, the wife of Iain Grant, the heir apparent to the Laird of Rothiemurchus, for a seat on Inverness-shire County Council. He was successful too. So by December 1945 Desmond had arrived on the political stage as an independent member representing Aviemore and Rothiemurchus on that council. (As for polling stations, so modest was Aviemore that the little hall of the former U.F. church and the garage at the rear of the Cairngorm Hotel served that purpose.)

On becoming a county councillor, Desmond's situation seemed to improve. His old battle dress, with a red and yellow muffler wound round his neck, was replaced by tweed plusfours, a duffle coat and a red 'toorie' hat. Brock's motorcycle combination provided the transport, the bulky Desmond packing himself into the sidecar for the bumpy ride along the bouldery track from Whitewell down to Coylumbridge. Like an emboldened species, he became much more visible on public hall platforms and at the station when journeying to and from Inverness. Thankfully, his finances were eased by a Leverhulme Award – just £150 for two years – which allowed him to engage in further research. His patience in lying for hours on his belly on some rugged moor or damp peat moss was legendary. Bird watchers had to bow to his sheer persistence in researching the territorial behaviour of rare birds. After sixteen years of painstaking work in Rothiemurchus, his ground-breaking monograph on the greenshank appeared in 1952. It was remarked that given his political leanings it should have been about redshanks! In 1966 his book on the snow bunting followed; it had involved 263 nights on the high plateaus and more years of assiduous observation. The whole family was engaged as a support team – Myrtle and Brock would be sent to collect water miles from the tent up on the mountain tops in order to brew up a pot of tea.

Desmond stood twice for Parliament as the official Labour candidate fighting the Inverness-shire constituency and polling a record vote for his party of over 11,000, but this was not enough to win the seat. He would have brought colour to the House of Commons and would have revelled in the cut and thrust of debate. His soft, but educated, Irish voice sometimes through sheer enthusiasm tumbled into a stutter. He disliked party labels believing that in the Highlands 'we must unite or perish'.

Aviemore and Rothiemurchus Village Council, revitalised by new blood after the war, called meetings of ratepayers with Captain Thompson in the chair. Housing, drainage and water supply plus other matters of local importance were on the agenda. Desmond, having nailed his political colours to the mast, soon showed that these were vibrantly socialist. He had fallen foul of the landed interests and their supporters, who were predominantly Conservative and Unionist, which did not make progress easy. Meanwhile, the Labour Party in the south emphasised the need for a speedy solution to the housing shortage even although one of its leading lights, Aneurin Bevan, condemned the principle of prefabricated houses. This was a shame as 'prefabs' were practical and proved exceedingly popular. Demand for new homes across Britain was estimated at not less than 100,000; nearly all people married during or after the war and thousands of returning servicemen were waiting with growing impatience to hear of a plan to build houses in quantity. Regarding the population of the gateway parishes, Duthil and Rothiemurchus were experiencing slight growth but Abernethy and Kincardine were in continuing decline – at just over 1,000 people being less than half the total in the former districts.

A breakthrough in the post 1945 years was the construction of council houses. Cairngorm Avenue in Aviemore was completed in 1949 (A. E. GLEN)

There had been a poor record of housing provision in the inter-war period. The whole of Inverness-shire only managed to have 434 new dwellings built in 22 years. Low standards and overcrowding were the outcomes. The new council was faced with constructing 2,000 homes and clearly this would take time. Conditions were appalling in the gateway as Desmond graphically disclosed. In Boat of Garten, three families squatted in dilapidated saw mill bothies vacated by the Newfies; the windows were broken and the roofs leaked. In Rothiemurchus a tiny cottage accommodated a family of seven; in Aviemore, nine people occupied a two roomed council flat. Altogether he computed that 25 families lived in 'bestial conditions' around Aviemore and 19 were in a similar plight near Boat of Garten. Desmond knew what it was like to endure inadequate housing which was only too common in the Highlands − a dwelling without proper sanitation, without running water, without electricity and with poor road access. His family occupied such a place. No wonder he was determined to improve services in the district.

First Desmond targeted empty properties in the gateway − villas, shooting lodges and hotels which shut for the winter − with a view to seeking their requisition as emergency accommodation. In this he was supported by the British Legion which was only too aware that it had taken seven years after the First World War to produce any new council houses in Inverness-shire. His proposal however provoked an outcry as people recalled the damage done to houses by some evacuee families. Not even the promise of compensation would win over the owners who were 'jealous of the sanctity of their homes'. There were bitter letters in the local papers but Desmond's appeals to their sense of decency fell on deaf ears.

So acute was the housing situation that ten Newfie huts at Kinveachy were adapted as temporary accommodation. Desmond admitted that they were not ideal but he did as much as he could in those days of austerity to have them made comfortable. By 1949 the first of the new council houses of four and five apartments at Cairngorm Avenue in Aviemore, built to a pleasing but standard design by the county architect, were becoming available at rents of £26 and £30 a year. A register of possible tenants was drawn up to ensure a fair allocation. New houses also followed at Boat of Garten and Kincraig. Later in Aviemore there came Myrtlefield, named after his daughter, the Collie Cottages for the elderly and Dell Mhor in Rothiemurchus. Even those who did not go along with Desmond's socialist views had to admit that no one worked harder or had done more good for gateway families than he. One of his famous dictums as a prospective parliamentary candidate was, 'The drift from the Highlands has been halted for the first time since Culloden'. Improving the quality of life for gateway folk certainly contributed to that welcome trend. The council house schemes were a bonus for the nearest shopkeepers, like Jock Garrow's grocery store and Charlie Stewart's butcher's shop by the Aviemore burn. Outlying places were served by their vans and a series of others. In keeping with the socialist vision of the time, a 'Co-op' store appeared in virtually every village when the Scottish Co-operative Wholesale Society bought out family businesses and put up its 'SCWS' signs.

There were numerous scarcities in the early post-war period. In some ways circumstances were more straightened than in wartime for extra items such as bread, oats and soap came to be rationed. On the farms everything from boots to machinery was lacking as it was difficult to turn round the war economy to meet the pent up demands of peacetime. For instance leather footwear for civilians became very limited. Purchasing a thermos flask required a permit, only made available to bona fide outdoor workers. It took determination to find any new furniture of the 'utility' type and old household plenishings sold at 'roups'(country auctions) fetched good prices. The Scottish Women's Rural Institute was still concerned with making lean resources stretch to lunches 'costing not more than 6d (2.5p)' and to doing wonders with 'mock cream'. Coal supplies were very short with local fuel overseers ensuring that no household exceeded a half ton of fuel in twelve months. In every sense, 'make-do-and-mend' continued.

There was to be no let up on the land either; farmers were urged to keep up production as the food situation world wide was reckoned to be critical. In fact potato and grain acreages in Britain were raised again and any surplus land was put under grass for three years. Even the aerodrome at Forres was ploughed up. In 1946 a hill cattle subsidy was introduced and it was to prove the salvation of many an upland farm. With so much reconstruction in progress, labour was insufficient for the harvests and P.O.W. and soldier assistance was welcomed. School children had to help with the potato lifting for a fortnight in October and with the school age raised to 14 years this duty was seen as 'very unsettling'. Thus began the 'tattie holidays' but they were not much fun – often chilly, muddy and back breaking. Shortly the little 'Fergie' tractors in their grey paint arrived on the scene; being 'made in Britain' they saved on imports too. Their three point hitch and hydraulic controls revolutionised farm work and they were affordable. Another boon to some farmers were the milk marketing boards guaranteeing a monthly milk cheque in return for 365 days of careful and unrelenting attention to a dairy herd. Germans had a name for being hard working and thorough and ex-P.O.W. Helmut Fritzche at Avielochan won an award for clean milk supplies.

There were other new trends, especially in the matter of transport. The postmen who served remote districts got vans instead of making deliveries on cycles. Far from speeding up the mail there was little benefit to customers as the time keeping of the train now known as the 'Postal' was too unreliable to give an improved service. No wonder – after five years of severe strain the railways were almost clapped out. School buses were introduced to transport the youngest pupils from outlying places to such schools as Rothiemurchus but in the cause of centralisation small schools such as Dorback, Glen Feshie and Insh were closed. Primary schools had once been about five miles apart to make them within 'walking distance' of most pupils. As the 'schoolie' and its teacher had been the hub of many a small community, folk were sorry to see them go. Those schools that survived had new 'canteens', even the name aping the military. Tighter planning controls provoked shock in many quarters and from now on 'no sheds or outhouses were to be erected without authority'. It was an edict which gateway folk resented because they had been accustomed to constructing what they pleased and it was described as 'more Hitlerism' in the Highlands.

Nevertheless, normality was returning. Men in the Forces were demobbed, 'welcome home' parties greeted them and in 1947 time-honoured events such as the Strathspey Farmers' Club Show and the Abernethy Highland Games were revived. The young Nina, Countess of Seafield, on coming into her inheritance of the vast Strathspey Estates, was received at Kinveachy Lodge by the tenantry and was carried over the doorstep by her husband, Derek Studley-Herbert whom she had married in secret in the 1930s. Football teams played again and the first 'Football Queen' was chosen by a ballot of the lads present at a dance; older heads shook in disbelief over the very idea that there should be a 'pin up' in their midst. At the 'Harvest Home' in the Dell of Rothiemurchus over 300 folk danced the night away and it was just like old times, 'up the howe an' doon the howe, ye never saw such jinkies'.

Having been without holidays for so long, more summer visitors than ever were coming back or were sampling the district for the first time. The legislation of the Holidays with Pay Act of 1948 had presented new possibilities to folk so long denied such pleasures. If they intended to stay five days or more they had to remember to take their ration books with them, otherwise emergency food cards had to be obtained. Such was the press of traffic on the railway that extra coaches were put on the trains and these once again ran in several portions in the high season. Youngsters counted the days until their Highland holiday in the strath would begin:

> Lying in bed at night and hearing the engines whistling and hooting in the station and the echoes in the hills were a joy to me. Their puffing gradually became fainter and fainter as they laboured up the long bank to Carrbridge . . . The scent of pines and heather wafted on the air and I felt I could burst with happiness.
>
> – PEIGI HIGSON

The Highland line continued to be very busy with heavy freight traffic but to some the 'nocturnal noises' at Aviemore Junction were spoiling the reputation of the whole district as a 'restful holiday resort'. Threats to the railway were becoming apparent – a furniture remover proposed taking Aberdeen-Angus stock to the cattle sales at Perth by road which was the beginning of the challenge to rail's monopoly of livestock in transit.

To promote the holiday revival, thousands of letters had been sent out to people 'in the Empire and overseas' to persuade them to come to Scotland. By taking a flight from New York a visitor could reach the Highlands in just 46 hours. It was urged that information bureaux to assist tourists should be set up and many more camp sites made; it might be thought that holidaymakers with recent experiences of the forces would have had enough of these – but no. This was the era of the holiday camp but none appeared in the gateway.

Although there was renewed apprehension with the onset of the Korean War in 1952 – yet another Comforts' Fund was started and men were encouraged to enlist in a revived Home Guard – peacetime pursuits predominated. An entertainment revolution was on the horizon – television. Faint signals were detected from the Kirk o'Shotts transmitter when it went into action. Soon the new houses were sprouting TV aerials and in the churches ministers were pondering whether programmes would strengthen family circles or subject people to even more distractions and stress. Aviemore folk were renowned for the success of their drama club in the Scottish Community Drama Association competitions, but would such activities now suffer?

A key organisation at the railway junction was the 'Mutual Improvement' class. Railwaymen throughout the country organised these self help groups with the aim of raising standards of proficiency in their work – in locomotive management and so on. The knowledge gained there could lead to promotion. It was the railwaymen who still gave the celebrated children's party at Christmas. So a Mutual Improvement Social

Community activities resumed in peacetime. Aviemore's football team of 1949–50 were champions, winning the Strathspey & Badenoch Welfare League plus several cups: (left to right) back row: James Anderson, Lewis Grant, Bob Ingram, James Mitchell, Donnie Maclennan, Calum Gault. Front row: Alan McBean, Hamish McLeod, Jack McDonald, John Brown, Sandy Gordon. The majority were railwaymen (Glen Collection / Irene Gordon)

Club evolved and it held whist drives and dances to raise funds for that event which was still very much part of the social calendar.

Football prompted similar ventures. Such was the game's popularity that by 1953, Aviemore had another team, Aviemore Thistle, formed to give younger lads a game. There was a new ground too, thanks to support from the National Playing Fields Association and to volunteers who carted earth and gathered tons of stones off the surface as these worked their way through the subsoil.

On the other side of the political spectrum from Desmond Nethersole Thompson was the prospective Unionist candidate for Inverness-shire, Lord Malcolm Douglas-Hamilton, a son of the Duke of Hamilton. (The Unionist Party was a Scottish clone of Britain's Conservative Party.) A man of action, he was an aviator of note who came to know the Cairngorms well as he skimmed their plateaus and corries in a Tiger

The low-cost accommodation of Aviemore's Youth Hostel, which was opened in 1933, was appreciated by cyclists, hill walkers and hikers. The photograph was taken in the mid-1950s when the original 'hut' had been considerably enlarged (I. W. CUMMING)

Moth biplane. He believed that youngsters should have the same possibilities of adventure as he had – 'For a nation to be healthy in every sense, its young people should know and revere their country'. Outdoor activities would be an 'antidote to much of the evil which arises through too much urbanisation'. Pioneering ventures in which his brother David had been involved pre-war in Glen Affric and in Morayshire were the prototypes for centres 'heralding a new era in educational methods'.

The time was ripe. The trek to the countryside which had begun in the inter-war years was reinforced by war time experiences which took men into hill country to train and ski where some got a real liking for it and for its folk. In time they returned and brought their families. At Glenmore, the lodge and huts vacated by the Norwegians lay empty and so youths from Clydebank came on a skiing holiday there in 1945. It happened that Lord Malcolm was the Commandant of the Air Training Corps in Scotland and the following year 200 cadets took part in a course in rock and snow climbing where 'initiative and resolve, observation and alertness' were enhanced. More week long courses were set up. Meanwhile, the Balavil Arms Hotel in Newtonmore advertised the

Bracken Ski School and ski racing; Bill Bracken was a former captain of the British ski team and guests used the slopes of bleak Drumochter for their practice. The demand from university ski parties was such that several hotels in the gateway opened early in the season.

Shortly the Scottish Education Department took a ten-year lease of part of Glenmore Lodge from the Forestry Commission as a training base for a range of outdoor activities. While the premises were being prepared for their new role, the 'students' were billeted at Aviemore Hotel, spruced up after its military occupation. The chief instructor was Lord Malcolm, heading the mountain adventures by day and entertaining the parties with film shows and ceilidhs in the evenings. In September 1948, Glenmore Lodge was officially opened by the Secretary of State for Scotland, Arthur Woodburn, as the 'first civilian mountain school in Britain'. Administered by the Central Council for Physical Recreation, courses of one to four weeks were organised 'to assist the individual to discover his or her physical, mental and spiritual potential . . . through the medium of nailed boots, skis or hand-on-the-tiller'. The choice of Glenmore, described as 'a region of high beauty and rich in natural treasures', was praised.

The first warden was the Rev R.J.V. Clark, an Episcoplian clergyman who was well known as a mountaineer and organiser of mountain rescue teams in Lochaber. He set about involving education committees around Scotland in his marketing drive for Glenmore and even lured the directors of education to a conference at the Aviemore Hotel. To give them a taste of the great outdoors, they were taken on a 'tramp' to the Pass of Ryvoan where the more venturesome bathed in the Green Loch (Lochan Uaine). Clark found an enthusiastic ally in Glasgow's influential Director of Education, Stewart Macintosh, a man of Highland descent who presided over the largest education authority in Scotland. Over the years hundreds of Glasgow children were to go to Glenmore. Indeed, the experience had such a profound effect on many youngsters, who had never had the opportunity of enjoying wild countryside, that a Glenmore Club was formed in Glasgow and regular reunions were held. Clark was followed as warden by Charlie Cromar who was on the staff of the Central Council for Physical Recreation. Their wives had to double as both housekeepers and secretaries looking after 35 to 40 students who were typically senior school pupils in term time. Arriving by train at Aviemore, they were conveyed by Johnnie Fraser's coal lorry to Glenmore – a cold and bumpy journey to a then reclusive place. During the school holidays courses for adults were held at a cost of just six guineas (£6.30) a week.

One of the more colourful 'amateur' instructors at Glenmore was Valdemar Axel Firsoff, of Swedish-Polish descent who came to the gateway as a convalescent in 1943. He was an astronomer and an able linguist who had escaped over the Tatra Mountains and made his way to Britain. Acknowledged as an expert in mountain warfare training, he was already the author of several books. First lodging in Glen Feshie, he explored the surrounding hills there. Moving to a cottage near Granish with his wife Marjorie and little son, he was seen regularly on skis in Aviemore whenever snow allowed. In 1949 his masterly book 'The Cairngorms on Foot and Ski', which was enlivened with his own sketches and photographs, was published. It was a ground-breaking effort.

Firsoff was not the only writer to revel in the mountain grandeur of the Cairngorm gateway at that time. The naturalist Richard Perry, based in Glen Tromie, produced his book 'In the High Grampians'. He was an experienced observer having written about Lindisfarne and having spent time as a shepherd on Skye. The recognition of the Insh meadows as a valuable wet land habitat owes much to his efforts. The work of the outstanding photographers, Robert M. Adam in landscape and Eric Hosking in birds, brought the natural history of the gateway region increasingly to public attention. Adam made his retirement home in Kingussie while Hosking was a regular visitor to Coylumbridge. Jack Drake, a retired Army officer, set up his alpine nursery on his family's estate at Inshriach. He had gathered seeds of rarities in the Himalayan foothills and from such small beginnings, Inshriach has become a mecca for rock gardeners, continued for many years by his business partner, John Lawson.

The upheavals of wartime had accelerated the disappearance of old Highland ways. Even before the conflict Dr Isabel F. Grant, a remarkable woman and capable scholar, had resolved to try to save the material settings in which folk had lived in several districts. She first bought a disused but small church on Iona and so, when her collection threatened to overflow, bigger premises had to be got. In 1946 the old Pitmain Lodge, a large house with some land attached, was acquired in Kingussie for *Am Fasgadh*, the Highland Folk Museum. A series of cottage types from various parts of the Highlands was reconstructed on the site and many gifts were made by local folk to the enrichment of the collection. It was a brave venture which in time was supported by the Scottish universities and is now administered by the Highland Council.

National Parks were back on the agenda. Hugh Dalton, the Labour Chancellor of the Exchequer, came on holiday to the Cairngorm gateway. He saw enough of the mountains and their surroundings to convince him that 'the area is indeed most suitable for a National Park'. The English examples established in 1949 were under the umbrella of the

Department of Health at the time. Five years earlier a survey committee had been at work on a similar proposition in Scotland and in January 1945 it presented its report with a selection of suitable places, although it admitted being spoilt for choice. Five won its recommendation – Loch Lomond and the Trossachs, the western glens of Inverness-shire – Affric, Canisp and Strath Farrar, Ben Nevis with Glen Coe and Blackmount, the Cairngorms, and Wester Ross with Loch Torridon, Loch Maree and Little Loch Broom. The Cairngorms were 'fourth in order of suitability' for reasons that make strange reading today – their distance from the main urban centres of population, their surprisingly low popularity as measured by the number of visitors at adjacent youth hostels and the inflammable nature of much of their surface, namely their peat, heather moors and pine forests. Nevertheless, the proposal was accepted and the Ramsay Committee was formed to consider the management and administration of National Parks in Scotland. An area of some 180 square miles (250km²), comprising the whole of the western and central massif of the Cairngorms and their intervening valleys, such as Glen Feshie and Glenmore, was earmarked. The key principles were:

> Country of outstanding natural beauty, preferably also of scientific, cultural or historic interest, owned and controlled by the Nation, accessible to all as a matter of right under suitable regulations . . . administered so that its distinctive values may be preserved unimpaired for the enjoyment and recreation of future generations.

Am Fasgadh, the Highland Folk Museum, was established in the former Pitmain Lodge at Kingussie by Dr Isobel F Grant. Close proximity to the railway line, however, led to replica buildings being set on fire by sparks from locomotives (A. E. GLEN)

Nor need the Scottish contenders be modelled on English lines for there were many other prototypes in Europe – from Norway and Sweden to Italy and Spain where National Parks had been established. But there was a problem. Most of the land in the proposed National Parks in Scotland was not owned by the nation. It was in private hands and so legal and other difficulties would be encountered; it was envisaged that the gradual acquisition of 3,000 square miles (4,140km^2) of non-cultivated land over a decade or two would be involved. This was not seen as an obstacle as the cost of mountain and moor was so low – a compensation estimate of 30 shillings (£1.50) per acre was described as 'generous'. On this basis the Cairngorms could have been acquired for £200,000. The landed proprietors were again thoroughly unimpressed especially over the threat to their inheritances, the potential loss of rent rolls, of sporting rentals and of rates' revenue to the counties.

The Ramsay Committee's other views were generally sensible. Traditional activities would be allowed to continue within a National Park as these must be productive areas supporting thriving rural communities, 'virile populations' instead of 'manmade wilderness'. For example, farming and forestry were seen as compatible with National Park objectives; quarrying was not. The control of deer and other game was accepted as was the need for the making and maintenance of paths and bridle tracks. While hostel accommodation was a possibility, camping would be limited and there would be no mountain huts as such. Scottish skiing interests were not consulted as the activity was of so little consequence at the time – 'facilities for winter sports' only received a mention. The existence of the National Park would ensure that there would be 'no defacement of the views from it' and the threat of a motor road through Glen Feshie would be forever removed. In 1947 the cost of establishing and developing the five Scottish National Parks was put at £3.2 million. The Labour government however had other pressing issues in mind – housing, health and its nationalisation programmes for the coal and steel industries, the railways and much else. By the 1950s nothing had happened.

Just when the holiday business seemed to be prospering once more, the gateway received a savage blow. On 26 September 1950 the Aviemore Hotel was destroyed by fire. It began around 8 am and within an hour the premises were gutted. When the outbreak was discovered in a small pantry on the first floor, the seventy guests were roused by the sound of fire gongs. Many clad only in their night attire escaped by lowering rope and chain ladders from their bedroom windows and scrambling to the ground. Others trapped on upper floors tore up bedclothes and made improvised ropes down which they slid to safety. Fire extinguishers proved of no avail as rescuers tried to crawl to the source of the blaze. Many brave attempts were made by hotel staff and by railway employees to carry out rescues. Especially courageous work was done by Donald Maclennan, a young railway porter; after tying two ladders together he had them placed on the back of a lorry which was then reversed up to the blazing building. With a car tow rope in his mouth he climbed up and joined the rope to a sheet lowered by an elderly couple from a third floor window. They then pulled up the rope and tied it to a bed. Maclennan could then climb into the room. After lowering them to the ground, he joined William Waterson, an electrician, and John Haggerty, a railway ganger, in rescuing an elderly woman. William Duff, an engine driver, also climbed to the roof but weakened by smoke and badly burned, he was forced to retreat. Maclennan also used the lorry, ladders and his fearless climbing skills to save a maid in an attic room. Fire brigades were summoned from Kingussie, Grantown and Inverness but there was little they could do. There were two fatalities. Only the servants' quarters and outbuildings escaped. George Maclennan's supreme courage was marked by the award of the George Medal, the highest recognition for civilian bravery in Britain.

In terms of fire prevention, it had been a case of too little too late. Permits had to be sought for all building work. Materials were scarce and demand was insatiable – so there were tight controls. In June 1947, the National Fire Service had made recommendations to the owners of the hotel – it should have been fitted with fire doors of a self closing type, steel fire escapes should have been installed and push button fire alarms on each floor. The cost was put at over £1,200, a sum which the hotel company was willing to pay but the work required over 10 tons of steel and 165 cubic feet (4.6m^2) of timber. Application was made for permits to cover these quantities without success. The enquiry reported sternly that public safety should have had priority over all other matters when a building was used for residential purposes. It was disclosed that the fire probably started from ashes emptied from a pail into newspapers which were then placed in a wicker basket in order to allow the pail to be used elsewhere. The extreme rapidity of the fire occurred not only from the lack of fire prevention measures but also from the nature of the interior walls – these were not of stone or brick but of timber, wooden lathes and plaster.

Many folk in the gateway area were thrown out of work and local trades people, who were the hotel's key suppliers, suffered in ensuing seasons. The large staff had also been good customers. The hundreds of well-to-do hotel guests, 'regulars' over many years, found other venues. Hugh Ross, the manager, who had worked tirelessly for a longer holiday season, especially for winter sports, hoped that the premier hotel in the strath, with its commanding views of the Cairngorms, would soon be rebuilt. Most regrettably it was not. What was left of the outhouses and staff accommodation was revamped as an improvised motel.

Shortly the Cairngorm gateway was in the news again and on a happier theme. 'Reindeer to return to Scotland' read the headline. Hunting legends from 800 years ago told of reindeer roaming the uplands of Caithness. After a long absence, a small herd from northern Sweden was to be introduced to the Highlands and where better than on the lower slopes of the Cairngorms? The moors of Rothiemurchus were the chosen terrain. The initiative came from Mikel Utsi, a member of a well-known Sami family in Norrbotten. For his bravery in helping Norwegians travel across the border between Norway and Sweden in the Second World War he had been decorated by King Haakon. First visiting the gateway in 1947, he saw the Cairngorms in a snow storm and was satisfied that they were 'reindeer country'. His wife was a distinguished American anthropologist, Dr Ethel Lindgren-Utsi. While Mikel was small in stature and ebullient, Dr Lindgren, as she preferred to be known, was tall, dignified and serious. Mikel was a recognised expert on all practical matters relating to reindeer but she too was very knowledgeable about the animals having accompanied them on migration across northern Europe.

It was no easy matter to bring eight reindeer to Scotland in 1951. The Scottish Home Department laid down strict conditions for the trial as there were fears about 'bovine diseases' which were quite unfounded. A Reindeer Council was set up with support from the Scottish Council (Development and Industry) with which Lord Bilsland of Kinrara was closely linked. The animals first had to be taken by lorry, then by train to Narvik in Norway where they were loaded on a freighter bound for Leith. The journey totalled 1,000 miles (1,600km). Months of quarantine then followed in Edinburgh Zoo which was a terrible hardship for beasts accustomed to range freely in tundra or forest and several succumbed. Those that survived the long incarceration emerged in poor shape and extra animals had to be imported.

The base for the experiment was Moormore, a former gamekeeper's cottage, leased from the Laird of Rothiemurchus, together with 3,000 acres (1,215ha) of land which had to be fenced. Only fourteen animals could be supported on such an area. It was an expensive exercise but it was believed that the Swedish government was involved. The Cold War was at its most bitter and the great resource of the Nordic reindeer herds was

Mikel Utsi, who re-introduced reindeer to Scotland in 1951 when he brought a nucleus herd from his homeland in Sweden's Norrbotten to the Cairngorm area (A. E. GLEN)

under threat. It was therefore thought wise to have a nucleus out with the northlands – hence the choice of the Scottish Highlands for the purpose. The Department of Agriculture for Scotland gave its approval and Mikel Utsi was officially 'Technical Adviser' to the Reindeer Company of the United Kingdom. His cousin, Niklaus Labba, came over as the first herder. He was totally different in both appearance and temperament from Mikel Utsi, being fair skinned, gloomy and very shy. The poor man was woefully homesick even although gateway folk were welcoming but without any English, he found it hard to make contact.

The Utsis' official home was near Cambridge and much time was spent travelling to Aviemore and to Glasgow where another batch of reindeer was quarantined in the city's dockland. Hospitality to the Utsis was generously repaid as gateway folk found out. These could be lively occasions as when Mikel took up the challenge of an American rancher to demonstrate his skill with a lasso by dropping it over the top of a telegraph pole in the main street of Newtonmore. Christmas treats in Aviemore were made more exciting by his arrival in Sami costume leading a sleigh pulled by reindeer; he enjoyed the fun and happiness it brought to gateway youngsters.

Although the Moormore reserve was at 800 feet (242m) or so, the herd was plagued by flies in summer and as the animals were fenced in there was no high ground to which they could escape to cool winds. They suffered dreadfully. After a couple of years, the Forestry Commission and the Nature Conservancy Council gave consent for a new reserve of 5,000 acres (2,024ha) to be formed at a higher altitude on Airgiod-meall (the silver hill) near the northern slopes of Cairn Gorm. It had been shown that the reindeer neither harmed native animals nor damaged commercial timber. They offered no competition to other creatures as their preferred food was reindeer moss, a type of lichen. By 1956, the experiment had cost over £8,000 but it had proved that reindeer could thrive and breed in Scotland. The herd was growing, two local men were employed as herders and visitors were welcomed at the reserve. In time the Utsis had a fine bungalow built in Glenmore with a superb view to the mountains and the grazings for their beloved reindeer. They named it 'Reindeer House' and within two decades they had 90 animals on the hill. It is now the base for the Reindeer Centre run by Tilly Smith.

There were memories of the war in 1952 when the new St Aidan's Roman Catholic chapel in Aviemore was dedicated to the memory of men of the 51st Highland Division in the presence of their colonel. The chapel on a hillock near the south entry to the village was mainly financed by Miss A. P. Keogh, a resident in Aviemore for many years who had been a nurse in the First World War. Hitherto the nearest chapel had been at Kingussie. The commandos from Highland Fieldcraft Training Centre, who had been under Lord Rowallan's command, were commemorated the following year when a cairn was unveiled in Glen Feshie. The military still kept a foothold in Rothiemurchus however where their ski hut below Airgiod-meall allowed practice for warfare in the tundra.

The solemn occasion of the coronation of Queen Elizabeth was marked by parades and parties; there was an upwelling of royal sentiment which showed in many strange ways – even gardeners planted up new varieties such as 'Elizabethan' strawberries and 'British Queen' potatoes. Gateway folk were well aware that Balmoral was the young monarch's favourite home and that she had a great attachment to the Highlands but they were dismayed by the use of the term 'the Second', which was quite inappropriate in a Scottish context. Many years were to elapse before she set foot in Strathspey.

The mountains again became the focus of attention in 1954 when the Cairngorms National Nature Reserve was created. Its purpose was to maintain 'as many as possible of the diverse animal and plant habitats which the reserve is capable of. generating, and where these have been destroyed in the past, of restoring them'. The Nature Conservancy, which was the responsible agency, was clearly edging towards the idea of sustainability. The Conservancy acquired only 10 per cent of the proposed reserve, the rest being managed in agreement with 'co-operative landowners'. The area chosen was the western massif centring upon Braeriach and Glen Einich which was mainly Rothiemurchus terrain. The laird received compensation for his land being 'regulated', or at least left untouched in order to achieve certain objectives in line with conservation. The reserve was not solely about preserving rarities, or keeping stretches of countryside unspoiled, or even about returning it to some primeval state – it was to be altogether more scientific being aimed at gaining understanding of its ecosystems, that remarkable interdependence of all living things in an evolving balance.

The reserve extended to 64,000 acres (25,910ha) and covered land ranging from 750 feet (228m) in the pine forests to over 4,000 feet (1,220m) on the arctic-like plateau of Braeriach with the Wells of Dee and the dramatic corries which girt its summit. With Glenmore and the segment with Cairn Gorm itself being increasingly disturbed by climbers, hill walkers and skiers, the western rampart was to be suitably protected and preserved. Even so in the 1950s 'people pressure' was not seen as a serious problem – it was 'just one more ecological factor to be studied'. There were no worries about restricting access; indeed the Conservancy was prepared to provide better facilities, such as bridges over difficult river crossings in remote locations to which parts would be flown by helicopter.

The NC agreements with landowners were for around twenty years, 'fairly short periods' in the Conservancy's view as it would have preferred to work on a much longer timescale. There was an obvious advantage in that the government was spared the expense of having to purchase estates outright. The whole business depended on keeping relationships with the landowners on a friendly basis for the latter 'had to make certain sacrifices in sovereignty' to further the programme. Iain Grant of Rothiemurchus was said to be paid handsomely for his involvement which must have eased the penurious state in which he appeared to exist. His threadbare tweeds seemed almost to put him on a par with many of his tenantry.

While the formation of the Cairngorms reserve was a premier prize for the Conservancy, another choice acquisition was the rock of Craigellachie where a second National Nature Reserve was established. It was geologically exciting as granite met Moine schist there. It also boasted an extensive birch wood with rare insects. Soon a nature trail was opened round Loch an Eilein and the task of informing visitors about the natural history of the gateway commenced, so that 'much that is now destroyed through ignorance may through better understanding be kept'. Auchantoul near Aviemore became the Speyside Research Station of the

Conservancy, later the Nature Conservancy Council.

It was inconceivable that Desmond Nethersole Thompson should remain silent when such events were happening on his patch. The county council supported a National Nature Reserve in the Cairngorms although it would have preferred a National Park. Desmond took the view that the latter would be 'the biggest thing for the district' and he foresaw improvements to approach roads, footbridges and high level huts for observers and wardens as an outcome. He believed that the Nature Conservancy alone would never be in a position to deliver these things and regretted that too little of the forest and moss was included in the reserve. There was personal bitterness over the employment of gamekeepers as wardens. He recalled his persecution by them – his tent with a notice pinned to it warning him off and an occasion when he arrived back with a fellow naturalist after a fifteen hour trek in the Cairngorms to find car tyres slashed and petrol adulterated. Desmond was also worried that increased access might spoil parts of the reserve unless 'proper planning' nurtured a harmony of interests.

And the ospreys were back. The Royal Society for the Protection of Birds was hot on their trail to guard their nesting sites from egg collectors. Desmond disclosed that the birds had been present in the gateway in 1954 and had then nested in several places with varying success. The public soon got to know of the ospreys' whereabouts near Loch Garten in Abernethy Forest; Boat of Garten being the nearest village to the ornithological activity saw a stream of eager, if confused, enquirers, 'Which is the road to the ostriches?' An egg collector robbed the nest in 1958 in spite of a watch being kept round the clock. Intruders risked fines or imprisonment. As nature programmes on television had boosted the popularity of bird watching, arrangements were made for visitors to view the favoured tree from a hide. By 1959, the RSPB had made application for a reserve of 400 acres (160ha) near Loch Garten to safeguard not only the nesting ospreys but also other rare species in the forest – capercaillies, crossbills and crested tits.

After the Second World War the railway had been nearing breaking point but now change was on the horizon. The railway network had been all but 'nationalised' during the conflict but in 1947 the private companies were formally taken over by the state as 'British Railways'. The new name and logo were soon displayed on the old lines' property but not before some of the worthies about Aviemore shed had chalked their own slogans on the locos –'It's our railway now'. There were high hopes for the new organisation and also for an integrated road and rail transport system in Britain from which the Highlands would be bound to gain.

New locomotives were a priority. In 1948 a series of engine exchanges between the different regions of British Railways was organised. The purpose was to find the best designs for a new generation of steam motive power. There was excitement among railway enthusiasts when it was announced that the Highland line would be one of the test routes. So it came about that a former Southern Railway locomotive of the West Country class and a former LNER B1 showed their paces against a LMS Class 5 from Inverness. One evening in early July round the curve into Aviemore Junction steamed *Yeovil*, the first Pacific style of engine ever to cross Drumochter summit. A throng of railwaymen and onlookers waited on the north end of the platform. It was a green engine with an 'air smoothed' appearance and it had a dynamometer car in tow. Its train was split at Aviemore – one portion to run to Inverness and the other to Forres. A friendly Southerner leant from the cab, 'I'm Driver Swain from Nine Elms shed, London, and this is my fireman, Bert Hooker'. Their engine was to excel on the climbs but lost time downhill; Driver Swain found the multiplicity of passing loops awkward. Nevertheless, the team

Highlights of 1948 were the Locomotive Exchanges between the constituent regions of British Railways. The former Southern Railway West Country class BR No 34004 Yeovil is seen at Aviemore (A. E. GLEN)

put up a heroic performance. If locomotives like the West Country class had been introduced on the Highland line, double heading could have been given up and economies made. The B1 driven by a canny Lowlander from Haymarket shed did not win many points. The best all rounder was the 'hiker' in the hands of Inverness men who knew the 'road' like the back of their hands.

Transportation was requiring a total overhaul. By 1949 the old 'Johnstone', the local train of happy memory, was winning few friends for rail travel; described as 'a three coach frigidity' it was withdrawn a year later. The 'London' (Euston to Inverness) had become 'one of the most capricious trains in the country' leading to many a bitter wait at Aviemore Junction. There was no bus service to Inverness and worse still no co-ordination between road and rail. There were cuts too prompting an angry passenger to complain that 'while Lochaber hungers on its train, Badenoch is hungering for a train' as some services no longer stopped at Newtonmore and Kincraig. New designs of engines, the BR Standard classes, did appear with convenient cab layouts and comfortable seats for their crews. Drivers like 'Slash' Cooper of Inverness and 'The Commando' from Aviemore responded to the problem of late-running trains; on one occasion they cut 28 minutes off the run from Aviemore Junction to Inverness. Allowing for the scheduled stop at Carrbridge and the climb all the way to Slochd, it was some achievement; the seventeen-coach 'Royal Highlander' with its two Black Fives hurtled down from the summit at over 90 miles per hour (140kph) arriving in Inverness on time. With hydro-electric schemes proliferating, the possible electrification of the Highland lines was held out and in 1954 a light railway up Ben Nevis was proposed. There were fears, however, about 'over modernising the mountains' – thereby removing their natural grandeur – and it came to nothing.

Shortly there were more profound plans for the railways on the table. In 1955 the British Transport Commission earmarked several Speyside stations for closure as 'poor use was made of the trains' and the cost of providing them was reported greatly to exceed the revenue earned. It wished to withdraw passenger services between Boat of Garten and Ballindalloch while shutting Nethybridge and Grantown East completely. The citizens of Grantown were up in arms – they argued that the railway was invaluable in snowy weather – and where would tourism be if rail links in the north were strangled little by little? British Railways seemed to make only half hearted efforts to encourage people to travel by train unlike the situation on 'the extremely efficient French railways'. For the time being, protests won a stay of execution for the line.

Fund raising for community projects was ongoing. This is the committee which raised so much money for the new village hall for Aviemore in 1949. Left to right, back row: William Grant, Mrs Rose, Mrs McBean, Mrs Fraser, Mrs Balfour, Mrs Matheson, Alec Matheson; front row: Mrs Sheriffs, Mrs Mackintosh, Mrs McCook, Mrs McSween, Mrs Garrow (A. E. GLEN)

By 1957, it was forecast that there would be diesel locomotives in the Highlands within four or five years. When this happened there would inevitably be redundancies at Aviemore. A year later a diesel rail bus was put on show at the junction and then began to operate on the threatened Speyside line between Aviemore and Elgin. A variety of these temperamental vehicles appeared; one type had to be run with its pneumatic windscreen wipers and doors in continuous action in frosty weather, otherwise the brakes came on! Nevertheless, the men who drove them relished the challenge as much as the close company and conversation of the passengers. Rumours circulated that certain 'motive power depots', as the engine sheds had been dignified, would close completely. This was a depressing prospect for the Aviemore area. Boat of Garten shed had already shut and its work had been transferred to the larger junction. The continuation and well being of the railway was crucial. Some 44 per cent of the working population of the district was employed on the railway with half on the motive power side; most families in Aviemore itself were dependent on it. Perhaps sensing that an era was drawing to a close, the BBC recorded a footplate journey on a Class 5 over Slochd to try to capture a piece of railway history. Soon men were being sent on courses to Edinburgh to learn about the new diesel locomotives and by 1960 class 26 machines were in action on the Highland line. In some desperation, Desmond Nethersole Thompson sought assurances from the British Transport Commission and from the Secretary of State for Scotland about the situation. The response was guarded – although Aviemore depot's activities might be 'restricted a little', it would remain open. Even Inverness-shire's Unionist Member of Parliament Neil McLean was misled in this matter.

A heartening project was a new hall in Aviemore which was the culmination of years of fund-raising, boosted by money from the Martineau Bequest and the Carnegie United Kingdom Trust. The land was gifted by the Countess of Seafield, who in this respect showed quite maternal support for the communities of the gateway. Construction began in 1954 on a site at the north edge of the village and it gave a real sense of pride to the community. Then there was the 'electric' brought to far corners of the gateway by the North of Scotland Hydro-Electricity Board; in 1954 a contract was placed to link up 500 farms and other premises east of the Great Glen at a cost of £250 per household. It was a lot of money to find; customers were advised to go 'all electric' and enjoy such wonders as kettles which would boil in two minutes. So candles and oil lamps, which had been the cause of fires in so many homes, and inconvenient radio batteries were at last given up.

Post-war there had been big plans to invest in forestry; in 1949 the Forestry Commission resumed planting in Glenmore where Swedish timber houses were erected for their workers. By the early 1950s however the hills of the Monadh Liath and many others were still bare after the wartime felling. The extensive scarred slopes caught the eye of King George VI en route to Inverness; questions were asked in high places, 'Why had the forest not been replanted?' The reply was that there were simply not enough foresters to go round. Shortly a joint scheme by the Forestry Commission and private estates was set up but a unique opportunity was again missed to help hill farmers become part-time foresters on Norwegian lines. It all hinged of course on land ownership and the entrenched attitudes to it. In 1944 Frank Fraser Darling, the noted naturalist, had declared at a conference that 'nothing beats a good laird' and that 'peasant ownership of the land is not common sense' to which a Norwegian replied that it worked very well in Norway! Dry weather brought fire risks to the forest – either from the cinders thrown out by steam locomotives or from unstubbed cigarettes. In spite of engines being fitted with spark arresters, over decades lineside fires ravaged Granish moor; one had threatened to destroy Boat of Garten and another

Nethybridge. The Crask near Carrbridge, being close to the railway, was repeatedly scorched. Once the peat was ignited, only the rains of autumn or a blanket of snow would finally douse the embers. There was a huge conflagration in Rothiemurchus forest in 1960; from the point where it commenced by the road to Loch Morlich, it fanned out to engulf not only Rothiemurchus woods but also large parts of the Forestry Commission plantations in the Sluggan pass and trees on Pityoulish estate. At one stage 1,000 men and ten fire brigades were at the site where over 1,600 acres (647ha) of vegetation were destroyed. There have been repetitions but none as serious; constant vigilance is always essential.

A new Glenmore Lodge with Murray Scott as warden opened its doors in September 1959. Located nearer the Pass of Ryvoan, it was a flat roofed, box-like construction of red cedar built to accommodate 60 students; unprepossessing it might be but at least it was relatively unobtrusive. The tentative act of faith at Glenmore had been fully justified and new courses trained instructors and leaders in a variety of outdoor activities. Now run by the Scottish Sports Council, it is the National Outdoor Training Centre for Scotland and specialises in mountain skills. The old lodge – which sadly lost its name to the new – was taken over by the Scottish Youth Hostels' Association as Loch Morlich Hostel and was renamed 'Cairngorm Lodge' in 2002. In the interval the barn and stable of the game keeper's farm had been converted by the Church of Scotland into the Sanctuary – a place of worship to serve walkers, climbers and users of the nearby campsite.

Two trends were emerging – the promotion of adventure tourism on a greater scale and in particular the expansion of skiing. More than ever skiing was welcomed as a means of hopefully extending the holiday season for 'the Happy Valley could be turned into a Ski Valley for at least two months in the spring'. The columns of skiers that ventured from Glenmore on to Cairn Gorm found it wearisome to wend their way up the mountainside for four miles (6.4km) only to have one run back down, or two if they were fit, for so much effort. Would a jeep road not make all the difference to their sport? In 1954 the Central Council for Physical Recreation appealed for one to be built as it was so depressing to see skiers 'trauchle up the hill in columns 200 yards (183m) long'. The district council argued in favour of a vehicle track plus a chalet on what was Forestry Commission land. There were flights of fancy too – 'Just imagine a motor road leading to a chalet at the top of the Lairig Ghru pass'. Even Desmond Nethersole Thompson thought the northern corries of Braeriach could be developed as one of the finest ski grounds in Scotland until he saw what downhill skiing involved.

Accordingly plans were laid for a Strathspey Winter Sports Development Association. Iain Grant of Rothiemurchus was a key player and endorsed these signs of enterprise. The visitors would bring social and economic benefits with winter sports filling a vacuum as the summer season was so short. As a laird he did not think that winter sports would conflict with other interests in the gateway at that time. To construct a sand and gravel track was estimated to cost only £2,500 but the idea soon evolved into something grander. Enquiries showed that there were 50,000 skiers in Britain but only 5 per cent ever came to Scotland. That number might be doubled if the facilities were right. There was always a key imponderable – the weather. While a ski road was being discussed, the elements again showed what they could do when a cloudburst in June washed away the road from Coylumbridge to Glenmore in two places.

There were also protagonists for a railway from Aviemore to the mountain, taking passengers to the same height as the proposed ski road but cost ruled it out. In the longer term it might have been more friendly to the environment demanding no massive parking lots on Cairn Gorm itself or in Glenmore. When the ski road was approved in 1958 Desmond Nethersole Thompson opposed it. He had no objection to a better road being made from Coylumbridge to Glenmore but he foresaw the ski development as the first stage in the commercialisation of the Cairngorms. The 2½ mile (4km) route up Cairn Gorm to the threshold of Coire Cas not only had tight hairpin bends but was only single track with passing places. Desmond argued that heavy costs in maintenance and snow clearing would be incurred – no wonder as the road itself cut through some of the best nursery slopes and the car park obliterated much of these too.

Nevertheless, the ski road project went ahead, kick-started by a donation of £170,000 from an anonymous source; by 1960 a single-track system had been constructed all the way from Coylumbridge up the slopes of the mountain to 'a smog free region of winter sunshine' – at least when the weather was kind. Meanwhile, the Forestry Commission had leased the skiing 'rights' on the higher ground above the tree line to the renamed Cairngorm Winter Sports Development Board, a non-profit making body representing mainly local interests. Iain Grant, now chairman, saw the road as 'a triumph of co-operation between the government, local authorities and private enterprise' which would bring gains to hotels, boarding houses and even farms, offering accommodation to skiers from Dalwhinnie to Grantown. This ski road was the first major incursion for winter sports into the unspoiled integrity of any premier Scottish mountain.

In October 1959 a public meeting in Newtonmore had introduced new players to the tourism stage whose actions were to have profound consequences for the region. Present that evening was William George Pottinger of the Scottish Home Department, seconded to a Scottish Tourist Board scheme for holiday development in the Highlands. Known to his fellow civil servants as 'Gorgeous George', he had a liking for the good things in life. The department stores magnate, Hugh Fraser (later Lord Fraser of Allander) was to mastermind the project. The village had been selected as a trial ground for plans to give it 'a new look'. Why Newtonmore? Probably because sports holidays, especially pony trekking, had been pioneered there by the Ormiston family at the Balavil Arms Hotel. It seemed to be a forward looking place.

Such a proposal from above struck the wrong chord with many local folk. They felt that initiatives were being taken out of their hands and there was resentment:

> Highland folk can only be horrified at the thought that they may suffer the desecration of being turned into a vast 'holiday camp'. They remain a stronghold of individuals in this mass-produced age.
> – GEORGIE HENSCHEL

Desmond Nethersole Thompson also tabled his concerns. He deplored the lack of consultation with the district councils and feared that tourism in the gateway would become 'an ugly haphazard thing, leading to a bed and breakfast state, rather than a great Highland movement for our people'. With respect to bed and breakfast provision, Desmond has proved mistaken. 'B & B' has in fact been a success story – a grass roots initiative which puts money into local pockets and has enabled a rising standard of living to be achieved throughout the Highlands. Others wondered what a draper could possibly know about tourism. 'Only a little' would have been a fair answer. From 1948 Hugh Fraser had been the proprietor of Nethybridge Hotel and he also leased the nearby farm of Coulnakyle. The latter was for his son, young Hugh, who had a wish to be a farmer. Hugh senior occasionally played the part of 'mine host' and appeared in the kilt. When the Aviemore Station Hotel Company sought premises after the fire of 1950, Hugh Fraser sold out. His frenetic pattern of take overs, targeted at department stores and culminating in 1959 with the acquisition of Harrods in London, was to follow; all this brought him fame, if not notoriety, as he built up the legendary House of Fraser.

After further explanation the so-called 'Fraser Plan' got off the ground.

In Newtonmore all disruptive elements and distractions would be removed, derelict sites cleared, new signs applied to shops and free paint made available in a range of approved colours. There would be improvements to hotels and 'the well cared for surroundings would encourage visitors to stop and explore'. Hugh Fraser believed that his Highland Tourist Development Company, with expert advice from the Scottish Tourist Board and the co-operation of public authorities and private individuals, could bring new prosperity to many villages. Later that year Hugh Fraser received a baronetcy, the lowest hereditary title in Britain, and became Sir Hugh. The title was conferred for charitable work but Sir Hugh was a staunch supporter of the Unionist Party, the Scottish arm of the Conservatives who were in power at that time, and helped to manage its funds.

For its part the Scottish Tourist Board wished to encourage tourist associations to help co-ordinate accommodation, transport and information; a paltry £10,000 was made available for the purpose. Shortly, George Pottinger recommended that such an organisation be set up to cover the whole of the upper 'Spey Valley' – the old terms of Badenoch and Strathspey were not trendy enough. Since 1956 there had been an association for hotel and boarding house interests headed by Alistair McIntyre of Carrbridge Hotel. In fact the latter village, spurred on by the Austrian Karl Fuchs, was determined to become a ski resort on Tyrolean lines with ski hire and transport to the slopes. Throughout the gateway, ski schools of European provenance appeared staffed by instructors with exotic names – Hans Kuwall, Rudi Prochaska, and Frith Finlayson, although the latter was a Scot from Clydebank who set up the Ski School d'Ecosse in Aviemore. A ski bus service was introduced and the vehicle's climb up the hills and s-bends of the ski road was quite an adventure; often as not passengers were asked to disembark and push the floundering bus up to the car park. The good-natured patrons took it as part of the fun of going skiing in the Highlands.

Scarcely had the ski road been in operation when early in August 1960 there was a disastrous washout on the route following a typical cloudburst on the mountains. Fed by the foaming burns streaming off the northern slopes of Cairn Gorm, the Allt Mòr was transformed into a raging torrent and rose 20 feet (6m) in little over one hour. It swept down the narrowing valley ripping out the thick deposits of sand, gravel and boulders which bordered its sides. A bridge was torn away and 300 yards (275m) of the ski road were destroyed trapping several vehicles and their parties on the hill. Once the water had subsided sufficiently, fallen trees were used as bridges by rescue personnel who were rushed to the scene. By midnight, the

In 1960 serious damage to the new ski road on Cairn Gorm was caused by a flash flood on the Allt Mor, a stream which drains the northern corries. Such events are not infrequent in the area (A. E. GLEN)

stranded had been brought safely to Glenmore. Gateway folk were not surprised. They had seen the results of such violent storms before and many had warned that the ski road's alignment was unwise. It was an area well known for such episodes and why had the Forestry Commission not been consulted about its weather history?

Events were moving ever faster. Soon the first chairlift on Cairn Gorm rose 1,000 feet (305m) to the shoulder of the mountain and conveyed 500 people per hour to within half a mile (800m) of the summit. Bob Clyde, its first manager, was also responsible for seeing to its construction for which he engaged some of his mountaineering companions from the famous Creag Dhu Club. Amazingly, demand proved brisker in the summer months than in the winter. A linking chairlift from the car park to save a twenty minute walk was soon proposed. The original White Lady Shieling was built in 1960 where the chairlifts met. But skiing did not generate a bonanza for local traders. Sam N. Mearns, who was the author of an informative guide book on Badenoch and Strathspey, observed that the main beneficiaries were hoteliers and boarding house keepers. Skiers were usually young folk with limited means who had spent a lot of money getting to the Highlands. They set off early for the ski grounds and by the time they returned the shops were closed. Hotels laid on entertainment in the evening which again brought little benefit to local businesses. What really allowed trade to flourish were the summer visitors who generally spent freely and the tourists who were passing through the strath. Activity holidays – pony trekking, hill walking, golfing, canoeing, dinghy sailing, angling and nature study – were widely advertised and growing in popularity every year. All these enhanced the summer season and met with local approval.

Touring the gateway together, it was inevitable that the eyes of Hugh Fraser and George Pottinger would fall on some likely places for a very ambitious scheme. One such location was in Rothiemurchus on the north side of the Coylumbridge road but the laird Iain Grant refused to sell on their terms – they proposed just £10,000 for 50 acres (20ha) of moorland. There was a determined rival in the ring however for the Rank Organisation offered £48,000 and secured the land. In 1961 planning permission for a 500 bed hotel and hostel on the site was given; so comfortable provision was certainly being made for more visitors to the gateway. Designed by Dundee architects, the structure, to be known as the Rank Motor Inn, had the attention of the Royal Fine Arts Commission and adopted an outline 'no higher than the trees' so as not to intrude upon the view to the Cairngorms or be too obvious in the Rothiemurchus landscape.

The easier access via the ski road took more climbers and skiers on to the hills throughout the year and accidents were increasing. A mountain rescue team, led by Peter Bruce, a telephone linesman, was officially constituted in 1962 with the local GP, Dr T. W. Palmer as chairman; twenty climbing enthusiasts joined up and fund raising began – just £500 was thought sufficient to equip such a team. Dealing with the casualties was another matter and every winter the hard pressed doctor found the injured from the slopes queuing up or deposited on his front doorsteps awaiting his attention. Thirty years on, mountain rescue sorties absorbed the local team in almost 1,400 man hours each year, mainly arising from incidents in winter.

Aviemore's shopkeepers had plans to replace their old shacks with a set of new shops in a simple line-up fronting the Great North Road. Grass roots enterprise was clearly at work. So a terrace of shops was built on former railway land to house a pharmacy, a general merchant, a butcher, a tea room, a sports outlet and a garage. Opened in 1963, it was a modest scheme financed by the business people concerned, notably the McCook, Grant and Lorimer families and was a genuine attempt to provide better facilities to meet 'the tremendous increase in the tourist trade'. It was sad to see the old 'shoppies' disappear. Syd Garwood's hairdresser-cum-shoe shop had been a village institution; purchasers of shoes, who generated far more revenue than hair trims, always had priority. So Syd would confidently abandon his scissors and his customer in the back shop in the certain knowledge that no one would dare leave with a style half cut.

In 1962 a project to build 'a unique tourist centre' on the northern approaches to Aviemore, was announced by a group of Highland hoteliers from Carrbridge, Lynwilg and Blair Atholl plus some Strathspey financial interests. (At the time there were just 135 beds available for tourists in and around Aviemore.) They had taken an option on land on both sides of the Great North Road for a motel and chalets to accommodate 120 guests, together with a restaurant and recreation centre including an indoor swimming pool, bowling alley, indoor curling and skating rinks. The project was estimated to cost £250,000 and the designs showed it to be in a 'ranch' style with a low profile. The Royal Fine Arts Commission was again consulted at the planning stage about its suitability. It was the first of a stream of plans aimed at cashing in on the skiing and tourist boom.

By 1963 developments were coming thick and fast around Aviemore. South of the village another hotel project – the High Range which was based on chalets – was in progress. It caused the licensing court sitting at Kingussie a headache because it had 'no sleeping compartments in the main building' and would not therefore qualify as a hotel. Nevertheless, it was approved and quickly completed for Graham Mackay and his partners at a cost of £80,000. Then came proposals for a development right in the core of the village. The site was occupied by the buildings of the old Aviemore Inn and its adjoining farm, the land being feued by the Seafield Estates for the purpose. The intention was to demolish some of the historic structures and replace them with a motor inn and restaurant, to be known as the 'Red MacGregor', a ski school and other facilities – three separate projects using the same architects. A piecemeal approach to the overall 'look' of the village was becoming only too obvious. 'New' was perceived with narrow vision as 'good'; 'old' was out of date, an obstacle to progress, maybe just a liability – and few appreciated what 'heritage' even meant.

In the same year, Dr Beeching's report 'The Reshaping of British Railways' was published. Described as 'rough, ruthless and reckless', it proposed numerous closures and cutbacks in the railway system. Roads and motorways were the special enthusiasm of Ernest Marples, Minister of Transport in the Tory government; he had links with the construction industry and was responsible for commissioning Richard Beeching's investigation. The old Highland route over Dava to Forres, the Speyside line to Craigellachie and the Coast 'road' of the former GNSR were to be shut. Aviemore Junction would inevitably be hard hit. Consequently men were transferred to other sheds – to Perth, Fort William, Glasgow's Eastfield and even down south; some were second and third generation railwaymen and proud of their lineage. The close-knit community bound by ties of intermarriage and family, which had evolved over a century, was torn apart. Railways were out of favour and even the hotel company erased the word 'station' from its registered name. The passenger services on the Forres and Speyside lines were withdrawn in October 1965 and the following year the Aviemore depot was finally abandoned. The big engine shed was taken over as a workshop by Tommy Mackenzie of Rothiemurchus smithy. Only freight services to Craigellachie to meet the needs of the Scotch whisky distilleries continued until 1968.

The neat railway terraces in Aviemore were sold off en bloc and the foursquare granite cottages in Boat of Garten found new owners. With Aviemore, shorn of its junction status, a 'bothy' on the island platform sufficed as a base for staff. A few were left to reminisce about the hard but satisfying days when drivers such as Bobbins, Washie, the Mole, Von Kluck, Suet and Adequate, or firemen like the Dancer, Honk, Snappy, Flash and Shortie manned the five 'links' or duties for which Aviemore was responsible, supported by such shed staff as Bouler, Snuffie, the Wizard and Banana. A few were unperturbed by nicknames but most objected and hence these were rarely used to a person's face but always when speaking about them. A terrible hush would fall on the bothy by the engine shed if a byname should be let slip within earshot. Some nick names had been acquired in school days but railwaymen were quick to find a good fit if one was lacking.

So there was much concern about employment in the gateway and prospects did not seem hopeful. Then came the bombshell – a £3 million tourist project to create a massive centre in Aviemore was announced in September 1963. Immediately it had a chilly reception from local people – especially those in the tourist trade. William McEwan Younger, the chairman of Scottish and Newcastle Breweries, disclosed that 'several parties were interested in the scheme . . . there was the Winter Sports Development Board, the Scottish Development Department, British Railways and at least one petrol company'. He hoped that there would be several hotels with perhaps up to 100 rooms each, possibly shops and various indoor amenities. It was a vague but frightening prospect for those already committed to smaller projects as the giant could be expected to swamp them. What he did not say was that the Unionist Party, of which he was the Scottish chairman, was also acutely interested in the project's vote-catching potential in the county. The sitting Unionist MP, Neil McLean, had only a slender majority.

Nationally the Tory party faced an election that would be close run. The new Aviemore Centre would undoubtedly be an 'employment generating' plank in the manifesto. From that point of view the ploy did not work. In 1964, after well over a decade of Tory rule, a Labour government came to power and Inverness-shire reverted to its old colours when it returned the young Liberal, Russell Johnston, a Skyeman and a former teacher, as its Member of Parliament.

The statement that local interests 'would require to co-operate' in what would be a blue print for other Highland locations produced indignation. The gateway missed its most potent personality – in 1964 Desmond Nethersole Thompson had retired as a county councillor and had already migrated to Sutherland. The response from local representatives was therefore cool – here was a scheme of profound magnitude being prepared without sufficient consultation or thought and based on the false premise that every winter would be like the last two which had seen exceptional snow falls. While developments were not opposed, it was firmly believed that these should not upset existing well considered proposals. And why Aviemore where plenty was already happening? Why not in some Highland district needing assistance on a greater scale?

The site under consideration by Fraser's consortium was the ample grounds where the Aviemore Hotel had once stood amid its gardens, tennis courts and golf course. Hugh Fraser envisaged a Highland equivalent of St Moritz arising there. He knew the latter town well as he spent his holidays in the Alps twice a year. John Poulson, a Yorkshireman who had no formal qualifications in architecture but was intent on having the biggest architectural practice in Europe, was waiting in the wings. He had set up an office in Edinburgh and had become a confidant of George Pottinger at the Scottish Office; the project would be eligible for a government grant of 25 per cent. A model of the 'Aviemore Centre' was unveiled; at the outset, it had four hotels (although ten were 'a possibility'), a group of hostels, a cinema, a curling and skating rink, a swimming pool, restaurants plus general purpose buildings for conferences. Presented as a bold plan to give Scottish tourism a new image, it had brewery chiefs Sir William McEwan Younger (by 1965 he too was a baronet) and W. R. Elliott of United Caledonian Breweries joining forces under Sir Hugh's chairmanship with A. W. Hardie representing Shell BP. Launched with the headline, 'How Scotland can help itself', the irony was that these big tycoons had just taken the initiative away from local business people and effectively torpedoed their plans.

The major involvement of brewery companies created a furore in the gateway. Some 18 licences were sought for the numerous outlets for alcohol which the centre would have. Aviemore had just four premises with licences. A petition was organised with a view to having a veto poll and it got over 90 signatures. A decade earlier the Licensing Court had expressed worries about 'over licensing' when one six day licence was requested for a hotel in Boat of Garten. The Chief Constable had warned then that issuing a single licence was 'a very serious responsibility'. The efforts of the Good Templars in encouraging sobriety were remembered as were the inebriates of epic proportions which the gateway had produced. There had been ones who were regularly wheeled home on barrows and others, who when confined to their houses by their families hiding their boots, thought nothing of walking in their carpet slippers through rain or snow to present themselves as 'bona fide' travellers at Lynwilg or Carrbridge just to get a dram.

With the lure of 800 to 1,000 jobs – at least 650 in the hotel trade and 110 in shops were mentioned – planning permission was given for the 69 acre (28ha) site at Aviemore. It was expected to double the population and necessitated major changes in the development plan for Strathspey. Regional water supply, sewerage, roads and much else would be affected. Furthermore at least 100 extra houses would be required in addition to those to cover 'normal growth' in the area. In time, villas which were once let to visitors by the month or longer would be converted into boarding houses or small hotels to cater for new types of holidaymaker – people on short breaks or bus tours exploring the Highlands. Similarly 'bed & breakfast' would be bound to expand and flourish.

It might have been thought appropriate that a competition be held for the design of such a huge complex but it was not. At first a five storey building was proposed for the old hotel site. Four months later it had grown to six storeys and eventually it was nine including basements. Likened to a skyscraper and dubbed the Aviemore 'Hilton', its architecture was condemned in Inverness-shire's planning committee as 'quite out of character with the surrounding area' and 'just an eyesore'. Even so this 'focal point' for the village went ahead with consultation promised with the Royal Fine Arts Commission – for what that was worth. (Aspects of the 1960s are now seen as a nadir in architecture and planning at least in Scotland.) The work was not even put out to tender. The firm of Bovis got the job and no contract was ever signed for it. The structures were put up – perhaps thrown up would be more exact – as quickly as possible. The entire design was prepared by the architects in just six weeks. Poulson was actually having the plans delivered in batches to the site as Bovis was building floor by floor. Inevitably he and the Bovis chairman Harry Vincent fell out, especially when the latter asked for more money.

Rank's Motor Inn at Coylumbridge was opened in 1964 by the Duke of Edinburgh. With its indoor swimming pool and outdoor ice rink, it was an immediate success. Furthermore the design of the 'mountain lodge' blended with its surroundings of moorland and Scots pines while its presence was relatively unobtrusive in the landscape. To avoid upstaging the Fraser scheme – Sir High shortly received a peerage becoming Lord Fraser of Allander – care was taken to maximise publicity for the Aviemore Centre by having the duke visit the construction site where 500 workers toiled and the shells of the steel framed buildings were taking shape. He was told that Aviemore was going to have 'the amenities of a town of 60,000 people'. Meanwhile, the Scottish Youth Hostels Association completed modern premises with accommodation for 60 on a splendid site adjacent to its old huts on the southern margin.

To mastermind the 'tourist village', as the Aviemore Centre was described, Captain John Wells RN was appointed general manager. His photograph appeared in the local papers – he was in naval uniform and in a pose resembling Caesar. This heightened apprehension. After a distinguished naval career the captain had recently retired from HMS *Kent* and was clearly selected for his leadership and disciplinary skills, but what did he know about business, tourism, or for that matter, the Highlands? According to one local hotelier, the answer was 'damn all'!

By December 1966, the Aviemore Centre was set to commence. The loss of the ailing Lord Fraser a month earlier cast a shadow over the event. His son, known as Sir Hugh and now chairman of the House of Fraser, had taken over the stores' empire; his widowed mother opened the premises. John Poulson had a silver salver waiting to present to her – he felt Bovis would attempt to outdo him which they subtly did by gifting a cheque to a Salvation Army home. Sir Hugh gave a speech composed by George Pottinger, his father's old assistant who was ostensibly back at the Scottish Office. Pottinger had in fact been acting as an intermediary between the warring factions at the Aviemore Centre for months because the participants were by then scarcely on speaking terms.

There were mixed reactions to the new centre. People flocked to see it and satisfy their curiosity. Money appeared to be pouring into the tills but backs were turned on old Aviemore whilst the local authority and community were left to wrestle with the problems which the complex unleashed on the Cairngorm gateway.

EXCURSION

The Pass of Ryvoan

With its long established National Forest Park, Glenmore is a highlight for visitors to the Cairngorm gateway. Follow the road from Coylumbridge to Loch Morlich, a distance of 4½ miles (7.5km). Forest Enterprise has a visitor centre where a leaflet about the many walks in the area is available (contact: 01479 861220). One of these goes to the Pass of Ryvoan with its mysterious Lochan Uaine, the Green Loch. This route follows part of the old *Rathad nam Mèirleach*, 'the path of the cattle thieves'. Rising above the valley is *Tom da Chomhaid*, the hillock of the two lookouts from where a watch could be kept on the robbers' movements. Continuing through the pass, the Ryvoan bothy is reached; it marks a croft which was worked until the 1900s. The track can be followed to Rynettin, then onwards to Forest Lodge, a headquarters for the RSPB, about 5 miles' distance (8.5km), and to Nethybridge about 9 miles (14km) away.

A view from 1930 of the Pass of Ryvoan which was followed
by the Rathad nam Mèirleach, 'the path of the thieves or cattle reivers'.
The route continued past Loch an Eilein south west to Lochaber (A. E. GLEN)

CHAPTER 8

Partnerships for Progress?
1965 to the Present

The ski and tourist boom of the 1960s brought expansion to all the settlements in the strath from Newtonmore to Grantown but none experienced the unrelenting growth of Aviemore. It could boast of having the first all year round leisure complex in Britain; the weather proof facilities were praised as positive measures enhancing Highland tourism. On the other hand, there were many who believed that the Aviemore Centre development, carried out with indecent haste, had not only spoiled the look of the place but would inevitably distort its character and that of the Cairngorm gateway in which it was set.

By January 1967, thousands of skiers were flocking to the slopes of Cairn Gorm. Traffic was intense on the widened ski road and the top chairlift was taking 600 passengers an hour up the hill. Visitors' reactions were mixed as patrons of the Aviemore Centre were disappointed to discover that unlike some Alpine resorts you could not ski from the front door of your hotel or hop on a lift close by and in any case the runs were short. Excavations on the mountain and more bulldozing were urged to make better pistes – snow was becoming 'white gold' and in 1968 the Ptarmigan Restaurant, at 3,650 feet (1,112m) the highest in Britain, was opened. Many local youngsters had taken up the sport with enthusiasm and seven out of the first ten juniors at the British Alpine Ski Championships were Scots. More women than men were skiing but not all found it to their liking:

> The worst thing about Scotland is the wind . . . it blows the snow away leaving ice, and it is so cold and raw on the slopes.

With more people on the mountains in winter there came a greater awareness of avalanches. Local observers knew that they happened – one day a corrie would be plastered with snow, the following it would reveal bare rock. When thousands of tons of snow collapsed in Coire Cas in February 1969, the vulnerability of the ski area was revealed. So many skiers were using mountain areas inadequately geared to their numbers that the litter deposited on Cairn Gorm was gross – all was hidden until the snow melted and revealed the masses of multicoloured garbage.

Inevitably, the skiing casualties soared and local doctors – both MacDonalds but unrelated – disclosed how burdened they were in winter – 'about one third of the work is directed towards accidents mainly on the ski slopes'. With the help of their wives they were running a 24 hour service and sometimes the doctors had to carry patients with skiing injuries on sledges to their own cars. Yet despite their persistence and that of MP Russell Johnston it took until 1974 for a proper health centre to be placed in Aviemore. The seriously injured had to be taken to Inverness for treatment. Clearly the tourist developments led by 'high finance' had outpaced this element of the infrastructure.

Although the Royal Fine Arts Commission had agreed that the arrangement of the Aviemore Centre was 'acceptable', there were renewed misgivings about its practicality. No thought had been given to the effects of heavy snowfall on its layout. When blizzards blew, its 'piazza', Allander Square, became a snow trap. The planning officer for Inverness-shire (who was also responsible for architectural matters) voiced his regrets about the new centre's brash style – 'people cannot be forced to design with a degree of sensitivity when they don't want to'. This was a curious admission when exactly that pre-condition had been applied to Rank's Coylumbridge development in Rothiemurchus. Had the big moneyed interests and the political clout mustered in favour of the project at Aviemore something to do with it? It gave rise to a feeling that in design terms, as far as Aviemore was concerned, anything went.

Where were the employees to come from? It was never going to be easy for ex-railway staff to be converted to hotel work. Contrary to the sanguine forecasts, two years after its opening the Aviemore Centre was only employing 360 people of whom just 65 per cent belonged to the local area. A third were outsiders and the existing community was feeling overwhelmed. Staff dismissals took place amid widespread publicity when employees 'failed to come up to the standard of a first-class hotel' and apart from the chef, the rest walked out in sympathy. There was trouble when a local councillor disclosed that the first fifty new council houses, which were sited on a peat bog, were to be allotted to Fraser's Highland Tourist (Cairngorm Development) Ltd – in other words to the Aviemore

Centre for its staff – a policy condemned as being 'greatly at variance with the interest of rate payers'. There was an acute shortage of sites for private housing and these were expensive – at least £1,600 was being asked for an eighth of an acre (500km²), a rise of 40 per cent in three years. Yet it was obviously undesirable for sites to be allowed to go 'ribboning' along the main road. Old villas – in fact any four walls which could support a roof – changed hands at inflated prices and new bungalows begun at the Craig-na-Gower site were quickly snapped up.

There was a noticeable drop in business for hoteliers in neighbouring places and as they had made the running in tourism for many years there was bitterness. Accordingly the new Highlands and Islands Development Board, which had been established in 1965, tested a system offering big reductions on mid-week bookings to try to offset the adverse impact of the Aviemore Centre. As a novelty the new venue was winning an astonishing range of conference activity – from the Scottish Licensed Trade and the Master Bakers to the highbrow Mount Pelerin Society and the National Mod. The organisers of the latter were angered by the excessive charges – it turned out that the Centre managers gave some sponsorship and then put the amount on the bill. The spotlight again fell on the Aviemore Centre in a more positive manner when it was chosen by the BBC for its New Year celebrations on TV in 1969 and 1970 – with the slogan, 'it may be cold but it won't be dry' – and from then on 'Aviemore', having won an audience of millions, was a destination known nation wide.

Unlike the rival hoteliers, some others counted benefits. A regional scheme drawing water from Loch Einich was soon in place and for the first time a mains supply was assured. There would be no more worries on farms and crofts about springs or 'fuarans' running dry in summer or freezing up in winter which was just as inconvenient. Then there was the need for sewage treatment; for years this had been euphemistically described as 'drainage'. With an outstanding sporting river so close, there were concerns about possible harmful discharges into it. Poulson had designed a private scheme for the use of the Centre but it was quite inadequate and regularly broke down whereupon the effluent spilled into the Aviemore burn and so to the Spey. The smell which permeated the place was 'nauseating, challenging its image as a health resort'. There was an additional nuisance when gulls pulled refuse from the poorly concealed and overflowing bins beside the hotels. It was most uninviting.

There were also new roads to consider. In addition to a ring road around the perimeter of the Aviemore Centre, by 1967 there were new bridges across the railway and the Spey giving easier access to

The Aviemore Centre when new – the Badenoch Hotel is on the left with the swimming pool and ice rink on the right. In scale and style, the complex was plainly out of harmony with its setting (JOHN PETER)

Rothiemurchus and Glenmore. Save for pedestrian use, the dangerous tunnel bridge was abandoned. On summer days 13,000 vehicles were pouring through the gateway area, the vast majority via the village. In 1969 the A9 was realigned through Aviemore in what was described as a 'mini-scheme'; it led to road widening, straightening and the loss of garden frontages which inevitably reduced the attractiveness of the village. Worst of all, the demolition of the old inn, which stood at a bend in the road, ripped the historic heart out of the place. Telford's toll house was also removed. Nothing was done to stop such destruction. Those elements which had given character to the built environment were reduced to rubble and Aviemore was dragged towards modernity whatever the cost to the community or its heritage with scarcely a word of protest.

With the road lobby dominating transport strategies in Britain, the proposal for a two-lane highway through Glen Feshie – 32 miles (51km) long from Kingussie to Braemar – had been revived by the Scottish Development Department and other agencies. Described as a route of 'primary importance' it was seen as a major trans-Scotland link not just for east-west tourism but also for such trade as timber haulage to the new pulp and paper mill at Fort William. Its protagonists argued that in winter it would allow advantage to be taken of the best snow conditions prevailing in the Cairngorms massif. Estimated to cost not less than £2 million, the scheme rightly incurred the wrath of those eager to protect the mountains, nature and solitude. Thankfully the road's high price in both money and conservation terms prevented its construction.

So the Cairngorm gateway was under intense strain because of the phenomenal pace and scale of development. Ecologists, geographers and naturalists expressed their concerns. As a gesture to the environment, an exhibition of stuffed Highland fauna with an uninspiring backdrop was displayed in the Aviemore Centre. The Nature Conservancy Council was alarmed about the 'massively mounting tourist pressures' and its chief wrote about the need 'to protect the land from people'. It proposed a survey of soil erosion and of plant and animal populations disturbed by skiing. Iain Grant of Rothiemurchus was worried about unrestricted freedom to camp in the Cairngorms leading to 'mountain slums'. He urged preserving the pristine beauty of certain areas despite the immense demands; he plead for 'polite notices' to engage people's attention believing that these were 90 per cent effective whereas threatening ones were not. Others wrote of the urgent need for a warden service, for footpath repair, for parking areas and much more. Only rangers could keep tourists 'well informed' but also 'under reasonable control'. It was suggested that some locations should be made car free. The Aviemore Centre was seen to be cashing in on an infrastructure largely developed through local initiative and on an environment that was manifestly fragile.

There was dismay too that the concentration on tourism was placing too many eggs in one basket. Farming was diminishing in importance in the gateway. Farms were being amalgamated as '100 acres of arable' (40ha) was no longer thought enough to make an income which would give an improving standard of living. Farming families also expected to have cars, TV sets and the domestic appliances which other folk had. A new form of clearance was taking place in the countryside and farmhouses and workers' cottages left empty were quickly converted to holiday homes.

A bitter letter in the *Scotsman* highlighted the plight of 'old Aviemore', now a neglected village of railway sprawl and derelict installations, 'more like an industrial slum than an international sports resort . . . split down the middle by road and rail and subjected to an assortment of styles sprouting uncontrolled amid the weeds'. The writer suggested that the whole place should be re-vamped to make it look like the new Centre. Gateway folk were horrified and there was a swift reaction from the Aviemore and Rothiemurchus Village Council. It declared that the character of the place had merit and that the aim should be to make it worthy of its magnificent setting, by clearing waste land, smartening up frontages and co-ordinating colours throughout its length. Superimposing the Centre complex on a modest village had unleashed a host of problems but there was a determination to tackle these, notably on the part of Father David Keith, chairman of the Village Council. Some feared that the settlement would simply become a dormitory for those employed at the Aviemore Centre. A scheme for village refurbishment was drawn up with support from local business people and householders but regrettably it could not be implemented for lack of funding and from the obstinacy of British Railways – the latter would not release any land as they 'had plans to develop the railway'. Strangely the Seafield Estate, as the largest landowner in the Cairngorm gateway, had no representation in such deliberations. It stood to make a great deal of money by selling land to developers.

As the threat to close rural railways grew so did rail enthusiasts begin flexing their muscles in a more active way. In 1961 an 'Association for the Regeneration of Unremunerative Branch Lines' was mooted. With a more realistic purpose and title the Scottish Railway Preservation Society

Aviemore's railway terraces were sold off to private owners and now white-wash hidees the years of lineside grime (JOHN PETER)

was also established in that year and its prospectus set out its aims — 'to keep alive the majestic blast of the smoke-plumed steam engine' and 'the magic of the railways in their hey day'. This would be achieved by 'a branch line operated by vintage locomotives and rolling stock . . . a reminder of the splendid past of the railways of Scotland'. Before the uprooting of the old Highland mainline via Forres in 1968, the SRPS had taken an interest in reviving part of that scenic route, namely the section from Aviemore to Boat of Garten and Grantown. It spoke of running steam-hauled trains at weekends in the principal holiday months. Although this tourist railway would be a volunteer effort, there might be some employment for local people. Shortly the Strathspey Railway Company was formed with a capital of £10,000. British Rail, meanwhile, was asking £46,000 for track and other installations on the route. It seemed an exorbitant sum. With the line being so far from SRPS support in the Central Lowlands, that society pulled out and resolved to find tracks elsewhere. For the Strathspey supporters many problems lay ahead, not least the intransigence of BR over access to Aviemore Station and the fact that the old engine shed there had been rented out. A separate station had to be constructed for the use of the Strathspey Railway; it was part of the abandoned one at Dalnaspidal and became 'Aviemore Speyside' but it was reached by such an awkward approach that it was difficult to advertise its presence. At Boat of Garten, which increasingly evolved into the volunteers' base, residents were worried that the revived railway would bring the rabble, which was seen to be frequenting Aviemore, to their sedate village. Nevertheless, the patience of the enthusiasts paid off and the line re-opened in 1978 with steam locomotives, including a former LMS Class 5, hauling the trains.

In the media, attempts were made to gloss over the obvious difficulties caused by the Aviemore Centre — at least by the interested parties. Scottish and Universal Investments, the Fraser power house, controlled the *Glasgow Herald* and over several years there was vigorous promotion for the complex in its pages. The House of Fraser had a third stake in the Aviemore Centre and new attractions were always being displayed to catch public attention. A trampoline park and crazy golf ('attractively constructed in green concrete') appeared in 1968. Why had a premier 18-hole golf course not been part of the big project from the outset? Probably because it would not have made enough money. Soon there was a pool for radio-controlled model boats where a shilling (5p) bought a shot at steering a ship. Go-kart racing was introduced to be followed by 'ice karting' with young Sir Hugh Fraser, an experienced kart racer, being roped in to try the experiment. The ice rink was adapted for other sports

– badminton, five-a-side football and table tennis – and tournaments were held to pull in the crowds.

In 1969 damaging criticism came from the British tourist industry. An article in the *Travel Trade Gazette* advised agents not to recommend the Aviemore district to clients who were accomplished skiers. It continued:

> The chances of creating a national winter sports area are remote. It appears that the winter sports interest is confined primarily to local weekend traffic.

This has largely proved to be true. The design of the developments was ridiculed as 'unhappy' being a mixture of 'Alpine/Scandinavian' when the ambience should have been 'uncompromisingly Scottish'.

While tourists welcomed the all weather facilities, the accountants were still dissatisfied. The Aviemore Centre was simply not making enough money. There were alarms over its slack times – especially in April-May, October-November and January-February as 'it was tremendously expensive to run such a centre with so many attractions on a year round basis'. The unpredictability of the snow fall put winter sports on a see-saw. A run of mild weather produced pay offs and short-time working in hotels and ski schools. The Selective Employment Tax imposed by a Labour government and the ending of investment allowances were reported to be denting 'this triumph of the market economy' and by 1970 it was clear that the Aviemore Centre's aims and clientele were going to alter. From Britain's biggest banqueting, conference and recreation complex in Manchester came Morris Marshall as the new general manager. A string of positions in the leisure industry had launched him into the entertainment world – Blackpool's Three Piers and the Golden Mile Centre, The Talk of the Town in London, Coney Beach at Porthcawl, caravan and amusement parks. He had recently been elected chairman of the Circus Proprietors' Association of Great Britain. Was his type of experience relevant to the Highlands? He was determined to make Aviemore 'popular' and profitable by importing the attractions which had succeeded at seaside resorts in the south.

This appointment caused further alarm and so early in 1970 a public forum sponsored by Aberdeen University drew a capacity audience to the Cairngorm Hotel. With Father Keith in the chair, Colonel Iain Grant of Rothiemurchus, Scottish Nationalist Councillor Sandy Lindsay and Highland transport expert Dr Iain Skewis were joined by Morris Marshall. In this debate the Seafield Estate was again not represented; a new Earl of Seafield had fallen heir to the lands, then one of the largest private holdings in Scotland. As for Aviemore, it was forecast that the village might swell to three to four times its size. The opinion was that it had become over dependent on tourism and visually was an ugly conglomeration lacking any proper structure and enduring nightmare traffic. The laird painted a depressing picture; the Aviemore Centre had attracted 'an element of riff-raff' with escalating vandalism, thefts, drunken fights and drug dealing – this was the era of the hippies – so another growth activity was policing with more officers and an ever larger police station. Crime had risen five fold. (By 1996–97, 22 officers were required for the Aviemore area alone and the crime total was over 600; many incidents were said to be alcohol related.) The pressures on the countryside were by now 'very severe' and the only way forward was by access agreements, by a warden service and by discipline on the part of visitors which recognised the priorities in the Cairngorms, then one of the largest nature reserves in Europe.

Marshall's view was completely different. He wanted 'more conferences, more investment' as Aviemore was just on the threshold of its future if it concentrated on the holidaymaker, 'we want his money' and must lure him to come to 'this sunny alpine garden of Scotland' – quite ignoring the fact that the Highlands were not the least like the Alps and that the weather was entirely different. According to Marshall, congestion was a long way off and tourism had little effect on the environment but a big effect on the economy – maybe he was thinking of Clacton or Southend-on-Sea. It was a frightening prospect which Councillor Lindsay deplored. He advocated light industry to give a better balance of employment throughout the gateway; he disliked what he saw of Aviemore – the Centre had made it a lop-sided place, grown piecemeal with poorly designed terraces of indifferent housing. He longed for a by-pass road and suggested a gondola chairlift to take visitors up Craigellachie for the view.

That summer a possible blue print for the route the gateway and the village should take was on view when the Landmark Visitor Centre was opened at Carrbridge by the Duke of Edinburgh; it was a heartening sign. Housed in an entirely modern building in harmony with its surroundings, it offered presentations about the heritage and natural history of the district. There was a restaurant and shop together with outdoor adventure features in a forest environment. Its founder was David Hayes who had been schooled in visitor attractions management in the National Parks Service in the United States. The duke delivered a timely warning – 'unless we take care how we exploit the raw material of the countryside, we may very easily destroy it' because 'mechanical devices' such as cars

The Highland Folk Museum at Newtonmore displays many heritage buildings. This reconstructed water-powered saw mill from Ardverikie estate, and a pole wagon for transporting large logs, are reminders of the importance of forestry in the region (ANN GLEN)

and chairlifts gave the means to do so. With the population's growing mobility, the threat to vulnerable areas was only too apparent. While understanding was required for paintings or music – why not also for the countryside? This message was in tune with the duke's key role in heading conferences on the countryside which in turn led to the Countryside Commissions being constituted. Apparently, he had a blind spot for the miles of bulldozed tracks disfiguring the Cairngorms.

That year also saw Rothiemurchus school, which had been replaced by a new primary in Aviemore, converted into a visitor centre for the estate. (There had been reports since 1875 which suggested that the school should be on the Aviemore side as rather more children came from that area.) With the adventure programmes at Glenmore Lodge proving so successful, these were modelled elsewhere; in 1969 a water sports centre had been opened at Loch Insh and within two years Abernethy Outdoor Centre with its Christian emphasis was established at Nethybridge. A sailing club on Loch Morlich and gliding at Glen Feshie also began. In 1972 the Highland Wildlife Park, which was a branch establishment of Edinburgh Zoo, opened at Dunachton near Kincraig. All these projects were much more in accord with the character of the Cairngorm gateway.

For many people holidays in the region were not what they had been.

The old style of visitors who had rented houses for a month at a time or sought out 'rooms with attendance' for shorter periods were priced out. They had been accustomed to make their own entertainment – they read, they sketched, they botanised and bird watched; some played golf or tennis and swam in lochs and rivers. They seemed impervious to the weather in their stout shoes and waterproofs as they explored on cycle or on foot. Families had put up with varying degrees of discomfort in their holiday homes – such as the cottage which slept six but had only five teaspoons and three glasses. Now as 75 per cent of the visitors came by car, a ceaseless stream of traffic – the volume had doubled since 1961 – jostled for position in the congested streets and limited parking places of the villages of Badenoch and Strathspey. Summer was still the top season for tourists, and wealth had risen in line with their numbers, most of it going into local pockets. Many trippers, however, wandered around apparently at a loss about where to go or what to do. The traffic, the crowds, the noisy entertainments seemed to herald the end of leisurely pursuits in a tranquil region which might lose its dignity and much of its beauty for ever unless stock was taken.

In the spring of 1971 a biography in praise of Lord Fraser was published. It was entitled *The Winning Counter*. The author was none other than George Pottinger and it was launched in style at the Savoy Hotel in London which had been Lord Fraser's preferred base in that city. Shortly Pottinger was promoted at the Scottish Office where he was made Secretary to the Department of Agriculture and Fisheries – obviously he was destined for a high position to match his membership of Edinburgh's New Club and of the Honourable Company of Edinburgh Golfers. Then in July 1972 in distant Yorkshire there was an enquiry into a bankruptcy at Wakefield. John Poulson was the centre of attention. Where had his wealth gone? The proceedings revealed that he had made absurdly generous gifts – one for £21,000 being to George Pottinger. There were parliamentary questions about 'a substantial gift accepted from a person engaged in government financial contracts'. Worse was to follow. It was divulged that a donation of £22,000 had been made by Poulson to a pet charity of Reginald Maudling, the Conservative MP, when he was Chancellor of the Exchequer.

At first Pottinger appeared unperturbed by the disclosures of 'his very good friend'; through solicitors he refuted the allegations being made in some quarters – 'any government grants paid have no connection, direct or indirect, with his duties or responsibilities' – and he threatened legal action if any other inferences were drawn and went off on holiday. One inference which did not disappear was that he had used his position to benefit John Poulson particularly over the Aviemore Centre. Soon police enquiries were taking place and the trustee in the bankruptcy raised an action against Pottinger to recover money. By the following year, both men were charged at Leeds Assizes with 'conspiring together so that Pottinger should corruptly receive £30,000 in relation to projects with which the Crown was concerned'. Pottinger was said to have been at dinner in Muirfield's exclusive clubhouse with a Court of Session judge and two sheriffs when the Fraud Squad summoned him.

The trial opened in the autumn and, as far as the Aviemore Centre was concerned, it was most revealing. It appeared that files in relation to that project had been 'doctored' in the Scottish Office. Letters had been removed and one file which focused on the Aviemore Centre was missing. Someone had extracted the correspondence to and from Poulson, presumably Pottinger in an attempt to conceal his true relationship with the architect. In a letter which did survive the latter had stated that his friend at the Scottish Office could 'influence a great number of people to give us work' as he certainly appeared to do over Aviemore. Indeed the impression among staff at the Scottish Office was that Pottinger had obtained the Aviemore Centre contract for Poulson. When Poulson fell out with other participants in the scheme, Pottinger was persuaded to draft conciliatory letters to Lord Fraser and Sir William McEwan Younger to try to smooth the path for him. Poulson also had other ends in view as he had a wish for honours believing that Pottinger had been responsible for Lord Fraser's knighthood and baronetcy; meanwhile, the civil servant had not done so badly out of the honours system himself having received a CVO in 1953 and a CB in 1972.

In these circumstances it was inept for Poulson to argue that his gifts were just ordinary presents and had no ulterior motive. Civil servants could only accept presents of 'low value' and according to the rules these had to be reported. Poulson's gifts were lavish – Pottinger had received a Rover car, expensive holidays abroad, tailor made suits, bottles of brandy and an extraordinarily fine house at Gullane close to his favourite golf course, Muirfield. His opulent lifestyle and smart apparel were explained away at the Scottish Office because 'Lord Fraser had shown him how to invest in the Stock Market'.

Colonel Iain Grant of Rothiemurchus was called to give evidence and this showed that pressure had been put on him to sell land to Lord Fraser's consortium. In fact, Pottinger had warned him that 'he would be playing with fire' if he did not sell to Lord Fraser and that government ministers would take a serious view of his intransigence. Subsequently, the laird found that planning permission for Rank's Coylumbridge project had been 'unduly delayed' by the Scottish Development Department, presumably to pay him back for not co-operating. Pottinger had been present at all meetings relating to the Coylumbridge plan. Lord Fraser had even threatened to arrange an announcement of a deal in the House of Commons to force Iain Grant's hand when no agreement about selling the land existed. With the parties at loggerheads, the laird had felt free to advertise the ground for sale but the Fraser faction persisted – they wanted the Rank Organisation to be part of the Fraser consortium but Iain Grant flatly refused to do business with the latter. Although Iain Grant gave an impression of diffidence, he could also be stubborn – in this instance to his great credit. Curiously, the Stakis Organisation was also mentioned in connection with the Aviemore Centre. Reo Stakis was described as 'a rising man in restaurants' when he was offered the chance of financing or running chalets there. This was, at best, only crumbs from the rich men's table and he declined. Strangely, in the years ahead the Stakis Organisation would become heavily involved in the gateway not only owning key properties at the Aviemore Centre but also at Coylumbridge.

When the court's attention turned to Bovis there was further embarrassment. Their chairman Harry Vincent had been made a director of Fraser's development company responsible for the Aviemore Centre. It had been very much 'a wheels within wheels' affair. The explanation for the absence of a contract was that 'Lord Fraser did not like written contracts' – an odd method for someone who dabbled in company take overs. Bovis had only produced estimates and it was suggested that this practice was simply a licence to extract high prices from the consortium. With Bovis giving separate figures for each hotel or other project, a higher profit was inevitable – the system had proved 'a very good thing' for Bovis. Poulson stood to gain too as his fee was 10 per cent of building costs – the higher these went the more he would get. Harry Vincent argued however that with Aviemore being 'a remote place' where there were 'very severe winters' there were bound to be extra costs.

Sir Hugh Fraser was also called as a witness and described his father's relationship with Pottinger as that of 'a business acquaintance'. Others saw him as a really close friend who had Lord Fraser's ear because he ' knew the ropes' about roads, legislation, grants and so on. Lord Fraser had treated Pottinger generously, to the point where the civil servant and his wife had accompanied him abroad on 'business trips' to study features of the tourist trade in well-known foreign resorts. These had taken Pottinger to North America and Switzerland 'in connection with the Aviemore project'.

Sir William McEwan Younger of the brewery company also appeared. Considered intellectual, he was also politically astute and was perhaps more perceptive than the rest. Mountaineering was one of his recreations. He stated that he was very dissatisfied with the work done at the Aviemore Centre especially in relation to the swimming pool. There had been a rumpus with the county engineer over the water supply – 'you will have hotels completed without water' was the threat. There was a similar fracas over the heating plant for the centre. Sir William had preferred caution – for example, a modest scheme with not more than three new hotels; the ten which had been modelled at the outset were 'a cloud cuckoo land, a fantasy which bore no relation to reality' but these of course represented possible fees and self aggrandisement for Poulson. As built the centre brought the architect a quarter of a million which was generous recompense at the time.

When the trial came to its conclusion, Poulson had been shown to be wildly ambitious and Pottinger to be utterly venial. Poulson gave without feeling as 'the all embracing and insidious process of buying the man' was at work. His desire to gain extra business at any cost had led to the biggest tax fraud in Britain since the Second World War; his debts were over £1 million. The pair were found guilty and sentenced to five years imprisonment each. Poulson was visibly a broken man, Pottinger seemed untouched by events but it was a humiliating outcome for one who had been acknowledged as well educated, hard working, a good conversationalist and an excellent sportsman. The trial was the longest and most expensive of its kind at that date, taking 52 days and involving 100 witnesses. It was widely held that 'only the tip of an iceberg of corruption' had been detected. An unfortunate consequence was that Reginald Maudling, by then Home Secretary in a Tory government, had to resign.

The Aviemore Centre was shown to be what shrewd observers had suspected – a tainted enterprise for which the village and the Cairngorm gateway had to pay a heavy price. Even basic contraventions of Scottish building regulations were exposed when the premier hotel of the complex was set on fire in 1995. The outstanding location within the Cairngorm gateway did not receive the treatment it rightly merited and the accusations that the place was 'prostituted for the sake of gain' have rumbled on and on.

While the trial was in progress, further developments at Aviemore were unveiled. A Post House Hotel was opened for Trust House Forte. It was expected that the Aviemore Centre would soon show its first profit. Marshall excused its slow performance on the grounds that it was so far ahead of its time that it left many seaside resorts standing. There was no admission that it was perhaps inappropriate in both scale and philosophy. More hotels were planned and a variety of other leisure proposals was published. Steered by Marshall, the decision was taken to go 'down market' and Lord Fraser's vision of a Highland version of St Moritz was to evaporate in the years that followed. The proposed additions were a weird and wonderful collection – a planetarium, a dolphin pool, a craft centre, squash courts, a solarium and an 'aerobus terminal' for journeys to Cairn Gorm – this monorail system on stilts would have ferried thousands of passengers per hour at speeds of up to 70 mph (112kph) to the mountain. Most controversially a Santa Claus Land on Disney principles was proposed for Aviemore. Both the monorail and mountain lodges in Coire Cas – even a three storey hotel was suggested at one stage – were opposed by the County Council.

Criticism was becoming more vocal and 'greedy and uncaring speculators' whose sole motive was to make money, even if it meant ruining the mountains, were condemned. There were however extensions of the ski areas into Coire na Ciste where an access road had been constructed by the Royal Engineers in 1968. On the sporting estates bull-dozed tracks – gouged into the slopes without the need for planning permission or environmental assessment – snaked ever further into the mountains. All this was in the cause of modern mechanised stalking practices. Walking in or riding ponies had been abandoned but it meant that remote wilderness in the Cairngorms was being substantially lessened and in some instances reduced to mere fragments.

At the Aviemore Centre only part of Morris Marshall's dream became a reality; in 1975 Santa Claus Land, 'one of the largest and most comprehensive children's paradises in Europe' was created. Marshall was said to have travelled the world to collect ideas for it and, with its gingerbread house, penguin pool with its own North Pole, plus a special post office and toy factory, its 'twee-ness' was only too plain. Despite the fact that there was a real steam railway in Aviemore, Santa Claus Land had to have a railway too. As a super amusement park, its aim was to make money – children would patronise it and parents would pay up. It was severely criticised as ill-suited and expensive. Why did families come to the Cairngorm gateway? What was special about wild and unspoiled country that attracted them? The artificiality of Santa Claus Land seemed shameful to many.

The HIDB was seen as favouring all out development; in 1970 it had acquired the upper slopes of Cairn Gorm which it then leased back to the Cairngorm Sports Development Council. This was the era of 'growth points' and the Aviemore Centre was seen as one of these. The idea was that a large investment in a big venture, whether it was an aluminium smelter as at Invergordon or a pulp and paper mill at Fort William, would trigger many benefits in the surrounding area in line with the multiplier effect in economics. After a decade of the Aviemore Centre's existence, there certainly were new shops and business premises, craft works, some light industry, sporting and recreational facilities plus greatly expanded hotels and guest houses. Unemployment was low; conference and trade fair activity was high with 750,000 visitors descending on the Centre itself. To keep its appeal fresh, ever more attractions were in view – this time a tartan bureau with a computer to pinpoint clan links to 8,000 surnames in four languages. Determined to wring every penny from the venture, Santa's Post Office had been turned into a gambling arcade of fruit machines from which staff carried off the coins in pailfuls. Many blenched at the turn that Aviemore had taken. Extra chalets were in the pipeline at the Centre while council houses of mediocre design and built to 'the lowest fixed price tender', were spreading sporadically. Meantime the Scottish Development Department had finally approved two sections of a new A9 trunk road between Kingussie and Aviemore which would create a 4¹/₂-mile (7.2km) by–pass round the troubled village.

In 1979 there was another revelation concerning an enormous complex – this time on the northern margins of Aviemore – when it was announced that the housebuilders, Barratt were to invest £12 million in a sports and residential project at Dalfaber. Nationally the company was well known through its advertisements on TV showing a helicopter in flight. Dalfaber, which was historic farm land, would become a time-share scheme with over 190 self catering holiday chalets, luxury lodges and 240 private houses on a roomy site. Barratt also mentioned a 100-bedroom hotel and an indoor sports centre to rival the Fraser effort, all to be built over six years. There was immediate concern in the local press; conservation doubts too were cast over the scale of the project which would effectively double the built up area of Aviemore:

> The people of the Spey Valley have to live with the ugliness of piecemeal development designed to make money out of tourists without preserving the natural splendours which attract them in the first place.

The plan had taken the community by surprise. A year earlier, Highland Regional Council had given approval to a discreet planning application by the Seafield Estate which then sold the land to Barratt who were all set to deliver. Both the Nature Conservancy Council and the local tourist board had been kept in the dark. Having seen the Aviemore Centre and the problems which it had precipitated, the Scottish Tourist Board had changed its tune about grandiose complexes; it was now worried about 'the sensitivity of the countryside' and about any ventures which might reduce its attractiveness. The Countryside Commission for Scotland objected to the Dalfaber scheme:

> There is a scale beyond which you change the character of an area and
> we are concerned that this large extension to Aviemore is going to
> have another significant adverse effect on the area.

Even if Dalfaber would have timber chalets in a traditional style, a low-rise hotel and housing which might be better suited to the landscape, the Cairngorm gateway risked being 'overdeveloped' and the urban sprawl already besetting Aviemore was a warning to other villages in Badenoch and Strathspey.

Undoubtedly local folk were growing more pro-active and the community council became highly critical of the proposal. People complained that Aviemore lacked any real focus or heart and that it was a split and straggling settlement with a caravan park at one end, private and council housing at the other and a haphazard mix of shops strung between. A disused railway goods yard still lay in the midst of the village and the elements of countryside within it, which had once given the place its green freshness and rural quality, were being eaten up by building. Lack of foresight and lack of cash had led to the cheapest options being chosen again and again. With the village growing into a small town – its population had risen from 600 in 1960 to over 2,000 – there was plenty of talk but no concerted effort to tackle its manifest defects. Now residents feared that 'a wealthy ghetto' would be built on the outskirts when basic amenities such as a worthwhile range of shops and bus services were still inadequate for local folk.

The time-share scheme at Dalfaber, known as the Scandinavian Village, was the second largest such development in Britain where visitors could 'buy outright chosen holiday weeks in luxury accommodation for their use each year'. A purchase gave 96 years' lease and membership of 'Resorts Condominium International' enabling holiday weeks to be swapped for other resorts world wide. Some saw timeshares as fashionable and flocked to buy; others saw them as a scam. When payments fell behind in recession the hapless 'owners' found that their holiday weeks were taken back without compensation and put on the market for auction to others. Nevertheless, Dalfaber's country-club image and golf course attracted plenty of customers.

Gradually local opinion appeared to be carrying more weight when British Railways Property Board agreed in 1981 to a shopping centre and mall being constructed on the unsightly yard near Aviemore Station. There was relief that 'the horrible goods wagons in the midst of the village' would go for ever. The obstinacy of BR had meant that the eyesore had not even received a facelift – there had been talk of a heather garden – on a temporary basis. With its additional shopping facilities and tourist outlets, the mall complemented an existing small shopping-cum-housing precinct, built in 1971 on the site of the old inn's garden. The new premises were opened by the Earl of Mansfield, then the Scottish Office Minister with special responsibilities for tourism – which was at last being taken more seriously by government.

In 1983 the House of Fraser disclosed that they would sell the Aviemore Centre for £3 million. Sir Hugh described the decaying complex as 'a concrete jungle'; he admitted that his father had seen it 'as a bit more up market than it is'. Comedian Billy Connolly had berated the place as 'air raid shelters with windaes'. Just 200 staff were employed. Reo Stakis, the restaurateur and casino owner, was approached. In 1978 his Stakis Organisation had acquired the hotel and time share chalets at Coylumbridge and Sir Hugh believed that the Aviemore Centre would fare much better in the hands of a firm in the hotel and leisure business. The prime hotels – the Strathspey and the Badenoch – had already been sold. Yet four years before the Fraser decision to be rid of the Aviemore Centre, it had surprisingly got a 'Golden Jubilee' award for tourism perhaps because the Scottish Tourist Board's Travel Trade Fair and a Highland Craft Fair had chosen it as a venue; staff had worked hard to win conference business which was lucrative. Visitors to such events had been found to spend three times as much as ordinary tourists.

There had been those who liked the Aviemore Centre and those who hated it but its lean years had easily outnumbered the more successful ones. There were no immediate takers and the following year it was losing £10,000 a week. It was even more tatty and one third of the staff at all levels were sacked. Fraser, hesitating to close anything down, framed a stop gap budget of half a million pounds to smarten it up and decided that Santa Claus Land would open only at weekends. From now on the accountants would 'look at a bottom line – without the brackets for a change'. Eventually, in 1986 the Fraser group did sell out to Stakis and two years on, a further array of elaborate proposals was unveiled – the prospect of 'Britain's largest multi-feature water park with its own tropical environment under a giant glass dome', a 400-seat cinema and much more. In deference to the locality, a Highland heritage display on the lines of Jorvik, the Viking Museum in York, was to be 'supplied'. The deficiencies of the Aviemore Centre prompted the Free Church Assembly of 1989 to condemn it as:

> a hideous piece of Highland exploitation, damaging the resource it feeds on, importing urban triviality and godless values and exporting most of the profit south.

With some truth it appeared to be reaping what had been sown.

Nothing came of the Stakis vision and in 1991 they scaled down their plans aiming instead for a low-key 'Swiss style' mountain village 'more in keeping with the area'. Again architectural idioms that were Highland or Scottish were ignored – why had Austrian, Scandinavian, or other styles to be aped? This redevelopment was however conditional on a new access road being made off the A9 trunk route into the centre. The company's intention was to pull down much of the complex but shortly this was sold to Marrside Ltd, part of Sheffield based Berkeley de Vere; it chose to trade under the name of Aviemore Mountain Resort but also failed to produce results or enhancement. Referred to as 'AMR' in planning circles, its story was to become a running saga.

With snowy winters in 1979 and 1980, the Cairngorm Winter Sports Development Company had expansion plans. It proposed new tows and uplift facilities to ease the weekend queues. In fact it wished to double capacity but it ran into an immediate conflict of interest because its eyes had fallen on the unsullied slopes of Lurcher's Gully west of Coire an Lochain. Battle was joined between the downhill ski lobby and the growing band of conservationists. The continuing problem of climate was of course glossed over by the ski protagonists – the snow incidence was unpredictable and that is why Aviemore and the gateway settlements would never match Andermatt or Chamonix. Occasionally the perfect combination did arrive in the Cairngorms with calm weather, sunshine and powder snow but it was infrequent. The weather reports were often depressing – 'only high level runs possible', 'just a dusting of snow', '50 mph (80kph) winds with strong gusts' or 'blizzards'. Serious mountaineering accidents – the worst in 1971 involving a group from an Edinburgh school – had polarised opinions about the wisdom or otherwise of having high level bothies to give shelter in the Cairngorms. The huts of St Valery and Curran on the plateau, Jean's Hut in Coire Cas and Sinclair Hut at the mouth of the Lairig Ghru have all since been removed. Alamein hut is still there, but in an area off the plateau and seldom visited.

Concerns about the lack of knowledge of Scottish mountain weather led in 1978 to an automatic weather station being set up near the summit of Cairn Gorm by Heriot-Watt University. Recording only temperature and wind speed, this soon showed just how changeable and ferocious conditions on the high tops could be; there were gusts of hurricane force 12 on one day in three and frequent blasts of gale force. The wind chill factor was formidable. It added up to some of the worst weather in Britain.

Even so, in 1981 proposals to develop facilities for downhill skiing west of Cairn Gorm were backed by Highland Regional Council and the HIDB. However, because the Nature Conservancy Council and the Countryside Commission for Scotland objected, there had to be a public enquiry at which the northern corries and Lurcher's Gully were described as of 'outstanding scientific, scenic, educational and recreational importance'. The upshot was that any intrusion of skiing into these areas was rejected, and access by road beyond the existing car parks was explicitly ruled out.

Three years later, National Planning Guidelines on Skiing Developments again stated that there should be 'a presumption against road extensions beyond the existing car parks' on Cairn Gorm, but the green light was given to plans for Aonach Mor in Lochaber, for Ben Wyvis and for two areas at Drumochter.

In spite of this statement, Highland Regional Council published its new draft Structure Plan late in 1988 which included a policy for downhill ski projects in Lurcher's Gully. Both the Nature Conservancy Council and the Countryside Commission for Scotland, acting as the government's environmental advisers, expressed strong opposition to such development and they were backed by a tide of objections from influential organisations such as the Royal Society for the Protection of Birds (RSPB), the National Trust for Scotland (NTS) and from many individuals. There was international opposition too from the World Wildlife Fund for Nature (WWF), the International Union for the Conservation of Nature and Natural Resources (IUCN, The World Conservation Union) and mountaineering interests. A 'Save the Cairngorms' campaign, a coalition of fifteen voluntary bodies, was mobilised to repel any threats to the mountains. Founded in 1976 its purpose was to urge better management for the whole Cairngorms region from low levels to the plateau tops. These issues have proved a momentous battleground for Scottish, and indeed European, conservation. In 1990 Ian Lang, as Minister of State, Scottish Office, and himself a skier, modified Highland Regional Council's plan review by deleting its westward expansion policy and initiated a further examination of the ski location guidelines.

Strategically located within the Cairngorm gateway is Rothiemurchus. It has great variety of landscape and habitat – loch and river, mountain, moor and forest plus a share of farm land. Of the once great forest of Caledon now only 1 per cent remains and of that fragment a tenth lies in the woods of Rothiemurchus, Abernethy and Glenmore – hence their exceptional ecological interest. Rothiemurchus is also a transit zone between Aviemore and Glenmore with its twin tourist magnets of Loch Morlich and Cairn Gorm. As almost two-thirds of the estate is in a National Nature Reserve, the laird John Grant receives payments for managing this unique land in the interests of conservation. It has been in part compensation for foregoing such activities as large-scale commercial forestry, heather burning and sheep farming. In addition there has been money for maintaining Special Sites of Scientific Interest and 60 per cent of rangers' salaries on the estate have been met. The funding package was £297,000 during 1999–2000; Scottish Natural Heritage (SNH) foots the bill with some assistance from the Forestry Commission. The system is controversial and lampooned in the national press as 'dosh for the posh' but the level of support only puts Rothiemurchus on a similar footing to Mar Lodge estate and Pentland Hills Regional Park. The emphasis however has increasingly shifted away from compensation for refraining from certain activities to a concentration on business plans, payments for work done and projects carried out; the theme is now sustainability wed to accountability.

John Grant is not undeserving; commendably he resides on the land of his ancestors and takes a pro-active role in its management. The family mansion of the Doune is being imaginatively restored. He has turned a moribund estate round by cashing in on its now critical location. His wife Philippa, a former member of the Scottish Tourist Board, has played a significant role in its success. Rothiemurchus logs 270,000 non-paying visitors a year and employs 30 full time staff plus extra help in summer; its first countryside ranger, Willie McKenna, was appointed in 1976. Visitors are welcome to use the 50 miles (80km) of footpaths and cycle tracks within it. The most profitable element on the estate is the fish farm. The laird has developed a range of other activities from corporate entertainment and clay pigeon shooting to picnic areas and camp sites. Accompanied by a keeper, deer stalking at £300 a day is possible. (To encourage re-growth of the Caledonian forest and of montane vegetation, the herds of red deer have been severely reduced in recent years as a policy requirement of funding.) Rothiemurchus is now almost entirely geared to tourism. Its visitor attractions' business tries to be in accord with perceptions of the Highlands and to maintain an 'unspoiled' image. Rothiemurchus represents an attempted solution to the problems of tourism and nature conservation which is peculiar but pragmatic.

And what of the vast Seafield estates? In 1970 Ian Derek Francis Ogilvie-Grant, the present Earl of Seafield, with 185,200 acres (74,980ha) at his disposal, was ranked fourth among Scotland's private land owners. With Abernethy forest and Forest Lodge sold (first to the Naylor family, descendants of the Holts, and then to the RSPB), with Lochindorb and Tulchan disposed off, and the assigning of Revack and Dorback to his sister Pauline (and subsequently purchased by new owners – Revack is also now owned by the RSPB), the Seafield patrimony has been much reduced. Strathspey portions have been further shared out between the earl and his family; even so Seafield land is still one of the largest non-public holdings in Scotland. Those who have experienced the estate's intervention as feudal superior are unimpressed and speak of slow response, if not opposition. The paternalism of the 'Good Sir James'

In the Lairig Ghru, a school party from Glenmore Lodge rests beside the Sinclair bothy which has since been removed (B. H. HUMBLE / GLENMORE LODGE)

appears to have been replaced by profit and loss accounting; feudal rights were reported as used to exact payments. Whereas the late Countess of Seafield, although described as 'painfully shy', was often present at local events – Highland games, Grantown Show or the opening of a football field – Lord Seafield is seen very little. Concern and support for the community and the environment of the gateway thus seem minimal. Nevertheless, the Seafields are in the tourist business, albeit at the upper end of the market, with celebrities enjoying country house splendours in Kinveachy Lodge and participating in fishing and shooting. It is alleged that some of the most invasive tracks in the Highlands have been bulldozed on Seafield land in the Monadh Liath for their greater convenience.

Notwithstanding the Rothiemurchus 'model', questions about how the Cairngorms should be managed persist. There have been calls from the Scottish Wild Land Group for the Cairngorms to be taken into public ownership; the Prince of Wales, showing a continuing concern for conservation, suggested in 1988 that National Parks should be considered in Scotland. In 1990 it was announced that the government intended to seek tentative listing for the Cairngorms as a World Heritage Site and a working party (chaired by Magnus Magnusson, then chairman of SNH) to review the management of the area was proposed. Within six months the Scottish Office had produced a document on yet another landscape designation – Natural Heritage Areas – and there were hopes of co-ordinated protection for the mountains. Two years later the straths of the Cairngorms were earmarked as Environmentally Sensitive Areas (ESAs). The region was gaining an astonishing concentration of protected terrain, being 'positively plastered with designations' emphasising that 'if there is any treasured land in Britain, then this surely is it'.

Then there was the matter of the Glenmore National Forest Park. In 1991 an international conference report entitled 'Forests in Trouble' pointed out that Scotland is one of the worst examples of forest mismanagement in the world with four-fifths of its remnant native forest under threat from overgrazing by sheep and deer. There may be plenty of crop timber, but slabby plantations of exotic conifers in close array are no substitute for natural habitats with their rich variety of life forms. Since 1946 the area of commercial forest in the Cairngorms massif has increased fourfold with most of the planting happening unbelievably on so-called protected areas such as Sites of Special Scientific Interest (SSSIs) and in the National Nature Reserve itself. Although from the 1920s Scots pine was planted in Glenmore by the Forestry Commission, such species as Sitka spruce and lodgepole pine from North America were also introduced;

meanwhile, the 'natural' Scots pine forest declined by 25 per cent. So in 1992 the first conservation forestry reserve of 1,850 acres (750ha) was established at Glenmore as part of an ambitious programme by Forest Enterprise to encourage the restoration of native pine woods in its care. The exotic species have been cleared and surviving indigenous trees allowed to seed. Working on a lengthy timescale, the benefits for the landscape and wildlife should be outstanding. There is plenty of scope for similar projects in the gateway encouraged by the Forest of Spey Challenge Fund.

Meanwhile, the Cairngorms Working Party had began its deliberations and in March 1993 it published its report, 'Common Sense and Sustainability'. This contained plans for a Cairngorms Partnership to co-ordinate a management strategy for the whole area but it was immediately criticised for relying on the voluntary principle and having neither the statutory powers nor funds to give results. There was a minority report which questioned its capabilities without those elements. Before the new group had even been constituted the Cairngorm Chairlift Company upstaged it by announcing plans for a funicular on Cairn Gorm. It raised very sensitive issues and was clearly a response to downhill skiing demands. Only in November 1994 was the Cairngorms Partnership established with David Laird as chairman. Although he had served on a SNH board, he also had a background in factoring estates and the appointment was interpreted as political. Nevertheless, the partnership was soon holding community meetings and taking soundings of local opinion with a view to producing its management strategy – no easy task when an area covering one-tenth of mainland Scotland and 100 various interest groups, plus 24 communities from Aboyne to Laggan, were involved.

The Cairngorms were a constant focus of media attention – the estates of Mar Lodge on Deeside and Glenfeshie[8] were both for sale and hopes were high that conservation interests would secure them. The outcome was that Mar Lodge went to the National Trust for Scotland but Glenfeshie to a charitable trust whose purposes soon appeared to lean in the sporting direction. In 1997 Glenfeshie was put on the market again, its English owners probably unable to stomach the requirements for the regeneration of the pine forest placed on them by the Forestry Commission, Scottish Natural Heritage and the Red Deer Commission. There was also the likely attitude of a new Labour government towards land management in the Highlands to be considered. Revack and Dorback, estates with a mix of farming, forestry and sport held by the Seafield family, came up for sale in 1998 at an asking price of £6 million.

There is astonishment over such prices but land values on Highland estates are not derived on a 'per acre' or 'per hectare' basis – instead they relate to yearly returns from sport together with forestry, farming and residential components.

By far the most controversial element in the Cairngorms was the funicular railway proposed as a replacement for the ageing, two-stage chairlift system. Estimated initially to cost £17 million and using steel cables powered by electricity, together with a two-metre gauge track, its protagonists argued that it would address winter ski pressures when 6,000 or more skiers per day – mainly at weekends – thronged the slopes. By conveying 120 a time, standing in two coaches for a six-minute trip, they would be able to have more skiing, or increasingly popular snowboarding, for their money. The opportunist character of Scottish skiing had undoubtedly benefited from the improvements to the A9 which reduced journey times from the Central Lowlands to 2½ hours compared with four hours or more in the 1960s; day visits to the mountain are now possible. As the funicular would be almost 'gale proof' its advocates said it would enhance passenger comfort and assist the winter evacuation of skiers from high level grounds if the weather should deteriorate. The gamut of facilities proposed included restaurants and creches.

Over the years the Scottish chairlifts have generally attracted more users in summer than in winter. So the funicular lobby stated that the system would offer a more agreeable 'year round' jaunt for the less able – a possible figure of 225,000 non-skiing visitors a year was quoted. Its statistical basis was questioned and this total has since been revised downwards to an average of 160,000 but by any standard it is a frightening increase. (Levels in the 1990s were just 50,000 to 60,000 visitors in summer – the latter being halved since the 1970s but there is now competition from other Highland chairlifts and from the gondola system on Aonach Mor.) The funicular figures may be wishful thinking; the most popular Highland visitor venue is currently Urquhart Castle by Loch Ness, effectively a dual attraction with 244,700 (1998); Landmark at Carrbridge had 90,000. If the funicular forecast, which pins its hopes on bus parties, is correct, visitor attractions – ranging from heather centre to water spectacle – may lose out. Other ski centres especially have cause to fear for their numbers and for their trade.

There are also the likely effects of global warming to consider. Although the 1998–99 and 2000-01 winter seasons produced plenty of snow at high levels and were consequently good for business, the summer snow fields on the mountains have declined. Record warm days have been noted each year and climate predictions suggest that by 2100

Scottish snow fall will decrease to about one-tenth of its present average – an outcome which has serious implications for funicular usage in winter.

While the Cairngorm Chairlift Company believed that the funicular would be less intrusive than the existing paraphernalia of the chairlifts, the likely appearance of the system was severely criticised; it was described by the Badenoch and Strathspey Conservation Group as 'rather like a tube train on a motorway flyover – 93 concrete columns, each two metres thick and up to six metres high, supporting a massive linear steel and concrete track, stretching for two kilometres up Cairn Gorm . . . ' Worse still there would be a 250 metre (270yds) tunnel blasted out of the mountain. It was feared that the 'negative effects' on the visual environment would be so adverse that the possibility of the Cairngorms ever achieving World Heritage Status might be ruled out. It was however the increase in visitors during May to November, hauled up on 8 to 12 minute trips, to be given a mainly indoor visual experience of what mountains are like, that was most contentious. Would they really wish to be whisked up the hill, latterly in a tunnel, to emerge into an enclosed space? Tourists have become ever further travelled and more discerning – so how would such a funicular stand in comparison with those of the Alps? The alpine ranges, both in sheer scale and angularity, are far better able to conceal such structures than the low-keyed, relatively smooth shoulders of Cairn Gorm. Strangely SNH failed to object to the funicular's potential for construction damage and landscape intrusion. The Cairngorms Partnership and others advised that the Secretary of State should call in the controversial proposal and launch a public inquiry. It was not done.

Regarding the chairlifts, a survey showed that half the patrons during May to November lingered around the Ptarmigan restaurant, while some 36 per cent made for the summit via the path and only 14 per cent went further; even so this has meant a very large escalation on Cairn Gorm compared with a ten times increase by people visiting other Scottish summits – the latter explained by the surge in hill walking and the lure of 'Munro bagging'. The danger of easier accessibility was foreseen by Sir Hugh Munro as long ago as 1895 when he described funiculars as 'crowning abominations' and gave thanks that so far no Scottish mountain had been 'desecrated' by one.

SNH seemed mainly to have misgivings about the containment of the likely visitor influx. If Cairn Gorm had been a discrete hill mass, then this aspect of the funicular might have been less disquieting but the mountain is part of a vast plateau and serves as a bridge to other summits and remote corries. SNH was the principal objector to the scheme and sought discussions on a visitor management plan – the notorious VMP. By the summer of 1996 it revealed that it was 'minded' to withdraw its objections in the light of amendments to the latter and in March 1997 it left the way clear for the Highland Council to grant planning permission for the funicular. Only a legally binding agreement under the European Community Habitats Directive would suffice and there would be no wandering up to the mountain top by funicular passengers. Charges would be payable by any walkers and climbers who tried to use the hill side car parks – even if as tax payers a share of their money had gone into the funicular development which was seeking £12 million of public funding. The arrangements for such visitors were described as 'draconian'.

By contrast, on Ben Wyvis in Easter Ross, SNH was resolute in its opposition to any development of downhill skiing and to all year round tourism involving a railway. The SNH as a landowner there had 'a heavy responsibility to look after this precious mountain environment'. Not to have objected would have been 'a betrayal' leading to 'unacceptable damage to the fragile ecology of the mountain'. Perhaps Cairn Gorm was seen as too much compromised by skiing over three decades to be other than sacrificed.

In defence of Cairn Gorm as a mountain habitat, heavyweights on the conservation side, including Sir David Attenborough and Professor David Bellamy, called for a public enquiry. They urged a strategic assessment of all the alternatives – notably of a gondola system as unveiled by a consortium of Scottish conservation groups. From Glenmore the gondola would feed a modern chairlift; this project would have been less costly than the funicular and would have removed the monstrous car parks on the hill and narrowed the road leading to them. The European International Consultation Group on Sustainable Mountain Development, meeting at Aviemore in 1996 under the auspices of the International Union for Conservation and Nature, not surprisingly voted against the development of a funicular on Cairn Gorm.

Attempts to block the funicular plan continued. Within a year the World Wildlife Fund for Nature and the RSPB were seeking a judicial review in the Court of Session of the Tory government's decision to exclude Coire Cas and other areas near Cairn Gorm – wrongly in their view – from a Special Area of Conservation under the European Union's Habitats' Directive. Meantime the Save the Cairngorms Campaign was put on a formal legal footing, transforming itself into 'The Cairngorms Campaign' the better to flex its muscle in defence of the mountains. A

Cairngorms Community Circle of concerned groups and individuals was encouraging debate on a fresh strategy for the region. In November 1997 the Scottish Office, with Donald Dewar, a Labour Secretary of State at the helm, and after reportedly agonising over a decision, announced that it backed the funicular development thus unlocking hefty public funding for it. Whilst an EC Objective One award of £2.7 million for the funicular was also approved, this payment was held over pending the outcome of the Court of Session case.

The declaration by the government that Loch Lomond and the Trossachs would become Scotland's first National Park, plus progress towards the Scottish Parliament, gave a sense of urgency to the politics of Cairn Gorm. The Cairngorms Partnership had unveiled its management strategy, described as 'a persuasive vision of how local communities can prosper through the effective safeguarding of this internationally respected environment'. Enunciating principles acceptable to all parties was hard enough, implementation of these would be much tougher.

Opponents of the funicular pointed out that it represented poor value for money in terms of job creation – each job costing nearly ten times the average for the Highlands -£100,000 compared with £10,000. Aberdeenshire Council, aware that the scheme would have far-reaching consequences, continued to press for a public inquiry. In November 1998 however the Highland Council and SNH had their position upheld by the Court of Session. It was a decision that disappointed the conservation lobbyists though they did not appeal. Highlands and Islands Enterprise (HIE) called on the conservationists to work with them on the 'approved plans' to develop 'a world class example of an environmentally sensitive tourist development'. Whether this was 'spin doctoring' or otherwise, the missing funding from the EC's Objective One sources was still held back awaiting a review of the whole project on both environmental and financial grounds.

Eventually in May 1999 the final £2.7 million from the European Regional Development Fund was formally offered but it came with strings attached. The project must create 65 full time jobs within three years while retaining 40 existing posts – otherwise HIE would be liable to pay back a portion of the funding. Early in August, Morrison Construction, commissioned by HIE, began the first phase of the infrastructure for the funicular scheme six years after the idea was mooted. There was immediate adverse comment as the firm was led by Sir Fraser Morrison who had lately chaired HIE; cronyism was mentioned but strenuously denied. As bulldozers once again churned up parts of the mountainside, the methods used brought the charge of 'official vandalism' from some ecologists; although HIE's stewardship of Cairn Gorm, which it now owned, might appear cavalier, SNH staff were monitoring the project. The main work started in the spring of 2000 with the contract for the railway itself being placed with the Austrian firm, Dopplemayer Seilbahnen AG, a company with wide experience of such installations. The vehicles were Swiss built.

By re-branding the old chairlift company, the new CairnGorm Mountain Ltd was launched, with Hamish Swan again as chairman, and a revised visitor management plan agreed. In the interim, HIE made purchases of buildings on Cairn Gorm, thereby putting the funicular on a firmer footing. It meant an extra £3 million for the scheme; there was also a loan of £1 million from the Highland Council. The whole funicular infrastructure is now in public ownership, while the railway system itself is leased to CairnGorm Mountain. Although logical, there were more protests about cash being taken from the public purse for the project. On a snowy 23 December 2001, the contentious funicular railway was opened − forty years from the day the first chairlift commenced − with the public admitted to try it on Christmas Eve. Only time would tell if the hoped-for boost to tourism in general would occur.

There have been those who have advocated retreat from Cairn Gorm with the removal of all ski installations and access roads, thus reviving 'the long walk in'. They resent the presumption that downhill skiing should have a first claim on the mountain and believe that there would be benefits for both the community of the gateway and its environment if this withdrawal took place. They affirm that the Cairngorms are too precious to be exploited in such a crude fashion and hail the rise of green or eco-tourism. Expenditure by 'mountain enthusiasts' benefits the Highlands by at least £104 million each year − in fact they contribute a quarter of all tourist spending in some districts − and their interests cannot be ignored. Walking whether on hills or in straths is the most popular main activity among both middle and high income groups in Britain. A legal right of access under civil law for hill walkers and mountaineers is proposed by the government. With 123,000 non-skiers using the Cairngorms footpaths every year, upgrading the most seriously eroded stretches alone is urgent and in the longer term there is much work to be done; the Cairngorm Partnership has priced repairs at £7 million spread over five years.

Scotland's population is now close to 90 per cent urban. More than ever town dwellers seek out the special qualities of the 'natural' environment 'for recreation, for escape from the stresses and artificiality of an urban existence − there is a yearning for wilderness with its fresh air and tranquillity'. Surveys show that people rate scenery highly, especially where lochs are surrounded by hills, as though they are searching for the elemental simplicity of rock and water. Wildlife and historic sites are well up their list of preferences too. The Cairngorm gateway answers all these needs in comprehensive and spectacular style.

Significantly in 1997 the first Cairngorms rally of ramblers took place in Glen Feshie to support conservation objectives and public ownership for the estate. That ambition was thwarted however when Klaus Helmersen, a Danish clothing and textile magnate with an interest in conservation, snatched the prize away in November 1997 by offering a higher bid – reputedly £7 million – than the consortium of Scottish organisations including the Highland Council. New European money was also in evidence in Glen Tromie where the French Vuitton brothers – associated with fashion and luxury luggage – bought the estate. Early in 2000 Castle Grant with its grounds, 'a real piece of Scottish history', was sold to an American-based group specialising in holiday rental property in Europe and the USA; but with Scotland's appeal as a destination sagging, together with the strength of the pound, by 2001 it was on the market again.

Later that year, with Helmersen's business interests in free-fall, Glenfeshie was sold in a secret deal to another Dane, Flemming Skouboe, whose wealth had come from wind turbine blade manufacture. The price paid was estimated at £8.5 million. Skouboe stated his intention to honour Helmersen's agreements and to co-operate with the environmental agencies in controlling excessive deer numbers, thereby allowing the natural regeneration of the indigenous Scots pine forest. Nevertheless, there was further disquiet. Land reform interests argued that Glenfeshie, one of Scotland's wilderness gems at the very heart of the proposed Cairngorms National Park, should be in the ownership of the Scottish nation.

From prosperity in the upbeat 1960s, agriculture in the gateway has been experiencing hard times and there are even fewer farming families now. Yet some 7 per cent of the working population in the Cairngorms area is still in farm employment, compared with 3 per cent in Scotland as a whole. Two, three or more holdings have become single units and the excess houses and cottages are second homes. Some estate owners have taken land back into their own hands, working it on their own account which makes it hard for young folk intent on being farmers to find a holding to lease. In the fields, the once ubiquitous Aberdeen-Angus herds, superseded by foreign breeds – Charolais, Limousins and the like – are making a comeback. Hill farming, which relies so heavily on cattle, has had to pay a heavy price for Britain's BSE misadventure. Yet for some families long-standing links with the land are retained in the face of adversity. In places new land uses – golf courses, nature trails, chalets and woodlands – have appeared in place of the traditional agriculture of stock rearing and the old rhythms of seed time and harvest.

With tourism in the Highlands currently flagging, what hope is there for 'sustainable growth' in the Cairngorm gateway? Firstly there is the built environment and the issue of the expansion of settlements, such as Carrbridge, Nethybridge and others, with Aviemore now an obvious target for suburbia. It has acquired urban trappings – estate agents, solicitors, traffic wardens, a supermarket and even a betting shop. (With incredible lack of judgement, the supermarket was put on a site cleared of two Victorian villas, thus further eroding the character of the village core.) Meanwhile, the smaller settlements have shed services which they formerly enjoyed – a variety of retail outlets, garages and petrol pumps – and their post offices, the hub of many a community, are also at risk. As Aviemore's resident numbers approach 3,000, there are plans to construct 500 houses on the heather moor of Cambusmore in Rothiemurchus which would be linked by a bridge across the Spey. As that resort amply demonstrates, growth has come at a price to the community and to the environment.

The clan warriors and cattle thieves of long ago have been replaced by more subtle and rapacious forces. For too long the developers and property speculators have been ranged on one side, the conservation and environmental interests on the other. Now moves are a-foot to market the Cairngorms as a 'green destination'. On the international scene, accreditation has been won by areas, such as Vilamoura in Portugal, which develop their tourist business along environmentally sustainable lines. Tourist facilities are monitored for energy efficiency, water use and waste disposal. A pilot scheme was launched in Aviemore in 1999 which it is hoped will eventually become gateway wide. Secondly, there is the realisation that appropriate 'niche' marketing, responsive to the sensitivities of the area, may encourage more visitors; for instance, the first Speyside Classic golf tournament, combining the gateway's major but seasonally underused courses at Boat of Garten, Grantown, Kingussie and Newtonmore, was held in 2001.

A third of the houses in the gateway are reckoned to be second homes; when time shares are added to these the impermanence and mobility of the population are exposed. How committed are these transients to the place or its people? True, there are many retirees who, having first sampled the Highlands on holiday, determine to settle. However, nowadays the floating population of the gateway area at high season times easily outnumbers the residents; the 'landward' parts have lost out whereas the settlements, especially Aviemore, have romped ahead. Both new and improved roads allow commuters to work in Inverness or the Moray towns and have their homes in the gateway itself. House prices have soared and many local folk have little choice other than council housing.

Although there are several industrial estates in the strath, worries over the lack of a range of worthwhile employment continue. The Cairngorm Technology Park at Dalfaber contains Spey House, built speculatively at a cost of £1.2 million, which has long lain empty, awaiting call centre or similar tenants. In April 2000, Telecom Service Centres, with an injection of £0.5 million from HIE and bringing an impressive client list, announced its intention to open in Aviemore with the prospect of 300 jobs – a major employment boost for the district – and latterly in 2002 some were hired. However, Aviemore ale is back again – this time made in a microbrewery which has paired up with a former rival in Tomintoul to try to capture the Highland market.

While the mountains were in a maelstrom of controversy, happily in the strath there was a fresh determination to repair the neglect and damage of the past. In 1997, there was a new style of 'master plan' in place for Aviemore which was a fundamental departure from the pattern of recent decades. The master plan had been worked out by public agencies such as the Highland Council and Moray, Badenoch and Strathspey Enterprise (MBSE), with the Aviemore Partnership as the spearhead and co-ordinator, by means of wide ranging consultations with community interests over a period of three years or more. So instead of big business setting the agenda and dictating the nature of development, it was hoped that the master plan, based on local consensus, would ensure that projects harmonised with their surroundings in scale and conferred some unity throughout the village. The aim was to seek out the best solutions which would give long-term benefits both to the community and the environment but unanswered questions remained over delivery and eventual timing.

With discussions with local people now accepted as pivotal, the strategy of revitalisation meant to give the 'village core' back to the pedestrians and create a 'high quality' street environment with buildings in traditional materials and with a Scottish idiom. A start has been made in giving some continuity to the place with drystone walls built by local men from granite hewn in re-opened quarries at Alvie, while the Dell of Spey scheme focuses on the Aviemore burn, transforming it into a key feature of the village; this has involved landscaping with rock from

Dunachton near Kincraig and re-circulating Spey water to create rills.

The Strathspey Railway with its steam-hauled trains is now a focal element at the heart of the former railway village. The trains run from the restored Victorian station which, in the absence of the historic inn, was until 2001 the only 'listed building' in the place. On the mainline, ScotRail's passenger business is growing while the expanding freight haulage of containers, cement and timber is helping to take pressure off the roads. Emphasising again the gateway's role as a corridor is the extension of the Speyside Way along the riverside from Aviemore down to the coast, which was completed in 2000 after prolonged negotiations over access through Dalfaber. The following year, the Badenoch Way, combining a network of community paths, linked Kincraig and Kingussie. The National Cycle Track from Inverness to Dover, proposed by Sustrans and instituted as a Millennium project, now traverses part of the strath.

Regarding the Aviemore Mountain Resort, there were repeated intentions to improve or replace it. In 1995 Premier Land PLC, which already had two hotels outwith the site, bought the largely derelict complex for £7.5 million. The lure was tranches of public money and an enterprise company waiting to dispense it to any entrepreneur with a feasible plan to transform 'this national embarrassment'. Although one ambitious rescue package after the other had been published, the former Aviemore Centre continued to decay. All those propositions left the community bemused and the local Chamber of Commerce disappointed. In 1997 Premier, with a revamped board headed by Neville Conrad, of Conrad Ritblat the exceptionally successful property company from London, paired up with Lars-Erik Magnusson, a Swede who fronts Larmag, a Dutch property group. They were joined by Donald Macdonald of Macdonald Hotels, another with a stake in the complex. The latter is a Harris man whose company has managed Barratt's timeshare resorts, including Dalfaber at Aviemore, for many years. (Indeed, Macdonald owns a half share in that enterprise making him effectively the owner and Britain's largest single timeshare operator.) Ikea, the Swedish furnishing stores giant, also invested a slice of capital in Aviemore Mountain Resort.

Soon Premier Land evolved into Probus Estates plc, with Magnusson as chairman. The plan was for that organisation to control 40 per cent of the Mountain Resort's capital but by 2000 with little happening on the ground, rumours were abounding. Probus was selling off assets. It withdrew from the project in May 2000 leaving its holding to be transferred to other parties and cancelling the inter-company debt owing to it by the loss-making mountain resort, which at £6.5 million it found 'extremely burdensome'. So Aviemore was exposed to the fast moving, wheeling-dealing circuits of international finance and to corporate organisations which, like amoebae, grow, divide and reform with rapidity. Other players had to be found urgently if both the fabric and image of the mountain resort· was to be rebuilt as promised early in the new Millennium. Together with Macdonald Hotels, the Bank of Scotland (now HBOS) and Tulloch Construction Ltd entered the ring.

The master plan proposals of 1997 for Aviemore were radical but the outline drew its inspiration from the planned settlements of two centuries ago. The Prince of Wales, with his well-known views on architecture and planning, held discussions with the Aviemore Partnership; arising from his concern, representatives visited his model settlement of Poundbury in Dorset. At Aviemore, the whole scheme was dependent upon a new street layout and a village square. In 1998 some dismantling began of derelict sports and other facilities; ultimately outworn hotels, chalets and the incongruous Santa Claus Land would go. Tree-planting on some cleared sites was to follow. Plans were approved for community leisure

The Dell of Spey on the Aviemore burn was the first project of the Aviemore Partnership. The aim was to create a sylvan corridor through the village. The assortment of architectural styles in Aviemore is revealed in this photograph (ANN GLEN)

provision and for a conference centre plus the extensive refurbishment of other structures. There were hopes for an environmental research base for the University of the Highlands and for a headquarters for SNH, in addition to a variety of accommodation for tourists and local people. There continues to be an unsatisfied demand for affordable houses in Aviemore. Overall the partnership team pledged a new beginning but the investment package was formidable − £30 million for the Centre itself in addition to £8 million for Project Aviemore; Barratt also scheduled a £10 million hotel and a championship golf course for their Dalfaber site. By 2001 there was alarm when a massive supermarket scheme was proposed by the AMR consortium, now re-named 'Aviemore Highland Resort Ltd'. Understandably, neighbouring places fretted over what they saw as excessive attention and potential investment being given once again to Aviemore and its environs.

Yet the village communities of the strath have not been mere onlookers. They have underlined their distinctive identities with publicity material and ingenious logos and, by means of heritage centres, interpretation at viewpoints and along walkways, they invite visitors to linger and to learn. The television series *Monarch of the Glen* has put a media focus on Badenoch and Strathspey, and by presenting the district so positively to millions of viewers in Britain and overseas, has helped to promote tourism. In fact, the image of 'Monarch Country' is now used as a marketing tool.

In the wider environment the 'too convenient' car is seen as destroying much of what people come to enjoy. Take Glenmore for an example. Consideration might be given to traffic calming or to extending car free zones. There has been talk of a narrow-gauge railway from near Aviemore to Loch Morlich; this is an old theme which has so far been shelved on the grounds of cost.

And what of the National Park for the Cairngorms? The fact is that the mountains and parts of their gateway already have a high public profile and are known to thousands of people who come to tour or cycle, to walk and climb or to enjoy other outdoor pursuits. A National Park has been signalled and this would hopefully bring not only status but proper funding and an overall strategy for the whole terrain. Wide consultations on the proposals for Scottish Natural Parks have been completed; these suggested that full planning powers should be given to National Park Boards and a preponderance of national appointees should serve on them. With respect to the Cairngorms National Park and in spite of the public consultation outcomes, SNH's advice to government ministers was that the board of this park should not have full planning powers (unlike that for Loch Lomond and Trossachs). Furthermore, 60 per cent of the board members should represent local interests, notwithstanding the fact that the park would be 'national'. The inference was that these arrangements were to placate the Highland Council which had long been opposed to the National Park idea.

Questions were aired over the extent of the National Park's boundaries. The SNH version would have created by far the largest National Park in Britain, involving five local authorities with limited experience of working together. This might be a prescription for discord. The anti-National Park lobby also pointed to the Lake District and the 'honey pot' effect which is supposedly attributed to that designation, but that region was over popular long before it became a National Park and it would be much worse without such stewardship.

Four objectives for the National Park have been set out: conservation of the natural and cultural heritage, enjoyment by the public, sustainable use of resources and the social and economic development of communities. Early in 2000, a few days before the launch of the Scottish Parliament's National Parks Bill, a management concordat with John Grant of Rothiemurchus was signed on the estate on behalf of the Scottish Executive by Environment Minister Sarah Boyack MSP, and key public sector representatives – the Highland Council, HIE, Scottish Natural Heritage, the Forestry Commission, the Cairngorms Partnership, and MBSE. Voluntary and non-government organisations (NGOs), such as the RSPB and the Mountaineering Council for Scotland, were noticeable by their absence. They were not invited – provoking charges of window dressing and that the concordat was flawed. Nonetheless, it came as no surprise that Rothiemurchus was seen as reflecting the official vision for Scotland's National Parks and the exercise in diplomacy would doubtless send a positive message to other landowners. To dispel misgivings on the agricultural side, funding had been made available earlier for farmers from the Cairngorms area to visit National and Regional Parks in France. A new expression had been coined too, namely 'agri-environment'.

Landscape protection in Scotland has long been criticised as 'chronically weak'. The Cairngorms Partnership relying on consensus has found it difficult to deliver conservation objectives and a National Park in the same mode could be relatively ineffective. A prototype National Park which would demonstrate good practice is long overdue and Loch Lomond and the Trossachs will be the trail blazer. To borrow a phrase from a Scottish Wildlife and Countryside Link report, such a 'greenprint', aimed at the better management of tourists and the fabric of the countryside, should seek to combine positive visitor experiences and local economic benefit with reduced environmental impact. Shortly, a National Park Management Group for the Cairngorms was put in place.

Then in May 2002 came a series of events which gave the Cairngorm gateway more headlines. On a positive note, the Strathspey Railway, after five years of largely volunteer effort, doubled its track length by opening to Broomhill, familiar as 'Glenbogle' station to TV viewers. There was a community buy-out of Anagach Woods at Grantown, thanks to the Scottish Land Fund Programme, and Kingussie's shinty team won the Camanachd Cup for a record sixth time in a row.

The Aviemore Highland Resort's financiers showed their hand when they got outline planning permission from the Highland Council for their big supermarket and housing development on the old Centre site. Tellingly, local councillors voted against the application. The developers claimed that they would spend £30 million on the scheme, seeking only £4 million of public funding. A new link road was stipulated. Villagers, ever more sceptical and vocal, were demanding that community facilities – a cinema, a public swimming pool, an exhibition and conference centre, so long promised – must be part of the deal. Although these would be written into a legally enforceable agreement, would a resort of quality emerge? Would the designs be in harmony with the natural environment and heritage? Would the materials be local and durable unlike those of the tawdry Centre? How much of the vision of a renewed green Aviemore would be retained? Past experience was not reassuring. Perhaps the application was a shrewd move to outflank any National Park Board position *vis-à-vis* the development of the village.

That same month, the Scottish Executive published its weighty Draft Designation Order for the Cairngorms National Park. It was heavily criticised. The park's area would be slashed by the exclusion of Angus and Perth & Kinross. Boundaries were drawn tightly round settlements, ignoring their hinterlands. There were tensions too over planning. Basically, this would be a shared responsibility, but the Park Authority could call in for its own determination planning applications of general significance to the National Park's aims. Bowing to pressure, the Executive's final proposal restored the Angus glens and stretched the boundaries to Drumochter and Laggan. Settlement hinterlands were largely recognised. At 3,800 sq.km, the Cairngorms National Park would indeed be the biggest in Britain, but the planning compromise stood. It was now decision time for the Scottish Parliament.

However imperfect, the Cairngorms National Park is on course to become a reality; the Cairngorm gateway is in need of being treated in a coherent and holistic way to give long term benefit and not simply short-term advantage:

> Scotland has been making a living out of the best of its natural heritage, especially tourism, for too long without investing in the care and sustainable development of this precious resource.
> – NATIONAL PARKS FOR SCOTLAND – SCOTTISH EXECUTIVE 2000

The Cairngorms National Park has a large measure of popular support. Cast in the right mould and extending from straths to summits, it would give a sense of proper esteem and distinction to some of the finest terrain and wildlife in Europe – and hopefully the guardianship which the international community considers the mountains and the gateway to

Which way will Aviemore and the Cairngorm gateway go? New signs and interpretative panels attempt to tell the story of the place and its people (ANN GLEN)

them deserve.

And what of the contentious mountain railway complex? The *Good Ski Guide* judged it the most improved European ski resort in 2001–2. Then it achieved 'gold standard' recognition after on-site audits of its environmental management won commendation for excellent practice from the Green Tourism Business Scheme in association with VisitScotland. An element in this success was the planting by local primary schools of *Coille na Cloinne*, the Children's Forest, which aims to re-create the tree-line scrub woodland of the mountains. Furthermore, and in spite of the restrictive visitor strategy prevailing, the railway's passenger numbers were said to be 'on target'.

EXCURSION

Cairn Gorm

The ascent of this impressive mountain was once a long slog, beginning near the Allt Mor in Glenmore. Now cars and buses whizz up the lower slopes to the huge car parks developed since downhill skiing claimed parts of the hillside and chairlifts were installed. The funicular railway now takes passengers over 3,600 feet (1,097m) to the top station. According to the visitor management plan, patrons are not permitted to make the short walk (about ¾ mile/1km) along a path built of pink granite boulders up to the summit cairn. Instead, those wishing to ascend the mountain have to climb from the car park. From the top, in clear weather, the grandeur and sheer scale of the Cairngorms can be savoured. It is worth going from the summit to a big tor or outcrop about ¼ mile (200m) due east for a glimpse of wild Loch Avon and its encircling crags.

For further information on skiing and other facilities, contact CairnGorm Mountain Ltd on 01479 861261.

SELECT BIBLIOGRAPHY

Firsoff, V. A., *The Cairngorms on Foot and Ski* (Robert Hale, London), 1949

Forsyth, *In the Shadow of Cairngorm* (Inverness, 1900, reprinted by Lynwilg Press, Aviemore), 2000

Giningham, C.H. (ed.), *The Ecology, Land Use and Conservation of the Cairngorms* (Packard Publishing Ltd, Chichester), 2002

Gordon, S., *The Cairngorms Hills of Scotland* (Cassell, London), 1925

Grant, E., *Abernethy Forest: its People and its Past* (Arkleton Trust, Nethybridge), 1994

Grant, E., *Memoirs of a Highland Lady* (Canongate, Edinburgh), 1997

Grant, I.F., *Highland Folkways* (Routledge & Kegan Paul, London), 1961

Haldane, A.R.B., *The Drove Roads of Scotland* (Nelson, Edinburgh), 1952

New Ways through the Glens (Nelson, Edinburgh), 1962

Nock, O.S., *The Highland Railway* (Ian Allan, Shepperton), 1965

Nethersole-Thompson, D. and Watson, A., *The Cairngorms, Their Natural History and Scenery* (Collins, London), 1974

Perry, R., *In the High Grampians* (Lindsay Drummond, London), 1948

Russell, H., *The Past Around Us: History and the Parish of Alvie and Insh* (Drumcluan Books, Feshiebridge), 1995

Smout, T. C. and Lambert, R. A. (eds), *Rothiemurchus, People and Nature on a Highland Estate, 1500–2000* (Scottish Cultural Press, Dalkeith), 1999

Taylor, W., *The Military Roads in Scotland* (House of Lochar, Colonsay), 1996

Wightman, A., Who Owns Scotland (Canongate, Edinburgh), 1996

Woodburn, D. A. (ed.), *Forestry Commission Guide*, 'Glen More Forest Park: Cairngorms', (HMSO, Edinburgh) 1975

NOTES

1. The Act for the Abolition and Proscription of Highland Dress: Enacted in August 1746, this was part of the Disarming Act and stated that 'no man or boy within that part of Great Britain called Scotland, other than such as shall be employed as Officers and Soldiers in His Majesty's Forces, shall . . . wear or put on the clothes commonly called Highland clothes . . . the Plaid, Philabeg, or little kilt, Trowse, Shoulder-belts, or any part whatsoever of what peculiarly belongs to the Highland Garb'. It forbade the use of tartan and the carrying of bagpipes, which were perceived as weapons of war. Offenders were imprisoned without bail for six months and a second offence incurred transportation for seven years. The measure was reinforced in 1748 when warnings were given from the pulpits in the parish churches. This Proscription Act was not applied to those chiefs who had supported the Hanoverian government but at the outset it was enforced against the Jacobite clans with brutal ferocity. By the 1760s, there was some relaxation in applying this harsh law. Eventually, efforts by a committee of the Highland Society of London, which contained leading members of the Scottish nobility, secured a repeal of the hated Act in 1782. In the circumstances, it is remarkable that an interest in Highland dress survived. The influence of royalty and the chiefs played a key role in its revival. (See Sir Thomas Innes of Learney in Frank Adam's The Clans, Septs & Regiments of the Scottish Highlands, Johnston & Bacon, 1975, pp. 370-3.)

2. Rents: In a Highland context these were different from fixed 'sum per acre' arrangements. Agricultural rent was basically a sharing of the produce between the owner and the occupier of the land. The harvest was divided into portions – one for seed, one for the tenant and one for the laird. Any increase in cattle stocks was split on similar lines. The parish minister also got his tenth portion or 'teinds' and if there was a mill, a 'multure' was due to the miller. As money payments became general and taxes had to be paid in money, it became usual to have part and then the whole of the rent paid in money. As money values and produce prices varied, the question of 'fair rents' arose. The old system avoided such disputes; the crop was shared whether good or poor – if the harvest was a success or prices were high, then the rent reflected this. 'Fair rents' based on the estimable produce of a farm, if worked in accordance with sustainable husbandry, might have some relevance today. (See Handley, J. E., Scottish Farming in the Eighteenth Century, Faber & Faber, 1953, pp. 82-4.)

3. The Entail Act: The wholesale improvement of estates was expensive but the situation was eased by the Entail Act of 1770. This permitted life renters of entailed estates to charge three-quarters of the costs to their heirs. As one-third of Scotland's land was soon on entailed estates, this measure hastened the transformation of the landscape. (See Caird, J.B. 'The Making of the Scottish

Rural Landscape' in the Scottish Geographical Magazine, 80 (1964), pp. 72-80).

4. The Public Money Drainage Act: Enthusiasm for drainage schemes led to the passing of an Act in 1846 which set up a fund from which landowners could borrow on long terms at low rates of interest. This offer was eagerly taken up by Scottish proprietors. A further Act of 1849, using private money, saw many companies formed to push forward drainage and land improvement. This took Scottish agriculture on to the flood plains and helped to create the level fields of parts of today's farming landscape. (See Fenton, A., Scottish Country Life, Tuckwell Press, 1999, p. 23.)

5. Easter and Wester in Place-Names: In Strathspey it was assumed that the River Spey flowed more or less northwards until modern surveying plotted its course with some accuracy. 'Wester' was therefore applied to those places that lay west of those of the same name which lay to the east or 'easter'. In some districts the terms were also used as the equivalents of higher or lower.

6. The Trespass (Scotland) Act: In common law, a walker might be exposed to prosecution if he trespassed in pursuit of game or, when trespassing, he or she commited some other offence. This is enshrined in what became known as the 'Scotch Trespass Act' of 1865, which also made camping an offence on private land without the consent and permission of the landowner. Walkers, following a right-of-way, had to affect as little as possible the interests of the proprietor or occupier of the land in regard to farming, forestry and sport. On the other hand, a walker or other user of a right-of-way, could not be molested or obstructed by the owner of the land. A voluntary Access Concordat, developed on the Letterewe estate in 1996, was a step forward in the 'right to roam' controversy. With the backing of Scottish Natural Heritage, an Access Forum proposed Scottish legislation in 1998, which would give the public the right of access to land and water in Scotland for informal recreation and passage, subject to responsible behaviour.

7. Parish arrangements:

    1631: Duthil and Rothiemurchus parishes were united due to a shortage of ministers of religion in the County of Moray, according to Lachlan Shaw in A History of the Province of Moray.

    1831: Rothiemurchus was made a Parliamentary parish and was disjoined from Duthil parish.

    1917: That portion of Duthil west of the Spey in the Aviemore area was placed in Rothiemurchus parish which was then described as the parish of Rothiemurchus and Aviemore.

    1949: That portion of the united parish of Kincardine and Boat of Garten constituting the National Forest Park at Glenmore was made part of Rothiemurchus and Aviemore parish area. Reflecting the shift in population, the parish is now known as Aviemore and Rothiemurchus and it is likely that the parish of Alvie will be an addition.

8. For the physical feature of the valleys, the spelling is 'Glen Feshie', 'Glen Tromie', etc. For the actual area of the estates, the name 'Glenfeshie' and 'Glentromie' has come into use.